TEXTBOOK OF
ECONOMIC ANALYSIS

By the same author

*

THE PROBLEM OF THE NATIONAL DEBT, 1954

THE MECHANISM OF CHEAP MONEY, 1955

CAPITAL FUNDS IN UNDERDEVELOPED
COUNTRIES, 1961; SPANISH EDITION 1963

A WORKBOOK OF ECONOMIC ANALYSIS, 1966;
SECOND EDITION 1969

THE LONDON CLEARING BANKS (WITH E. W. DAVIS), 1970

AN INTRODUCTION TO MICRO-ECONOMICS, 1973

TEXTBOOK OF
ECONOMIC ANALYSIS

EDWARD NEVIN
M.A. (Wales), Ph.D. (Cantab.)

PROFESSOR OF ECONOMICS
UNIVERSITY COLLEGE OF SWANSEA

Fourth Edition

Macmillan Education

First Edition 1958
Reprinted 1959, 1960
Second Edition 1963
Reprinted 1964, 1966
Third Edition 1967
Reprinted 1967, 1969, 1970, 1973
Fourth Edition 1976
Reprinted 1977

Published by
MACMILLAN EDUCATION LTD
Houndmills Basingstoke Hampshire RG21 2XS
and London
Associated companies in New York Dublin
Melbourne Johannesburg and Delhi

Printed in Great Britain by
Butler & Tanner Ltd
Frome and London

Foreword to the
Fourth Edition

ALMOST twenty years, and three editions, have passed since this book was first published; I find it a chastening thought that it will now be falling into the hands of young people who were not even born at that time. A great deal has happened in the interim, both to the world which is the subject-matter of the book and to the teaching of economics at the level for which the book is intended; sufficient has happened, indeed, since the third edition was prepared in 1967 to render that previous version obsolete in major respects.

So far as the world is concerned, the changes are well enough known. Inflation has long since become a daily diet and many of the monetary values used for purposes of illustration in that 1967 version now look frankly ridiculous. The British banking system has undergone its revolution and corresponding changes have occurred in official techniques of trying to tame the monster; even academic thinking on the subject of monetary policy has moved on – or, as some would have it, moved back. Britain is now a member of the European Economic Community, although the passage of time could conceivably render even this simple statement obsolete. The international monetary system is in greater turmoil than ever. Enough there alone for a new edition!

But the changes in the teaching of economics have been profound also. When this book was first written, economics was still a 'new' subject at Advanced Level and its teaching in schools tended to be relegated by headmasters to those members of staff whose time-table exhibited the most blanks or who were in other respects deserving of disfavour. Not any more: those of us who teach in the universities are only too aware of the degree to which the level of the teaching of elementary economics has risen in the past decade. It is now taught by specialists and frequently distinctly better than the job is done in some universities. The distinction between the good 'A' Level candidate and the average first-year university student is now much less clear than it was ten years ago. So much so that the universities simply cannot go on treating all their first-year students of economics as equally ignorant, Advanced Level or no. Not only is this an insult to an enormous number of first-class teachers: it is equally a gross and indefensible waste of the time and intellect of many first-class students. We simply cannot go on doing this and it is a matter of some pride to my colleagues in my own Department that we have for some years now allowed well-trained new entrants to proceed at once to the work of which they are perfectly capable rather than be bored and alienated by going over material in which they have already been well taught for two years or more.

All this is reflected in a general raising of the level of treatment in this new edition although I hope I have achieved this without in any way qualifying the usefulness of the book for the total newcomer to the subject, including those relying on their own resources to master the basics of what is not, and is not intended to be, an easy subject in which the refugee from the demands of a rigorous intellectual discipline can find a soft option.

Over these past sixteen years I have derived enormous pleasure and benefit from comment on the book, verbal and written, from users of it. I really am most grateful for this. I am especially appreciative of the comments I was sent by a group of members of the Welsh Branch of the Economics Association who were good enough to give the book a going-over at my request. It would be pleasant to think that they will continue to be my customers but in any event they will certainly remain my benefactors.

Swansea
June 1975

E.T.N.

Contents

PART I   INTRODUCTION

I THE NATURE AND SCOPE OF ECONOMICS

II THE ECONOMIC PROBLEM

PART II THE THEORY OF DEMAND

III INDIVIDUAL DEMAND

PART III THE THEORY OF PRODUCTION

V THE ORGANISATION OF PRODUCTION

VI PRODUCTION IN THE SHORT RUN: DIMINISHING RETURNS

PART VII MACRO-ECONOMICS

XXV AGGREGATE DEMAND AND SUPPLY

XXVI THE PROCESS OF INCOME FORMATION

XXVII MEASURING THE PRICE-LEVEL: INDEX NUMBERS

XXVIII MACRO-ECONOMIC POLICY

PART VIII INTERNATIONAL ECONOMICS

PART I

INTRODUCTION

CHAPTER I

The Nature and Scope of Economics

1   SCARCITY AND CHOICE

THE world in which we live is a desperately poor place. Today, three thousand million human beings crowd its surface, each one needing food and shelter in order to do nothing more than preserve his own life. But parts of the world, it may be said, are not poor; in America the family garage has two cars and indoors the deep-freeze contains ice-cream and chicken. Even in Europe the general standard of living is not bad; few people die of starvation or exposure; television sets and cars are not uncommon. The sad truth is partly that Europe and North America are not the world, or even the greater part of the world, and that for the majority of the world's population human life exists on the border between bare subsistence and extinction. It is also true that the relatively rich communities such as Europe and North America contain enormous pockets of real poverty, and the world is a long way yet from the day when they will be finally removed. Even if all the good things of the world were placed in a gigantic common pool, and shared equally amongst all the human race, therefore, the world's population would still have scarcely enough food and clothing and warmth and shelter to keep itself alive.

This is not all. If a situation could be conceived of in which every adult in the world was able to produce as much material wealth as the most highly skilled operative in the most modern American factory – and the situation, of course, is scarcely conceivable for many years to come – it would still be found that the world was dissatisfied with its living standards. This is a

familiar characteristic of human beings – their perpetual dis-
content with the material wealth they have and their incessant
desire for more, or for better. Nothing is more common than
people, or families, experiencing from time to time some degree
of envy for more fortunate groups in the same society or, indeed,
other societies. If only we had as much as they do, the less
fortunate are inclined to think, we would be absolutely content.
But it never works out like that; when the time comes when these
once unattainable standards have been reached, most of us go
on envying other people whose life contains all sorts of things
still beyond our grasp. And so it has been all throughout history
and with the whole human race. As the fundamental and essential
needs of life have been met, the realisation of the possibilities
of an easier and fuller material life has dawned and new wants –
as real and as pressing as those which have been satisfied – have
arisen. The lowest-paid worker in Britain today enjoys a standard
of living which would have seemed incredibly high to a
moderately wealthy man a couple of centuries ago; yet the worker
is probably conscious only of the things he lacks in comparison
with his neighbours. Even the much-envied prosperous American
family with its two cars and deep-freeze is nowhere within sight
of gratifying all its existing wants. By the time all those wants
have been satisfied, new ones, as yet not conceived but soon
to acquire enormous strength, will surely have arisen.

These two basic facts – that in its material wealth the world
is very poor and that its needs appear to be capable of infinite
development – explain the existence of the science of economics.
Since the productive powers of the human race are limited, the
dual problem must arise of (a) ensuring that all available
resources are used fully and to the best possible effect, and (b)
in allocating the wealth so produced, of choosing which wants
are to be given priority and which are to be left unsatisfied.
This problem – the *economic problem* as it is called – arises only
because of the insufficiency of the world's wealth in relation
to its needs. The extent to which needs can be met, or the
way in which the choice between the satisfaction of want A
and want B is made, is of the essence of economics. If ever
mankind found itself able to produce more material wealth than

it knew what to do with – which, unfortunately or otherwise, it never will – then the necessity for choosing between the satisfaction of one want and that of another, or of ensuring the best use of all available resources, would have disappeared; and with it would disappear the science of economics.

2 DEFINING ECONOMICS

Scarcity, then, is the foundation of economics, and as a first approximation the subject could be defined as the systematic study of the processes by which priorities may be rationally determined across the infinite range of desirable ends facing mankind at any moment of time and of the ways in which the means available to satisfy those ends can be most effectively used to attain those priorities once decided upon. In other words, to use the definition proposed by Robbins, economics is concerned with the analysis of the manner in which men determine the allocation of scarce means which have alternative uses between ends which are competitive or conflicting in nature.

It is clear, however, that the adoption of such a definition, literally interpreted, would make the scope of the subject impossibly wide. To begin with, it is usually said that economics is a *social* science – that is, it is concerned with human activities which in some way influence other members of a community as well as the person undertaking them. For example, time is always a scarce factor: a man will always have to choose between various ways of using his time. But if he is choosing between spending a particular Saturday afternoon in bed or on a long walk, his decision will have virtually no importance for other members of society and is therefore outside the interests of the economist. On the other hand, if the choice is between an afternoon in bed and an afternoon at work then society *is* interested, because the total amount of wealth produced, and therefore the general standard of living, is going to be influenced by the decision. Consequently, the economist is directly interested in the factors which enter into that choice between sleeping and working.

In general, this means that a choice is within the scope of economics only when it involves something which can be *exchanged* or resources which have alternative uses. The man deciding between bed and a walk cannot pass on to anyone else the benefit he derives from either; it is entirely personal and subjective. But he *can* pass to someone else the result of an afternoon's work in a factory – he can sell the goods he produces or the labour which helps to produce them. Economics is primarily concerned with exchange, including the processes which lie on either side of it – the production of the thing exchanged and the consumption of the thing exchanged. Anything which affects these processes is within the scope of economics.

Even with this reservation, a definition of economics which links it with the overcoming of scarcity as such remains too wide. The quantity of food which can be produced with a given amount of labour and land, for example, is not solely an economic question. It involves technological issues such as the application of chemistry to soil fertility, or mechanical engineering to agricultural processes. On the other side, the consumption of food will be influenced by such factors as racial characteristics, climate and physiology. An economist obviously cannot be expected to be a master of all the sciences and technologies which have a bearing on even the simplest acts and occurrences of everyday human life. His interest in and special knowledge of all these things extends only as far as they influence, or are influenced by, the actual process of exchange. The chemical properties underlying a particular fertiliser are quite outside his ken, and, as an economist, he has no special interest in them. But he *has* an interest, and *is* concerned, if the application of that fertiliser, whatever its physical properties may or may not be, results in certain types of foodstuffs losing some of their exchange value through increased abundance, or if some development in the market for chemicals, or labour, or land, stimulates or discourages the application of the fertiliser concerned.

Exchange is vital to economics, then, not only because it indicates that a particular human activity has a social, as well as an individual, significance, but also because the economist is competent to analyse only those aspects of individual and social activity which in some direct way influence or are influenced by the process of exchange. Not *all* acts of exchange are of economic significance, however; the object being exchanged must be something scarce in relation to the need which society as a whole feels for it; mad dogs may be rare, but they are not scarce in this sense. The exchange must be based on scarcity; and the overcoming of the scarcity must have a direct bearing on the process of exchange.

It follows that economics studies those aspects of decision-making processes and procedures of exchange which arise from efforts to overcome the scarcity of desirable goods and services which humanity will always experience in comparison with its demand for them. But at this point it is necessary to consider a dilemma faced by all branches of systematic study at some time or another: is the scope of a subject (and therefore the skills and knowledge required for its serious study) properly defined in terms of the kind of problem which it seeks to solve or, on the other hand, is its legitimate sphere of competence defined by the particular skills and techniques which its study may inculcate? In other words, do we identify the sort of problem we would like to be able to solve and define the scope of economics so as to include whatever skills or knowledge are necessary to solve them or, conversely, define economics as a specified set of techniques and its sphere of competence in terms of those problems which we are thereby equipped to solve? There are two reasons why this dilemma has become especially acute for economics in the last decade or so.

The first of these is a simple matter of age. In one sense economics is a very old subject. The word 'economics' is itself derived from the Greek for (roughly) household management and the reader of Aristotle and Plato will find many discussions of issues which would nowadays be described as economic. The determination of such popular concerns of modern economics as wages and prices much exercised the scholastic theologians of the Middle Ages, while the pamphleteers, tract-writers and politicians of the ensuing centuries were deeply and continuously concerned with the economic problems of their time. Yet economics as a systematic, intellectual discipline unconnected with any particular issue or doctrine of the day and worthy of separate status in the universities, is a relatively new subject. Adam Smith, with his *Wealth of Nations* published in 1776, has some claim to be the founder of the subject in this sense although it was another century before there appeared the great systematic treatises on which the modern development of the subject has rested, especially (for the English-speaking world) Marshall's *Principles of Economics* in 1890.

For the first half of the twentieth century, therefore, most of the exponents of the subject were necessarily drawn from other, older disciplines – mathematics, philosophy, history and so on – a fact which much enriched the subject but equally led to great differences of approach and of concepts of the nature of the subject. Only in quite recent years has it been true to say that the development of the subject has passed into the hands of a generation wholly trained as professional economists. With that coming-of-age of the subject, so to speak, has come also a sharper awareness of the difference of view which exists concerning its inherent character.

The second reason for the increased awareness of the dilemma facing economics in recent years is to be found in the experience of ambitious and detailed intervention by governments in the economic affairs of their countries, frequently with the aid of the new generation of professional economists imported into the ranks of the public service. Inevitably, if not always fairly, more attention has been paid to the apparent failures of such interventions than to their successes – the continuous recurrence of crises in the realm of world trade and payments, disappointing rates of growth in living standards from one year to another, the apparent powerlessness of government in the face of accelerating increases in the general price level and so on. Inevitably some soul-searching has gone on under the general heading of: why have we failed?

The problem is inherent in the way in which economics has developed and is common to any subject which is described, as economics generally is, as a *social science*. The theoretical structure of the subject rests on a basis of logical, deductive reasoning from certain basic assumptions or postulates; its conclusions have to relate, however, to the real world of people whose actions and reactions are by no means exclusively governed by logical and rational considerations. Economic theory can predict how decisions will be made if the object of the process is solely and exclusively to obtain the maximum material gain from the use of a limited volume of scarce resources; its predictions are liable to be falsified, however, if and to the extent that decisions are determined by other types of motivation – ethical, political, cultural or sociological.

It is not necessary for the validity of economic analysis that these non-economic elements in human action should be totally absent – which is clearly impossible anyway. But it *is* necessary that they should not collectively exert so substantial an influence on the situation under analysis as to make the basic postulates or the process of logical reasoning seriously unrealistic. Herein lies the explanation of what appears to many to be the unsatisfactory record of economics and economists in the realm of major issues of national economic policy; as the analysis moves from relatively small groups operating towards a single, straightforward end – for example, a firm or industry producing a particular product – to the higher levels of national policies where many different ends are being pursued simultaneously – so the influence of the political and social factors increases relatively to that of the purely economic.

Two alternative remedies are possible in such a situation and each has its exponents in the debate over the true nature and requirements of the subject of economics. On the one hand are those who would define the subject in terms of the sort of problem which needs to be solved and conclude that the importance of political and sociological factors in them implies that the economist should know more, and take more account, of these other social sciences. These may be called the exponents of the subject of *political economy* – the name by which it was known until comparatively recently. On the other hand there are those who wish to emphasis the need for economics as a *scientific* subject rather than an inherently *social* study and conclude that problem areas in which non-scientific (i.e. non-measurable) factors exert a predominant influence are by definition beyond its scope. That

is, they would define the subject in terms of what it can do
rather than in terms of the problems which we would like to
be solved.

Both views are important and it will be as well to consider
each in a little more detail before proceeding further.

3   ECONOMICS AS POLITICAL ECONOMY

Economics is a social science and if the emphasis is placed on
the first of these two words its main focus of attention is turned
on society as a whole and, in particular, those aspects of the
social system concerned primarily with the exchange of goods
and services – mankind, as Alfred Marshall put it, in the 'ordinary business of life'. This would not be to deny that Robinson
Crusoe, alone on his island, had to face and solve economic
problems. But such situations, while useful for some elementary
theorising purposes, would be, in this concept of the subject,
exceptional and peripheral rather than in the mainstream of its
interests. Any society at any time is able to dispose of only
a finite quantity of the material requisites of physical well-being,
and the method by which that limited supply is allocated to
competing ends is the proper study of political economy.

The logical inference from such a definition of the subject is
that the economist would need to know a good deal about the
other subjects concerned with the operation of human societies,
not merely in order to ensure that his basic assumptions and
postulates are realistic but also to enable him to take due
account of non-economic motivations in analysing the chain of
cause and effect lying between those initial assumptions and
the final conclusions of his study. He will need to know a good
deal of human *psychology*, for example, since he will be concerned
with social groups in their roles of consumers and workers, and
the way in which their behaviour is affected by a multitude
of considerations ranging from the impact of advertising to the
consequences of repetitive work operations. Equally he will need
to understand something of the processes of *political* decision-
making and the operations of the machinery of government –
whether it be at a national level or of a trade union – since these

may have a fundamental bearing on the nature and solution of the allocative problem which is his primary concern.

Much of this knowledge can be gleaned from the study of economic *history*, since this is concerned with the collection and analysis of the evidence of how mankind has reacted to change in the past. An understanding of how society has generated and absorbed changes in its supply of goods and services in the past does not guarantee an ability to predict how it will react to comparable changes in the future, but it is an essential first point of departure for it.

Finally, the political economist will inevitably find himself involved with matters of *ethics*, since any study of social inter-relationships leads to questions of what is or is not desirable, or lawful, or good, in some sense. If the ultimate aim of economic analysis is, as many would argue, to produce policy prescriptions as to what should or should not be done to bring about some improvement in the material well-being of society, or some section of it, then economics has become a *normative* subject, deeply and necessarily involved with ethical judgements as to whether one situation is in some sense 'better' than another and whether the costs involved in one course of action are (again, in some sense) 'worth' the benefits believed to follow from it.

This, then, is one conception of the true nature and scope of economics – it is the study of that part of social behaviour concerned with material wealth and of the methods by which the problems associated with the inadequacy of that wealth, or its distribution, may be reduced. Because mankind is a complex many-sided species, the study of economics, so defined, must be associated with that of other specialities within the social studies group. It needs a theoretical, analytical framework as does any systematic body of knowledge, but it also needs a substantial factual and institutional knowledge of society and an involvement with the normative issues of what *should* be as well as what is.

4   ECONOMICS AS A SCIENCE

The second view of economics places the emphasis on the word 'science' rather than the word 'social'. That is to say, it would attribute any lack of success in the record of economic analysis to too much involvement (often implicit and unconscious) with political or normative considerations, rather than too little. If economists have failed to achieve conspicuous success in their predictions, it would be argued, it is because of inadequate rigour in their analysis and a failure to rest their work firmly on scientific method.

The word 'science' is used in a wide variety of senses but in the present context it may be defined as a branch of knowledge which requires the formulation of hypotheses about reality in such a form as to make them testable against objective evidence, the rejection of hypotheses which prove to be inconsistent with that evidence, and the ranking of alternative hypotheses concerning the same phenomena in accordance with the degree to which predictions based upon them are capable of explaining or accounting for the observed events to which they relate. The emphasis is thus placed on propositions which are (at least in principle) testable against objective evidence – that is, observable data which exist independently of the person advancing the proposition – and on the empirical verification of the consistency of the propositions concerned with the appropriate evidence.

Interpreted in this way, economics becomes a *positive* rather than a normative study. By definition it aims to arrive at explanations of or predictions concerning the real world which are established as consistent with the evidence available rather than propositions which *recommend* some course of action as being by some standard desirable and which are inherently incapable of proof or disproof. Its particular concern is, of course, those aspects of human activity which deal with the allocation of scarce resources having alternative uses between conflicting ends, but since it seeks to adopt scientific method it can concern itself only with decisions involving measurable entities; normative aspects such as the relative *desirability*, on some ethical or political scale of judgement, of either the ends themselves or the consequences of different courses of action are incapable of objective resolution and are therefore beyond its sphere of competence.

The questions which positive economic analysis seeks to answer are thus fundamentally different from those which are the concern of normative economics. The latter seeks ideally to answer questions of the form: what *should* be done in a given situation in order to raise, or maximise, human welfare? The former asks: in a given situation involving the allocation of scarce resources amongst competing uses, what will be the consequences of alternative courses of action? Furthermore, it is concerned with answers which can be tested against the evidence in order to establish their empirical validity. The *measurement* of the resources involved and the consequences of their use is therefore of the essence of the subject.

Positive economics is thus in some ways much more restricted but in other ways more general than normative economics. It is obviously more restricted, in that areas of decision-making which involve inherently non-measurable considerations are by definition excluded from its scope; many of the great policy issues, involving ethical or political considerations, must be beyond its reach; the positive economist must leave decisions concerning what is desirable or preferable to others and address himself only to such propositions concerning the consequences of different courses of action as can be tested against objective evidence. On the other hand, the subject so defined is no longer restricted to the area of 'social' studies, as that term is generally understood. It can be applied to allocative problems in literally every sphere of human activity, ranging from the engineer undecided as to whether a machine is or is not worth further maintenance, to the military strategist seeking to balance the conflicting claims of different forces for limited nuclear weapons, or the health administrator torn between competing demands for qualified doctors for general practice on the one hand and cancer research on the other. As a scientific technique, rather than the handmaiden of politics or ethics, its competence is more narrowly defined but its range of application is virtually infinite.

5   METHODS OF ECONOMIC ANALYSIS

These two conceptions of the nature and scope of economics are obviously fundamentally different and it is quite conceivable that by the end of the twentieth century they will have developed into two more or less distinct subjects; on the one hand there will be the 'social' study in which the emphasis will be on the economic aspects of some particular branch of social science leading to studies labelled 'political economy', 'economic geography', 'economic philosophy' and so on, while on the other there will be a subject labelled 'economics' devoted to the study of the scientific processes of decision-making whose students will speak the language of mathematics and statistics but have no special contact with the social sciences.

This, however, is a long way ahead – fortunately perhaps. In the present state of the subject the dichotomy of view need not impress itself too strongly in the early stages of study – that is, at the level with which this book attempts to deal. The different concepts of the subject are by no means immaterial at this elementary level and from time to time, when the conflict emerges, this book will lean frankly to the positive rather than the normative. But in general the tools of the trade are common to both types of practitioner; it is in the way in which they are used, and the material on which they are used, that the fundamental difference lies. What, then, are these tools of the trade?

Unlike the physical scientist, the economist cannot carry out controlled experiments under laboratory conditions, where all factors except the one under examination are prevented from operating, so that conclusions can be arrived at with a fair degree of certainty. The subject-matter of economics, it was said earlier, was once defined by Marshall as 'man in the ordinary business of life' – and man carrying out the ordinary business of life under laboratory conditions is a contradiction in terms. This method of analysis being denied him, then, the economist has recourse to two other methods – the deductive method and the inductive method.

By the *deductive* method is meant the process of logical deduction from a given proposition; the method is characteristic of, for example, mathematics. A hypothesis is taken as being true, and a process of reasoning is applied to it so as to bring out all the implications which it contained but which were not immediately obvious. For example, if it is postulated that the producers of goods will always act so as to obtain the greatest possible money profit, certain testable predictions can be derived from that postulate (they are in fact implicit in it) concerning the number of goods which they will sell in a given situation and the price at which they will sell them. Or again, it can be postulated that the more of a commodity a person consumes the less enjoyment he derives from each additional unit of it; from this hypothesis can be derived certain testable conclusions about the nature of demand.

The bulk of the theorising in economics is based on this type of procedure. It should be clearly understood, however, that the truth of any conclusions arrived at in this way will depend on three things: first, the correctness of the process of logical deduction; second, the realism of the original hypothesis; and third, the degree to which man himself acts logically in the context involved. The first need not cause much concern. If I say 'A is true, therefore it follows that B will happen', and my reasoning is in fact faulty, clearly my conclusion will be wrong. However, as a science establishes itself, by constant discussion and development, errors of this kind are eventually discovered and put right. The basic theory set out in this book is, for the most part, the outcome of the analysis and criticism of many generations of scholars, and elementary logical errors are scarcely likely to have survived this process.

The second two limitations on the method are more serious. The problem of deciding upon a hypothesis having general usefulness is a difficult one for a science concerning itself with human nature in all its infinite complexity. The hypothesis that producers always seek to obtain greatest profit, for example, is falsified every day by producers who act in the interests of their workpeople, or society, or according to long-established routines, rather than in the pursuit of maximum profit. And conclusions drawn from a hypothesis are unlikely to be valid if that hypothesis is wildly unrealistic.

Similarly, assuming that a sound hypothesis is found, conclusions drawn from it by rigorous logic will be true of the real world only if mankind also draws the logical inference from a fact and acts upon it in practice. A worker might accept the hypothesis that he would prefer to work for a high wage rather than a low wage, but a deduction that he will therefore move from factory X, where he is paid £10, to factory Y, where he could get £12, might be falsified in the event because the man fails to act rationally – he may instead be influenced by instinct or laziness and so on. How many of us as consumers are perfectly rational in our purchases? Where is the person who has never bought something 'on the spur of the moment', i.e. quite irrationally?

Because of these limitations to the usefulness of abstract reasoning, economists must always have recourse to the essential second half of scientific method – the empirical (or *inductive*) testing of theoretical propositions. Here the appeal is to facts, rather than reasoning, and an attempt is made to verify conclusions from the known facts of actual life. Economic historians, for example, seek to find in the record of history explanations of important economic occurrences and developments. Statisticians collect data about production, prices, wages, and employment, and the figures are analysed to find significant trends or inter-relationships. Inductive work of this kind can in itself give rise to generalisations: the collection of data concerning the household expenditure of various classes in the community, for instance, might indicate some relationship between income, or social class, and spending habits which would not have been arrived at by logical argument alone.

It is in combination with the deductive method, however, that this type of analysis is most useful. By it one can test a theory arrived at through logical deduction against the experience of reality, and so expose unrealistic hypotheses or faulty reasoning. Empirical analysis can never *prove* a theory, since the world is so complex that the data never admit of only one explanation; facts seldom 'speak for themselves' and never with one voice. But a theory can be shown to be *inconsistent* with the facts, and therefore wrong. On the other hand, deductive analysis must come before inductive, since in empirical work a choice has always to be made from an infinite number of facts and figures, and this choice necessarily presupposes some theorising. If I am investigating the demand for eggs over the past ten years, and examine data concerning the price of eggs, the production of eggs and the price of bacon, then I have implicitly postulated a theory relating the demand for eggs to those factors, and I am now testing the degree to which the facts confirm that relationship. The two types of analysis are therefore interdependent, each being valuable and necessary.

One other distinction needs to be made clear at this stage. Contemporary economic analysis is usually classified into either *micro-economics* or *macro-economics*. The former is the branch of theory which concerns itself with individual units or particular sectors of the economy – such as the demand for a particular product or its relative value, or the output of particular firms or industries. Macro-economics, on the other hand, considers the economic system as a whole and the relationship to the whole and to each other of broad aggregates – such as the general price level, the rate of investment and changes in overall industrial production – and concerns itself with individual groups of producers or consumers only in so far as they influence the economy in its entirety. Broadly speaking, Parts II–V of this book are devoted to micro-economics, while Part VII is an introduction to macro-economics.

6 ECONOMIC LAWS

From a systematic analysis of a deductive and inductive nature what is called an 'economic law' is frequently arrived at – for example, discussion will later centre on the law of diminishing utility, the law of decreasing returns and other generalisations. Unfortunately economics can have no pretensions to arriving at immutable and universal truths such as those resulting from the development of physics and chemistry. The law of gravity, or Boyle's laws, will always remain valid so long as the natural order prevails. But economics is concerned with human beings, and human beings, unlike inanimate matter, have minds and wills of their own, with the result that one can never be *certain* as to how they will react in any given situation. All that economics can do, and all that it attempts to do, is to indicate from its deductive and inductive analysis certain generalisations which are *likely* to be valid of human beings in the mass and in the long run. The 'laws' which are arrived at, in other words, are statements of *tendencies* that are likely to result from certain causes.

For example, the law of demand indicates that, generally, the lower the price of a commodity the greater the amount of it which will be consumed. That could not be relied upon to be true of any single individual; some people, for example, may already have enough of it and will not increase their consumption of it however cheap it becomes. For the whole body of consumers taken together, however, it is very likely to be true, since both reason and experience indicate that sooner or later some people are bound to increase their consumption of the commodity involved.

Although economic laws can never be treated as if they were as universal and as certain as physical laws, therefore, their significance should nevertheless not be under-rated. They rest on the behaviour of people in fairly large numbers; they express what the normal and natural reaction of people will be to economic forces. This is a weakness in so far as no single individual can be relied on to behave in precisely the way that the group as a whole is likely to behave. But it is a strength in so far as such laws rest on the firm foundation of human nature which, although unpredictable in the individual, is immensely powerful in the community as a whole. If a parliamentary law is passed which conflicts with an economic law (i.e. with the natural inclination of ordinary people in matters relating to their economic welfare) it is doubtful if the parliamentary law will long survive as an effective measure. The experience of rationing and price regulations during wartime, for example, shows that it is only with the aid of determined enforcement and a lively social discipline amongst the community that economic laws can be prevented from asserting themselves in the form of black markets, as they did in many countries. Even in countries where the effects of conflicts of this kind have been successfully repressed, it is fairly clear that as time passes the tendencies described by economic laws become increasingly powerful. Even if they cannot claim anything approaching universal validity, then, economic laws are firmly rooted in human nature or experience, and although human nature can be restrained, and sometimes altered, neither is an easy task.

FURTHER READING

C. NAPOLEONI *Economic thought of the twentieth century* Martin Robertson, London 1972, Chs. 1–2

K. E. BOULDING *Economics as a science* McGraw-Hill Book Company, New York 1970

E. MANSFIELD *Micro-economics* Norton, New York 1970, Ch. 1

R. WEISS *The economic system* Random House, New York 1969, Ch. 7

E. H. PHELPS BROWN 'The under-development of economics', *Economic Journal*, Vol. 82, No. 325, March 1972

M. FRIEDMAN 'The methodology of positive economics', *Essays in positive economics* University of Chicago Press, Chicago 1953

CHAPTER II

The Economic Problem

1 WHAT IS THE 'ECONOMIC PROBLEM'?

IN the preceding chapter the *economic problem* was defined as
that of allocating scarce resources which have various alternative
uses amongst different desired ends which cannot all be satisfied,
and which therefore compete with one another for the use of
those scarce resources. At first sight this definition may seem
very far removed from the conception of economics held by the
man in the street: he thinks of the subject in terms of broad
national policies concerning budgets or wages or foreign
exchange rates – issues involving the Stock Exchange or central
banks or high-powered international conferences. Yet this essentially simple allocative problem is the underlying reason for, and
subject-matter of, these more sophisticated and glamorous
features of modern society. It is as well, therefore, to begin with
a careful scrutiny of the fundamental characteristics of the allocative problem: some general principles can be discerned which
recur time and time again when the discussion has to move into
these more arcane areas.

Every allocative problem involves three main ingredients –
first, a statement of the end it is desired to achieve, *second*,
a technical relation between the quantities of resources (or *inputs*)
used for the given purpose and the product resulting from that
use (or *output*) and, *third*, a limitation imposed by circumstances
on the quantities of inputs available. The economic problem is
invariably that of how to get the *most* out of the resources available to any person, group or society or, conversely, how to attain
a specified end with the use of the minimum quantity of those
scarce resources. In mathematical terms, the problem is always
that of maximising something subject to a constraint or, con-

versely, minimising the inputs required in order to achieve a specified end. The three elements are always present: a statement of the *object* desired by the decision-maker, a *technical* relationship between inputs and output and a *budgetary* constraint imposed by the scarcity of the resources available to any of us in relation to all the uses to which those resources could conceivably be put.

Now the first two of these are beyond the explanatory competence of the economist. The desired end he must take as given: he has no special authority to pronounce on whether it is good or bad, wise or foolish. Similarly, the technical relationships he must leave others, specialised in the relevant areas, to define and explain. As was noted in the previous chapter, if the agricultural scientist tells him that the output of a certain crop will be increased in a specified proportion by the application of a particular fertiliser, this is something he takes as a datum; other specialists must be left to explain *why* this should be so or to determine ways in which the effect of that (or some other) fertiliser on crop fertility may be improved. The technological or psychological relationships existing between scarce resources and the uses of which they are capable, in other words, are part of the essential data of his analysis but not the subject of it. In fact, economic activities such as consumption and production may well be bound up with almost every special study in existence, from psychology and physiology to chemistry, engineering and nuclear physics. Naturally the economist does not presume to trespass into these specialised fields of knowledge. He will not seek to enquire *why* people consume tea in one country and coffee in another, or *why* a combine harvester will cover a given acreage in a fraction of the time taken by a horse-drawn reaper. He leaves to other specialists the task of explaining what these technical realities are and why these things are so; he takes them as facts of the situation just as much as climatic conditions or the inherent qualities of the race.

When the third element – the choice between alternative uses of limited resources – is superimposed on these technical relationships, however, the problem ceases to be a purely technical one, to be decided by the specialist in the area concerned; it becomes an economic one – and hence within the province of economic analysis. Any decision which involves the achievement of a specified end – the production of a steel ingot or the baking of an apple pie – through the use of *less* of one or more inputs and without the *increased* use of any is a technical decision, since it involves no choice between conflicting uses; something is gained but nothing has to be sacrificed – the state of technology, in fact, has improved. But few decisions in real life are of this kind: most involve a choice between the use of more of one thing and less of another, so that the issue of selection between alternatives becomes inescapable: is the gain on one side more than counterbalanced by the loss on another – or not? Bearing in mind the fact that resources are scarce, their use for one purpose necessarily implies their loss for some other use – scarce resources, in other words, always have an *opportunity cost*. It is of the essence of the economic problem, as distinct from a purely technical problem, that the output obtained by the use of resources for any given purpose must be measured against this opportunity cost – that is, the output it was capable of attaining in some other (possibly quite dissimilar) use. It will be helpful to examine one very simple illustration of such a problem: the method of analysis, and some of the conclusions, will prove to be of very general applicability over the entire universe of economic analysis.

2 A TECHNICAL PROBLEM: LAND AREA*

Suppose that an official land agency has decided to offer land to new settlers for the construction of houses and provides a maximum of 160 metres of fencing which must be used to enclose each individual plot. Each applicant is told that he can have whatever space he can enclose with the official fencing, the only restriction being that the area enclosed must be rectangular in order to avoid the creation of small pieces of territory occupied by no one. Assuming that each applicant wishes to acquire as

---

* The example is based, in its initial stages, on K. J. Cohen and R. M. Cyert, *Theory of the firm,* Prentice-Hall, Englewood Cliffs, New Jersey 1965, Ch. 3, pp. 31–5.

large a site as possible for his house, each faces the problem of how to decide the dimensions of the area he will proceed to fence with his allotted material.

If any prospective settler were familiar with the techniques of the differential calculus he could reach an answer to his problem in the space of a minute or two, but it can be assumed for present purposes that this is not amongst his accomplishments. How is his problem to be solved?

Now it can be assumed that he *does* know that the area of a piece of land is the product of its width and length — i.e.

$$\text{Area } (A) = \text{Length } (L) \times \text{Width } (W)$$

It follows that any given area can be obtained with an infinite number of combinations of length and width and it will be useful to set these possibilities out graphically as is done in Fig. 2A(i).

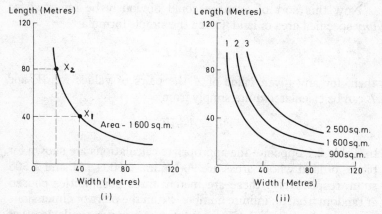

Fig. 2A   A technical relation: the area of a field and its dimensions

The curve in this diagram traces out all those combinations of dimensions which will give the same area of land — in this example, 1 600 square metres — measuring the length of the sides of the rectangle along the vertical axis and its width along the horizontal axis. Point X_1, for example, corresponds to a rectangle (a square to be precise) with length and width 40 metres;

point X_2 to one 80 metres long and 20 metres wide; other points would correspond to:

Length (metres)	Width (metres)
100	16
50	32
25	64
20	80
10	160

and so on. Clearly there will be an infinite number of such combinations; plotting them all and joining the points so plotted will result in the continuous curve shown in Fig. 2A(i). This curve is a graphical representation of the technical relation between inputs (dimensions of length and width) and a given, fixed output — an area of 1 600 square metres.

Now this sort of exercise could obviously be repeated for *any* specified area of land. Given the simple formula

$$A = W \times L$$

then, for any given value of A the pairs of values for W and L can be calculated quite simply from

$$L = A \div W.$$

In Table 2.1 opposite the appropriate calculations are shown for pieces of land whose areas are 900 sq.m., 1 600 sq.m. and 2 500 sq.m. respectively: these are merely three possibilities chosen at random from an infinite number. From the pairs of dimensions corresponding to each area a continuous curve similar to that of Fig. 2A(i) can be drawn up and these are shown as curves 1, 2 and 3 in Fig. 2A(ii). An infinite number of such curves could be constructed but the three shown are sufficient to illustrate the general principle. The *map* so formed represents the whole range of possible areas which the prospective settler could enclose within the limits of the dimensions shown, each curve representing an area greater than that represented by any to its left but smaller than that represented by any to its right.

But at this point the constraint under which the prospective settler is working has to be taken into account; while the number of possibilities technically open is infinite, his resources are not — he has only his allotted quota of a maximum of 160 metres

TABLE 2.1 *Technical relationships between area and dimensions*

Width of field in metres	Length of field in metres (area divided by width)		
	Area 1: 900 sq.m.	Area 2: 1 600 sq.m.	Area 3: 2 500 sq.m.
10·0	90.0	160·0	250·0
20·0	45·0	80·0	125·0
30·0	30·0	53·3	83·3
40·0	22·5	40·0	62·5
50·0	18·0	32·0	50·0
60·0	15·0	26·7	41·7
70·0	12·9	22·9	35·7
80·0	11·3	20·0	31·3
90·0	10·0	17·8	27·8

of fencing which must surround the chosen site. This, too, can be shown visually. For any chosen length of site he must allocate twice that length of fencing, there being two sides of that length to cope with. The fencing left for the remaining sides will thus be limited to

$$160 - 2L$$

so that the maximum width of his site will be determined for him — i.e.

$$2W = 160 - 2L$$

Once again an infinite number of combinations are possible but in this case they must all lie within the limits of $L = 80$ (i.e. $2L = 160$) and $W = 0$ at one (obviously silly) extreme to $W = 80$

(i.e. $2W = 160$) and $L = 0$ (equally silly) at the other. Now all these possible combinations are illustrated in Fig. 2B: in this PP′ represents all possible combinations lying between 160 m. length (i.e. two sides of 80 m. each) and 160 m (i.e. 2×80 m.) width. Any set of dimensions lying within this range — i.e. within the triangle POP′ — is open to the settler; any combination outside — that is, to the right of — this triangle is beyond his grasp, given the limitation of 160 m. of fencing imposed on him.

The solution to the settler's problem is now clear. Assuming that he wishes to maximise the area of land enclosed, he seeks to reach a combination of dimensions lying on a curve in Fig. 2A which is as far to the right as possible. The straight line PP′ of Fig. 2B embodies the constraint he is operating under and thus defines the combinations of dimensions *possible*. The obvious next step is to bring the two diagrams together and to trace out both the 'technical relation' curves of Fig. 2A and the 'possibility line' of Fig. 2B in a single diagram, as is done in Fig. 2C. It is clear that the solution of the prospective settler's problem must lie at the point where the 'possibility' line touches the furthest curve to the right attainable.

In Fig. 2C this is obviously point X on curve 2; any curve to the right (e.g. curve 3) requires combinations of dimensions beyond his capability (i.e. lie beyond his possibility line) while any other combination of dimensions on or inside his possibility

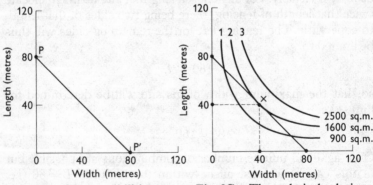

Fig. 2B   The possibilities open   Fig. 2C   The technical solution

line fails to attain curve 2 and gives an area less than 1 600 sq. in. Reading off from point X, it will be seen that this 'best' or *optimum* combination of length and width corresponds to a rectangle whose length and width is 40 m. – i.e. a square. Any other set of dimensions would *either* require more than 160 m. of fencing (which he does not have) *or* give him a smaller area of ground (which by assumption he does not want).

3   TECHNICAL BECOMES ECONOMIC

As so far stated, the settler's problem is not strictly an economic one. He is seeking to maximise the use of scarce resources – his quota of 160 metres of fencing – but those scarce resources *do not have alternative uses*. If he uses less than 160 metres there is no advantage to him: the authorities will not give him something else to compensate him for taking up less than his full quota. No problem of *choice* is involved – merely the technical matter of the relationship between area and dimensions which he has to accept as given and beyond his power to influence.

Consider therefore a somewhat more complex (but, equally, more realistic) version of the same problem. Suppose that the settlers are offered by the government not a maximum *quantity* of fencing but a grant of up to £800 with which to buy fencing but which cannot be used for any other purpose. They are told, however, that the type of fencing needed for the sides of the site running north to south (the 'length' sides) is different from that required for the sides running east to west (the 'width' sides). The settlers do now really face a choice of using resources which have alternative uses, since the total length of fencing available to each is not a fixed amount; it depends not only on the total grant but also on the relative amounts of *L*-type fencing and *W*-type fencing they choose to have. Each £1 spent on *L*-type fencing, in other words, has an *opportunity cost* amounting to the length of *W*-type fencing which that £1 would have been capable of buying. Fortunately, the apparatus of Fig. 2C allows this sort of complexity to be taken into account quite easily.

If the unit prices of both types of fencing are fixed, the immediate effect of defining a *monetary* limit to the resources available,

rather than fixing those limits in terms of a single type of fencing
applicable to both *L*-sides and *W*-sides, is again to fix unambiguously the limits of the 'possibility line' – or *budget* line as it
is known in economics – and thus the range of possibilities open.
Suppose, first, that both types of fencing have a price of £5·00
per metre. The limits of the budget line are thus set: £800 will
buy 160 metres of *either* *L*-fencing *or* *W*-fencing so that the
limiting dimensions are 80 metres long and 80 metres wide.
The line P_1P_1' in Fig. 2D(i) connects these two limits and any
combination of dimensions lying on or inside it will be within
the settler's maximum budget. The solution to his problem is
seen to be exactly as in Fig. 2C when he was dealing with a
single type of fencing – he can enclose a maximum of 1 600
sq.m. with a square 40 metres by 40 metres. This is hardly
surprising, since if both types have the same price they *are*
virtually the same thing so far as his budgetary limit is concerned.

Suppose now that the two types of fencing have different
prices – in particular, that *L*-type fencing has a price of £3·20
per metre while *W*-type fencing still costs £5·00 per metre. The
limiting points of his budget line are now different; £800 will
buy 250 metres of *L*-type fence and 160 metres of *W*-type. The
combination of dimensions open to him therefore ranges from
a length of 125 metres and zero width to a width of 80 metres
and a zero length. The budget line P_2P_2' in Fig. 2D(ii) traces
out all the possibilities open to him within those limits. Two
differences between this situation and that of Fig. 2D(i) are immediately apparent. First, the settler is now able to reach curve

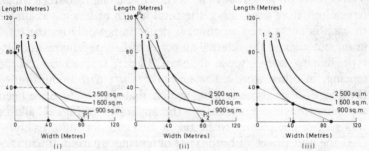

Fig. 2D   Solving the problem with prices

3 – i.e. enclose an area of 2 500 sq.m. Secondly, his optimum shape will no longer be a square; it will in fact be a rectangle 40 metres wide but 62·5 metres long. The fall in the price of *L*-type fencing has not only allowed him to stretch his £800 budget further and enclose a bigger area; it has also led him to give more emphasis to length than width in his chosen shape.

Consider finally a case where the different prices are *L*-type = £10·00 per metre and *W*-type = £4·42 per metre. His budget will now buy a maximum of 80 metres of *L*-type or about 181 metres of *W*-type. The limiting dimensions are thus 40 metres long and 90·5 metres wide and these are shown by P_3P_3' in Fig. 2D(iii). The combination of dimensions which enable him to reach the maximum area – 900 sq.m. in this case – is one of 20 m. length and 45 m. width. The change in prices has both limited the area attainable and given a bias towards a site in which the north–south dimensions are reduced and the east–west dimensions increased.

At first sight this example may seem rather far removed from what is commonly understood to be the subject of economics. Yet it illustrates both the characteristic elements of every economic problem and the essentials of the solution to all such problems. Every economic problem comprises three crucial elements: a *behavioural assumption*, specifying the objective which the decision-maker is assumed to be seeking, a *technical relation* – that between dimensions and the area of a building site in this example – and a *budget constraint* which imposes a limit on the resources available in the pursuit of the objective – the supply of fencing in this case.

The objective sought is, in general, much more complex than the area of a piece of land: so far as people in their capacity as *producers* are concerned, it will relate to the flow of output of goods or services over time, while so far as people in their capacity as *consumers* are concerned it will concern the level of welfare or satisfaction obtained by them (or those for whom they act) again over some period of time. The relationship between the degree of attainment of the objective and the resources used up will never be as simple and direct as that between length and width, on the one hand, and area on the other; a good deal more will need to be said about the nature of these relationships as the analysis proceeds. It may be as well, however, if a little more is said about the third element in the economic problem before proceeding further – the generalised equivalent of the fencing material.

4 FACTORS OF PRODUCTION

A community derives its income through the intelligent use of the resources with which it is endowed. Unfortunately manna does not rain from Heaven any more; everything society consumes or puts into its capital stock has to be *produced*. The resources which society employs in this production can be classified into four groups comprising resources of broadly similar characteristics. These groups are called *inputs* or *factors of production*, meaning (literally) the things that make the production of wealth possible. The factors are:

Land – meaning not only the fields and hills, but all the other resources endowed by nature: the sun, wind, rain, water-power and mineral wealth. The quality of land, of course, varies enormously over the globe, not only because of its geological qualities but also because of its position, the prevailing climate, etc.

Capital – briefly, capital may be defined as the stock of wealth existing at any moment of time; it comprises all those goods which are wanted by their owners because of the contribution they will make to the production or consumption of wealth in the future. It would therefore include manufacturers' or wholesalers' stocks of finished products.

Labour – the exercise of human physical or mental powers in the creation of wealth. The part played may be indirect, such as the manufacture of a single small component in a complex finished product. Or the labour may be directed not to the production of any tangible commodity but to the performance of personal services – as is the case with a teacher, or nurse, or lawyer.

Enterprise – a particular form of labour having such special characteristics, and playing such a special role in the economic system, that it is best thought of as a separate factor. It refers to the exercise of powers of *initiative* in the controlling of the other factors, to the supply of *enterprise* in seeking out, developing and applying new methods, products or inventions and above all to the bearing of the *risk* and *uncertainty* associated with these functions in a dynamic world.

On these four factors, operating together, depends the production of wealth. Different societies, or even different generations, are endowed with each of the four in varying measure; the production of wealth in a society will be at its maximum when the factors are used fully and combined with one another in the most efficient proportions.

The world 'efficient' has just been used, however, and this draws attention to the importance of two elements in the economic framework which influence the wealth-creating capacity of a society just as much as its endowment of these scarce factors of production: these are the state of technology and the capacity of decision-takers to apply the latest advances of technology in their use of scarce resources. The prospective settler in the earlier example was able to enclose the maximum possible area of land only if he *knew* the maximum feasible area to be enclosed with various dimensions: having sufficient fencing to enclose it would not have been enough in itself. Similarly, any member of or group in society will be limited in the output attained with any given quantity of inputs by its knowledge of what, according to the current state of the industrial arts, is technically feasible and by its ability to apply that technology. Two producers with the same usage of inputs will end up with quite different outputs if they differ in the degree of advancement of the technology they are employing in using those inputs.

A distinction must be drawn, then, between production and productivity. The latter refers not to the total quantity produced over a given period but rather to the quantity produced per unit of resources used up. Thus if a firm, through the adoption of better techniques, or more efficient equipment, or improved labour relations, manages to maintain its previous output with a smaller labour force, production is constant but productivity has risen. Conversely, if a firm increases its output but only at the cost of even greater increases in its outlays on labour and capital, production has risen but productivity has fallen.

In principle, productivity can only be measured by taking

account of all resources used up in producing wealth but in practice this is far from easy to do. Much attention has been given in economics to the problem of why productivity rises more rapidly in some economies, or in some periods of time, than in others. It has to be admitted that this is a branch of the subject which has so far succeeded in generating many more questions than it has answers.

5 THE MARGIN

The example of the settler enclosing a piece of land illustrates the two basic characteristics of the economic *problem* – the technical relation between inputs and outputs and the limitations imposed by the scarcity of available resources. It also illustrates a very important characteristic of the *solution* – the necessity of arriving at a position where the value of the addition to output achieved by an extra unit of any given input is exactly equal to its cost.

Consider the solution illustrated in any of the three diagrams of Fig. 2D. In each case the maximum area was achieved when the line showing the relative cost of the two inputs – i.e. the quantity of one which would have to be sacrificed in order to obtain one more unit of the other – was a *tangent* to the technical possibilities curve: that is, it had the *same slope* at that point. The precise significance of this equality will be explained in different contexts as the analysis proceeds but it brings out the crucial role of this concept of 'an extra unit' in problems of this sort – what is referred to in economics as the 'marginal' unit.

In almost all contemporary economic theory great reliance is placed on the use of this concept of the *margin*. The concept is an unfamiliar one, and it is essential that the student should be quite clear as to what it means. In the economic world adjustments are constantly being made by both producers and consumers. Producers are always increasing or decreasing their output in response to changes in demand, or using more or less labour or capital as new methods of production come along. Consumers, similarly, are constantly altering the pattern of their expenditure as the prices of some commodities change relatively to those of others, or as fashions die or are created. A great deal of economics, indeed, is devoted to the analysis of the effects of adjustments such as these on the economy as a whole.

Now although economic conditions are never completely stable, so that these adjustments of production or consumption are constantly occurring, the process of change is always a *gradual* one. An industry as a whole never comes into existence or goes out of existence *en bloc* and overnight. Firms gradually expand or reduce their output, one or two new ones may be created or may move into the production of some different commodity. As a result, for both the individual firm and the industry of which it forms part, the choice is seldom between producing or not producing. The choice is usually between producing a few extra units of output or a few less units.

The same is true of consumers. Only rarely do instances occur of people suddenly giving up altogether the consumption of a particular commodity; the usual situation is that in which a person decides to buy rather less of this and rather more of that. This is especially true when it is remembered that the economist is usually concerned with the *total* demand for products, rather than the demand of an individual. In a market where consumers number thousands, or perhaps tens of thousands, changes are bound to be gradual; even if some individuals give up the consumption of a commodity altogether, or if new buyers come in who previously bought nothing, the proportionate effect on *total* demand is bound to be small. Cases have been known in which consumer demand suddenly underwent a violent change upwards or downwards, but these are distinctly exceptional.

Given this inherent characteristic of the real world, where production and consumption are the outcome of decisions by a large number of separate individuals, economic analysis naturally concentrates on the places where the changes occur. If 99 people consume today the same number of apples as yesterday, but one man stops eating apples today, any effects on the price of apples can be connected with the one man who for some reason has altered his consumption; economic analysis can concentrate on this element of change and ignore the elements which have not changed. If 9 producers keep a constant output and the tenth expands his by 50 per cent, analysis will again concentrate on this one changing factor in the situation.

This frontier, so to speak, at which changes and adjustments are liable to occur is called in economics the *margin*. The particular commodities which someone starts to consume, or ceases consuming, are called the *marginal units*. The marginal apple is no different physically from any other apple; it is simply that apple which would not be bought if demand changed infinitesimally and left consumers buying one apple less than before; the man who would give up that apple would be the marginal consumer — the man who would reduce his consumption of apples by one if (for example) the price of apples rose very slightly.

Similarly, economists speak of the marginal producer — the man who is just induced to produce a certain commodity with the existing level of profits to be obtained from it, but who would give up producing it if his profits fell slightly. If a shoe manufacturer thinks that at the present price it is worth his while to produce 100 pairs of shoes over a given period, then the hundredth pair of shoes is the marginal unit. It is no different from any other pair; it could not be picked out of his production line. Nevertheless there is a pair of shoes which he would *not* produce if prices fell a little, and that is the marginal pair.

This concept will recur time and again in the course of this study, in all kinds of contexts. As it appears in each connection it will be defined for the special purpose for which it is being used. But the essential nature of the concept remains the same in all contexts; it always refers to that last single unit in the total supply which a person thinks is just, but only just, worth exchanging, and which would cease to be exchanged if its price or cost altered very slightly.

6 WEALTH AND WELFARE

For a commodity or service to enter into exchange, and therefore to fall within the purview of economics, it must be scarce and it must be desired for some purpose. If it is not scarce — that is, if there is more than sufficient for everyone to have as much as he wants — there will be no need for people to give something else in exchange for it. If the product concerned is not desired, no one will *want* to take it in exchange for something else. There is still a third requirement, however; it must be physically possible to exchange the commodity in question. My health is a real asset to me, and plenty of people would pay a great deal if I could somehow give them part or all of my good health in exchange for their indifferent health. But it just cannot be done; therefore my health, infinitely valuable though it is to me, has no exchange value — that is, it cannot be used to obtain goods and services through the process of exchange. The economic problem consists of allocating resources between various competing uses; hence it cannot arise in connection with entities which cannot be transferred or exchanged. Since economics is concerned with exchange in all its aspects, 'value' to the economist means *exchange value*, and the word will be used only in that sense in all that follows. However treasured a thing may be to an individual (a souvenir, a quality, an experience and so on), if that thing cannot be exchanged then so far as the economist is concerned it has no value.

In economic analysis, the word *wealth* means the total value of things possessed by a person or group of persons. Those things may be tangible goods such as houses, factories, land or cars, intangible assets such as skill or business goodwill, or sums of money. So long as they have value — that is, exchange value — they constitute wealth. Hence economists speak of individual, or private, wealth and of the wealth of a country or group of countries. As will be noted in a little while, wealth can be regarded as either the total stock existing at any one moment or a flow being acquired and consumed over a period of time.

It is not difficult to see that wealth is not the same thing as *welfare*. By welfare is meant the general condition of well-being of a person or group of persons, including their mental and moral as well as their material well-being. The assessment of general social welfare has to take account of considerations such as the contentment of society, its cultural level, the state of law and order, or the health and education of the people. Economic welfare is that part of social welfare arising from the

wealth-producing and consuming activities of a community.
Normally, a rise in economic welfare – people becoming materially better-off – will be associated with a rise in welfare as
a whole. Normally, but not necessarily. A despotic government
may force its subjects to work longer hours and produce more
goods, for example, but the people may well think that the loss
of their liberty (or even their leisure) more than offsets the improvement in their supply of goods.

7   CAPITAL AND INCOME

A second important distinction in connection with wealth revolves round the question of whether, in a count-up of a community's wealth, it is intended to calculate how much wealth
exists at a particular *moment* of time or to measure how much
wealth the community will produce, or has produced, over a
particular *period* of time – whether a flashlight 'still' photograph
is being taken, so to speak, or a moving picture. If the former
approach is followed, then the wealth is a certain stock which
exists and can be counted up and valued, and that stock is known
as *capital*. It would consist of what is usually called *fixed capital*
– factories, houses, roads, machinery, shipyards – or of *working* capital – raw materials, half-finished goods still in course
of manufacture, or stocks of finished goods. All capital is wealth
which will be consumed only some time in the future; the difference between working and fixed capital is that the former
is destined to be consumed on a single occasion, as particular
goods in which it is embodied are finished and sold, while the
latter will be consumed only indirectly as it contributes over
the years to the production of a whole series of goods, or yields
a protracted flow of services, and is gradually worn out.

If the second approach is adopted, however, and the amount
of wealth produced over a period of time is measured, *income*
is being calculated. Unlike capital, the total amount cannot be
visualised as one enormous collection existing at a particular
moment, because income is a *flow* which passes into consumption
or into additions to capital as it is produced. The economic
system can be likened to a river pouring through a pipe into

a reservoir and then out again into the houses of consumers. To measure the amount of capital, the amount of water existing in the reservoir on a particular day would have to be calculated; to measure income, the quantity of water which had passed in through the pipe during a given week, or month, or year would have to be calculated. The amount flowing into the reservoir during a particular week might be the same as the amount flowing out to consumers through the outlet pipe. In that case the volume of the water in the reservoir would be the same at the end of the week as at the beginning, except for any loss from leakage or evaporation. If more water flows in than flows out, then the reservoir level will be higher. Much the same is true in economics. If the inflow (income) is equal to the outflow (expenditure by consumers) then the capital stock will be unchanged except for a wastage economists call *depreciation*. (More will be heard of this a little later.) If income exceeds consumer expenditure, then the difference will take the form of a greater capital stock – a process economists call *capital formation*. If consumers spend *more* than they earn, then the community's capital is getting smaller – a process which can no more continue indefinitely than can the process of taking more out of a reservoir than is being put in.

8 CONCLUSION

To summarise, then, the economic problem consists of the allocation of scarce resources between competing ends in order to attain some desired objective. The simple example used earlier in this chapter demonstrates the three essential ingredients of the problem – the identification of the objective to be attained, the technical relations between what is sacrificed to attain it and what is obtained or produced and the constraint imposed by the limitation of resources available. In Part II this framework is used to analyse the behaviour of consumers in allocating their limited wealth between all the possible kinds of expenditure open to them; in Part III it is used to examine the behaviour of producers in allocating factors of production between all the kinds of product they are capable of making. Parts IV and V examine how these two sets of decision-making processes interact to determine the market values of both products and factors of production. From there on the analysis considers the operation and consequences of these economic decision-making processes in the wider context of society as a whole and the problems of policy which their interaction can and does generate.

FURTHER READING

K. J. COHEN and R. M. CYERT *Theory of the firm* Prentice-Hall, Englewood Cliffs, New Jersey 1965, Ch. 3

L. ROBBINS *The economist in the twentieth century* Macmillan, London 1954, Ch. 1

E. MANSFIELD *Micro-economics* Ch. 1

E. NEVIN *An introduction to micro-economics* Croom Helm, London 1973, Ch. 1

PART II

THE THEORY OF DEMAND

CHAPTER III

Individual Demand

1 TOTAL AND MARGINAL UTILITY

IN the nineteenth century the word 'utility' was defined, for the purposes of economic analysis, as the satisfaction, or pleasure, or benefit derived by a person from the consumption of wealth. A moment's reflection on those words 'satisfaction', 'pleasure' and 'benefit' will be enough to show that they are vague and elusive terms. In particular, they are essentially *introspective* terms – that is, they relate to inner sentiments and emotions and not to things having an objective, physical existence, although the phenomena they describe are none the less real for that. For example, Smith may derive intense enjoyment from wearing a tie which Brown can look at only with intense suffering; one man's meat is another man's poison, as we say. Utility is something experienced within a person and is not inherent in the physical commodity with the aid of which he experiences it.

Given its introspective nature there is obviously no way in which to measure *total utility* – that is, the total satisfaction derived by a person from a commodity – any more than any human sentiment or emotion can be measured. I may believe that my bad tooth is causing me more pain than yours is causing you, but there is no way of testing this belief; similarly, you can believe that you have enjoyed a certain film more than I have, but there is no way of proving it.

The position is not quite the same with *marginal utility*. By this expression 'marginal utility' is meant the addition to a person's total utility brought about through the consumption of the last unit of a commodity he consumes. If I use three gallons of petrol in a week, then my marginal utility is the difference between the total utility I derive from the three gallons and the total utility I would have derived if I had used only two. If I go to the cinema six times each month, then my marginal utility from seeing films is the difference between the total utility I derive from six films and the utility I would derive from seeing five. As will be established in a little while, this is·by no means the same thing as saying that the marginal utility of a commodity is the total utility a person derives from it divided by the number of units of it which he consumes.

The important difference between total and marginal utility is that although utility cannot be measured, it *is* possible to say that a consumer will derive the same marginal utility from the last value-unit (i.e. pound's-worth or dollar's worth) of each commodity entering into his range of expenditure. This may seem rather odd; if utility cannot be measured, how can marginal utilities be known to be equal? The answer is that a person's behaviour in spending his income indicates *how much he is prepared to pay* for the last unit of a commodity which he consumes, assuming that he is acting rationally and seeking to obtain the maximum possible satisfaction from his limited income. This amount can be taken as a comparative measure of the extra satisfaction which that last unit brings in to him – in comparison, that is, to the satisfaction he would have derived from whatever commodity he would otherwise have bought with the same money. For example, suppose that when a certain brand of shirt is selling at £5, a man buys three every year; from this it can be concluded that the marginal utility of a shirt to this particular man is roughly equal to the utility of the other things he could have bought with that £5. If the marginal utility was *less* than that of the other things he could have bought with £5, then presumably he would not have bought that third shirt (and perhaps not the second either) but would have spent the money on other things; if the marginal utility was *more* than that of the other things £5 could have bought, then presumably he would be buying more than three shirts and spending £5 less on other goods. The fact that he buys three shirts, but no more than three, suggests that the marginal utility is just equal to the

sacrifice represented by foregoing the other things which that
£5 could have bought.

Does it follow from this that the *total* utility derived from
a commodity can be measured by the total amount of money
spent on it? In the example of the man buying new shirts, can
it be said that, since he spends £15 a year on shirts, the total
utility he derives from new shirts is equivalent to £15. Unfortunately it cannot. Market price can be taken as an indicator of
comparative marginal utility, but the consumer buys *all* units
of any commodity at that price; total expenditure would reflect
total utility, therefore, only if the utility derived from each unit
of the commodity was equal to its marginal utility. There would
be no foundation at all for assuming that this is the case; in
fact there is good reason for supposing that it is untrue. This
limitation – that only marginal utility can be taken as reflected
in the price a consumer is willing to pay, and not total utility –
will not prove particularly inconvenient for the level of analysis with which this book is concerned. The fundamental conditions governing the price and output of a product can be
worked out by reference to marginal utility, and total utility is not
involved.

A more important weakness of this concept of utility emerges,
however, if it becomes necessary to compare not total and marginal utility but the marginal utilities of different persons. Although
it can be said that the comparative marginal utility of a commodity is reflected by the price which a consumer is willing
to pay for it, it does not follow that if two people pay the same
price for a commodity the marginal utility derived from it is
the same for each person. If I say that the marginal utility I
derive from a new shirt is measured by £5, I mean that it equals
the utility I would receive if I bought other things with the same
£5. But the utility represented by £5 *to me* may not be the same
as the utility represented by £5 *to someone else*. To a poor man,
£5 may mean a great deal; to a rich man, it may not be worth
the bother of picking up. Again, a man of education and culture
may derive a high degree of utility from commodities which
other people are unable to appreciate properly, and *vice versa*.
For reasons of this kind, it is impossible to make a comparison

of rigorous scientific validity — as opposed to one broadly amenable to common sense — between the utilities enjoyed by different people. So far as market equilibrium is concerned, this point is not of fundamental significance; it is important, however, in the context of judgements as to whether society is 'better off' or 'worse off' as a result of a certain act of economic policy. Judgements of this kind, assessing the total welfare of society or of different elements in society, must rest in the last resort on political convictions and can have no claim to rest on objective scientific analysis.

2 THE LAW OF DIMINISHING UTILITY

Personal experience, and observation of the behaviour of others, makes familiar a human characteristic which underlies the whole nature of demand. This characteristic is that in general, and if all other things remain constant, the extra satisfaction derived from the consumption of additional units of any commodity tends to decline as the quantity consumed increases. A second chair in my dining-room is not quite as essential as the first; a third is a little less useful than the second, and so on. By the time I am contemplating buying a tenth chair I am beginning to wonder whether there is much point in cluttering up the place with so many chairs.

This simple and familiar fact of life has been generalised by economists into *the law of diminishing utility* which states that, other things being equal and over any specified period, the utility derived by a person from the consumption of a commodity increases as his consumption increases, but not as rapidly. In other words, marginal utility gets smaller and smaller the more of a commodity a person has. It is important, however, to bear in mind the qualification 'other things being equal', since the law may not hold if factors other than the rate of consumption are changing. What exactly is involved in this qualification?

First, and most important, it is assumed that *income* is constant, since the satisfaction derived from a commodity will naturally depend on the number and quality of *other* commodities which the consumer has at his disposal. Hence, if over any period a person's income goes up or down, the marginal utility derived from a commodity may undergo a change as a result, and the person may find that the marginal utility derived from a unit of the commodity has increased or decreased since the beginning of the period concerned.

Secondly, it is assumed that the *nature* of the successive units consumed is constant. This means not only that they must be physically identical (i.e. one bar of chocolate must be identical in blend, quality, etc., with every other) but also that the consumption of successive units does not affect the consumer's basic attitude towards them. For example, certain drugs are habit-forming, and a person may become addicted to them as his consumption of them increases; naturally, his marginal utility will not necessarily decline under these circumstances. Similarly, consumption of a commodity may result in a person acquiring a taste for it, and his enjoyment may increase as his consumption increases. Or the nature of the commodity's primary purpose or function may change; for example, as a man's collection of a particular type of rare stamp increases, further acquisitions may become more and more not mere stamps but the means to attaining the world's biggest collection of something. Finally, if the period of time involved is very long in relation to the time taken to consume the commodity, successive units of consumption may be so far separated as to lose all connection with each other.

Summing up, then, the law of diminishing marginal utility holds only if incomes and tastes remain constant. If either changes, the law may become inapplicable; it will be only a temporary invalidity, however, since it will come back into operation as soon as the change has ceased and a new pattern of incomes and tastes has been established.

3   INDIFFERENCE CURVES

In discussing the concept of utility it has been made clear that there are serious limitations to its usefulness in the real world because, being essentially an introspective concept, it does not lend itself to measurement. It can reasonably be assumed that a person is able to assess for himself the relative marginal utilities of different commodities, and that the price he is willing to pay for different commodities is therefore a guide to the marginal utility he derives from them. But the fact remains that the utility derived by two people from a commodity which they buy at the same price may be widely different, so that the whole concept of utility is inevitably a somewhat vague and difficult one.

Primarily to place the theory of consumer behaviour, or demand, on a less nebulous basis, the technique of *indifference curve analysis* has been evolved. This analysis rests on the fact that, while utility cannot be measured, it is possible to observe from experience and experiment the *preferences* which people display when choosing between different commodities. Consider the case of a man buying a sandwich in a railway refreshment room. There are cheese sandwiches or tomato sandwiches, both being sold at the same price, and he decides to have a cheese sandwich. What conclusion can be drawn from this? It is certain that nothing can be said about the absolute magnitude of the satisfaction he derives from the cheese sandwich, since this is inherently immeasurable. But it *can* be said that that satisfaction – whatever it is – is *greater* than the satisfaction he would have derived from the tomato sandwich. Why else would he have chosen cheese rather than tomato? It is assumed always, of course, that people act rationally, that they use their resources so as to obtain the greatest possible benefit from them. Having made that assumption, it follows that if a man chooses to employ a certain amount of his wealth on buying one unit of commodity A rather than one of commodity B costing the same amount, he must derive more satisfaction from A than from B. In other words, even if nothing can be said about how much utility a person enjoys from any given commodity, it can still be said that that utility is greater or less than the utility he would obtain by the expenditure of an equal amount of money on some other commodity which he does *not* buy.

Now in actual life such preferences are being expressed every day by everybody. A woman spends her clothing allowance on a new hat rather than on a new scarf; a man buys a new record rather than a new book. Every purchase in a shop is an expression of preference as between different commodities, implying that greater satisfaction is derived from the goods which are bought than would have been derived from those which could have been bought but are not. The comparison need not be only between goods selling at the same price, of course. If I go once to the theatre instead of using the money to go twice to the cinema, then it follows that I derive from one visit to the theatre more satisfaction than I would from two visits to the cinema. (*How much* more, of course, no one can say.)

If people are rational, their actual expenditure behaviour can be interpreted so as to establish their scales of preference as between various commodities, and this will indicate which of two comparable expenditures gives the greater satisfaction. More than that, their expressed preferences as seen in actual purchases can be used to discover from which sets of commodities consumers derive *equal* satisfaction. Consider again the case of the man choosing his sandwiches. If he had expressed *no* particular preference as between cheese and tomato, and had left it to the waitress to give him whichever she cared to, then it could have been concluded that the man derived equal satisfaction from either kind of sandwich, although once again nothing need be said about the absolute magnitude of that satisfaction. Similarly, I may prefer a visit to the theatre to two visits to the cinema, I might have no particular preference between one visit to the theatre and *three* visits to the cinema, and I might definitely prefer four visits to the cinema to one to the theatre. Assuming that I am acting rationally, it follows that I derive *more* satisfaction from one theatre visit than from two cinema visits, *less* satisfaction from one theatre visit than four cinema visits and *equal* satisfaction from one visit to the theatre and three to the cinema. All this can be concluded without any necessity for knowledge about *how much* satisfaction I derive from either form of entertainment or about the precise relationship of that satisfaction to the price paid for it.

Indifference curve analysis uses as its basis this latter fact that if a person has no especial preference as between a given amount of one commodity and a given amount of another – i.e.

if he is *indifferent* as between these alternatives – then he derives an equal degree of satisfaction from the two sets of commodities. By experiment it is possible to discover what combinations of goods have this characteristic for any particular person. He can simply be asked 'Would you prefer x of commodity A or (x − 1) of A plus 1 of B?', 'Would you prefer x of A or (x − 1) of A plus 2 of B?' and so on, until the quantity of B is reached at which the person concerned expresses himself indifferent as between x of A and, on the other hand, (x − 1) of A and the given number of B. The questioning can then be recommenced, taking as the alternatives (x − 2) of A plus various quantities of B, so as to establish the quantity of B which, combined with (x − 2) of A, has equal attraction for the consumer as x of A and no B. And so the process can go on, the questioning being repeated for every possible combination of A and B. If quantities of commodity A are now measured along one axis of a graph and quantities of commodity B along the other, all the combinations of A and B which leave the consumer indifferent (i.e. all the pairs of quantities from which he derives equal satisfaction) can be plotted. If all these points are now joined, the resulting curve is known as an *indifference curve*; it shows the quantities of the two given commodities between which the consumer expresses no especial preference.

A simple example may make this clear. Suppose that there are only two goods in existence – apples and oranges – and that a person has a fixed income given to him in the form of ten apples. He is now asked how many apples he is prepared to exchange for one orange – i.e. he is asked what number of apples plus one orange is equally satisfactory to him as ten apples and no orange. Then he is asked how many apples he will sacrifice for another orange – again, what number of apples together with two oranges give him the same satisfaction as ten apples and no orange. The questioning is continued in this way, his answers being noted down, until the number of oranges needed to induce him to part with *all* his apples has been found. A schedule showing the different combinations of apples and oranges which give this consumer equal satisfaction could then be drawn up. It might be like this:

No. of apples	No. of oranges
10	0
9	1
8	2
7	3
6	5
5	7
4	10
3	13
2	17
1	22
0	27

As between all these possible combinations, the consumer will be *indifferent* – he will feel himself no better off and no worse off whichever combination he has. If all these points are now plotted on a graph – measuring apples along the vertical axis and oranges along the horizontal axis, as in Fig. 3A – the result will be an indifference curve, II', a schedule showing the various combinations of commodities which give the consumer equal satisfaction.

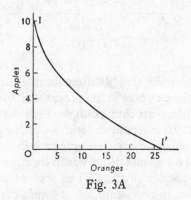

Fig. 3A

So far the discussion has proceeded as if there were only one indifference curve for each person, but in fact there will be an infinite number of them, corresponding to each possible level of the consumer's satisfaction. The previous example was one of a consumer indicating every equally satisfactory combination of apples and oranges between 10 apples and no oranges at one end of the scale, and no apples and 27 oranges at the other end. But the process could be repeated on the assumption that the consumer began with 11 apples rather than 10, and again with a starting position of 12 apples, or 20. Each time a new schedule of equally-satisfactory combinations would be obtained, and an indifference curve could be constructed from each. The final result would be, as in Fig. 3B, an indifference 'map' showing the equally-satisfactory combinations with each level of total income, $I_1 I'_1, I_2 I'_2$ and so on.

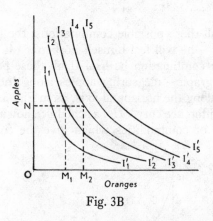

Fig. 3B

The analogy between this 'indifference map' and the technical relation lines of the example in the previous chapter (Fig. 2A(ii)) is obvious and direct. In that example, each curve showed the various combinations of length and width which together resulted in the same area of land. Here the curves are showing the various combinations of two commodities which together yield the same utility to the consumer of them. The area of land, unlike the utility derived from the consumption of goods, can be objectively measured but this difference need not qualify the analogy between dimensions yielding a given area and commodities yielding a given utility. After all, the 'area' lines could have been drawn up for areas such as x, $2x$ and $3x$ – spelling out that in each case combinations of L and $W = x/L$ would yield the same total area, x — without necessarily knowing what x was.

Just as with the 'area' lines, one curve to the right of another necessarily corresponded to a larger area of land, so any indifference curve to the right of another indicates combinations each of which yields a higher total satisfaction than any combination on a curve to the left. For example, $I_3 I'_3$ indicates the combinations of goods giving the same satisfaction as (say) ON apples and OM_2 oranges. Every point on $I_2 I'_2$ indicates a level of satisfaction equal to that derived from ON apples and OM_1 oranges. Since the consumer must derive greater satisfaction from a combination comprising a given number of apples and a larger number (OM_2) of oranges than from the same number of apples and a smaller number (OM_1) of oranges, every point on $I_3 I'_3$ must represent a higher level of satisfaction than any point on $I_2 I'_2$.

Similarly, it is clear that indifference curves cannot intersect. If they did it would mean that a consumer was indifferent as between a point on a high indifference curve and one on a lower curve (i.e. the point at which the curves intersect and which represents the same combination of goods on each). This would contradict the previous finding that an indifference curve must represent at *every* point a higher level of satisfaction than every point on a curve to the left of it. Hence it is impossible for indifference curves to intersect just as the 'area' lines of the example of Chapter II could not logically intersect.

Another generalisation can be made about the shape of indifference curves. This is usually taken to be similar to that of the curves shown in Figs. 3A and 3B — i.e. convex to the origin, which implies that as his stock of one commodity diminishes a consumer will require greater and greater quantities of the other commodity to compensate him for sacrificing further units of it. This *diminishing marginal rate of substitution,* as it is called, is merely the indifference-curve expression of the law of diminishing marginal utility. If it was desired to generalise this tendency from the case of only two commodities to the case of all commodities, then 'all other commodities' (i.e. total income) can simply be substituted for one of the commodities along the horizontal or, more commonly, the vertical axis.

The indifference curve apparatus can show why a consumer will benefit from exchanging goods rather than consuming only a single commodity. Suppose the consumer has an income of ON apples, and that his indifference 'map' is that shown in Fig. 3C. By definition his satisfaction will be maximised by achieving a combination of apples and oranges which lies on the highest possible indifference curve. Suppose also that in the world as the consumer finds it the current rate at which apples are being exchanged against oranges is in the ratio $ON:OM$ – i.e. that ON apples can be exchanged in the market for OM oranges. This exchange rate can be shown on the graph by connecting the point on the vertical axis representing ON apples with the point on the horizontal axis representing OM oranges. This line indicates every possible combination of commodities which the consumer's income could purchase; it is exactly analagous to the budget line of the example in Chapter II, which traced out all the combinations of length and width obtainable within the prospective settler's budget. Just as this line was bound to form a tangent to some 'constant area' curve, so the consumer's budget line must at some point form a tangent with an indifference curve. (Since there is an infinite number of curves in an indifference map, as has been seen, the budget line is *bound* to be a tangent to one of them.) That point of tangency, P, indicates what combination of apples and oranges the consumer will choose, given both his relative preference for apples and oranges and the current rate of exchange. In terms of Fig. 3C this means that the consumer will exchange NN_1 apples for OM_1 oranges, consuming only ON_1 apples out of his total apple-buying-power of ON apples and taking the rest of his income in the form of oranges.

Why is this? The explanation is that by entering into exchange the consumer has been able to reach a point on the indifference curve $I_4I'_4$. Given his initial stock of apples and the current apple–orange exchange rate, the budget line NM shows all the possible ways of consuming his income which are open to him. It is not possible for him to reach a point on any curve higher than (i.e. to the right of) $I_4I'_4$. But he *can* reach $I_4I'_4$, and by obtaining a combination on that curve he will, by definition,

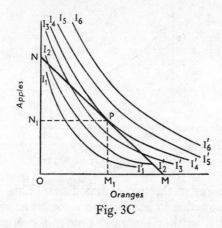

Fig. 3C

obtain more satisfaction than from any other combination which would lie on a lower curve. Hence the point *P* — where the budget line is tangential to an indifference curve — indicates the combination of apples and oranges from which (given his initial income and the exchange rate between apples and oranges) he will derive the maximum satisfaction.

This conclusion can be generalised into a very important axiom of consumer-behaviour, or demand, theory. The slope of an indifference curve at any point indicates the terms on which a consumer is prepared to exchange one commodity for another. Let Fig. 3D represent a magnified section of an indifference curve. The slope of the section *AB* indicates that in return for the sacrifice of 10 apples (given his initial stock of 70) the consumer will require an additional 30 oranges if he is to feel neither better nor worse off. If a smaller and smaller section of the curve is taken, and a smaller and smaller number of each commodity, the slope at one point only can be conceived of, and this will indicate the rate at which the consumer is willing to exchange *one* unit of one commodity for the other — i.e. his *marginal* rate of exchange of oranges for apples, or what is usually called his *marginal rate of substitution* of oranges for apples. If the budget line is a tangent to the indifference curve, this means of course that both lines have the same slope at that point — i.e. that the marginal rate of substitution is *equal* to

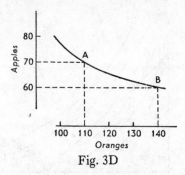

Fig. 3D

the relative prices of the two commodities. (This is parallel to the finding below that in equilibrium a consumer will distribute his expenditure so that marginal utility is everywhere in the same proportion to price.) Since it has just been established that at this point of tangency the consumer's total satisfaction from his income is maximised, it follows that any consumer can be said to be obtaining the greatest possible satisfaction from his income if his marginal rate of substitution between two commodities is brought into equality with their relative prices. The argument has been conducted here in terms of only two commodities, but since it could be applied to *any* two commodities it is clearly valid for consumer expenditure as a whole.

4   THE CONCEPT OF EQUI-MARGINAL RETURNS

This is a basic theorem describing the way in which consumers with limited resources (i.e. a finite income) will divide their expenditure as between the infinite number of different goods and services they could enjoy. It holds, of course, only if it is postulated that consumers wish to get the maximum utility from their limited income, and that they act rationally in seeking to attain this end. It is possible to argue that in real life people do not always have the aim of getting the greatest enjoyment of material things which is open to them; they often act in a way which is contrary to their best material interests – for example, because of religious or political convictions. Similarly, it can be argued that people are by no means rational in their behaviour, but allow their judgement to be influenced by irrational forces (such as superstition or strong emotions) or are in ignorance of the most logical course open to them.

There is a substantial amount of truth in these arguments, but the economist would justify the retention of his basic postulate of utility-maximisation on two grounds. First, although people may not always be strictly rational in either their motives or their actions in so far as economic affairs are concerned, it is only by the process of logical deduction that a good deal of analysis can be carried out; if the assumption of rationality is abandoned, then systematic analysis becomes impossible and economists would be reduced to stating that there is an infinite number of possibilities in any given situation: a conclusion of singularly little usefulness. Secondly, although the assumption of rationality on the part of everyone all the time may not always be realistic, experience shows that it is realistic for *most* people and for *most* of the time. Few generalisations about human behaviour can hope to be true of all times and all people; the economist, being usually concerned with society as a whole rather than with particular individuals, regards his assumption concerning human economic behaviour as certainly the most realistic generalisation which can be made.

Given this assumption that in general people seek to maximise their utility and act rationally towards that end, then, indifference curve analysis arrives at the generalisation that people will distribute their expenditure as between various commodities so as to ensure that the marginal utility obtained from every commodity purchased is in the same relationship to price. This is usually known as the law of equi-marginal returns. The previous section has established this generalisation in broad terms but the proposition is important enough to justify a little closer attention.

Suppose that Fig. 3E(i) represents a 'close-up' of the tangency point reached by a consumer allocating his expenditure between two commodities 1 and 2. The slope of the line P_1P_2 represents their relative prices. Now consider the question: how much extra of product 2 will he need to compensate him for the loss of a small quantity AX of product 1 ? The answer

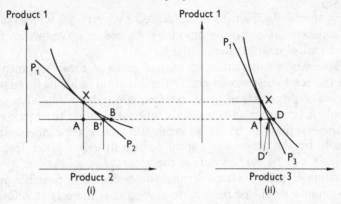

Fig. 3E   The marginal rate of substitution

given by the indifference curve is, of course, the quantity AB of product 2, and if the quantities involved are small enough this will closely approach AB', where B' is the closest point on the price line P_1P_2. Now AB'/AX is, of course, the slope of that line – in other words, another way of expressing the relative prices of the two products concerned: P_2/P_1. So we have the marginal rate of substitution, AB/AX, equal to relative prices P_2/P_1, given that B and B' are so close that AB can be taken as equal to AB'. Hence

$$\frac{AB}{AX} = \frac{P_2}{P_1} \text{ and } AX = AB \cdot \frac{P_1}{P_2}.$$

Turn now to Fig. 3E(ii) which represents exactly the same kind of 'close-up' but, in this case, of the allocation between product 1 and another commodity, product 3. By exactly analogous argument, the marginal rate of substitution between the same quantity of product 1 and product 3 is given by AD/AX, while the price ratio P_3/P_1 is given by AD/AX, so that

$$\frac{AD}{AX} = \frac{P_3}{P_1} \text{ and } AX = AD \cdot \frac{P_1}{P_3}.$$

Now if AX – the quantity of product 1 being sacrificed – is the same in both cases, it must follow from these two equations that

$$AB \cdot \frac{P_1}{P_2} = AD \cdot \frac{P_1}{P_3}$$

and, dividing each side by P_1,

$$\frac{AB}{P_2} = \frac{AD}{P_3}$$

i.e. $\qquad\qquad AB/AD = P_2/P_3.$

But of course this simply says that AB/AD, the marginal rate of substitution between products 2 and 3, is equal to their relative prices P_2/P_3. And what is true of products 2 and 3 will be true of *any* two products if the consumer is making the optimum use of his limited income.

This can be inverted to make an important truism – rational behaviour of a utility-maximising consumer implies that relative prices must be equal to the marginal rates of substitution between any two commodities which he consumes. *Given the law of diminishing marginal utility, in fact, this requirement that marginal rates of substitution should be everywhere equal to relative prices must be met if the maximum utility is to be obtained*; increasing consumption of one commodity at the expense of another after this point has been reached necessarily means that the marginal utility gained from each extra pound spent on the one is smaller than that sacrificed through spending a pound less on the other. The fact that we cannot measure utility in no way affects the validity of this generalisation; we do not need to know the magnitude of something in order to know that it is reduced through the process of adding to it units which are smaller than those which are simultaneously being taken away from it.

5   THE ANALYSIS OF PRICE EFFECTS

With the aid of indifference curves it is possible to take the analysis one step further and to investigate the effects on a consumer's expenditure-pattern of a change in the relative prices of two commodities. Suppose that at all times a consumer's real income is just sufficient to enable him to attain the level

of satisfaction represented by the indifference curve shown in
Fig. 3F. When the relative price of oranges is such that a quantity
OA can be bought with OP apples, the budget line will be PA
which just touches the highest attainable indifference curve at
point X_1. The consumer will therefore purchase OM_1 oranges
and ON_1 apples.

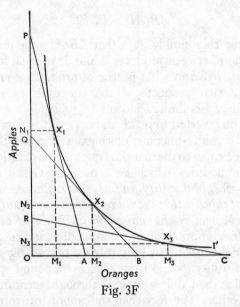

Fig. 3F

Now suppose oranges become cheaper, so that a quantity
OB of oranges can be bought for the equivalent of OQ apples.
The budget line swings across to QB, which just touches the
indifference curve at X_2. At this point the consumer will purchase
OM_2 oranges and ON_2 apples. Similarly, if oranges become even
cheaper, so that a quantity OC can be bought with the equivalent
of OR apples, the budget line becomes RC and the consumer
will purchase OM_3 oranges and ON_3 apples.

The pattern emerging is thus fairly clear. As the price of
one commodity falls in relation to the other, the consumer shifts
his expenditure pattern so as to consume more of the relatively
cheap commodity and less of the relatively expensive commodity.

This, of course, is only another way of expressing the principle of equi-marginal returns. If a consumer starts from the equilibrium position described earlier — i.e. that in which the marginal rate of substitution between any two products is in the same ratio as their prices — a fall in the price of one commodity, all other things remaining unchanged, will naturally leave its marginal rate of substitution above its relative price. The consumer will therefore be able to increase his total satisfaction by buying more of the product whose price is reduced and less of others. Given the law of diminishing marginal utility, the marginal satisfaction derived from the additional units of the (relatively) cheaper commodity will tend to fall, while that derived from the commodities whose consumption is reduced will tend to rise, until, eventually, the equality between relative marginal utilities — the marginal rate of substitution — and relative prices is restored. The consumer will then be back in equilibrium at, of course, a higher level of total satisfaction.

The analogy with the land-enclosing example of the previous chapter may again be useful. In that example it was shown that when L-type fencing became cheap in relation to W-type, the settler would be best advised to go for a long, narrow site; when L-type fencing was expensive in relation to W-type, on the other hand, his best choice lay with a relatively short, broad site.

This, then, is the normal, or usual consequence of a fall in the relative price of a product; it is the first, and basic, law of demand that *all other things remaining equal* as a commodity becomes cheaper its consumption will rise, and as it becomes dearer its consumption will fall. The qualification 'all other things remaining equal', however, is an important one — and one which is encountered very frequently in economic analysis. In the present context, one of the most important implications of it is that the consumer's total *income* is assumed to remain constant; if this assumption does *not* hold, the consequences of price movements may differ significantly from those suggested by this basic law of demand. The analysis must now turn, therefore, to consider the effects of changes in income on consumption patterns.

6 THE ANALYSIS OF INCOME EFFECTS

Assuming that the relative prices of all commodities remain unchanged while the income of a consumer rises, what changes will follow in the pattern of his expenditure? The rise in income, of course, could come about in either of two ways: the consumer's money income could increase without a corresponding rise in the general price level of goods and services, or, alternatively, the general price level might fall without an equal fall in the consumer's money income. In either event the consumer's ability to purchase goods and services would be increased; how would he use this increased buying-power?

In order to generalise the analysis, the indifference curves shown in Fig. 3G relate the weekly consumption of a typical product, milk, to the consumer's average daily income in pounds, rather than to the consumption of a single other product. The consumption of milk, in other words, is related to that of *all* other goods and services, as represented by the general purchasing-power of total income. Now suppose the initial situation is one in which the consumer has a daily income equivalent to £6·00 or 30 pints of milk (i.e. milk sells at 20p a pint) and an indifference map similar to that in Fig. 3G. From this map it can be deduced that in the initial situation he will spend £3·00 a week on 15 pints of milk. When the consumer's daily income

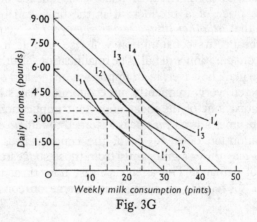

Fig. 3G

increases to £8·00, the budget line has an unchanged slope, since a constant price of milk is assumed, but it shifts upwards and to the right. It now touches $I_2I'_2$, and at that point the consumer will spend £4·20 a week on 21 pints of milk. Let his daily income increase again to £9·00 ($= 45$ pints of milk). He will now attain curve $I_3I'_3$ and will spend £4·80 on 24 pints of milk. Setting these results out in the form of a schedule gives:

Daily income (pounds)	Weekly consumption of milk (pints)
6·00	15
8·00	21
9·00	24

and by continuing in this way the effects on demand of changes in income with a constant level of relative prices can be traced out.

This, again, is the usual case: increases in income, other things being equal (in this case, relative prices), lead to increased consumption. With certain types of commodity, however – usually goods of comparatively low quality – consumption may *fall* as income rises, precisely because the consumer feels sufficiently better-off to afford something better. Hence economists speak of this as the case of *inferior goods*. Here an indifference map of the kind illustrated in Fig. 3H showing a consumer's preference as between margarine and all other goods and services – represented by total income – is encountered. As the consumer's total income rises he moves from curve $I_1I'_1$ to $I_2I'_2$ and then to $I_3I'_3$. On each occasion he feels sufficiently better-off to replace some of the margarine he was previously consuming with some more attractive substitute – butter is the obvious choice. Hence the 'perverse' income effect is seen in his demand for margarine; his consumption of it falls from OX_1 to OX_2 and then from OX_2 to OX_3.

At any moment, then, there are two major influences which can lead a consumer to increase or reduce his consumption of a particular commodity – a change in the relative price of the commodity (the *price* or *substitution effect*) or a change in his

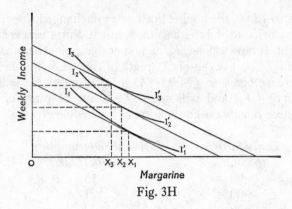

Fig. 3H

real income – i.e. the goods and services which can be bought with total money income – (the *income effect*). In the actual world the situation is complicated by the fact that a change in the price of a commodity also, and *ipso facto*, changes the consumer's real income. If the commodity is dearer, his real income is reduced since he can now buy a smaller volume of goods and services with any given money income; if it is cheaper, he is better off (his real income is increased) since a given money income will now purchase a larger volume of goods and services. The price and income effects are therefore operating simultaneously.

Again the analogy with the land-enclosing example of the previous chapter will be helpful. It will be recalled that when the price of *L*-type fencing was reduced from £5·00 to £3·20 the result was not only to lead the settler to choose a long, thin site rather than a square one (the substitution effect); it also enabled him to enclose an area of 2 500 sq.m. rather than one of 1 600 sq.m. (the income effect). Similarly, when *L*-type fencing became more expensive in absolute and relative terms the effect was again two-fold – a bias towards a shorter, wider site (the substitution effect) and a restriction to a smaller overall area of 900 sq.m. (the income effect).

Fig. 3I illustrates how the relative magnitude of the two effects can be discovered in such a case. Here the effect of a change in the price of petrol is examined. In the initial situation the

price of petrol is given by the line *PA*; the consumer is able
to reach the indifference curve $I_1I'_1$ and consumes a quantity
OM_1 of petrol. The price now falls, so that the budget line moves
over to *PB*. The consumer increases his consumption to OM_2
and reaches the curve $I_2I'_2$ (i.e. his real income has risen). How
much of this increased consumption is due to the relative
cheapening of petrol as such, and how much to the raising of
the consumer's real income? To answer this question it is only
necessary to draw the *new* budget line, showing the new price
of petrol, as a tangent to the *old* indifference curve; this will
tell us how much petrol the consumer would have bought at
that price if his real income had *not* been raised. It will be seen
that the answer is the quantity OX; the rest of the increase
– i.e. the quantity XM_2 – is attributable to the income effect
alone.

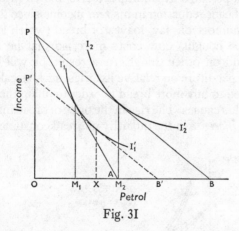

Fig. 3I

As a general rule the two effects will operate in the same
direction, as in the example of Fig. 3I. That is, a fall in price
will normally increase the consumption of a commodity *both*
because it is now cheaper in relation to other commodites *and*
because the consumer, being better off in real terms, is able
to increase his consumption generally. In certain cases, however,
the two effects may operate in opposite directions, one effect
moderating to some degree the influence of the other. In extreme

instances, the income effect may operate so strongly as to more than offset the influence of the price effect; commodities of which this is true are often called Giffen goods, since Sir Robert Giffen is generally credited with first drawing public attention to the curious fact that the poor in the England of his day consumed more bread when it was dear than when it was cheap. Giffen goods are often commodities of a relatively low quality which form an important element in the expenditure of the poor, the best-known examples being staple food-stuffs such as bread and potatoes. Because of their bulk, such foods are important in the diet of poorer people; as people become richer they prefer to buy the more expensive and attractive foodstuffs (for example, dairy products or confectionery) and so reduce their consumption of these coarser foods. If such commodities form an important element in a person's expenditure, a rise in their price can cause a very significant reduction in his *real* income since the purchase of a given number of, say, loaves of bread (which are essential and *must* be bought) now costs more, so that he is left with less to spend on other things. As a result, he will have to cut down his expenditure on relative luxuries, such as cakes or meat, and will need to buy more bread in order to fill up the nutritional gap which this causes. The rise in the price of bread may therefore result in an *increase* in the quantity of bread consumed.

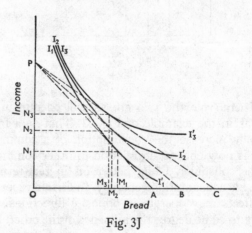

Fig. 3J

This sort of case is illustrated in Fig. 3J with bread as the commodity in question. In the initial situation, with the price of bread implied by the budget line *PA*, the consumer is able to reach the indifference curve $I_1I'_1$ and consumes a quantity OM_1. The fall in the price of bread shifts the budget line over to *PB*; the consumer is now able to move up to the higher indifference curve $I_2I'_2$ (his real income is raised), substitutes other more attractive foods for bread and reduces his bread consumption to OM_2. Similarly, if the price of bread falls further, and the budget line moves over to *PC*, his bread consumption will be reduced further to OM_3.

Summing up, then, certain generalisations emerge about the principles governing the behaviour of a consumer in distributing his limited income amongst the infinite variety of goods available. First, he will so arrange his expenditure that the relative marginal utilities of all the goods he consumes (their marginal rates of substitution) are everywhere in the same proportion to their relative prices. Secondly, a fall in the price of a commodity, other things being equal, will increase its consumption while a rise in its price will reduce its consumption. Finally, a rise in the consumer's real income, whether brought about by a price reduction or otherwise, will *normally* result in an increased consumption of goods and services but *may*, in certain cases, result in a reduction of consumption. A fall in real income, of course, will have the reverse effect.

FURTHER READING

H. A. JOHN GREEN *Consumer theory* Penguin Books Ltd, London 1971, Chs. 1–5

R. T. NORRIS *The theory of consumer's demand* Yale University Press, New Haven 1952, Part 1

E. MANSFIELD *Micro-economics* Norton, New York 1970, Chs. 2–3

A. M. LEVENSON and B. S. SOLON *Outline of price theory* Holt, Rinehart and Winston, New York 1964, Ch. 5

J. HADAR *Elementary theory of economic behaviour* Addison-Wesley Publishing Co., Reading, Mass., 1966, Ch. 12

K. LANCASTER *Introduction to modern micro-economics* Rand McNally, Chicago 1969, Ch. 7

CHAPTER IV

Market Demand

1 DEMAND CURVES

IT has been seen that people desire goods and services because they derive utility from them, that the utility derived from consumption will vary as between different commodities and different people, and that in general the additional utility derived from any commodity by any one person diminishes as his rate of consumption rises. In economic analysis it is convenient to express all these things in the form of a *demand curve* for each individual commodity, such as that shown in Fig. 4A. This curve

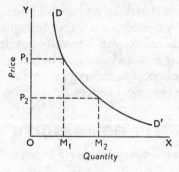

Fig. 4A

is a line connecting the various possible prices charged for the commodity (measured along the vertical axis) with the amounts of the commodity which the people will be prepared to buy at each different price. For example, the curve shows that if price was OP_1 consumers would purchase a quantity OM_1, whereas if price fell to OP_2 consumers would purchase a total quantity OM_2.

These curves are most easily understood if they are thought of as derived from the indifference maps of all the individuals entering the market for the commodity concerned. The indifference-curve diagrams of the previous chapter were concerned with the reactions of a single individual to changes in prices and incomes. As was remarked earlier, however, the economist is usually concerned with the actions of people as a group, rather than with the individual, and with the total demand for a product rather than individual demand. In principle, therefore, the transition from indifference curves to demand curves presents no difficulty: the latter are simply derived by aggregating the former. The various individual demands for a product at each price are summed to give the market demand at each price. The resulting curve, of course, will normally slope downwards from left to right, as in Fig. 4A, reflecting the law of diminishing marginal utility and the basic characteristics of consumer behaviour summarised at the end of the previous chapter.

In practice, however, it is seldom possible to draw up a schedule of this kind showing the amounts purchased (i.e. the 'demand') at every conceivable price, since in the real world only a limited range of prices has usually been experienced. Still, it may be possible to draw up a more limited schedule of prices and quantities demanded from the statistics of different markets or by experiment. For example, it may be known that for a certain type of motor-cycle the numbers demanded at recent prices have been as follows:

Price (£)	Quantity sold per annum (000s)
1 000	150
900	300
800	400
700	550

From these data the demand schedule shown in Fig. 4B can be drawn up, although it is necessary to *assume* that the curve joining the four observed points is a smooth one – the quantity demanded at a price between £900 and £800 is not *known*, but it can be assumed that the rise of the quantity demanded from 300 000 at £600 to 400 000 at £550 will be a gradual and continuous one.

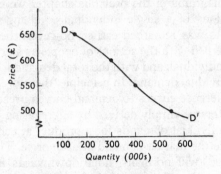

Fig. 4B

The relationship illustrated by a demand curve can be stated (often more conveniently) as a simple equation relating the quantity demanded in the market over a particular period of time to the prevailing price of the product. Such an equation (or demand *function*) might take the form

$$Q = 200 - 10P$$

where Q is the number of units sold per interval of time (e.g. each week) and P the market price. By inserting hypothetical values for P the volume of sales can easily be calculated. For example:

$P(£)$	$10P$	$Q(= 200 - 10P)$
20	200	0
18	180	20
16	160	40
14	140	60

It will be observed that plotting these pairs of values of P and Q will result in a straight-line demand schedule and there is in fact no special reason why demand functions should take this form. Equally it is unlikely that the function should have a constant slope throughout its length, as this one does; the effect on quantity demanded of a small change in price is likely to be different when price is very high from its effect when price is very low. Nevertheless a straight-line (or *linear*) demand relationship is often a useful and reasonable approximation for price changes within the sort of range actually experienced in reality.

Assuming that it is statistically possible to construct a demand curve of this kind, it could be drawn up only on the assumptions which underlay the law of diminishing utility (since the normal demand curve is no more than a graphical expression of that law) – that is, that income and tastes are constant. If either of these changes, then it will be necessary to draw up an entirely new demand curve. For example, let the curve $D_1D'_1$ in Fig. 4C represent the demand schedule for oranges at a particular

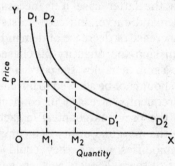

Fig. 4C

moment. Now imagine that the public suddenly becomes more conscious of the nutritional value of oranges; individual indifference-maps will undergo a corresponding change and a completely new curve, $D_2D'_2$, will need to be drawn. A similar shift would occur if people in general became richer and if the income effect led people to buy more oranges at any particular price.

Another factor assumed constant in the construction of these demand curves is the price level of goods which are either near substitutes for or closely competitive with the commodity in question. As will be seen in a later section of this chapter, some commodities may be related to one another in an especially close manner, so that a change in the price of one commodity may cause a shift in the whole demand schedule for another commodity.

Put briefly, then, the demand curve for a commodity is drawn up on the assumptions that the incomes of consumers are constant, that their tastes are constant, and that the price level of closely related commodities is constant. It is important therefore to distinguish between a change which occurs in the consumption of a commodity as a result of a change in its price, and one which occurs because of a movement in one of these factors which are assumed to be constant. In the former case the movement in consumption is measured by moving along a single demand curve; it is usual to speak then of a *contraction* or *extension* of demand, according to whether the quantity consumed is reduced through a rise in price or increased through a fall in price. In the latter case it is necessary to draw up an entirely new demand curve, and economists speak of a *shift in demand*, or an increase or decrease of demand.

In all this discussion the quantity purchased by consumers has been related to a sum of money, the price. This is a convenient simplification but should not be allowed to obscure the underlying reality. As was frequently stressed in connection with indifference curves in the previous chapter, in fact consumers are always comparing the marginal utility of a commodity with that of the other commodities which they could obtain with the resources available to them. Money, as is shown at a later stage, is merely the medium through which the exchange of goods is most conveniently carried out. The consumer is always assessing the relative attractiveness of all the commodities he could conceivably purchase, and ideally along the vertical axis should be measured not money but the *utilities* which a consumer is sacrificing in order to consume a particular commodity. It is impossible to do this, since utilities are neither measurable nor additive between people, but if it was possible to do this it would make clearer this important fact that consumers are always seeking to bring into equality the marginal utility derived from each commodity and the marginal utility they sacrifice by buying it rather than some other commodity.

2 'PERVERSE' DEMAND CURVES

It has been seen that demand curves normally slope downwards from left to right, reflecting the fact that a fall in the price of a commodity will usually stimulate an increase in its consumption while a rise in its price will usually reduce consumption. Is it possible for *perverse* demand curves to exist – that is, for this normal price–quantity relationship to be reversed? Instances of this can be conceived of, but it will be found that it is usually more useful and revealing to consider them as cases in which *shifts* occur in a 'normal' demand curve, rather than as 'perverse' curves which defy all the rules.

The first, and most important, case is that of the Giffen good. As was shown in the previous chapter, the income effect associated with changes in the price of this type of commodity is so powerful as to more than offset the usual substitution effects of such price changes. Since the shifting or re-aligning of individual preference maps normally resulting from changes in real income do *not* occur in these Giffen cases, it would be justifiable to conclude that the demand curves derived from their preference maps would be perverse – i.e. that they would show consumption *increasing* with price rather than varying inversely with it. On the other hand, there is a good deal to be said for retaining the basic assumption of demand curves – i.e. that real income is constant over the whole range of prices covered by them – and treating the case of these Giffen goods as a *shift* of the demand curve as price rises and real income falls – from $D_1D'_1$ to $D_2D'_2$, from $D_2D'_2$ to $D_3D'_3$, and so on, as shown in Fig 4D(i) – rather than a movement along the upward-sloping demand curve, DD', such as that shown in Fig. 4D(ii), which would result from simply connecting up the various prices and the quantities purchased at those prices.

Similar considerations apply to the two other situations in which there may seem to be perverse demand curves. In one, an increase in price gives rise to expectations on the part of consumers that *further* price increases are likely, so that they rush to buy a commodity before its price rises even more – a sequence of events frequently underlying Stock Exchange

transactions in securities. Here again, at first sight, is a case
where a greater quantity is purchased at a high price than at a
lower one; in reality, however, it is one in which the whole state
of demand is changing, this time because of consumers' expectations as to future prices. A series of demand curves shifting
to the right or left is more appropriate than a single upward-sloping curve.

In the remaining type of situation, the commodities involved
are demanded specifically because of their high price and therefore

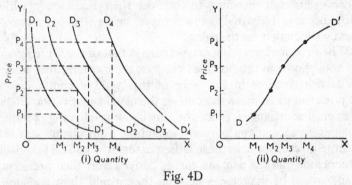

Fig. 4D

exclusive nature – especially precious stones and other means
of human ostentation. If these commodities were reduced in
price so that they were within the means of a large number
of people, they would thereby lose their exclusive character and
hence their appeal. Apparently a fall in price would result in
a fall in the quantity demanded, but the situation is in effect
one which involves different commodities; although the commodity is physically unchanged by a change in price, its character
so far as the consumer is concerned *has* changed, and it is
therefore a different commodity from the economist's point of
view. As in the other cases, therefore, new demand curves (of
normal slope) are really involved, rather than a single perverse
curve.

3   INTER-RELATIONSHIPS OF DEMAND

Before concluding this examination of some fundamental characteristics of the demand curve, a word is necessary about inter-

actions which may occur between the demands for commodities which are physically distinct. As was noted earlier, a demand curve is drawn up on the assumption that the prices of other goods are constant at a time when a change is taking place in the price of the commodity whose demand is being analysed. In real life prices are constantly changing, so that this assumption seldom holds. This would not matter too much if all commodities were related to one another only in the sense that all of them compete for the limited income of consumers. If I spend £1 more on books, the demand for other commodities is bound to be affected, since I have £1 less to spend on other things. But if there is no *special* relationship between commodities, the effects on the demand for commodities in general of a change in the demand for one in particular can safely be ignored; even if the change is large for the one commodity (say a doubling of total expenditure on it), the total number of commodities in existence is virtually infinite; if the effects of this change in the demand for one commodity are spread evenly over all other markets, it will not have any significant effect on any one of them.

Occasionally, however, inter-relationships exist which result in an uneven spread of such changes, so that the markets for physically separate commodities are intimately linked with one another. Three important inter-relationships of this kind are worth noting. The first is known as *joint demand*; this exists when the satisfaction of a want involves two or more physically separate commodities used in conjunction – the demand for petrol is closely linked to the demand for motor-cars, and similar links exist with pipes and pipe-tobacco, pens and ink, knives and forks, etc. The effects of this inter-relationship are easily visualised. A shift in the demand for one product, or a movement along its demand curve as a result of a change in price, will cause a shift in the same direction in the demand for the related product without any causative change in its price. Commodities linked in this way are known as *complementary* goods. (The opposite situation prevails, of course, with goods which are closely *competitive* – electric cookers and gas cookers, cigarettes and pipe-tobacco, rail travel and motor-coach travel, etc. Here, a movement in the demand for one product will cause an *opposite* movement in the demand for its substitute, again without any causative change in the price of the latter.)

Suppose, for example, that the weekly demand for condensed milk is approximated by

$$Q = 17 - 0.80\,P_1 + 1.40P_2$$

where Q is monthly condensed-milk consumption per head in ounces, P_1, the average price in pence of a 4-ounce tin of condensed milk and P_2 the average price in pence of a pint of fresh milk. It is clear that condensed and fresh milk are closely competitive. If the initial prices were 25p for a 4-ounce tin of condensed milk (P_1) and 20p for a pint of milk (P_2), a rise of, say, 5 per cent in the price of fresh milk will cause a *rise* of about 1.4 ounces in the monthly per capita consumption of condensed milk, the price of the latter remaining constant.

Secondly, there is the case of *derived demand,* which exists when a commodity is demanded not for its own sake but by virtue of its contribution to the manufacture of another product. Few people want steel as such; the demand for it is derived from the demand for the commodities made of steel – cars and washing machines and railway lines. Similarly, the demand for bricks is derived from the demand for houses and factories, and that for raw cotton is derived from the demand for dresses and shirts. This relationship is basically similar to that of joint demand, and a similar connection will exist between the markets concerned.

The final type of inter-relationship is known as *composite demand.* This exists when a single product is wanted for a number of different uses, as contrasted with joint demand where several products are wanted for a single use. Instances of composite demand are found with, for example, sugar (used for direct consumption, or baking, or jam-making, or even fire-lighting), sheep (for wool, or meat, or skins) and coal (households, gas-making, electricity generation, ships' bunkers). The interaction between different markets in cases such as these operates through supply rather than demand. An increase in the demand for one type of use will tend to draw supplies of the product away from its other uses, causing a relative scarcity in other markets and therefore influencing price and consumption in those markets.

In dealing with all these types of demand, then – and they cover a wide range of the whole economic system – it must always be borne in mind that the assumption of the independence of demand curves by no means always holds. The demand for any given commodity will depend on its price; but it may also depend on the prices and supply of, and demand for, many other commodities having at first sight no connection with it.

4 PRICE ELASTICITY

At the beginning of this chapter, reference was made to the reason why a 'normal' demand curve is drawn sloping downwards from left to right, reflecting the basic law of demand that, other things being equal, more of a commodity will be purchased at a low price than at a high price. It is now necessary to continue the discussion a little further so as to decide the meaning and significance of the *rate* at which a curve slopes downward – i.e. to discover why some demand curves may be relatively steep and others nearly horizontal.

The steepness of the demand curve at a particular point reflects what is called the *price elasticity* of the demand for a particular commodity; by elasticity is meant simply the degree to which demand responds to price. Consider the demand curves shown in Figs. 4E(i) and (ii). In Fig. 4E(1) the curve is fairly steep, so that a fall in price from P_1 to P_2 results in a relatively small increase in the quantity purchased, from OM_1 to OM_2. Contrast this with the curve shown in Fig. 4E(ii); here the curve slopes much less steeply, and a similar fall in price, from P_1 to P_2, results in a relatively large increase in the quantity purchased, from OM_1 to OM_2.

The concept can be made a little more precise than this: the expressions 'relatively small' and 'relatively large' are very vague after all, and convey little. The simplest way in which price elasticity of demand can be measured unambiguously is by reference to the total amount of money which consumers spend on any given commodity at different prices. This total, of course, is the product of the number of units purchased and the price at which they are sold. When the price of a commodity falls, the total amount of it sold will normally increase. If the increase in sales is more than sufficient to offset the fall in price, then the total amount of money spent on it will *increase,* and demand is then said to be elastic. If the increase in sales is relatively small, however, and insufficient to offset the reduction in price, the total expenditure on the commodity by consumers will *fall* as the price is reduced, and the demand is then said to be inelastic. Finally, if the increase in sales is just sufficient

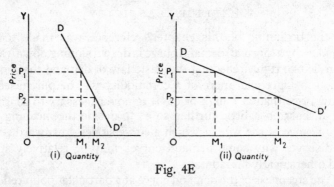

Fig. 4E

to offset the reduction in price, so that the total amount of money spent on the commodity remains constant as the price falls, then elasticity of demand is said to be equal to unity. Thus if the quantities of a commodity sold at various prices were as follows:

Price (pounds)	Sales (000s)	Total amount spent (£000s)	
10	10	100	>1
9	12	108	
8	14	112	1
7	16	112	<1
6	17	102	

elasticity of demand would be said to be greater than unity at the prices of £10 and £9, equal to unity at £8 and less than unity at £7.

A rather more refined, but essentially similar, procedure is to express the actual change in the quantity purchased as a proportion, and similarly express the change in price as a proportion. Elasticity of demand can then be defined very clearly in terms of these proportions. Suppose that the initial price of a commodity is denoted by P and the quantity being sold per unit of time at that price by Q. Price now changes by ΔP where the Greek delta, Δ, is used to denote 'a very small change in'; the corresponding change in the volume of sales as a result of that price movement can then be denoted by ΔQ. Given this bit of notation, price elasticity of demand, e, can be defined as

$$e = \frac{\Delta Q}{Q} \div \frac{\Delta P}{P}$$

or

$$e = \frac{\Delta Q}{\Delta P} \cdot \frac{P}{Q}.$$

This method of measuring price elasticity has the advantage of enabling a relative measure of the *magnitude* of the elasticity to be calculated rather than being confined to a statement of whether it is or is not greater than unity. Thus, in our example, when price falls from £9 to £8 (i.e. $\Delta P = -1$) the volume of sales rises from 12 000 to 14 000 (i.e. $\Delta Q = +2\,000$). Using the formula,

$$e = \frac{+2\,000}{-1} \cdot \frac{9}{12\,000} = -1\cdot50.$$

Unfortunately this method does not always lead to an unambiguous result. The elasticity calculated will depend on whether the price used in the calculation is the *initial* price or the price *after* the change. Suppose the previous calculation were repeated for a *rise* in price from £8 to £9 (i.e. $\Delta P = +1$) when the example indicates that sales fall from 14 000 to 12 000 (i.e. $\Delta Q = -2\,000$). Again using the formula,

$$e = \frac{-2\,000}{1} \cdot \frac{8}{14\,000} = -1\cdot14.$$

One method of avoiding this ambiguity is to calculate the *arc elasticity* of demand – in effect, the average elasticity over the range of the 'before' and 'after' prices: the changes in price and quantity are expressed as proportions of the *sum* of both old and new prices and quantities. In terms of the formula,

$$e = \frac{\Delta Q}{Q_0 + Q_1} \div \frac{\Delta P}{P_0 + P_1}$$

$$= \frac{\Delta Q}{\Delta P} \cdot \frac{P_0 + P_1}{Q_0 + Q_1}$$

where P_0, Q_0 are the initial prices and quantities and P_1, Q_1 those prevailing after the change. It now makes no difference whether elasticity is measured before or after: in terms of the change from £9 to £8 in the example, the calculation becomes

$$e = \frac{2\ 000}{-1} \cdot \frac{17}{26\ 000} = -1 \cdot 31$$

or, for the change from £8 to £9,

$$e = \frac{-2\ 000}{1} \cdot \frac{17}{26\ 000} = -1 \cdot 31.$$

It will be noted that the arc elasticity is an *average* of the elasticities previously calculated for the two extremities of the range of prices. The calculation of *point* elasticity – that is, the elasticity at one single price – would require the measurement of the quantity response to an infinitesimally small change in price. This requires the techniques of the differential calculus and will not be investigated here. For most purposes, calculating price elasticity at the initial price will be a sufficiently close approximation, *provided that the price change in question is a small one.*

Strictly speaking, a price elasticity calculated by any of these methods will have a *negative* value, since the price and quantity changes are normally in opposite directions. In practice the negative sign is usually omitted, so that an elasticity of, say, 2 would mean that the quantity change is twice as great as the price movement stimulating it and in the *opposite* direction.

It follows from all this that the fact that a demand schedule has a constant slope does *not* imply that elasticity of demand is the same throughout the length of the schedule, since the measurement of elasticity involves the *initial* price and quantity purchased as well as the *changes* in each. For example, suppose that the price of a certain product whose demand schedule is a straight line fell from £10 to £9 and that the quantity purchased increased from 50 to 100 units (see Fig. 4F(i)). The formula

$$\frac{\text{Proportionate change in quantity purchased}}{\text{Proportionate change in price}}$$

gives an elasticity of $(50/-1)(10/50)$, which equals -10. If the price now falls a further £1, the quantity purchased rises from 100 to 150, so that the elasticity of demand at that price is given by $(50/-1)(9/100)$ which equals -4.5. By continuing in this way it will be found that the elasticity of demand is different at every point on the curve – when price falls from £2 to £1, for example, the elasticity of demand is found to be only 0.22. It follows, then, that elasticity can be spoken of only as the elasticity at a particular point on the curve (i.e. at a specified price) or over a specified range of prices.

It is possible, however, to conceive of a demand curve which has the same elasticity throughout its length. Such a curve would have the shape of that shown in Fig. 4F(ii); it is what the geometers call a rectangular hyperbola, which is a curve such that the rectangle formed by abscissa, ordinate and the axes (e.g. $OP_1Q_1M_1$ or $OP_2Q_2M_2$) has a constant area at all points of the curve. The area of this rectangle, of course, is equal to the product of the lengths of two sides, one of them measuring the price and the other the quantity demanded. It therefore measures the total amount spent on the commodity at any price, since the number is being multiplied by the price at which each is purchased. The rectangular hyperbola is therefore a demand curve which indicates that the total amount spent on the commodity is unaffected throughout by a change in price; as has already been seen, this means that elasticity of demand is everywhere equal to unity. The 'area curves' of the example in Chapter II were of course of this type.

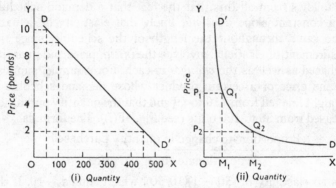

Fig. 4F

Summing up, it can be said that the concept of price elasticity of demand is concerned with the relative responsiveness of the demand for a commodity to changes in its price. Two limiting cases can be formulated. If a change in price has no effect whatever on the quantity purchased, then demand is said to be *infinitely inelastic* at that price. If a small change in price has an infinitely large effect on the quantity purchased, then demand is said to be *infinitely elastic* at that price. It is a useful exercise to draw a graph illustrating these two extreme cases.

5   FACTORS GOVERNING PRICE ELASTICITY

Having discussed the methods by which price elasticity may be measured, it is necessary to consider the factors which tend to make the demand for a particular commodity more, or less, elastic than the demand for other commodities. It is useful to bear in mind in this connection the fact that a change in the quantity of a commodity sold on a market may come about through *either* a change in the average quantity purchased by each consumer *or* a change in the number of consumers, although both effects may (and usually will) occur simultaneously. The immediate task is to discover why in some cases a change in price will have a marked effect on the average amount of a commodity consumed or on the numbers consuming it, while in other cases the effect will be only slight.

The first, and most important, factor is the extent to which fairly close *substitutes* can be obtained for a commodity. If a commodity can be easily replaced by others, then a small rise in its price will have a relatively large effect on its consumption, as people switch to other commodities which are fairly similar but have not changed in price. For example, most people regard lamb and beef as reasonably close substitutes. If lamb becomes dearer, therefore, it may not induce people who eat only lamb to buy much less of it but it will induce a good many people to substitute beef for lamb on the Sunday table. Hence, the demand for lamb will be relatively elastic.

Conversely, a commodity having no close substitutes is likely to have an inelastic demand, since it is not possible for a switch to or from other commodities to occur on any substantial scale. If the cost of sending a letter through the post increases, for example, people may be stimulated to some extent to use tele-grams or telephones instead. These are not very close substitutes, however, and the falling-off in demand which will occur as a result of such substitution is unlikely to be significant.

This possibility of substitution is at the root of the usual assumption that the demand for necessities is likely to be inelastic while the demand for luxury goods will generally be elastic. By definition, a necessity is a commodity which has no adequate substitute, while a luxury is something which can be replaced fairly readily by something else. The adequacy or inadequacy of substitutes, however, is largely a matter of upbringing and habit, rather than a question of physical similarity or dissimilarity between commodities. A person of modest means, for example, would consider milk a reasonably close substitute for cream, and a change in the relative prices of milk and cream would probably cause significant changes in his consumption of each. By contrast, a person accustomed for many years to drinking only cream in his (or her) coffee would probably regard milk (for this purpose, at any rate) as a very imperfect substitute and would replace cream with milk only reluctantly as cream became relatively expensive. Again, tobacco is by any physical standard a luxury; it is in no way necessary to human existence. Nevertheless many people become addicted to tobacco, with the result that in the past fairly large increases in price have had only small effects on consumption. What is a luxury and what is a necessary commodity, then, turns largely on whether there are *thought* to be adequate substitutes, rather than on the physical nature and quality of commodities.

Another aspect of this same factor is the number of uses to which a commodity can be put, which is in a sense the inverse of the extent to which it can be substituted for a particular use. Generally, a commodity which has several uses will have a relatively elastic demand because of the range of markets in which a price change can exert its effect. Electricity, for example, can be used for lighting, cooking, space-heating and motive-power. Even though a fall in price has only a small effect on its consumption for each purpose, the aggregate effect of a small increase in each might amount to a substantial change in total demand. Conversely, there is not much to be done with wheat except make flour of one kind or another from it, so that a price change must have a substantial effect on this single use if total demand is to be significantly changed. The fact that a commodity has only a single use, then – which usually means, of course, that it has few or no close substitutes – will tend to reduce the elasticity of its demand.

A second major influence on the price elasticity of the demand for a product is its *durability*. Generally speaking, the more durable a commodity the greater is the scope for postponing its replacement when its price rises and the greater the incentive to replace it if price seems unusually low. An electric light bulb, for example, wears out fairly rapidly and will then have to be replaced, even if its price has risen in the meantime. A rise in the price of cars, on the other hand, may well lead people to hang on to their old car rather longer than they would otherwise have done, so pulling demand down. The more durable a product, in other words, the greater the ability of consumers to lengthen or reduce its effective working life in response to increases or reductions in its price.

A third factor governing elasticity is the *relative importance* of a commodity in the total expenditure of consumers. If the purchase of a commodity forms a significant proportion of a person's total expenditure, either because its price is high or because the amount consumed is large, then his demand for it is likely to be more sensitive to price changes than if the expenditure involved had been only a minor element in his total spending. A person in the habit of visiting a cinema every night of the week, for example, is likely to cut out one or two visits a week if cinema prices rise 50 per cent, simply because the extra cost involved is a substantial one. On the other hand, a person who visits a cinema only once or twice a year is likely to be unmoved by the same price change. A doubling of the price of newspapers or salt is unlikely to seriously reduce demand because, despite the frequency with which these commodities are purchased, their price is so low that the total amount spent by each person on them is relatively small. On the other hand, a doubling of the price of, say, meat would have a much bigger effect on household expenditure if consumption was not reduced.

6   OTHER TYPES OF ELASTICITY

So far the discussion has been concerned with price elasticity of demand, which is in fact the most important type of elasticity for economic analysis. Other types exist, however; two of which need to be mentioned here. First there is *income elasticity* of demand; just as price elasticity corresponds to what was called in the previous chapter the substitution effect, so income elasticity corresponds to the income effect. It was established in the previous chapter that demand is influenced by income as well as relative price; by income elasticity, therefore, is meant the response of the demand for a product to changes in the real income of consumers. Its measurement is exactly parallel with that of price elasticity – i.e. the division of the proportionate change in quantity demanded by the proportionate movement in income which gives rise to that change. By analogy with the formula for price elasticity, if the consumer's initial income is Y and the change in it ΔY, then income elasticity is given by:

$$e_y = \frac{\Delta Q}{\Delta Y} \cdot \frac{Y}{Q}$$

where, as before, Q is his initial consumption of the commodity in question and ΔQ the change in the quantity consumed when income changes.

Unlike price elasticity, which is always negative, income elasticity can be positive or negative, since the income effect can reinforce or offset the substitution effect. Supposing that in response to a 10 per cent rise in consumers' income the demand for electric irons moves as shown in Fig. 4G(i) – i.e. the demand curve shifts over from $D_1D'_1$ to $D_2D'_2$, and weekly demand at a constant price rises from 40 000 to 50 000, or by 25 per cent. The income elasticity is thus $+25/10$, or $+2\cdot5$. Now suppose that as a result of the same rise in income the demand for potatoes moves as shown in Fig. 4G(ii) – i.e. the curve shifts to the *left* and weekly demand drops from 150 000 tonnes to 120 000 tonnes, or by 20 per cent. The income elasticity is then $-20/+10$, or $-2\cdot0$.

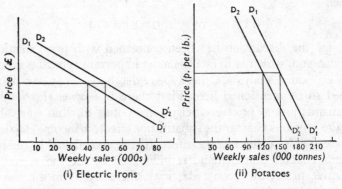

(i) Electric Irons   (ii) Potatoes

Fig. 4G

The other important type of elasticity is that between commodities – *cross-elasticity*. As was shown in an earlier section, most commodities are substitutes for one another, so that a cheapening of one will lead to a downward shift in the demand for others whose price is unchanged. If goods are *complementary*, however, the opposite happens: if one becomes cheaper, and its consumption rises, the demand for the complementary good will shift upwards. By analogy with the formulae for price and income elasticity, the cross-elasticity between two products X and Y can be defined as

$$e_{xy} = \frac{\Delta Q_x}{\Delta P_y} \cdot \frac{P_y}{Q_x}$$

where Q_x is the quantity of product X consumed initially and P_y the initial price of product Y. Like income elasticity, then, cross-elasticity may be positive or negative; if the goods are substitutes their cross-elasticity will be positive (i.e. a fall in the price of Y will cause a fall in the demand for X), while it will generally be negative if the goods are complementary.

7   THE SIGNIFICANCE OF ELASTICITY

It is not difficult to see why a knowledge of the size of the elasticity of demand for a commodity would be extremely useful. A manufacturer contemplating an expansion of his output, for example, will need to make some estimate of the level to which his price will have to be reduced in order to sell the extra volume of goods he is thinking of producing. If elasticity of demand is less than unity, he will actually find himself selling a larger quantity of goods in return for a smaller total sales revenue, a development which he is unlikely to regard favourably. Conversely, if the elasticity of demand for his product is greater than unity, it will mean that through a relatively small reduction in price he can secure a large increase in his sales. The market research specialists are constantly trying to obtain precisely this kind of information, even though they may not speak of the concept of elasticity of demand as such.

Another case in which a knowledge of the elasticity of demand could play an important part in policy decisions is that of indirect taxation. For example, consider a commodity on which the government is levying a tax. If the rate of tax is raised, will total tax revenue increase? This will depend on the elasticity of demand at the ruling price. If it is less than unity, the quantity consumed will not decline in as great a proportion as the rise in the rate of tax, and total tax revenue will increase; on the other hand, if the demand is highly elastic, purchases may be reduced in a greater proportion than the increase in the rate of tax, and the result will be that the government obtains a smaller revenue from a high rate of tax than from a low one – clearly a possibility needing to be taken into account. Two examples are given in Fig. 4H. In the first the tax P_1T_1 on tea is increased to P'_1T_1; since the demand is inelastic, the quantity consumed falls only slightly, and the total tax revenue rises from $P_1Q_1R_1T_1$ to $P'_1Q'_1R'_1T'_1$. When the tax P_2T_2 on oil heaters in the second example is raised to P'_2T_2, however, the consequent rise in price causes a substantial drop in sales; the existence of several fairly close substitutes makes the demand a highly elastic one. Hence the new tax revenue, $P'_2Q'_2R'_2T'_2$, is smaller than the previous revenue $P_2Q_2R_2T_2$.

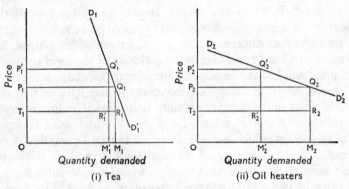

Fig. 4H

In the light of all this, it would appear that, other things being equal, a government would be well advised to levy indirect taxes on commodities having an inelastic demand. In practice other things are not always equal. Many commodities have an inelastic demand, as has been seen, because they are considered to be necessary for a tolerable standard of life, and precisely because of this a government might hesitate, on social or political grounds, to make such commodities more expensive by taxing them. Nevertheless, this consideration of elasticity explains why commodities such as tobacco, wines and spirits contribute a very important share of the government's total revenue from indirect taxation.

Given the obvious usefulness of a knowledge of the elasticity of demand for different products, can elasticity be measured in practice? It is in fact difficult to do so. It might seem straightforward to discover from the statistics of production and sales of various commodities how demand has responded to price changes in the past. To translate such calculations into a demand curve, however, is another matter. An increase in consumption following on a fall in price *might* be the result of that fall in price. But it might also be due to a change in tastes (which is not measurable) or to changes in the prices of other goods (which are constantly occurring) or to changes in the income of consumers (such changes are never absent). It is difficult, therefore, to make a clear distinction between changes in consumption occurring because of a movement *along* a given demand curve (which is what price elasticity involves) and those occurring because of *shifts* in the demand curve. Nevertheless statisticians have grappled with these problems and their findings suggest that in Britain, at any rate, price elasticities are very low for food, drink, tobacco and clothing generally (around 0·2 only) but higher for groups such as vehicles (probably around 0·75). For individual products *within* each broad category, however, price elasticities are certainly much higher and are probably substantially in excess of unity with products such as consumer durables. Income elasticities are easier to measure from household budget data; in Britain they range from about 0·5 for foodstuffs generally to over 2 for consumer durables and 2·5 or higher for travel and holidays.

Even if they have no statistical estimates of the price elasticity of the demand for their products, however, most producers usually have a fairly shrewd idea of the likely effects of a small change in their current price, although their ideas will admittedly be rough and ready and based on 'hunch' or instinct rather than statistical calculation. In any case, the fact that elasticity is seldom accurately measurable in practice does not make it a useless or unrealistic concept for the analysis of market behaviour. By employing it, economists are merely using in a clear and precise

way a concept which plays an important part, although in a
less well-defined manner, in the decisions of producers and the
determination of market price.

FURTHER READING

E. MANSFIELD *Micro-economics* Ch. 4
H. A. JOHN GREEN *Consumer theory* Ch. 9
A. M. LEVENSON and B. S. SOLON *Outline of price theory* Ch. 6
K. LANCASTER *Introduction to modern micro-economics* Ch. 3

PART III

THE THEORY OF PRODUCTION

CHAPTER V

The Organisation of Production

1 INTRODUCTORY: THE ENTREPRENEUR

ECONOMIC activities can be broadly classified into consumption, production and exchange. The preceding Part was concerned with the factors underlying the rate of consumption of one commodity in comparison with that of other commodities. The next problem to be dealt with, therefore, is that of analysing the forces which determine how wealth is produced. All wealth is created, as was noted earlier, by factors of production; these are labour, land, capital and enterprise. By the process of *production* is meant the use of any of these scarce resources not for the personal gratification of the user (which would be consumption) but for the creation of a flow of commodities or services which are desired by other people or organisations − either for *their* consumption or for use in the production of some other form of wealth.

Now this obviously creates an organisational problem. A pack of cards thrown on a table will not deal itself into hands; a pile of eggs, butter and flour thrown into a basin will not form itself into a pudding; similarly, a collection of land, labour and capital will not form itself into a wealth-producing relationship. For any group of individual entities to be placed in some purposeful and systematic association with one another, a controlling intelligence must be at work. For cards, it is provided by the dealer, for the pudding, by the cook; for the production of wealth, by the *entrepreneur*. This last word is perhaps a strange choice (its translation into English is particularly misleading) but it has now an accepted place in the technical jargon of economics. By the entrepreneur is meant the person (or group of persons) who brings the other factors of production into an organised relationship, decides on the quantities of each factor to be employed, and on the product which they are to be used in making. He provides the factor called *enterprise*.

There would be a great deal to be said for treating this factor, enterprise, as a form of labour and the supplier of this factor, the entrepreneur, as merely one special type of labourer. Labour has been defined as any exertion of the human mind or body directed to the production of wealth, and this process of assembling and organising factors certainly comes within that definition. For the purposes of analysis, however, it is helpful to treat this particular form of labour as a separate factor (just as it is helpful to treat land separately rather than as a form of capital) because of the rather special forces which operate on it and of the distinct role which the entrepreneur plays in the economic system of a country.

The essential point about the entrepreneur is that he incurs the cost involved in obtaining the services of the other factors, which is known beforehand, in the hope of a return from the sale of the product, *a return which lies in the future and is uncertain*. The other factors – land, labour and capital – are engaged for a specific rate of payment which is agreed before their services are used; the entrepreneur has no such guaranteed return, since his judgement as to what a product will cost to manufacture and what it will fetch when it is sold may prove to be wide of the mark. In this possibility lies one of the characteristics which distinguish enterprise from the other factors; although the other factors may receive a small reward, only the entrepreneur can receive a *negative* reward – that is, make a net loss. If the judgement of an entrepreneur proves to be defective, he may end not only with no payment in return for his exertions but – if the costs incurred exceed the price at which a product has to be sold – with less wealth than that with which he began, some of it having been lost in his unsuccessful productive venture.

The function of an entrepreneur, therefore, is to shoulder the *risks and uncertainties* involved in assembling the other factors in an efficient productive relationship and in making the decision as to the type of commodity those factors should produce. Now, if the world was a static sort of place where the amounts of various goods and services which people consumed remained more or less the same from month to month, and where production methods also remained unchanged, this job of organising and directing production would be a matter of administrative routine. In fact the world is not like that at all. The demand for different commodities is constantly changing as fashion and habit change, or as people find themselves worse off or better off, or as new products or new substitutes come along to tempt the consumer away from established buying habits. Modern production requires resources to be laid out (i.e. costs to be paid out) months or even years before the finished article reaches the shop window, and the task of anticipating correctly how many units of a product will be sold, and the price they will fetch, four or five months hence, is by no means an easy one. Nor are production techniques constant; an entrepreneur may buy machinery and organise his productive flow only to find a few months later that a new device has been invented, or new process discovered, which makes his methods out-of-date and expensive in relation to the methods now open to his competitors. The primary job of the entrepreneur in a dynamic world is therefore to assess and bear the *uncertainty* inherent in the modern economy – uncertainty as to future demand, prices and productive methods. It is possible to insure against certain business risks which operate with sufficient regularity to permit an insurance company to calculate their probability – losses such as those occurring through storms, fires, or theft – but the uncertainties attaching to future demand or supply conditions are of their nature unpredictable, and the entrepreneur must undertake the responsibility for assessing and bearing them.

2 INDUSTRIAL ORGANISATION

Who *is* the entrepreneur? Theoretically the answer is clear – the person (or group) ultimately responsible for production policy decisions and bearing the uncertainty inherent in the process of producing in advance of demand. In practice it is by no means always easy to be quite sure who actually performs these functions. This fact is brought out by a brief survey of the various forms in which economic enterprises are organised; such a survey will also make it easier for this theoretical discussion of the factor of enterprise to be related to the actual economic world.

The simplest form of industrial structure to be found in Britain is the *one-man business,* the firm which is owned and controlled by a single individual who takes an active part in the productive process but who may employ other people to assist him. This type of firm is most often seen in trades which of their nature favour small-scale output – agriculture, retail trade, professional services, etc. – but is occasionally found in some branches of manufacturing industry. Here at least there is no difficulty in identifying the entrepreneur. A similar type of organisation is that of the *partnership,* where two or more individuals own and control the firm. In general, such firms do not have limited liability – that is, there is no limit beyond which the private wealth of the partners cannot be claimed by creditors of the firm so as to secure payment of a debt – although there are exceptions to this rule. Once again the problem of identifying the entrepreneurs is not very great, since the responsibility for policy decisions and the burden of uncertainty obviously is with the individual partners. In practice, however, some partners may take little active part in the running of the business, so that they implicitly transfer their entrepreneurial powers to the active partners.

The most important form of business structure in this country is the *registered joint-stock company,* and the vast bulk of private industry is organised in this form. With a few special and relatively unimportant exceptions, such companies register under the provisions of the various Companies Acts, comply with the requirements of those Acts, and are granted limited liability. This means that the persons who invest funds in the company, and therefore own it – the shareholders – cannot be held responsible for any debts incurred by the company except to the extent to which they have contributed funds. For example, if a person holds shares to the value of £1 000 in a registered company, he could lose his £1 000 if the company was forced into bankruptcy, but a creditor would have no claim on the rest of the shareholder's wealth even if some of the company's debts remained unpaid.

These companies may be of two kinds. *A private joint-stock company* is one in which at least two but not more than 50 persons hold shares. It is private in the sense that it is not required to publish an annual balance-sheet; on the other hand it is not permitted to appeal to the public at large to contribute new capital. More important in practice is the *public joint-stock company*. Such a company is required to hold an annual meeting of shareholders and publish an annual balance-sheet, as well as to comply with a great many other legal requirements aimed at the protection of the investing public from mis-information and fraud. On the other hand, they can offer securities for sale to the general public and so attract funds for the business.

These securities may be of three main types. *Debentures* are acknowledgements of a debt amounting to a specified sum on which a fixed rate of interest is paid annually; often they carry a promise of capital repayment by or on a certain date. Persons who purchase debentures are in no sense shareholders of the company; they are simply *creditors* of the company entitled to the fixed annual interest payment and sometimes capital repayment on a specified date. If a company fails to meet these contractual interest or capital payments, for whatever reason, the debenture holder can have the company declared bankrupt and have its assets sold in order to regain his capital.

The second main type of security is known as the *preference share*. Unlike the debenture holder, the holder of this type of security is not a *creditor* of the company – he is a *shareholder*. This means that he has a claim to any profits the company may make, but has no claim on the company if it fails to make any profit and is unable to pay him any return on his investment as a result. Like the debenture, however, the preference share bears a specified rate of dividend which must be paid before anyone else can share in the profits. The debenture interest has to be paid before profits are arrived at; the preference shareholder then has first claim on the profits, and until the specified rate of dividend has been paid to him no one else can share in the profits. Some preference shares are *cumulative,* which means that if profits in any year are insufficient to enable the company to pay the full rate of dividend on its preference shares, then the deficiency must be made good in subsequent years before any other claimants to profits can receive anything. Usually, preference shareholders have no voting powers in the control of the company so long as their specified rate of dividend has been paid out.

The third type of security is the *ordinary share.* The purchaser of an ordinary share has no guaranteed rate of dividend whatever; he is simply entitled to share in whatever profits are made by the company over and above those needed to meet the prior claims of the holders of preference shares. The ordinary share-holder therefore bears the greater part of the risks of the enterprise; the return on his investment may be zero for years on end, while, on the other hand, it may be very high indeed if the company succeeds. In normal times, the ordinary share-holders attend an annual general meeting at which the policy of the company is explained by a board of directors elected by them to manage the company on their behalf. If the shareholders are not satisfied, they may refuse to re-elect the board of directors and elect new directors from amongst their number.

When an attempt is made to identify the entrepreneur in a private or public joint-stock company, the task is frequently difficult. In theory, the uncertainty inherent in economic enterprise lies unambiguously with the shareholders; so does the ultimate responsibility for the policy decisions necessary to the running of the company. In practice, however, the degree of true control exercised by the shareholders of a company is often very small; provided a company continues to pay a reasonable dividend, most shareholders are content to let the board of directors look after the affairs of the company and do not even trouble to attend the annual general meetings. Hence the management of a large established company tends to take on an identity of its own, with the active directors and salaried managers regarding the general body of shareholders as a set of creditors who have to be placated but who in no real sense participate in the policy-making. Ownership and control, therefore, the two ingredients of entrepreneurship, become divorced and the identity of the entrepreneur often tends in practice to be somewhat nebulous.

This is even more so with other types of industrial organisation. *Co-operative societies,* for example, have a large number of small shareholders who theoretically control the societies but who in practice take little active part in policy-making. *Public corporations* or *nationalised industries* such as the Central Electricity Generating Board, the B B C, the British Gas Corporation, coal-mining, railways, etc., are theoretically owned by the citizens of the whole country, but it is stretching the imagination to treat every voter as an entrepreneur in these industries. Effective power rests in the hands of the chairmen of the Boards concerned and, of course, the Minister responsible for them.

3   OPTIMUM FACTOR COMBINATION

The entrepreneur, then, has to decide what is to be produced and in what quantities; if his judgement proves to be wrong, the reward he receives will be small and may even be negative. Having decided what to produce, however, he still has the problem of the way in which the commodities are to be produced. Very few commodities have only a single method of production; almost all can be produced in a large number of different ways. Catching fish might seem as straightforward a form of economic activity as any, but the methods by which fish can be caught range from, at one extreme, the man with a rod and line (i.e. much labour and relatively little capital) to the modern trawler with complex radar and echo-sounding equipment (i.e. much capital and relatively less labour) at the other.

On what basis does the entrepreneur decide the factor-combination with which his commodity should be produced? It is assumed that the entrepreneur, like the owner of any other factor of production, seeks to obtain the maximum possible monetary reward from his economic activities. If he decides to produce a certain quantity of output and to sell at a certain price, he will seek the factor-combination which results in the production of the goods at the lowest *cost*. His reward consists of the difference between what he has to pay for the factors he uses (i.e. the cost) and what the product brings in; the lower the cost the greater his reward.

Once again there is a close and immediate analogy with the example of the settler seeking to maximise the area of land discussed in Chapter II. Instead of the size of a building site, the entrepreneur has as his focus of attention the output of a particular product or group of products, but the essential problem of maximising some desired result within the constraint of a limited supply of resources is assumed to be common to both. Now it was noted in connection with the analysis of consumer behaviour that the behavioural assumption being made — the first element in the analysis of every economic problem — might not always be realistic. The consumer may not always seek exclusively to maximise his own welfare, nor always act rationally in his spending decisions. A similar note of warning must be sounded concerning the behavioural assumption being made here — that the entrepreneur seeks to maximise the profit he receives from his business and thus to minimise the cost of whatever he produces. Like the consumer he may have regard to other consequences of his decisions: the number or welfare of his work-force, the impact of his business on his locality or even the country generally, his public 'image', the prestige of his firm and its position relative to competitors — or just a quiet life and two rounds of golf a week. Like the consumer, he may not always act rationally in seeking to achieve his desired ends, whatever they may be; he may not possess adequate information to do so, even if he wished.

The assumption of an aim of profit-maximisation can thus be only a first approximation to reality. But, like consumer rationality, it is probably the best *general* assumption which can be made of most entrepreneurs most of the time. The conclusions which follow from it will always need to be tempered in fact by these many other influences acting upon the entrepreneur: but they constitute a reasonable point of departure.

Given this basic assumption, there is once more a close analogy between the settler of Chapter II and the consumer of Chapter III. The settler was seeking the maximum area it was possible to enclose with a limited stock of fencing material; the consumer seeks to attain the maximum possible utility from the expenditure of a given sum; the entrepreneur is trying to get the maximum output from a given quantity of factors. Not surprisingly, then, the analytical tools used to study consumer expenditure need only small modification to handle the case of an entrepreneur combining productive resources. An example is given in Fig. 5A. Here the curves Q_1Q_1', Q_2Q_2', etc., are obviously comparable with the 'area lines' of the settler problem or with indifference curves, but for the producer they represent different levels of *output* of his product, not satisfaction; they are called *isoquants,* since every point on each curve represents the same quantity of output, just as every point on the area lines in Fig. 2A represented the same area. Along the axes are measured the amounts of factors of production, in their various possible combinations, required to produce those outputs, just as the axes of an indifference map measure the quantities of commodities from which the consumer derives the satisfaction represented by the indifference curves.

The curve in Fig. 5A(i), for example, shows the combinations of capital and labour (assumed to be the only variable factors) which will all result in an output Q. If the relative price of one unit of capital and one unit of labour is represented by PA – the equivalent of the consumer's budget line – the point of tangency, X_1, gives the combination of factors which will produce the output Q at minimum cost – in this case, OC_1 units of capital and OL_1 units of labour. This point, of course, is that at which the marginal rate of substitution of the factors (given by the slope of the isoquant at that point) is exactly equal to their relative price (given by the slope of the price line); it corresponds with the consumer's equilibrium point at which marginal rates of substitution (relative marginal utilities) were equal to relative commodity prices. Why should this particular point indicate the factor combination which gives a defined output at minimum cost? To establish that it is so, it is only necessary to compare the cost of this combination with that of any other giving the same output. If the producer adopted the combination at X_2, for example, he would reduce his use of labour by EX_1.

The price line PA shows that this saving of EX_1 units of labour is equal to the cost of EF units of capital, but the producer is actually using FX_2 units of capital *more* than this at point X_2; his total costs would clearly have risen. Similarly, if the producer adopted X_3 he would be saving X_1G units of capital, sufficient to pay for GH extra units of labour; his additional labour requirements, however, will be HX_3 more than this. The combination X_1, at which the marginal rate of substitution of factors is equal to their relative price, is thus the cheapest possible for the postulated output Q.

Similar isoquants can obviously be drawn for every practicable level of output, such as the examples shown in Fig. 5A(ii). If the line embodying the prevailing price ratio of capital and labour is drawn at a tangent to each, the combination of factors giving each level of output at minimum cost can be discovered. Connecting up these points of tangency gives the expansion path SS', which records the quantities of factors which the entrepreneur will use in order to produce different levels of output.

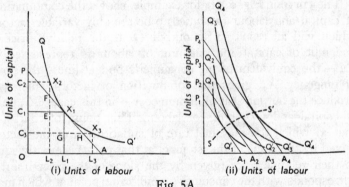

(i) *Units of labour*   (ii) *Units of labour*

Fig. 5A

This combination of factors resulting in the production of a given output of a commodity at minimum cost is called the *optimum,* or best, combination. It is the collection of land, labour and capital which, with the directing and organising control of the entrepreneur himself, constitutes the best (i.e. cheapest) way of producing the article concerned – it is the productive method which involves the smallest sacrifice of the community's scarce resources in the production of a given amount of wealth. Naturally this optimum will involve different proportional combinations of the various factors for different types of commodity; some commodities are produced most cheaply with a lot of land and relatively little labour and capital, while others are best produced with large amounts of capital but relatively little land and labour. The optimum combination for any given commodity will also vary from time to time as new techniques and inventions occur. Changes of both of these will involve shifts in the position or slope of the isoquants. Finally, the optimum is closely related to the relative costs of the various factors; one combination may be the optimum for a particular commodity when land is relatively plentiful, and therefore cheap, but a completely different combination may become the optimum if land becomes dearer relative to labour; such a change can be analysed by an appropriate adjustment of the slope of the price line. The analogy with the settler of Chapter II varying the dimensions of his site with the changing relative prices of the different types of fencing is both obvious and direct.

4   THE SIGNIFICANCE OF TIME

In dealing with the effects of a change in price on demand, or of changes in demand on price, it was reasonable to ignore the possible delay which might elapse between the change in one and the change in the other. In practice, such delays are unlikely to be long; even if they occurred they would not materially affect the previous analysis of reactions between demand and price. In considering the output of goods, however, delays, or time-lags, are of considerable significance; this is because in the real world considerable time may elapse before production is fully adjusted to changes in price (factories and shipyards cannot be built overnight) and also because such time-lags have important implications for theoretical analysis. To be more precise, economists distinguish between the short and long periods. By the *short period* is meant that space of time in which the productive capacity of an industry cannot be fully adjusted to a change in demand; by the *long period* is meant the space of time in which capacity can be so adjusted, either through changes in the normal capacity of existing firms in the industry (i.e. the increase or reduction of factory space, the installation or elimination of plant and machinery, and so on), or through the entry of new firms into the industry, or departure of firms from it, or, of course, some combination of the two. For example, if the demand for transatlantic sea-travel increases, shipping firms will be forced to meet the increase by working their existing ships and crews on more frequent trips and by bringing into use ships and crews which for one reason or another had previously been laid up. This will seldom be satisfactory as a permanent solution, however, and if the increase in demand is believed to be permanent new ships will be ordered and new crews recruited and trained. When the new ships and crews are finally put into service, and capacity is fully adjusted to the new level of demand, then the long-period equilibrium will be reached; prior to that time the situation prevailing will be a short-period one.

The actual length of the short and long periods in terms of calendar time will naturally vary from industry to industry. In the cotton spinning trade, for example, it may only be a matter of a few months before new equipment can be installed and additional operatives trained; in the case of air transport, five or six years may elapse before new aircraft can be delivered and additional crews be provided. A second point to note is that the long period may have different lengths in terms of calendar time according to whether capacity is being expanded or contracted. In general, a factor such as labour can be dismissed more rapidly than it can be obtained, especially if a fairly high degree of skill is required. On the other hand, capital wears out relatively slowly; it may take several years for a machine to pass out of use through wear and tear, whereas a new one could perhaps be manufactured in a few months. A producer faced with a reduced demand, and therefore with excess capital equipment, can reduce his capital only at the rate at which it wears out. (There will be no point in deliberately destroying it; he would obtain no benefit from that.) The best he can do is to spend no more money on it – i.e. omit to maintain it in a full state of repair and allow it to wear out gradually. This process may take several years.

It will become clear as the analysis proceeds that there are many reasons why this distinction between the short period and the long period is important in economic analysis.

5 JOINT PRODUCTS

So far the discussion has proceeded in terms of a single producer concerned with the provision of a single product or service. It is therefore as well to refer briefly at this point to the possibility of a single firm making more than one product. Where the products concerned are not the outcome of a single productive process no special problems arise. Although production may be located in a single factory, the firm can be conceived of as two or more separate enterprises operating in two or more industries and independent cost calculations can be made for each product.

The situation is less straightforward, however, if the process of producing one commodity is technically connected with that of producing another, as frequently happens. In such a situation, the commodities involved would be spoken of as *joint products,* meaning that a single productive process results in the production of two or more products. The production of coal gas, for example, inevitably involves the production of coke; rearing beef cattle necessarily results in the production of hides; supplying planks for a timber-yard also increases the supply of sawdust.

The major problem raised in these situations, where an increase or decrease in the production of one commodity automatically involves an increase or decrease in the output of another, is that of attributing costs of production to either. If gas and coke are produced by the same operation, how can the total cost of production be allocated between the two products? More important, how can the *marginal* cost of either product be calculated? – further analysis will show that it is marginal cost which plays the vital role so far as an individual producer is concerned in determining the equilibrium level of price and output in a free market.

Two types of situation can be distinguished. In one it is technically impossible to vary the relative amounts of the products emerging from the productive process – the cultivation of raw cotton, for example, involves the production of a more or less constant proportion of cotton-seed. Here, the marginal cost of one product can only be taken as the total cost of producing an extra amount of *both* products *minus* the extra revenue brought in from the increased output of the joint product. Where the proportions *can* be varied, however (the amount of straw produced in conjunction with wheat can be altered by changing the type of seed employed, for example), the marginal cost of one product can be defined as the cost of increasing its output by one unit in such a way as to maintain an unchanged output of the joint product.

The same distinction must be borne in mind in considering the effects of an increase in the supply of one product on the price of the product associated with it. If the proportions of the joint products cannot be varied, an increased output of one, called forth by a rise in demand, will necessarily result in an increase in the output of the other and therefore (assuming the demand for the latter is unchanged) a fall in its price. On the other hand, if the proportions *can* be varied, an increase in the output of one product can occur without any increase in the output of the other (or, indeed, may be associated with a *fall* in the output of the other) so that the price of the joint product may be unchanged or may even rise.

Once again the time element is frequently important. It often happens that the proportions in which joint products are supplied can be altered in the long run but not in the short run. The relative amounts of wool and mutton produced by a sheep-farmer, for example, can be varied by switching from one breed of sheep to another, but obviously this is a process which will take some considerable time. In the short run, therefore, an increased output of one joint product will usually involve an increase in the output of the other, and hence a fall in its price. In the long run, on the other hand, the proportions in which the products are supplied can usually be varied, so that an increased demand for one can be met without depressing the market for the other.

6 OPPORTUNITY COST

Throughout this discussion of the organisation of production, the expression 'cost' has been taken to mean the money payments which an entrepreneur is forced to make in order to obtain the services of the various factors of production. In reality factors are obtained through money payments, and in economic analysis 'cost' is therefore generally used in this sense.

There is another, and more fundamental, sense in which the word 'cost' can be used, however. Money is merely a device which is used in the everyday world because of its great convenience; underlying monetary transactions, however, are the real sacrifices inherent in the scarcity of resources in relation to our needs. Hence the concept of 'opportunity' cost has already been used to get behind the monetary veil to the fundamental realities which it tends to conceal. By the *opportunity cost* of production is meant the alternative uses of factors of production which are necessarily sacrificed by using those resources in a particular way. The money cost of a table is the total paid out in the course of its production by way of wages, rent, interest and profit; its opportunity cost is the desk, or chairs, or cricket bats which *could* have been made with the same resources but which are sacrificed by using them to make a table.

This concept of the opportunity cost of production is constantly recurring in various contexts. For example, wages in a particular industry are determined partly by what labour could obtain in other industries, and this will be a measure of the opportunity cost of labour. Again, a country may find that to increase a defence programme it is necessary for it to go without motor-cars which would have been supplied to it by an industry now occupied in making tanks and aircraft. For the community as a whole, as opposed to the individual producer or consumer, this concept of opportunity cost is more meaningful than that of money cost. The reason for this is that it brings clearly and unambiguously before our minds the fundamental reality of the economic world – that resources are scarce in relation to the goods and services we should like to consume; that, given full employment, using resources in one way implies a sacrifice of their alternative uses; that we cannot eat our cake and have it.

The concept was encountered in its simplest form in the land-settlement example of Chapter II : each settler could extend the length of his site only at the expense of reducing its width. The same dilemma runs through the whole of economic life to the very highest levels of decision-making at which, for example, the advantages of using more doctors in hospital treatment have to be balanced against the potential gains of using them in medical research; the need to repair and improve existing roads has to be judged against the gains from building new motorways; the devotion of increased productivity to higher levels of output and consumption has to be balanced against its allocation to environmental protection or improvement with unchanged consumption.

The economist, therefore, can never interpret reality in the politician's terms that we must have more of X or that Y is manifestly desirable; decisions, to the economist, imply *choices* between more of X and the alternatives which must be foregone if more of X is in fact to be provided, between Y, which is doubtless desirable, and the opportunity cost of Y – which is also doubtless something desirable. His trade is not to *make* such choices: it is rather to reveal them and their nature to the decision-makers in the hope that thereby better-informed decisions will be made.

FURTHER READING

K. LANCASTER *Introduction to modern micro-economics* Ch. 4

J. HADAR *Elementary theory of consumer behaviour* Ch. 3

D. F. HEATHFIELD *Production functions* Macmillan, London 1971

A. BEACHAM and N. J. CUNNINGHAM *Economics of industrial organisation* 5th ed., Pitman, London 1970, Ch. 1

A. M. LEVENSON and B. S. SOLON *Outline of price theory* Ch. 7

R. S. EDWARDS and H. TOWNSEND *Business enterprise* Macmillan, London 1965, Part I

CHAPTER VI

Production in the Short Run: Diminishing Returns

1 THE CASE OF LAND

THE preceding chapter has introduced two concepts – that of the optimum factor combination for any given level of output of a product and that of the short-run situation in which the quantities of one or more factors in use may not be capable of variation. The two can now be brought together in order to examine the relationship between inputs of factors of production and the output of a product as the level of production is varied in the short period. (The same relationship between inputs and outputs in the long period will be considered in the next chapter.)

The significance of this relationship first received public notice in the late eighteenth century in connection with the productivity of farming as the level of agricultural output expanded. This was natural enough in the circumstances of Britain at that time, when population was beginning to increase and press upon the capacity of what was still an essentially agricultural economy. The economic commentators of the time, examining the evidence of history and relying on their own observations, advanced the proposition that if a farmer is able to choose the amount of land he cultivates, the land being free in the sense of having no price (as it would be for settlers in a new country, for example), he will apply his labour and capital to the area which gives him the highest average return. If to that area he subsequently applies more labour or more capital, or both, the average output per unit of labour or capital will sooner or later begin to diminish.

His total output will rise, that is, but eventually *not* in as great a proportion as the amounts of other factors being employed.

This *law of diminishing returns* is best illustrated by means of a simple diagram, as are a good many economic concepts. Consider an example of a farmer producing a single crop, wheat, with a fixed acreage of land. In the diagram (Fig. 6A) the number

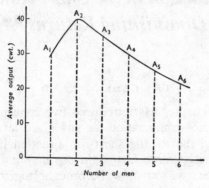

Fig. 6A

of men whose labour is used on the given acreage is measured along the horizontal axis; on the vertical axis is measured the average yield of wheat per man – the total output divided by the number employed. If the farmer used only his own labour, he would attain an output of 30 cwt. (A_1). If he employed an additional man, however, believing that the area was too big for one man to cultivate efficiently, total output would be 80 cwt., giving an average of 40 cwt. per man (A_2). The average return would have risen, and the amount of labour employed would be in just the right proportion to the acreage being cultivated. If he now applied further units of labour the law of diminishing returns would begin to operate. If he employed another man, total output would rise (say to 105 cwt.) but not to the same extent as the increase in the labour force; average output would fall to 35 cwt. (A_3). As the amount of labour increases, so the returns per unit of labour will continually decrease.

In view of the fixity of the supply of land, this feature of agricultural production was regarded by nineteenth-century economists as one of considerable importance. It implied that, if population increased, the additional food supplies required could be produced only by applying further units of labour and capital to the fixed supply of land, and therefore only under conditions of diminishing returns – less and less food would be produced per head of the population. The law was extended to other uses of land. As further units of labour and capital are applied to mines, for example, the average output will tend to fall as seams are worked out and mining has to go deeper and deeper (although mineral deposits are wasting assets in the sense that, unlike fields, their fertility cannot be maintained indefinitely by careful cultivation). *Building land* is similarly subject to diminishing returns; after a certain point, as labour and capital are applied, sites become crowded and congested and each building added reduces the average value of the existing buildings.

As a generalisation concerning economic activity, the law is unquestionably valid. Some important points about it should be noted, however. First, the formulations of the law by the nineteenth-century writers explicitly or implicitly assumed that the state of technical knowledge remained unchanged while the additional factors were being applied to the fixed area of land. If this was not the case, average output per man might well increase rather than diminish as the scale of production expanded. If six men are employed in cultivating an area which was previously worked by three men, average output may well decline *if the same methods of production are employed*. But if new techniques or equipment are developed simultaneously, the six men may well have a *higher* average output than the three. The output curve shown in the diagram would be shifted bodily upwards by the improved production methods, although its shape would remain unchanged. This is in fact what has happened in history, so that the gloomy predictions of an increasing population being driven towards starvation by diminishing returns have not been borne out. Technical development has more than offset the law of diminishing returns, and average output in agriculture has risen rather than fallen. But in the short run, of course, when significant technical developments cannot be looked for, the law can and will come into operation.

Secondly, in formulating the law it is assumed that there is no change in the *quality* of the units of the variable factors being applied to the constant factor, and also that the fixed factor is capable of being spread over different amounts of the variable factors. If the quality of the variable factors was not constant, or if the fixed factor could be used only in conjunction with a specific quantity of the other factors, then the law might not hold.

The final point about the law is that *it is not uniquely associated with the factor of land*; it can and does apply to other factors. Nineteenth-century writers formulated the law in connection with land because of their awareness that land was fixed in supply and therefore likely to be the constant factor to which varying quantities of other factors would be applied. But under certain conditions other factors may be fixed in supply, at least for a time, and diminishing returns will be experienced if a constant amount of *any* factor is used in conjunction with increasing amounts of other factors. If a farmer commences from a position in which the right amount of land and labour are being combined and then proceeds to spread his fixed labour force over a greater and greater area by taking new land into cultivation, average output per unit of resources used will diminish in exactly the same way as when increasing amounts of labour were applied to a constant area of land. It is not land as such which gives rise to diminishing returns; it is the *fixity* of factor supply. In the long run only land is completely fixed in supply, but in the short run (i.e. as a temporary state of affairs) other factors may be fixed in supply and will thus give rise to diminishing returns. The proposition is essentially simple; it amounts to saying that an aircraft which has two pilots in its crew cannot fly twice as far, or carry twice as many passengers, as when it is flying with a single pilot. Generalising the law, it can be said that in all productive activity there is an optimum combination of the factors of production which results in the maximum average output per unit of the resources used; *if additional amounts of factors are now applied to a fixed quantity of one factor, total output will increase in a smaller proportion than the amounts of variable factors being used.*

2   THE GENERAL CASE

It has just been noted that under certain circumstances the quantity of any factor being used in a particular productive process may be fixed, and not merely the quantity of land. It will be obvious that such a fixity is not only possible but, by definition, *inevitable* in the short period, especially as regards the fixed capital usually involved. The buildings, plant and equipment being used by any enterprise will have been designed for a specific level of operation which may conveniently be referred to as the *capacity* of that enterprise. The use of the word 'capacity' does not imply that the firm's output cannot possibly exceed the specified level but rather that at outputs below or beyond that level the buildings and equipment are not being used to the intensity for which they were initially designed. A car engine, for example, operates most efficiently at a specified number of revolutions per minute but it is quite able to operate at speeds below or above that rate. The fixed capital equipment of a productive enterprise can similarly be operated below or above its design capacity.

It follows that for any capacity level there will be a short-run expansion path as variable factors – labour, materials, fuel and so on – are employed to bring the capital into use and gradually increased as output rises up to, and if necessary beyond, the capacity level. After that capacity is reached, the law of diminishing returns will apply just as inevitably as with the farmer applying increased manpower to a fixed area of land.

A simple example of the phenomenon is illustrated in Fig. 6B. Suppose that this relates to the production of a certain type of casting by a process which involves a combination of semi-automatic machines and workers, a combination which can be varied within fairly wide limits by changing the number of men working with each machine and adjusting operating speeds accordingly. The isoquant map in Fig. 6B shows the sets of machine-men combinations capable of producing weekly outputs ranging from 5 000 to 25 000 finished castings.

Suppose the entrepreneur decides initially to aim at a weekly output of 10 000. His optimum combination of machines and men will be governed by their relative costs; if these are £64 a week for a machine and £40 for each man employed this price ratio will be shown by a line connecting $5x$ machines on the vertical axis with $8x$ men on the horizontal axis. It is clear that for a weekly output of 10 000 the tangency point – i.e. the combination yielding minimum cost – will be X_1, at which he will operate with 25 machines and a labour force of 40. He accordingly arranges for this capacity to be built.

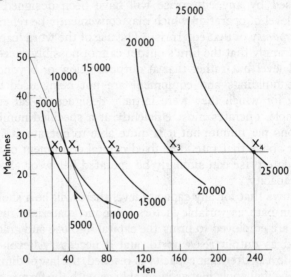

Fig. 6B   Production in the short run

Now it is unlikely that he will be able to proceed immediately to an output of 10 000 a week from scratch. If he begins operations at 5 000 a week, however, the 5 000 isoquant indicates that with his *fixed* capacity of 25 machines he will need about 22 men, with all of the machines running at less than full capacity because of undermanning. In due course he can expand to the desired weekly output level of 10 000 by increasing his labour force to 40.

Suppose now that he obtains large orders for his product which justify him in raising output further. Unless he is to wait until additional machines are delivered and installed, higher outputs can be attained only by increasing the labour force operating his 25 machines; the 15 000-a-week isoquant indicates that about 85 men will be needed to reach that output (point X_2), while 150 men will be needed for 20 000 a week (point X_3) and no less than 240 men for an output of 25 000 a week (point X_4).

The operation of diminishing returns can now be clearly seen. Setting out the labour force associated with each level of output gives:

Weekly output (1)	*Labour force* (2)	*Output per man* $(1 \div 2)$ (3)
5 000	22	227
10 000	40	250
15 000	85	176
20 000	150	133
25 000	240	104

It is clear that the situation is exactly comparable with that of the farmer in Fig. 6A. Once the design capacity of the firm has been reached, weekly output can be increased only at the expense of a steady fall in output per man. (As will be seen a little later, this is frequently but not necessarily associated with rising cost per unit of output.) Inspection of Fig. 6B indicates clearly enough why this is happening: as output expands along the path dictated by the fixed capital capacity – the line $X_1X_2X_3$ etc. – the feasible factor combinations are departing increasingly from the optimum points on the isoquants concerned. (These can be located, of course, by finding the tangent of the machine-men price ratio line to each.)

3 AVERAGE AND MARGINAL PRODUCT

From the example just discussed it is possible to introduce a concept which, in various forms, will prove to be of considerable significance in subsequent analysis. The figures of output per man quoted in it could be alternatively labelled as *average product,* since they are calculated by dividing total output by the number of men engaged in producing it. (One should beware of assuming that this is a measure of labour productivity – the capital equipment in use is also making a contribution.) It is also possible to derive estimates of *marginal product* – that is, the addition being made to total output by each batch of extra men. For example, when the labour force rose from 22 to 40 in the example, output rose from 5 000 to 10 000; hence the extra men added 5 000 to output and their marginal product (per man) was thus 5 000 divided by 18 – i.e. about 278.

Continuing in this way, a schedule of average and marginal products at each output level can be set out:

Output (Q)	ΔQ	Labour force (L)	ΔL	Average product (1)÷(3)	Marginal product (2)÷(4)
(1)	(2)	(3)	(4)	(5)	(6)
5 000	5 000	22	22	227	227
10 000	5 000	40	18	250	278
15 000	5 000	85	45	176	111
20 000	5 000	150	65	133	77
25 000	5 000	240	90	104	56

The relationship between these two concepts of average and marginal product may best be appreciated by referring to Fig. 6C in which these numerical data are approximated by curves – assumed for the sake of simplicity to be continuous between the observed points. The relationship between the two curves is in fact one of very general applicability.

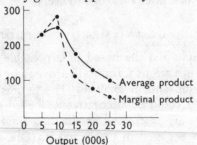

Fig. 6C   Average and marginal product

In the first place it will be noted that the marginal curve moves between wider limits than the average and is in general more variable. This is of course a result of the damping effect of averaging on any series of numbers. If the first two batsmen in a cricket team score 70 and 80 respectively, the average score is 75 and the marginal score – the runs added by the second batsman – is 80. If now batsman number 3 is out first ball without scoring, the marginal score falls catastrophically from 80 to zero but the average score falls only from 75 to 50.

Secondly, as long as the marginal curve is *above* the average curve (even though it may itself be falling) the average will be rising; conversely, if the marginal curve is *below* the average curve the average will be falling – again even if the marginal curve is rising. From this follows an important characteristic of the two types of curve: if the marginal curve is neither above nor below the average curve – that is, the values of each are *equal* – then the average is stationary. It will be seen later that this property has important implications for competitive price and output levels.

Finally it should be noted that the marginal product curve may well become negative if output is expanded far enough while it is almost inconceivable that average product should become negative. The economic meaning of this is that a variable factor is being used in such quantities that total output is actually being reduced by employing them. This may seem a highly unlikely state of affairs but it is by no means impossible: it is often suggested that in badly under-developed countries the number of peasant farmers cultivating the limited ground available is too great to allow any of them to adopt efficient techniques of cultivation – they are literally getting in one another's way.

The curves demonstrate, then, that the behaviour of the marginal product curve identifies three phases of the productive process. When it is *rising* employment of the factor concerned is clearly too small; the fixed factors are being used below their proper capacity and output will rise more than in proportion to the increase in the use of the variable factors. Equally, if the marginal product is *negative* employment of the variable factor is too great; production is being reduced in absolute terms by the last units of the factor employed. Hence the only region of doubt is that over which marginal product is positive but falling. Here the question of whether too much or too little output is being produced can be answered only in the light of cost and revenue considerations which have yet to be explored.

4   CONCLUSION

The phenomenon of diminishing returns occurs when the application of increased quantities of variable factors of production to a fixed quantity of one or more factors results in a declining average output per unit of variable input. While the phenomenon was first observed and discussed in the context of agricultural land, it has been seen that it can be, and is, associated with *any* factor of production whose quantity cannot be varied. Any period of time which is too short to permit of such a variation in any necessary input is referred to as the short period and the situation can be referred to as a short-run situation. The phenomenon of diminishing returns is characteristically associated with such a situation and must indeed inevitably be encountered in it, sooner or later.

No such generalisation can be made in the long period, however, when by definition any factor of production can be increased or decreased in supply to whatever extent is desired. It is to this more complex situation that the analysis must now turn.

FURTHER READING

E. MANSFIELD *Micro-economics* Ch. 5
J. HADAR *Elementary theory of economic behaviour* Ch. 2
E. NEVIN *An introduction to micro-economics* Ch. 2

CHAPTER VII

Production in the Long Run: Increasing Returns

1 RETURNS TO SCALE

IN the short run, the entrepreneur seeking to expand his output has to ignore the concept of the technical optimum combination of inputs: his capacity – usually his buildings, plant and equipment but conceivably a nucleus of key personnel whose number cannot be varied – is fixed, and expansion proceeds by increasing variable inputs to whatever levels are necessary to produce any given output with that fixed capacity. After passing the output for which that capacity was designed, diminishing physical returns are inevitable – although this does not necessarily imply, of course, that his profits are falling after that point. As will be seen in succeeding chapters, the behaviour of profit is determined by factors of a monetary as well as of a technical character.

In the long run, however, the limitation imposed by a fixed capacity is by definition removed. In expanding output, therefore, the entrepreneur will ideally select for any given output level that combination of inputs which minimises total cost for that output – in graphical terms, the combination of inputs defined by the point of tangency between the relative-price line of the inputs concerned and the isoquant corresponding to the level of output in question. The entrepreneur will follow the 'expansion path' of Fig. 5A(ii). Can anything be said concerning the behaviour of the increases in the quantities of inputs necessary to bring forth successive increases in quantity of output?

Unlike the short-run situation there is no *general* rule. If the movement from one output-level to another (with appropriate adjustments to *all* inputs) leads to an increase in output which is proportionately bigger than the increase required in inputs, then it is appropriate to refer to the situation as one of *increasing returns to scale*. If the movement involves equal proportionate increases in both inputs and output, then the situation is one of *constant returns to scale*. Finally, if the movement necessitates a larger proportionate increase in inputs than is attained in total output, then *decreasing returns* are said to apply. (Note that the term '*decreasing* returns' implies that a long-run situation is in question in contrast to '*diminishing* returns' which refers to the short-run situation.)

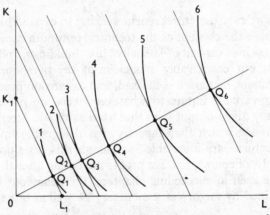

Fig. 7A   Increasing and decreasing returns to scale

Consider the hypothetical example illustrated in Fig. 7A and suppose that the isoquants 1 to 6 correspond to weekly output levels ranging from 10 000 to 60 000. Along the vertical axis, *OK,* are measured inputs of capital and along the horizontal axis, *OL,* are measured the inputs of labour. The relative price of units of capital and labour is denoted by the line K_1L_1 and this price is assumed constant throughout. If the entrepreneur steadily expands his output from 10 000 to 20 000 and from 20 000 to 30 000 and so on, making a full adjustment of his capital and labour inputs on each occasion, he will employ in succession the quantities of capital and labour indicated by the points $Q_1, Q_2 \ldots Q_6$.

Now in the first stage of expansion from the starting point of isoquant 1 to isoquant 2, the necessary increase of inputs is measured by the distance Q_1Q_2, which is clearly less than that of the initial distance OQ_1; similarly, when he expands from isoquant 2 to isoquant 3 the increase in inputs, Q_2Q_3, is smaller again than Q_1Q_2. Over this range of expansion, therefore, the enterprise is enjoying increasing returns to scale – measured against the scale of inputs the isoquants corresponding to equal successive increases in output are getting closer together. After this point, however, the opposite happens: Q_3Q_4 is greater than Q_2Q_3, Q_4Q_5 is greater than Q_3Q_4 and so on: expansion is occurring under conditions of decreasing returns to scale. Obviously there might well be an intervening range over which expansion would be associated with constant returns to scale.

What then are the forces which determine the behaviour of the productivity of an enterprise as its size increases? It will be convenient to consider this question separately for the two major types of input into the productive process: labour (including for this purpose the special kind of labour known as enterprise) and capital (including, again for this purpose, the particular form of capital known as land).

2   THE DIVISION OF LABOUR

A man may run a farm or workshop on his own and so necessarily undertake all aspects of the work involved. If his business grows he will need other men to help him and in the process it is likely that he will concentrate his own efforts on some parts of the work and leave other parts largely to his helpers. An increased scale of output, in other words, is typically associated with specialisation.

Indeed, in considering the role of human beings in the process of production, the first and most striking fact which is to be observed in the modern economy is that of the *division* or specialisation of labour – that is, the employment of the overwhelming majority in narrowly defined occupations or even in narrowly defined tasks. There are farmers, factory workers, doctors, teachers, bus drivers, and so on; few people attempt to supply

all their own economic needs, or even the greater part of them.
People do not (most of them) try to build their own houses,
grow their own food, and make their own clothes. Indeed, they
specialise even within their particular occupations; the factory-
worker specialises in a particular process or the use of a particular
machine, the farmer usually specialises in certain branches of
agriculture, the teacher specialises in certain subjects, even
medical men specialise in certain branches of medicine —
although only to them, for some reason, is the title of 'specialists'
actually given in ordinary parlance.

Why is the human contribution to production organised in
this peculiar (and at first sight rather unnatural) way? The
answer is that experience has long since shown that specialisation
leads to an immense increase in the amount of wealth which
any given number of people can produce in any given time. There
are a number of reasons for this. First, and most important,
is the familiar fact that specialisation leads to a high degree
of *skill and dexterity* — practice makes perfect, as the saying
has it. The constant repetition of particular activities accustoms
minds and muscles to the procedures involved, and enables them
to be carried out rapidly and with less effort. Compare the speed
and accuracy of the professional typist with the amateur, the
drill of the trained soldier with that of the raw recruit, or the
tennis of someone who practises frequently with that of a person
who plays once in the proverbial blue moon. And increased
speed and dexterity mean, in economic life, increased production
and increased wealth.

A second advantage of the division of labour is the fact that
it enables substantial *time* to be saved. On the one hand, a man
turning from one job to another even in the same factory inevitably loses time in doing so and in settling in at the new job.
On the other hand, the time taken to train a man to become
proficient at a wide range of tasks is naturally longer than that
involved in training him for one particular task. An unskilled
person can be trained to watch and operate a particular machine
in the average factory in a few weeks; the training of a fully qualified turner or electrician or toolmaker will take six or seven years.

Thirdly, specialisation allows people to exploit their own individual *aptitudes*. Some people are naturally clever with their hands and some are the reverse; some take readily to indoor work, others cannot stand it; some move and think rapidly, some are naturally slow-moving. Through specialisation there is a greater chance, to put it no higher, that people can find jobs for which their particular talents are best suited.

Finally, by breaking up complex processes of production into separate tasks, specialisation encourages the *use of machinery* and its introduction. The use of machinery is encouraged because the breaking-up of production into separate tasks permits a person to devote his whole time to that task, producing a much larger output of components than if he were trying to carry out every stage in the process of manufacture. Since a machine is economically used only when its capacity is being employed fairly fully (which means when it is producing large numbers of units), the division of production into stages, each involving a high output, enables a machine to be economically employed. If a man made every part of a shoe himself he might produce only two or three pairs a week, and at this level of output it would scarcely be sensible to use machinery at any stage. If he concentrates only on, say, cutting out the sole of each shoe his output of soles might reach several hundred a week, so justifying the introduction of machinery to help him. What is more, the breaking-down of production into separate processes means that an engineer can develop a high degree of familiarity with every detail of a process. As a result he may be able to see ways in which tasks could be carried out mechanically – something he could not do without that breaking-down of particular processes which specialisation permits.

Division of labour, then, has considerable advantages, and the high standard of living now enjoyed by the population of a country such as Britain is probably due more to it than to any other single factor. But society cannot afford to be unaware of the dangers and disadvantages. In the first place, this high degree of specialisation makes each person dependent on millions of other people completely unknown to him and quite beyond his control. Britain specialises in manufacturing, which means that it relies even for food, without which life is impossible, on countries thousands of kilometres away; perhaps only war really brings home the enormity of what is involved in that. Again, if that part of the population which specialises in driving railway-engines for some reason cannot or will not drive engines, then the entire economic life of the country finds itself threatened with dislocation. Further, specialisation increases the risk of unemployment for the individual; the narrower his training and experience, the more difficult it may be for him to find alternative employment if he is forced to seek it.

More generally, there is the danger that a narrowness of specialisation will cause a narrowness of personality and outlook. A man or woman engaged all day and every day on some wholly mechanical and repetitive task finds little scope for creative impulses or the exercise of mental faculties. This may generate its own inefficiencies if frustration and boredom lead to low quality work or frequent industrial disputes, as is believed to be the case in highly mechanised industries like car assembly. Indeed, wider social issues are raised. Can a community employed in this way on monotonous and mechanical tasks, largely under factory conditions, really develop to the full its intellectual and moral qualities? It is an important question. In answering it, many would point out that the infinitely higher living standards and shorter working hours enjoyed by the present generation in comparison with the people of, say, three hundred years ago make for a fuller and more wholesome human life than was even conceivable when men found themselves hard put to it to attain even bare subsistence. Present generations, they would say, have in return for specialisation an infinitely more varied and satisfying life than their predecessors. Ultimately, only opinions can be expressed on an issue of this kind; the important thing is that society should be aware of, and guard against, the dangers which over-specialisation in any field may involve.

3   OTHER FACTORS IN LABOUR EFFICIENCY

It would be wrong to imagine that the extent of specialisation is the only factor determining the productive efficiency of a nation's labour force. The amount of capital with which labour is equipped, or the nature of the land on which it is engaged, naturally play an extremely important part. The significance of such factors will be considered at some length when the discussion passes to the subject of capital in the next section.

A great many other considerations have a bearing on the efficiency of labour as such. Some people are endowed to a higher degree than others with certain qualities favouring economic efficiency – qualities such as adaptability, inventiveness, perseverance and energy. Physical strength as such has played an important part in the past but is diminishing in importance with the spread of mechanisation. A country's climate may be an important factor in this context, since a temperate climate tends to be more conducive to the exertions of economic life than a tropical climate, for example.

The general condition under which a nation's labour force lives, as well as its innate qualities, will also affect its efficiency. An underfed, badly housed and inadequately clothed population can hardly be expected to provide a fully efficient labour force. Nor is it merely a question of the physical requirements of life. A first-rate labour force will develop only in conditions which offer adequate personal freedom, variety of life and scope for ambition. A slave is seldom a really efficient worker.

Many elements therefore contribute to the efficiency of a country's labour force. Some of them are scarcely within human control – innate qualities, or climate – but many can be provided, or at least encouraged, by adequate welfare provision and by careful design of education and vocational training. As the benefits of such measures accrue to the community as a whole, and seldom to a single individual or institution, the responsibility for them is generally agreed to lie primarily with the government. The use of resources in them can raise the wealth-producing capacity of a community just as surely as, if somewhat less dramatically than, some revolutionary development in the field of technology.

4 CAPITAL AND CAPACITY

The second major set of factors determining the effect of size on the productivity of an enterprise is concerned with technical rather than human forces. In the earlier discussion of the law of diminishing returns it was emphasised that it could be formulated only in terms of a situation in which the state of knowledge and technological possibilities remained unchanged. Now it is a feature of industry generally that an increase in the scale of output often does not leave technological possibilities unchanged: methods and techniques become practicable which were not open to the entrepreneur so long as output was maintained at a lower level, with the result that average returns to the factors employed will increase. What are these technical economies which are reaped by a producer as his scale of output increases?

They are best classified under the two headings *internal* and *external*. Internal economies are those which result from the expansion of an individual firm and are enjoyed only by that firm; they may be technical, marketing or financial in nature. By technical economies are meant reductions in the cost of the manufacturing process itself. Increased *division of labour* is of course a major source of economies under this heading and this may apply to management as well as operatives; the small firm may have only one manager who has to concern himself with all aspects of management from labour relations to sales promotion, but a big firm may be able to employ specialists in these activities. A second possibility is the increased use of *machinery*; a high-speed drilling machine, for example, would be largely idle in a firm whose weekly output could be handled by it in an hour, and it would therefore be uneconomic; its possibilities might be fully exploited, however, in a bigger firm. Not only will the use of machinery be more widespread in a large rather than a small firm; frequently, equipment is cheaper to construct and operate (per unit of output) as its size increases. Doubling the area of the sides of a furnace, for example, will result in considerably more than a doubling of its capacity. A large lorry needs no more drivers than a small one, and so on. Further, a large plant may be able to take advantage of the *linking of processes* – that is, to arrange production in such a way that the work is carried on in a continuous sequence, avoiding the wastes involved in breaking production up into separate stages. A large steel mill, for example, may be able to convert ore into pig-iron, iron into crude steel and crude steel into finished steel strip without any break in the sequence, so reducing the transport costs and costs of heating and re-heating incurred if the process were carried on in its separate stages by smaller plants.

The *marketing economies* may be of buying or selling. On the buying side, gains will arise if the orders for raw materials are large enough to justify the employment of a skilled buyer. Buying in large quantities is in any case cheaper than in small lots, since the costs of handling and transport rarely increase in the same proportion as the quantities purchased; further, sellers frequently offer more favourable terms to important customers placing large orders. Selling, also, is generally less expensive per unit in the case of large quantities, since a selling organisation of a given size is often necessary whatever the volume of sales handled. Commercial travellers may secure a large order with the same expenditure of time and effort as that involved in securing a small order; the costs of book-keeping and administration are frequently the same for a large as for a small sale. A high turnover of goods may justify specially designed transport facilities or sales outlets which handle the selling process with maximum efficiency and effectiveness.

The *financial economies* are fairly obvious. A big firm is usually regarded by investors as less risky than a small one, so that they are often willing to lend capital to it at a lower price. Banks are less likely to refuse accommodation to a large concern in times of credit stringency; important customers are too valuable to be lightly refused help. The costs of raising funds on the capital market do not increase proportionately with the size of the sum borrowed, so that the average cost of borrowing in this way is smaller for a large-scale borrower.

All these economies accrue to an individual firm as it grows, and are known as internal economies. By *external economies* are meant the gains arising from the growth of an *industry* and which accrue to all firms in that industry, irrespective of their size. When an industry becomes big enough, for example, *disintegration* may occur — that is, one process may be split off and performed on a large scale by a specialist firm which can gain all the economies of large-scale operation in that particular process. All firms in the industry will now be able to have this process carried out for them at a low cost instead of attempting to meet their own needs by carrying it out themselves on a small scale and at high cost. Subsidiary trades doing specialised processes may spring up when the industry has become big enough to support them, and all firms will benefit from this. Specialist buying and selling agencies may be established; waste-products on a sufficient scale may justify the formation of firms utilising them, so reducing total costs; research and information bureaux may supply services for an industry which no individual firm could afford to provide from its own resources. Frequently such economies are associated with the specialisation of a given area in a certain type of activity, but they will not necessarily take this form.

All these economies, internal and external, in a sense arise from the fact that some of the factors of production are *indivisible* — they are available only in lumps, so to speak. If labour were completely divisible into small units, the optimum division of labour could be adopted however small the labour force, a fractional amount of labour being employed on each separate process. In fact, however, one man (or woman) is the smallest unit of labour which exists, and a man may therefore have to be employed on several processes so long as the scale of output is too small to justify his specialisation on one. Similarly, all the technical economies arising from the increased use of machinery are denied the small-scale producer because he cannot install a fraction of a machine; he can use the machinery only when his output is big enough to keep at least one machine in fairly full employment. The full benefits of technological development and inventions, in other words, often accrue only to those enterprises which are large enough to take proper advantage of them.

5 RETURNS IN PRACTICE

What is the quantitative importance of these economies of large scale? It might appear relatively easy at first sight to discover the answer to this question but in practice it is in fact very difficult to do so. By no means all enterprises are able to allocate costs precisely betwen the various products they make; such data are seldom prepared by different firms in such a way as to make them directly comparable – even assuming that they are not treated as highly confidential; comparisons between firms, or between a given firm at different points of time, are invariably complicated by the fact that influences other than the size of firm are affecting the comparison; and so on.

One way to avoid some of these difficulties is to make comparisons based on purely engineering data – that is, scientific estimates of the technical efficiency of given types of equipment when constructed at various sizes. Over a very wide range of equipment and structures such studies have tended to establish a 'six-tenths rule' – that is, the average cost of the output of a large machine or container tends to approximate 60 per cent of the cost associated with a smaller machine or container of similar design. While to some extent this confirms the existence of the economies of scale, it must be treated with some caution. The technical efficiency of a piece of equipment at various design sizes, taken in isolation, is one thing; the efficiency of the entire environment in which it has to work – bearing in mind the human and technical complexities involved in increasing the whole enterprise – may be quite another. Engineering efficiency and economic efficiency are by no means synonymous.

Investigations into the comparative costs of whole enterprises operating at different sizes have had to grapple with difficulties of the sort mentioned earlier. To the extent that they have proved feasible, they have tended to suggest marked economies of scale in the early stages of industrial expansion followed by constant returns over a fairly extensive range of establishment size. One recent study has taken this point at which average cost per unit of output flattens out as the 'minimum efficient scale' of output for the product concerned and then examined the behaviour of average costs in firms of less than this size. Some of the results of this analysis are shown in Table 7.1. This indicates how costs in establishments operating at about a half of the minimum efficient scale for the product concerned compared with those at the minimum-efficient-scale level of output.

TABLE 7.1 *Estimated economies of scale in British manufacturing industry*

Product	Minimum efficient scale (MES) output	Average cost per unit (excl. materials) at 50% of MES: as% of MES cost
Beer	1 mn. barrels p.a.	155
Books	10 000 copies	150
Ethylene	300 000 tons p.a.	130
Bread	30 sacks flour per hour	130
Refined oil	10 mn. tons p.a.	127
Polymers	80 000 tons p.a.	123
Cement	2 mn. tons p.a.	117
Steel	9 mn. tons p.a.	112–117
Electric appliances	500 000 p.a.	112
Cars	500 000 cars	110
Footwear	300 000 pairs p.a.	105

Based on C. F. Pratten *Economies of scale in manufacturing industries* Occasional Paper No. 28, Department of Applied Economics, Cambridge 1971.

It will be seen that average cost fell by anything between 5 and 50 per cent (of the minimum) as the firms concerned increased in scale from a half of the optimum size to the optimum itself. As might be expected, the fall in average cost was particularly marked for products involving a high proportion of capital to labour (e.g. brewing or chemicals) but was less marked for products in which capital is used less intensively, such as footwear.

It follows that the phenomenon of increasing returns to scale is encountered most markedly in the context of manufacturing industries in which the scope for a high degree of mechanisation is greatest but to a much lesser degree in those sectors of the economy concerned with the provision of individual services – sectors which account for a steadily increasing proportion of total employment. For manufacturing industry, in other words, the advantages of scale appear to be overwhelming.

6 SMALL-SCALE OUTPUT

In view of the fact that large-scale industrial production often results in important economies which reduce average costs of production, how is it that small-scale enterprises survive? That they do survive is shown by the fact that in 1968 about 60 000 of the 92 000 or so establishments operating in manufacturing trades in the United Kingdom employed less than 25 people (although they provided only about 7 per cent of the total employment in manufacturing). Many of these establishments may have been jointly owned by a single firm, of course, but it is obvious that even so small firms are by no means extinct in British industry. Several factors underlie this stubborn survival of small-scale enterprise. The most important is probably the limitation of the *size of the markets*; there is no point in producing on a large scale if only a small proportion of the output can be disposed of in the market. Many markets are severely limited by transport considerations – people like shops to be close at hand, bread cannot always be transported very far, garages and laundries and hotels have to established in the areas where they are needed. Milk-processing costs might be reduced to a minimum if all the milk in the country was handled by one central establishment, but for this industry the effective market in fact is the local market and it is pointless trying to organise it on a national scale. Similarly, the production economies of one central brickworks might be very great, but these would be more than offset by the heavy transport costs involved in taking the finished product to the large number of scattered localities where it is wanted.

Secondly, the *nature of the industry* may be such as to require small-scale production; in agriculture and building, for example, activity is necessarily carried on over a wide geographical area and cannot be centralised.

Thirdly, the small firm (being less complex in its organisation and having less extreme specialisation of capital and labour) is frequently *more flexible* in its output, and can often respond more quickly to changes in demand. The change-over from one model to another in a mass-production car factory may involve the dislocation of output for several weeks or months, and will certainly involve enormous sums of capital; a small and less specialised plant could probably absorb changes in design without any serious inconvenience. In markets where fashion is liable to dominate, or where demand is likely to oscillate for any other reason, this consideration may be of considerable importance. It is obviously crucial where each finished product is made to individual requirements (as in tailoring or repair work) rather than to some standardised pattern.

Finally, forces of a technical nature are sometimes at work *limiting the continued growth* of a firm. A firm may become too complex for any single entrepreneur to control efficiently; funds may not be available to finance further growth; expensive selling and advertising campaigns may be necessary if a firm is to dispose of output by breaking into a competitor's market; and entrepreneurs are as subject to human inertia as most other people, with the result that they may not wish to expand their output (and therefore their responsibilities) even though they could increase their profits by doing so.

Small-scale enterprise survives, and is likely to go on surviving, then, despite the apparently overwhelming technical advantages of large-scale production. In any industry, and at any time, there will theoretically be an *optimum size* for firms; this will embody a compromise between all these conflicting forces – technical factors tending to favour the large-scale firm, and market (and other) factors tending to favour the small firm. It is seldom possible in practice to identify this optimum size, because it will depend on factors such as the quality of the entrepreneur (it is the amount of enterprise combined with the other factors which matters, not the number of entrepreneurs), and will in any case vary from time to time and industry to industry. All that can be said is that such an optimum can always be conceived of – the size of firm which is such that, taking account of all the forces at work, its costs of production are reduced to a minimum.

FURTHER READING

E. MANSFIELD *Micro-economics* Ch. 6

J. HADAR *Elementary theory of consumer behaviour* Ch. 4

A. BEACHAM and N. J. CUNNINGHAM *Economics of industrial organisation* Ch. 5

C. F. PRATTEN *Economies of scale in manufacturing industries* Cambridge University Press, London 1971

R. S. EDWARDS and H. TOWNSEND *Business enterprise* Chs. 7–8

CHAPTER VIII

The Cost Curve

1 THE NATURE OF COSTS

IN the analysis of demand in a previous chapter it was noted that consumers could conceivably purchase commodities by offering other commodities in exchange for them – i.e. through the process of barter. In fact, the modern economic world finds it more convenient to use money as an intermediary – for reasons discussed in detail in Chapter XX below. Similarly, although the owners of productive inputs could barter the services of those inputs in return for a share in the goods they help to produce, in practice it is infinitely more convenient for all concerned if they place the services of those inputs at the entrepreneur's disposal in return for a money payment. Hence, labour is paid for by wages (and salaries), land by rent, loan capital by interest and enterprise by profits. Later discussion will be concerned with the forces determining these factor-prices.

Now, just as it is convenient to translate indifference maps into market demand curves, so the isoquant maps of the previous chapter need to be translated into cost curves. Demand curves trace out the relationship between the quantities of a commodity purchased and its various market prices; cost curves trace out the relationship between the quantities of a commodity which enterprises are producing with its cost of production at the appropriate levels of output.

The relationship between output and cost is a little more complex, however, than that between demand and price. To the consumer the price paid is a fairly unambiguous concept: it is the sum of money he must hand over to the seller in order to obtain ownership of the product or its use for a specified period of time. The calculation by an entrepreneur of his cost of production, however, raises two important matters of principle.

The first concerns the distinction between short run and long run discussed in Chapter V above. Just as the short run is a situation in which some inputs are fixed in supply while in the long run all inputs are variable, so some types of cost are fixed in the short run while others are not. That is to say, when an entrepreneur is increasing or decreasing output certain costs (notably labour costs) can be increased or reduced without great difficulty whenever output changes, but others (notably capital costs) cannot be changed for a considerable period, however much output may vary. This distinction, between factor costs which can be varied whenever output changes and those which cannot, is of great theoretical and practical significance. The former are usually called prime, or variable, costs and the latter overhead, or fixed costs.

By *variable* costs are meant those which vary directly with output, even over a short period of time; the major costs involved are those of labour and raw materials. If a firm making television sets finds that demand and price have fallen, so requiring a reduction of output, it can reduce its labour force more or less immediately, so cutting its total labour costs; similarly, it will need fewer cathode-ray tubes, cabinets, etc. and can reduce its purchases of these forthwith. Certain costs cannot be changed so quickly, however, and these are called *fixed* costs. These are commitments which remain at a constant level so long as the firm remains in existence at all, whatever its level of output, or can be changed only after the lapse of a considerable period – for example, the rent of the land on which the factory stands, the interest on the capital locked up in the form of plant and machinery, and the salaries of the essential managerial and administrative staff. The payments under these headings are usually fixed for long periods at a time and have no direct connection with the rate of production at all except in the long run. A striking example of the independence of such costs is provided by the publishing trade. Once it is decided to publish a book, the entrepreneur must incur the cost of having it set up in type, ready for printing; however many copies he subsequently produces, this cost remains fixed. The larger the number of copies which are in fact printed, the greater the volume of production over which this fixed (and major) element in total cost can be spread. (See Table 7.1.) Similarly, once the Central Electricity Generating Board has built and equipped a power-station, it incurs a fixed charge in respect of the cost of the buildings and equipment concerned, whatever the rate at which the station is generating electricity.

As a result, there can be, and usually is, a significant difference between the *average* cost of a unit of output and the *additional* cost incurred in increasing production by one unit – i.e. the *marginal* cost. The average cost of a particular unit, of course, is the total cost incurred by the entrepreneur divided by the total number of units produced. The marginal cost of a unit of production, say the xth unit, is the difference between the total cost of producing x units and the total cost of producing $(x-1)$ units.

The second problem of principle in defining the cost of production of any commodity concerns something closely connected with this distinction between fixed and variable costs – the calculation of the cost of capital. The problem is this: output is necessarily expressed as a number per unit of time – litres per month or tonnes per annum – and the costs corresponding to this output must therefore be expressed in the same time dimension if average cost is to be calculated. For inputs which are being paid for on a similar time scale this creates no problem – the cost of labour, or rented land, or borrowed funds, can also be calculated per month or per annum and related to the corresponding output. The same, obviously, is true of materials or components embodied in each unit of output. But the capital of an enterprise – its plant, machinery, buildings and so on – may last for an indeterminate period of time and its costs cannot be attributed to individual units of output in any unambiguous way. Yet the cost of capital clearly enters into total costs of production. How is its cost per unit of output to be calculated? To answer this question it is necessary to consider at some length the nature and characteristics of the productive input known as capital.

2   TYPES AND FORMS OF CAPITAL

In a first preliminary discussion of capital in Chapter II it was said that capital was the wealth of a community regarded as a stock existing at any moment of time, unlike income which can be measured only as a flow over time. The essential feature of capital in practice is that its full value is enjoyed only indirectly, after it has contributed to the production of goods and services which are themselves consumed, or over a long period of time. For example, a house renders utility directly to its occupier, and is not wanted for the contribution it can make to the production of other goods. On the other hand, a house is a long-lived asset and continues to render its services for many years after it has been produced. If a house was treated as being consumed in the year it was produced (which it clearly is not) estimates of the amount consumed in that year would be violently exaggerated and consumption in later years would be underestimated since the house would not then be included but would still be entering into consumption. Strictly speaking, indeed, other durable consumer goods such as furniture and motor-cars should be treated as capital for the same reasons. Like houses, these things yield their full utility only over a period of years. The difference is only one of degree; houses generally last much longer than these other goods.

If it were possible to take a flashlight photograph of the economic wealth of a community at any moment of time, all these things *would* be included and counted in the total capital stock. In fact, this procedure is not possible year by year, and in the usual calculations of annual additions to or reductions of the total stock of capital, houses are the only commodities included which render service directly to consumers. It is possible to estimate the total change in the value of the houses in an economy, but the task of valuing changes in the total stock of furniture, pianos, cars, etc. would be a gigantic one. An increase in the number of cars used by industry for production purposes, however, *would* be counted as an addition to capital, not because a car is a durable commodity but because, like other industrial capital, cars used by an industry are valuable for the indirect contribution they make to the production of the final output of that industry and are not wanted for their own sakes.

For practical purposes, then, and not through the application of strict logic, annual additions to the total stock of capital belonging to a community are usually classified under personal, industrial and social capital. As has been seen, under *personal* capital is included only new dwelling-houses. Under the heading of *industrial* capital are included fixed and working capital, the distinction between these two, as was seen in Chapter II, being that fixed capital can be used many times whereas working capital is embodied directly into final output and can therefore be used only once. Fixed capital comprises the plant, machinery and buildings used by industry of all kinds for the purposes of production; working capital includes, on the one hand, stocks of finished goods in the hands of producers, wholesalers and retailers and, on the other hand, raw materials and semi-finished goods still awaiting embodiment in finished goods. Under *social* capital are included all the assets belonging to the community as a whole rather than to particular persons or industries – for example, roads, schools and hospitals.

It will have been noted that in this discussion the word capital has been identified with physical assets – houses, factories, roads and so on – and no mention has been made of stocks of money or claims such as mortgages or securities. From the point of view of the economy as a whole, money or claims to money are not capital, although in ordinary speech people are inclined to speak of 'capital' when they really mean 'money'. To an individual, money is capital because it represents a claim on goods and services; the community as a whole, however, cannot enrich itself by merely producing claims on itself. Money or securities of all kinds represent claims on other members of a community, just as a debt is an acknowledgement of such a claim, and for the community as a whole such claims and debts naturally cancel themselves out. As will be seen later, money or monetary instruments are wanted not for themselves but for the goods and services which can be obtained with them, and an increase in the amount of money in a society in no way makes that society richer; only an increase in its stock or supply of goods and services can do that. But claims on *other* societies (i.e. foreign countries) *are* capital, because a society can add to the total supply of goods available to it by exercising those claims. Printing more pound notes cannot make Britain as a whole better off, because pound notes represent a claim on Britain itself; but a sudden gift of dollars *will* make Britain as a whole better off, because they can be used to add to the supply of goods available to Britain's population. A country's stock of claims on other countries, then – gold and dollar reserves and titles to physical assets abroad – is part of its capital; it is the only monetary item which can be included as part of the national capital. For the world as a whole, such claims cancel themselves out with the corresponding debts or liabilities, of course, and the world's capital stock will include only physical assets.

3   GROSS AND NET OUTPUT

If a statistician is trying to estimate how much wealth a country has produced over a given period – say a year – it is obvious that he cannot add together raw materials used to make final products *and* the final products themselves. If he did, he would be counting the same thing twice. For example, if Crusoe produces x kilograms of wheat in a year, all of which is used to make flour which in turn is used to make, say, fifty loaves of bread, he could not say that his total output of wealth is x kg of wheat *plus* 50 loaves of bread. The bread contains the wheat, and in producing the one he has used up the other; only the bread represents the net amount of wealth he has produced during that year. Final products *and* the resources used up in making them cannot be added together if the true production of wealth is to be measured.

In the same way, statisticians cannot count as wealth produced in a given year any goods, or parts of goods, which are in fact drawn from a stock with which producers began that year. Just as a producer may use up in manufacturing a commodity resources which have been produced during the same period – Crusoe and his wheat – so he may use up resources which have been inherited from a previous period – i.e. capital.

To the extent that capital has been used up, of course, a society is poorer afterwards than it was before, and this consumption of capital has to be subtracted from total output to find how much new wealth that society has created. For example, if a country starts the year with a stock of 1 000 pairs of shoes, consumes 500 pairs in the course of the year and ends with a stock of 900 pairs, its true output of shoes during that year must have been 400 pairs, even though its consumption was 500.

For capital in the form of stocks of goods this is obvious enough. In the case of fixed capital, however, it is less obvious, although the point is equally important. Say a country produces 400 pairs of shoes and ends the year with the same plant and machinery as it began; assuming its stocks are unchanged, is its true output of wealth 400 pairs of shoes? The answer is no: in the course of the year the machinery has been in use, and will have been worn out to a greater or lesser extent. Even if it has not deteriorated from this wear and tear, technical developments are almost certain to have made it to some degree obsolete. Whichever is the cause – and usually both factors are operating – the fixed capital will be worth less at the end of the year than at the beginning; it will have *depreciated*. Before the true value of output can be assessed, then, some allowance must be made for this depreciation associated with it. Unless sufficient resources are set aside each year to replace the fixed capital which is being used up or is wearing out (the setting-aside being known as *amortisation* of capital) the society concerned will one day find that its equipment has reached the end of its life and its powers of production will be seriously affected.

Exactly the same is true of the individual productive enterprise. In computing the cost of the year's output it must take account not only of the out-payments it has made in producing that output – wages and salaries, rent, purchases of fuel and materials and so on – but also of the decline in the value of its capital equipment and buildings over the period in question, despite any maintenance expenditure incurred in order to keep it in running order. Because of physical and/or technical obsolescence that capital stock has a finite life and one day it will have to be replaced if the enterprise is to continue in business. Unless an adequate amount is set aside year by year for this purpose under the heading of amortisation, therefore, the enterprise is under-estimating its true operating costs.

Precisely how this amortisation is calculated is a matter for debate and accountants are liable to differ considerably in their practice. Perhaps the simplest method is that known as straight-line depreciation – that is, the assumption that the value of a piece of capital declines at an even rate throughout its working life and the setting-aside of constant annual sums whose aggregate value will equal the cost of the capital at the end of its estimated working life. Thus, if a piece of equipment is estimated to have an effective working life of three years, one-third of its value would be set aside annually as amortisation.

The matter is more complicated than this, however. Quite apart from its steady loss of value through depreciation, capital imposes a cost in that it embodies resources which have an opportunity cost. Consider a man who borrows £2 000 to buy a new car and commits himself to repay the loan at the end of four years. He will clearly need to set aside £500 a year in order to amortise (i.e. repay) that debt. But he will certainly have to pay interest on that loan in the meantime: this also is part of the cost of the car. Even if he financed the car from his own resources the costs would be the same: he will need to set aside depreciation against the day when the car has to be replaced but he should also treat as part of the cost of the car the interest he *could* have obtained by investing the £2 000 in some interest-bearing asset rather than using it to buy a car.

The productive enterprise is in exactly the same position. The annual cost of its capital will consist of (a) the appropriate amortisation charge and (b) the annual interest cost of the capital. The fact that most industrial investment is financed from undistributed profits rather than with borrowed funds on which interest has in fact to be paid does not affect the second half of the calculation: the undistributed profits *could* have been invested and earning the company interest and they thus have an opportunity cost. It can be shown that the total annual requirement under both headings will be

$$k = \frac{r(1+r)^n}{(1+r)^n - 1}$$

where k is the fraction of the price of the capital which should be set aside annually, r the current rate of interest and n the estimated working life (in years) of the capital.

For example, consider the man buying a car for £2 000 out of his own accumulated savings. He estimates that it will last him four years (and he treats its scrap value thereafter as zero) and the current rate of interest he could earn on a bank deposit account is 8 per cent. What is the annual capital cost of his car? Putting $r = 0.08$ and $n = 4$ into the formula,

$$k = \frac{0.08(1.08)^4}{(1.08)^4 - 1} = 0.3019$$

which gives him a true annual capital cost of £2 000 × 0.3019 = £603.8.

For the modern business there is one other important complication — the steady rise in the general price level. If the business is to survive, enough must be set aside annually to cover not merely the original cost of the capital but *the cost of replacing it* with a similar piece of capital. The man in the example is unlikely to be able to replace his car by accumulating £2 000 since in four years the cost of a similar car will certainly be more than £2 000. Again it can be shown that if the price level of the type of capital involved is expected to rise at a rate of g per cent per annum the amortisation formula would become:

$$k = \frac{r(1+r)^n}{(1+r)^n - 1} \cdot \left[1 + \frac{(1+g)^n - 1}{(1+r)^n} \right].$$

Suppose the expected rise in prices is 10 per cent per annum; putting $g = 0.10$ into the example, the true annual capital cost of the car would become £2 000 × 0.4049 = £809.80. After paying out 8 per cent interest each year on the original £2 000, the balances set aside will accumulate by the end of four years to £2 928 — the estimated price of a replacement car at that time.

Without bothering overmuch about the details of the precise formula adopted, then, it is clear that the problem of converting a capital stock into an annual capital cost can be overcome given an estimate of its working life and the likely rate of increase in its price level and of the current rate of interest. The way is thus clear for the conversion of the quantities of real factor inputs required for different levels of output into a cost curve corresponding to those outputs.

4 THE SHORT-RUN COST CURVE

It is convenient, once again, to examine the behaviour of production first in the context of the short run – that is, when the capacity (i.e. the capital stock) of a firm is fixed at some predetermined level and only the variable inputs (e.g. labour) can be increased or reduced in order to vary the level of output. The consequences of changes in the rate of production need now to be examined in terms of the effect on costs rather than output per head as in Chapter VI.

Consider the simple example shown in Fig. 8A, supposing that the production possibilities open to the entrepreneur are represented by the five isoquants shown in Fig. 8A(i), relating to monthly outputs ranging from 1 000 to 5 000 units. Suppose

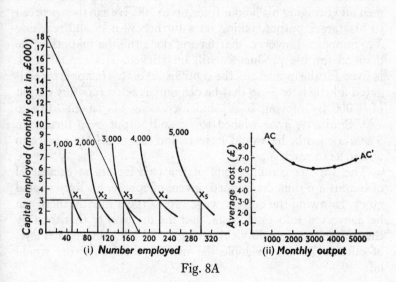

Fig. 8A

also that the prevailing wage-rate for the type of labour he needs is £100 a month and that the entrepreneur decides to construct a factory designed to produce a monthly output of 3 000.

For the sake of convenience, the amount of capital employed is measured in Fig. 8A(i) in terms of its monthly cost – i.e. the annual cost (interest and depreciation) of the buildings and machinery divided by twelve. The relative price of capital and labour is thus registered by a line connecting £1 000 of capital with ten men, and so on. The analysis of the previous chapters has established that for his target output of 3 000 a month, the entrepreneur will achieve minimum unit cost at the tangency point X_3 – i.e. with a capital stock whose annual cost is £36 000 (£3 000 a month), which in practice would probably represent a *total* capital stock of around £250 000, and a labour force of 150 men.

Having built his factory, the entrepreneur gradually brings it into full operation. He begins with a level of production which corresponds to 1 000 a month; the relevant isoquant shows that, given his (fixed) capital stock, he will need to operate at point X_1 – i.e. with 50 men. When he steps up output to the 2 000-a-month level, he will move to point X_2, employing a further 50 men and bringing his labour force up to 100. He can then proceed to his target output, taking on a further 50 men and reaching X_3. Suppose, however, that having done this he finds that the demand for his product is still unsatisfied. His capital stock is fixed for the moment – the significance of this factor is investigated a little later – so that he can only reach a monthly output of 4 000 by moving to X_4 and increasing his labour force to 220. Similarly, if he wished to expand output even further to 5 000 a month, he would have to increase his labour force to 300 so as to reach X_5.

The various combinations of the two factors at each level of output are thus determined, given, of course, his fixed capital stock. Knowing the current wage-rate (£100 a month) these can be converted into total costs, and the division of this total by the rate of output will yield average cost per unit at each level of output. In this example the monthly cost structure would be:

Monthly output	Capital costs (£)	Labour costs (£)	Total costs (£)	Average cost (£)
1 000	3 000	5 000	8 000	8·0
2 000	3 000	10 000	13 000	6·5
3 000	3 000	15 000	18 000	6·0
4 000	3 000	22 000	25 000	6·25
5 000	3 000	30 000	33 000	6·6

If these average costs are now plotted on a curve, an *average cost curve* such as *AC* in Fig. 8A(ii) is obtained. Theoretically, of course, such a curve will trace out average costs at *every* level of output open to the entrepreneur, and not just five arbitrary levels such as those used in the example.

The average cost curve therefore represents the cost to the entrepreneur of the average amount of the factors used up in producing one unit of a commodity at different levels of output – i.e. the total payments of wages, rent, interest and profits divided by the number of units produced. In other words, it reflects the costs of *all* the factors required to produce a commodity, including the factor of enterprise. Unless an entrepreneur receives a certain rate of profit from his activity, he will go to some other industry or perhaps become a wage- or salary-earner instead. Hence, a certain rate of profit – the 'normal' rate of profit for the entrepreneur concerned – is part of the cost of production of a commodity, and is included as an element of the average cost curve. If price *equals* cost, therefore, this does not mean (as it might in everyday speech) that the entrepreneur is making no profit; it means that he is receiving the 'normal' rate of profit on each unit of the commodity.

In the discussion of demand curves, it was established that such curves would normally be falling from left to right, although their exact slope would vary as between different commodities. In the case of cost curves, no such normal rule can be laid down, since average cost of production may increase, decrease or remain constant as output expands. In other words, the production of a commodity may be taking place at any moment under any one of three broad types of supply conditions – falling, constant or rising cost – depending on the behaviour of the average cost curve as output rises. It is often convenient to draw cost curves with the same direction (falling, horizontal or rising) throughout their length. In practice, however, it seems likely that most average cost curves will probably be more like that shown in Fig. 8B – average cost falling as output expands and as the optimum combination of factors with a given level of 'normal' capacity is approached, reaching a minimum at some output *OM*, where the optimum factor-combination is reached, then beginning to rise again as output expands past this level

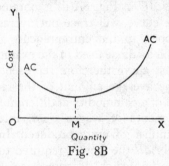

Fig. 8B

and the law of diminishing returns comes into effect. For example, most commodities require some minimum capital equipment, such as a factory building, however small output is. As output rises, this capital is used more and more fully until at last its normal capacity is reached. Thereafter it may not be worthwhile to install more capital (build another factory, say) until output is considerably greater, so that costs rise again as more and more labour is employed until the output is big enough to justify a second big 'lump' of capital and the cost curve commences to fall once more.

This emphasises the distinction between increasing (physical) returns, on the one hand, and falling average cost on the other – and, conversely, between decreasing (physical) returns and increasing average cost. Average cost *may* be falling because an enterprise is experiencing increasing returns in the sense that output per man is rising but it may also be falling because the effect of decreasing returns is being offset, in a financial sense, by the further spreading of fixed costs over a larger output.

Conversely, average cost may begin to rise before the technical economies of scale have been exhausted if the expansion of output has had the effect of forcing up input prices – for example, through the necessity of paying overtime rates to labour.

5   AVERAGE AND MARGINAL COST

The distinction between average and marginal cost was discussed earlier in connection with fixed and variable costs. As later analysis will show, the distinction is a critically important one in the context of entrepreneurial decisions as to what is or is not a profit-maximising output. By *marginal cost* is meant, of course, the addition made to total costs when output is raised by the smallest practicable amount from any given level. If the average cost curve is a smooth and continuous one, as in Fig. 8B, then marginal cost can be expressed as the change in total cost induced by an infinitesimally small change in output. Put in mathematical terms, if C is the total cost of some output Q of a product (so that its average cost $= C/Q$), then marginal cost $= dC/dQ$.

A numerical example may be more helpful. Suppose that the data shown in Table 8.1 overleaf represent the short-run cost structure of a small firm engaged in making wooden tables. Its fixed capital stock generates fixed costs of £100 a week and consists of a set of tools designed to turn out five tables a week. Each table requires labour and materials costing £50 each for outputs up to and including three a week, but at higher outputs these variable costs begin to rise sharply because overtime has to be paid and higher transport charges are incurred on the raw materials.

For the first table, the total cost of production will therefore be £150; since only one table is involved, this is also its average cost. The difference between the total costs of producing this table (£150) and the total costs of producing one fewer (i.e. none at all) is £150, so that this is also its marginal cost. Thereafter, however – as Table 8.1 shows – total, average and marginal costs differ considerably. The marginal cost at first falls rapidly as the fixed cost is spread over an increasing number of tables,

TABLE 8.1 *Average and marginal costs of producing tables*

(1) Weekly output of tables	(2) Fixed costs £	(3) Variable costs £	(4) Total costs £	(5) Average cost [(4)÷(1)] £	(6) Marginal cost £
1	100	50	150	150	150
2	100	100	200	100	50
3	100	150	250	83	50
4	100	210	310	78	60
5	100	287	387	77	77
6	100	384	484	81	97
7	100	503	603	86	119
8	100	653	753	94	150
9	100	825	925	103	172
10	100	1 035	1 135	114	210

and average cost also falls, though not so violently. When output rises above that of 3 a week, however, marginal costs begin to rise. For a time the effect of this is more than offset by the gain arising from spreading the fixed cost over a larger output, and average cost continues to fall. So long as marginal cost is less than average cost, of course, the average *must* fall; a smaller amount than the average is being added to the total and naturally the overall average is reduced. Ultimately, however (in this example when output rises to 6 tables a week), marginal cost becomes greater than the average cost, and the average begins to rise; the increasingly high variable costs become more than sufficient to offset the spreading of the fixed cost. Once again, however, the average will change less violently than the marginal cost.

The relationship between average and marginal costs can be shown more generally with the familiar curve diagram. In Fig. 8C which is based on the data contained in Table 8.1, the curve *AC* is the type of cost curve which was discussed earlier; it shows the average cost of production at various levels of output. On the same axes *OX* and *OY* can be drawn the *marginal cost* curve, *MC*. Certain general rules can be laid down about the behaviour of these two curves. First, so long as the marginal cost curve is below the average cost curve, then average cost must be falling as output rises. This is straightforward enough; as has already been noted, if marginal cost is below average cost expanding output must be adding a smaller amount to total costs than the previous average, so that the new average will be smaller than the old. Similarly, if marginal costs are in excess

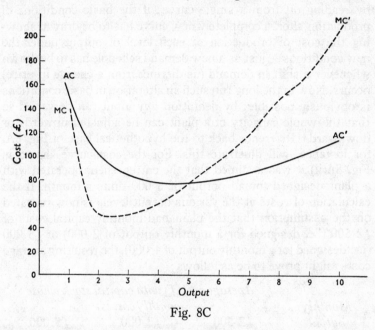

Fig. 8C

of the average it means that the average must be rising; a *bigger* amount is added to total cost than the previous average as output rises, and the new average must therefore be bigger than the old. Finally, if marginal cost *equals* average cost, then average cost is neither rising nor falling at that point – in other words, average cost is at its minimum; it has ceased falling but has not yet begun to increase.

These relationships are obviously very similar to those of the average and marginal product curves discussed in Chapter VI and are, indeed, closely related to them. It will be found that they have considerable significance in the determination of equilibrium prices and outputs discussed in Part IV.

6 THE LONG-RUN COST CURVE

As with demand schedules, the effects of output changes on average cost in any given production situation are examined by reading off from a single curve; if the basic conditions of production alter, a completely new curve has to be drawn, showing the cost of production at each level of output under the new conditions – just as a new demand schedule has to be drawn whenever a shift in demand (as distinct from a change in price) occurs. Now in the long run such an alteration in basic conditions is obviously possible; by definition *any* input can be varied so that the whole capacity of a plant can be adjusted upwards or downwards. Reference back to the hypothetical case of Fig. 8A, for instance, will illustrate this. For the cost curve shown in Fig. 8A(ii) it was assumed that the entrepreneur operated with a plant designed for an output of 3 000 units a month. If the calculation of costs at the various output levels is now repeated on the assumption that the plant had monthly capital costs of £2 500 (i.e. designed for a monthly output of 2 000) or £5 000 (i.e. designed for a monthly output of 4 000), the resulting average costs might prove to be as follows:

Monthly output	*Average cost (£) with capital stock whose monthly cost is:*		
	£2 500	£3 000	£5 000
1 000	7·50	8·00	9·50
2 000	6·30	6·50	7·10
3 000	6·90	6·00	6·20
4 000	8·00	6·25	5·80
5 000	9·40	6·60	6·10

Clearly the whole cost structure is different in the three cases and in the long run the entrepreneur will select that level of capacity – and thus that cost structure – which gives him the lowest average for what he considers to be the most probable level of permanent output. The figures above show, for example, that an entrepreneur anticipating a normal monthly output of 2 000 will aim at a capital stock whose monthly cost is £2 500, since the average cost of such an output is lower with that capital capacity than with any other. Similarly, at an anticipated monthly output of 4 000 his average costs will be minimised with a capital stock whose monthly cost is £5 000.

It follows that the long-run cost curve of a firm will be derived from a whole series of short-run average cost curves, one corresponding to each adjustment of capacity made by the firm over time. An example is given in Fig. 8D(i). Suppose that in the first instance the firm is operating at output OM_1, at

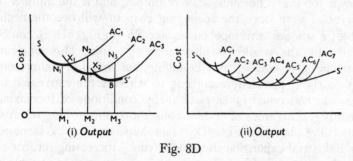

(i) *Output*   (ii) *Output*

Fig. 8D

which the operative average cost curve is AC_1; average cost is therefore MN_1. Demand now rises, and output increases to OM_2. In the short run, capacity is fixed and the curve AC_1 remains the operative one; the output OM_2 can be achieved, therefore, only at the average cost M_2N_2. After sufficient time to adjust capacity, however, the cost curve shifts over to AC_2 and the average cost of output OM_2 can be reduced (to M_2A), and this would be true for all outputs corresponding to points to the right of X_1. On the other hand, for outputs smaller than this – corresponding to points to the *left* of X_1 – the original capacity level, reflected in AC_1, would yield lower average costs than that reflected in AC_2. Similarly, if output rises further to OM_3 costs will rise in the first instance to M_3N_3; when suffi-cient time has elapsed for capacity to be properly adjusted, however, the operative cost curve will become AC_3 and the cost of output OM_3 will be cut to an average of M_3B. Once again, this third level of capacity will yield lower average costs for any output corresponding to a point to the right of X_2; for outputs between X_1 and X_2 the second level of capacity will be preferable.

In other words, when time is allowed for capacity adjustments at all points, two facts emerge: first, average cost becomes the determining factor, not marginal cost; secondly, only those parts of the three curves shown in Fig. 8D(i) by a heavy line become relevant and operative; the *long-run cost curve* of the firm, that is to say, is given by the scalloped curve SX_1X_2S'. Theoretically, short-run average cost curves can be drawn for every possible scale of output, and if the number of curves is very large the scalloping element will become negligible; a smooth 'envelope' curve, like SS' in Fig. 8D(ii), can be drawn for the whole possible range of output. This long-run cost curve, of course, may be falling, horizontal or rising from left to right, primarily according to whether the expansion of the firm concerned takes place under conditions of increasing returns – economies of scale – constant or diminishing returns. The curve shown in Fig. 8D(ii) has the shape usually assumed for industrial expansion in the long run – increasing returns as the firm grows sufficiently to exploit the economies of scale, a period of constant average costs and then rising average costs as the complexities and limitations of very large-scale enterprises give rise to diminishing returns. When the average or marginal cost of production is in question, therefore, a great deal may turn on whether the operative cost curve is a short-run or long-run curve.

FURTHER READING

E. MANSFIELD *Micro-economics* Ch. 6

K. LANCASTER *Introduction to modern micro-economics* Ch. 5

A. M. LEVENSON and B. S. SOLON *Outline of price theory* Ch. 8

P. J. D. WILES *Price, cost and output* Blackwell, Oxford 1961, Ch. 12

CHAPTER IX

The Supply Curve

1 FIRM AND INDUSTRY

UP to this point the discussion has been confined to the individual firm − the curves which have been considered show the relationship existing between the output of a particular firm and its average or marginal cost of production. For many purposes, however, the total supply of a commodity on the market may be of more interest than the output of one firm producing only a fraction of that total; in considering how the price of milk affects its supply, for example, it is the total output of milk which will be the object of interest, not the production of any individual dairy farmer. For problems such as these, it is necessary to shift the emphasis away from the firm and on to the industry − i.e. the group of firms which together produce the entire supply of the commodity concerned to the market. In other words, the discussion must move away from the cost curve of the individual enterprise and focus attention on the supply curve of the industry as a whole; cost curves are concerned with the relationship between the output of a product and its cost, whereas supply curves illustrate the relationship between the total output of a product and its market *price*.

Before considering the way in which such a supply curve can be built up, it must be made clear that the question involves certain rather difficult issues which are better dealt with separately at a later stage and which will have to be left on one side for the moment. For example, it is by no means easy to define what exactly is meant by an 'industry'; if firms are selling products which are similar but not identical − such as Ford cars and British Leyland cars − are these firms in the same industry or not? How similar do products have to be before they can be regarded as the same commodity? A second, and related, difficulty is that of the relationship which is assumed to hold between the different firms in the industry – how far they are regarded as competing with one another, and how far some form of monopoly element exists. These issues have a great deal to do with the relationship between price and output, as will be demonstrated at length in Chapters X–XIII.

In order to examine the essential nature of the concept of the supply curve, however, these complications can be left on one side. For the moment it can be supposed that there exists an industry in the sense of a group of firms whose products are more or less identical, so that they can be regarded collectively as forming a single commodity being sold in a single market – the word 'market' denoting any organised relationship between potential buyers and potential sellers and not necessarily a single place or building. Further, let it be supposed that these firms are in full competition with one another, the output of each individual firm being so small a share of total production in the industry that changes in it have no effect on either market price or the output of the other firms. The market price for the product, in other words, is something each firm has to take as given. In such a situation it is clear that a change in the market price for which the commodity is being sold will affect its total supply in one of two ways. First, the more or less immediate effect will be to stimulate changes in the output of each individual firm in the industry, within the broad limits imposed by their (for the moment fixed) capacity in terms of capital equipment. Secondly, however, if the change in price is sufficiently permanent, existing firms will ultimately make appropriate adjustments to their basic capacity and new firms will enter the industry (or existing firms leave the industry).

Yet again the distinction between short run and long run is obviously crucial. In the short run, by definition, capacity is fixed and the total supply of a product can be varied only through an expansion or contraction by firms already within the industry whose capital equipment is fixed. In the long run capacity can be varied *both* through a readjustment of the capacity of firms already in the industry *and* through increases or decreases in the *number* of firms in the industry. As usual, it will be convenient to examine each of these situations in turn.

2   THE SHORT-RUN SUPPLY CURVE

Firms are in business to make profit. A 'normal' profit, it has been assumed, is included in their cost curves. Hence at first sight it would appear axiomatic that if the price obtainable in the market for their product equals or exceeds their cost of production at any output then that output will be supplied. *A fortiori*, if market price increases firms will increase production up to that point at which costs rise into equality with price. The industry's supply curve would appear at first sight to be nothing more than an aggregation of the individual cost curves of the firms in that industry with the simple substitution of 'price' for 'cost' along the vertical axis.

In reality the problem is not quite so simple, since the question arises: *which* cost curve is relevant here – average cost or marginal cost? Consider the example of a firm, Excel Products Ltd, whose cost data are summarised arithmetically in Table 9.1 and geometrically in Fig. 9A. Its capital costs, fixed in the short run, amount to £500 a week, and its weekly output can be varied only in one-hundred units. At relatively low levels of output – between 100 and 400 units a week – its unit variable costs (labour, materials, fuel and so on) decline because of gains derived from division of labour, bulk purchases, etc. but thereafter they tend to increase because of the need for overtime, more distant sources of materials and so on. At its 'normal' output of 400 a week a price of £3·50 is sufficient to cover all its costs and provide a normal profit – total costs amount to £1 400 and total sales revenues (400 at £3·50) are sufficient to cover these. If it expanded output to 500 a week at this price, total revenues would rise to £1 750 (i.e. by £350) but costs to £1 800 (i.e. by £400) – profits would fall by £50. To be precise the revenue from the extra 100 (£3·50 each) would be less than the extra (i.e. marginal) cost of £4·00 each.

Suppose that the market price now fell to £3·00: what output, if any, would the firm find it worthwhile to produce? At

first sight the answer is none, since the average cost of the
product is greater than £3·00 at any feasible level of production.
Here the distinction between short and long run becomes
crucial, however. In the short run the fixed costs of £500 a
week are an inescapable commitment even if production stops
altogether. The relevant question is therefore not whether total
revenues exceed *total* costs but whether or not a reduction of
output would increase profits or reduce losses. A cut in output
from 400 a week to 300 a week, for example, would reduce
revenue by £300 (100 at £3·00 each) whereas costs would fall
by only £210 (from £1 400 to £1 190). Revenue would fall, in
other words, by more than costs and profits would fall (or losses
increase). In the short run, that is, *marginal* cost is the determining factor, not average cost. If sales revenue exceeds
marginal cost it is worthwhile to increase production, since each
unit sold is covering its extra cost and making some contribution to the inescapable fixed costs; if revenues fall below
marginal cost, profit will be raised, or losses reduced, by cutting
back on production.

One more complication remains, however. Suppose in Fig. 9A

TABLE 9.1   *Weekly cost structure of Excel Products Ltd*

Weekly output (100s)	Fixed costs £000	Variable costs £000	Total costs £000	Average cost (£) (4÷1)	Marginal cost (£) Δ4÷Δ1	Average variable cost (£) 3÷1
1	2	3	4	5	6	7
1	500	300	800	8·00		3·00
2	500	500	1 000	5·00	2·00	2·50
3	500	690	1 190	3·97	1·90	2·30
4	500	900	1 400	3·50	2·10	2·25
5	500	1 300	1 800	3·60	4·00	2·60
6	500	1 920	2 420	4·03	6·20	3·20
7	500	2 800	3 300	4·71	8·80	4·00

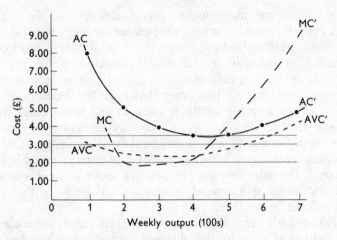

Fig. 9A   Excel Products Ltd

market price falls to £2·00. As will be seen, this exceeds marginal cost at an output of 300 a week and the considerations just discussed would suggest that it will still be worthwhile for Excel Products Ltd to stay in business at that level of output. It will be noted, however, that at that level market price has fallen below *average variable cost* – which is £2·30 at that output. The significance of this is that the total variable costs being incurred at that output (300 × £2·30 = £690) exceeds total revenues (300 × £2·00 = £600). While the marginal cost of the last hundred produced is covered by revenue, therefore – i.e. the rise in costs from £1 000 at 200 to £1 190 at 300 is less than the revenue of £200 brought in by that extra hundred – total revenue is still not covering the extra costs incurred by continuing production. Since marginal cost exceeds price, an output of 300 is more profitable (less loss-making) than one of 200. Since price is less than average variable cost, however, an output of zero would be even more advisable. At zero output losses consist of the £500 a month fixed costs; at an output of 300 losses consist of total costs (£1 190) minus total revenue (£600) and come to £590 a month.

So two rules appear for the output of a firm in the short run.

First, it will stay in production only if sales revenue per unit (in this case the 'given' market price) exceeds average variable cost at some positive output. Secondly, even if this condition is satisfied production is still only worthwhile if the revenue brought in by any unit of output exceeds (or at least equals) the marginal cost of producing that unit. By definition, fixed costs are inescapable whatever happens and thus cannot enter into production decisions *via* the average cost curve; the short-run supply curve of a firm can be defined as that part of its marginal cost curve which lies above its average variable cost curve. If the sales revenue per unit lies above this curve at any output, output will expand; if revenue falls below it, that output will not be produced.

It is a fairly easy step to move from this supply schedule for an individual firm to the short-run supply schedule for the industry as a whole — it is simply a matter of aggregating the individual supply curves of the firms existing in the industry concerned at any particular moment of time. A numerical example may help to show how the total supply of a commodity will respond in the short run to changes in market price through adjustments to the output of firms in the industry. Suppose that the figures shown in Table 9·2 represent the marginal costs at different levels of output of an industry composed of five firms and that the period of time being considered is too short to allow either adjustments to the capacity-level of any of these firms or the establishment of new firms in the industry. For the sake of simplicity of exposition, it is assumed that each firm has rising marginal costs at all levels of production and that these are everywhere in excess of the average variable cost at each output level concerned.

Suppose the market price settles initially at £2; at this price each of the companies is able to cover its costs at an output rate of 100 units, but none can profitably produce more than this level of output. The total supply at the market price of £2 will therefore be 500 units.

Now suppose market price rises to £4. At this price, Company 1 will expand its output to 300 units, since it is only at levels of output higher than this that its marginal cost exceeds the

TABLE 9.2 *Marginal costs in a hypothetical industry*

Units of output	Marginal cost per unit in pounds:				
	Company 1	Company 2	Company 3	Company 4	Company 5
100	2·0	2·0	2·0	2·0	2·0
200	3·0	4·0	2·5	4·0	6·0
300	4·0	6·0	3·0	6·0	8·0
400	5·0	8·0	3·5	8·0	12·0
500	7·0	12·0	4·0	10·0	20·0
600	8·0	16·0	6·0	12·0	25·0
700	10·0	20·0	8·0	16·0	32·0
800	12·0	24·0	12·0	23·0	40·0
900	16·0	29·0	16·0	27·0	50·0
1 000	20·0	35·0	20·0	32·0	60·0

market price of £4. Companies 2 and 4 will similarly raise their output to 200 units each and Company 3 to 500 units, since price is high enough to cover marginal cost at these output levels. It is *not* high enough, however, to permit Company 5 to increase its output above the 100 level. Total supply at the market price of £4, therefore, will rise to 1 300 units — 300 produced by Company 1, 200 each by Companies 2 and 4, 500 by Company 3 and 100 by Company 5. If this process is continued for different market prices, a schedule can be drawn up which will show the total amount of the commodity which will be supplied at each price. The data in Table 9.2, for example, show that at a market price of £20 total supply will amount to 3 900 units — 1 000 produced by Company 1, 700 by Company 2, 1 000 by Company 3, 700 by Company 4 and 500 by Company 5.

If all these prices and outputs are now plotted in the form of a graph, the result is a short-run supply curve for the industry concerned. An example is shown by the curve SS' in Fig. 9B; this curve is in fact drawn from the data shown in Table 9.2 It is thus based on a highly simplified and not particularly realistic example; it is manifestly unlikely, for example, that the marginal cost of a product should rise, as it does for Company 5 in Table 9.2, from £2 for the 100th unit to £6 for the 101st. This does not affect the *principle* of the derivation of supply curves, however, and this is the only important issue here. Such curves, of course, will normally slope upwards from left to right, reflecting the familiar economic generalisation that a greater quantity of any commodity will be offered at a high price than at a low price. The higher price is, the more profitable production becomes

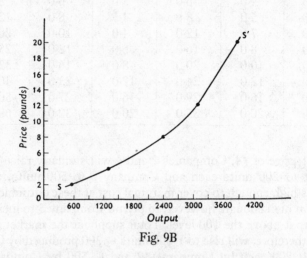

Fig. 9B

and the greater the output which each entrepreneur will find it worthwhile to produce.

The analytical rationale of this is now clear. The short-run supply schedule is, in effect, an amalgam of individual marginal cost curves and in Section 5 of the previous chapter it was shown that when average costs are at their minimum the marginal cost curve is necessarily rising. Hence if it is assumed that in the initial position firms are operating at the point of minimum average cost (reasons why this should be so in a competitive situation are examined in Chapter XI) then any increase in output must necessarily be associated with rising marginal costs — and therefore rising prices will be necessary to cover them.

In the short run, then, the slope of the industry supply curve is readily predictable; in the long run (as usual) matters are somewhat more complex and the outcome more uncertain.

3   THE LONG-RUN SUPPLY CURVE

The essential characteristic of the long-run situation is that all inputs into the productive process can be varied and, in particular, that capital capacity can be expanded or contracted. For an industry the consequences of this need to be considered from two aspects. First, existing firms in the industry can adjust their capacity levels; second, the number of firms in the industry will increase or diminish as new firms set up business in it or existing ones reduce their output to zero and, perhaps, transfer to some other industry. It will be useful to consider each of these in turn.

For firms already operating in the industry the fundamental difference between their short-run and long-run strategies is that in the long run *all* costs become variable. If profits are to be made, therefore, the revenue from output must cover *all* costs and not just marginal costs. To tolerate a price which falls below average cost of production in the short run is one thing; to tolerate it in the long run, when there are no inescapable fixed costs is quite another. It is in fact inconsistent with the basic assumption of profit maximisation. If market price has fallen below average cost,then, and looks like remaining there, the entrepreneur will reduce output until the deficiency is made good – if necessary to zero output. Market supply will contract. Conversely, if price has risen above average cost one of two things can happen. If unexploited economies of scale are available to the firm, the higher rate of profit now being enjoyed will stimulate an expansion of capacity so that a higher output will be associated with lower unit costs. If the firm is already at the minimum-cost output, on the other hand, there will be no point in expanding capacity (which would by definition involve higher average costs); the firm will raise output from its existing capacity, its extra profits being somewhat reduced by the higher unit costs. In either event, excess profits will appear and this is the mechanism

which motivates the second ingredient in the adjustment process – the attraction of new entrants into the industry.

The industry having become unusually profitable, firms will
be drawn into the industry. If these are assumed to be of roughly
the same level of technological efficiency as the old firms, it
might be supposed that this process would continue until the
excess profits are competed away – that is, until output had
expanded, and price brought down, sufficiently to restore the
initial level of profit, no more, no less. Market price, in other
words, would revert to the original level at which it equalled
average cost.

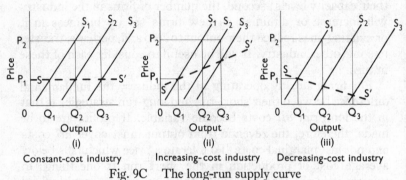

Fig. 9C   The long-run supply curve

This may indeed happen; it is the case illustrated in Fig.
9C(i). Suppose S_1 is the initial short-run supply curve in the
industry, P_1 the initial price and Q_1 the initial output. Let demand
now change so that the market expands to OQ_2. In the short
run, by definition, price must rise to OP_2 to call forth this output
(i.e. to cover short-run marginal costs). In the long run, however,
the mechanism just described begins to operate: the unusually
high profits attract new firms into the industry so that the expanded output Q_1Q_2 is taken away from the old-established firms
and produced by newcomers with similar cost curves. A *new*
short-run curve S_2 now becomes applicable, corresponding to
the expanded capacity of the industry. Reading off this curve,
the old price OP_1 is sufficient to call forth output OQ_2 and the
situation settles back to equilibrium. If now the market expands

again to OQ_3 a similar sequence will occur as price rises initially to OP_2, more new firms are drawn in and price falls back again to OP_1 and equilibrium is once more restored. The dashed line, SS', connecting these long-run equilibrium prices and outputs, is the long-run supply curve of the industry. Being horizontal, it indicates that expansion in the industry is associated with constant long-run costs.

But matters may not turn out this way. The entry of new firms into an industry may affect the underlying cost conditions of all firms in that industry, old as well as new. One possibility is that the expansion of the industry may generate external diseconomies, especially if the expansion drives up the prices of the industry's inputs of labour or materials or creates scarcities necessitating recourse to inferior substitutes. It is plausible enough to neglect such effects in considering the cost curve of an individual firm whose consumption of inputs is only a relatively small proportion of the industry's total: when the industry expands as a whole, however, such effects may be considerable. The consequences are illustrated in Fig. 9C(ii); expansion of the industry's output from OQ_1 to OQ_2 is associated with the same short-run price increase as before, but now the upward pressure on the costs of all firms as expansion proceeds requires a permanently higher price to generate the expanded output. The long-run supply curve will therefore be sloping upwards from left to right; expansion in the long run is associated with steadily rising average costs.

Things may go the other way, of course. The expansion of the industry as a whole may generate external economies of scale of the type discussed in Section 4 of Chapter VII, so that the unit costs of each producer are reduced not by his own increased output but by the expansion of the industry generally. Such a situation is illustrated in Fig. 9C(iii); the long-run supply curve is sloping downwards from right to left and the industry is one in which expansion is associated with falling unit costs.

The shape of the long-run supply curve is therefore dependent on the characteristics of the industry in question and there is obviously no reason why its direction of slope should be constant throughout its length. It is very likely that in its early stages expansion of an industry will be associated with decreasing unit costs; a period of constant costs may follow and possibly turn into a phase of increasing costs as the pressure on inputs steadily increases. There can be no *a priori* rule.

It was noted in a previous chapter that changes in tastes, incomes or the prices of related products could cause the demand curve for a particular commodity to shift bodily to left or right; similarly, a change in the fundamental conditions of production arising from the advancement of technology can cause supply curves to shift to right or left. Since these curves are in effect built up from a group of individual cost curves, it follows that they may shift over a period of time as the result of technological developments as well as of changes in the scale of the industry. Hence, if the market price ruling for a particular commodity and the quantities of it supplied by an industry were correlated *over a long period of time*, it might well be found that the supply of the commodity was greater when prices were relatively low than when the price had been high. This would not mean that the supply curve existing at any given point of time was downward-sloping, however, but merely that a short-run, upward-sloping supply curve has been shifting through time as the result of developments in the scale or technical methods of production.

Like demand curves, once again, supply curves can seldom, if ever, be constructed in reality. It is doubtful if many individual firms would be in a position to draw up curves showing their cost of production at various outputs, except in the very vaguest and most general terms; it would be statistically impossible to obtain such data on a comparable basis from all the firms in an industry (even assuming that the problems of defining an industry could be solved) so as to construct a supply curve for the industry as a whole. Such curves are nevertheless a valuable analytical device. They enable the principles underlying the relationships between price, cost and output to be embodied in a visual and convenient form, so that they can be set out against a similar representation of the factors at work on the side of demand. In this way, a large number of complex and interdependent influences can be brought together into a single analytical process, and their probable effects can be illustrated in a way which would otherwise be impossible without the use of fairly forbidding mathematics.

One final qualification is necessary. Throughout this discussion, output has been assumed to depend solely on price and cost, and supply has been identified with production. In the real world, neither procedure is wholly justifiable. The output of firms, or an industry as a whole, may vary without any change in prices or costs – because of adverse weather, for example, or an epidemic amongst the labour force, or bombing by an enemy during war. Economic analysis, of necessity, ignores these other influences on production, simply because they are not of an economic character, and the economist has no authority to pronounce on them.

The identity of supply with production is less defensible. If prices change in the market, an important consequence may be, and often is, the accumulation or running-down of stocks of goods by wholesalers and retailers, while such changes in stocks may in turn exert significant pressure on market price. The existence of stocks, in other words, breaks the direct connection between the current production and actual supply of goods offered to consumers. If traders believe that the price of a commodity is going to rise, they may try to accumulate stocks of it in order to sell the commodity after its price has risen, while expectations of a fall in price may result in an unloading of stocks on to the market in an attempt to sell before the price falls. Whether these expectations are well-founded or erroneous, stock changes of this kind can exert a considerable influence on the available supply of a commodity (and hence on its price) without any changes at all in current output.

The complications introduced into the analysis by the existence of stocks can be ignored at this stage, however, for two reasons. First, it is obviously desirable to obtain a clear picture of the fundamental relationships between price, cost and output, and to do this it is advisable to leave subsidiary considerations on one side for the moment, even though they may be of considerable importance in practice. Secondly, most commodities deteriorate in one way or another if they are stored for any length of time, so that over a fairly long period changes in stock positions tend to cancel one another out. The supply of a commodity over the long period is determined primarily by the level of production; stock changes can exert a significant but essentially *temporary* effect on its price.

4　ELASTICITY OF SUPPLY

In discussing demand it was noted that it was unduly vague to assert that the quantity consumed of a commodity will respond inversely to a change in its price: this could mean anything from an infinitesimal increase in consumption induced by a very large price reduction to an enormous expansion of the market caused by a very small price cut, and the differences between these two situations would obviously be of considerable consequence for any producer. Much the same is true of supply: the statement that the quantity of any product supplied to a market is responsive to the price prevailing for it is to indulge in generalisation too imprecise to be useful.

The solution is closely analogous to that adopted in the case of demand. Elasticity of supply, e_s, can be defined formally as

$$e_s = \frac{\Delta Q}{\Delta P} \cdot \frac{P}{Q}$$

where P and Q are respectively the market price of a product and the quantity of it being supplied at that price per unit of time and the Greek Δ denotes infinitesimally small changes in each. Translated into words, and in exact parallel with elasticity of demand, this expression defines elasticity of supply as the ratio between the proportionate change in the quantity of a product supplied to a market in response to a given proportionate change in price. Thus in the example of Fig. 9B a rise in market price from £8 to £12 was associated with a rise in supply from 2 400 to 3 100. Although these changes are in fact rather large to use in the formula (which strictly refers to elasticity at a point), they would in fact yield:

$$e_s = \frac{700}{4} \cdot \frac{8}{2\ 400} = +0.58$$

Using the formula for 'arc' elasticity described in section 4 of Chapter IV – in view of the large changes involved – the estimate would come out at + 0·64.

It will be observed that, in accordance with the reasoning of preceding sections, elasticity of supply is positive in sign, in contrast with price elasticity of demand. Theoretically it could vary between zero – when total supply is fixed whatever the price – and infinity, when supply will react infinitely in response to the slightest change of price. The former is by no means implausible (e.g. the total supply of Picasso paintings) whereas the latter is singularly improbable.

It will be obvious that the time interval over which elasticity of supply is being measured is of extremely great importance. With demand, time can reasonably be neglected in analysing elasticity; the response of demand to price can be assumed to be immediate without introducing too much unreality. In the case of supply, however, the time element must be taken into account, because short-run and long-run elasticities of supply are likely to differ considerably. Elasticity of supply cannot in fact be measured without specifying the period of time over which this responsiveness is examined. In the short run, as has been seen, cost curves tend to become steep fairly quickly, so that quite a large rise in price will call forth a relatively small increase in output. The longer the time allowed for the adjustment of capacity, however, the more elastic supply will tend to become.

As between industries, many factors will enter into the determination of relative elasticity of supply. An industry using highly specialised capital or labour, for example, will find it more difficult (and probably more expensive) to increase its capacity than one which uses relatively unspecialised and unskilled factors. Again, an enterprise making more than one product would possess an elastic supply potential for either one of them since it could switch its resources from one product to another fairly quickly if a change occurred in relative prices. Physical conditions of production may also influence elasticity – the supply of agricultural products is notoriously inelastic in the short run, for example, since a farmer, having once sown or prepared his fields, can do little about altering his output until the following season, however much prices fluctuate.

Later analysis will show that elasticity of supply, taken in conjunction with elasticity of demand, has an important bearing on matters like the impact on price of shifts in demand or the distribution of the burden of a change in cost or in taxation between consumers, on the one hand, and producers on the other.

FURTHER READING

J. DOWNIE *The competitive process* Duckworth, London 1958

E. MANSFIELD *Micro-economics* Ch. 8

P. J. D. WILES *Price, cost and output* Ch. 10

E. NEVIN *An introduction to micro-economics* Ch. 10

PART IV

THE THEORY OF PRICE

CHAPTER X

The Nature of
Market Equilibrium

1 PRICES, COMMODITIES AND MARKETS

HAVING discussed at some length the nature of the forces influencing, on the one hand, the demand for goods and services, and, on the other, the supply of goods and services, it is now necessary to turn to an examination of the way in which demand and supply interact, and thus to find an explanation of the determination of the price of any commodity in the market.

Before going further, the meaning of three important words in that last sentence must be made quite clear: price, commodity and market. The word 'price' will not give much trouble. In a modern economy goods are exchanged not directly but through the medium of money, and by price is meant the sum of money which a person hands over to a seller in order to obtain ownership of the commodity concerned. Nevertheless price is a little more complicated than this; in treating it an economist may be concerned with either *absolute* or *relative* prices – that is, he can be seeking to answer either the question 'Why are pencils 4p ?' or the question 'Why is the price of pencils only one-tenth the price of a packet of cigarettes ?' It is with the second kind of problem that the analysis is concerned for the moment – i.e. the problem of the causes underlying the value of one commodity relatively to that of other commodities. The problem of the absolute level of prices will be discussed later on.

An unambiguous definition of the word 'commodity' is rather more difficult. In a general, and rather loose, way a commodity can be spoken of as being a good, or service, for which there is no close substitute and which satisfies a particular, distinct want felt by consumers. Unfortunately, the identification of a particular commodity is very difficult in practice, since neither wants nor commodities are sharply distinct in the real world. Is the demand for tea a demand for tea-drinking as such, or is it simply one part of the demand for beverages, and hence met by coffee, cocoa and a dozen other fluids as well as tea? And is *tea* the commodity, or is Indian tea a different commodity from China tea?. Is Lipton's tea a different commodity from Lyons' tea? How close does a substitute have to become before it ceases to be a separate commodity? This kind of difficulty arises with almost every product in the economic system, and presents virtually insoluble problems. In speaking of 'a commodity' in the sense mentioned above, then, a fairly drastic over-simplification is being made in order to render the analysis at all manageable, and the real world is considerably more complex and less clear-cut than the analytical picture of it.

Finally, the word 'market' has to be defined. In everyday speech the word is frequently used to mean a building or area of ground in which trading takes place on certain occasions. In economics the word is used much more widely, and refers to all the persons and institutions concerned in the exchange of any commodity. In this sense it can include an entire country, or even the whole world, if people buying or selling a commodity are in contact with one another over those areas. On the other hand, a market may mean only a handful of people, if the persons in contact with one another for the purpose of exchanging some commodity are few in number. In any case, a market in this sense will have no single physical location; the person encouraged by an effective advertisement to buy a commodity in his local shop will be unknown to its manufacturer, who is perhaps thousands of kilometres away, but they are nevertheless both part of the market for that commodity.

2 INDUSTRY AND FIRM : THE DEMAND CURVE

Assume that an individual commodity can be defined closely enough for the present analysis. By a firm is meant any group of factors of production operating under the direction of an entrepreneur: by the industry is meant the collection of firms engaged in the production of the commodity with which the analysis is concerned.

Now this distinction between firm and industry is an important one, and it will underlie all the analysis of the various possible types of market situation with which this book will have to deal. In particular, the distinction has important implications for two things: the *demand curve* involved in the analysis and the *equilibrium conditions* which have to be satisfied. Consider the implications for the demand curve first of all.

For the industry as a whole, the relevant demand curve is that for the commodity (since it is *total* demand and supply which is involved when the industry is considered) and it will therefore be of the type discussed in Chapter IV. Now, in the earlier discussion of those curves the analysis was concerned with the relationship between the quantity purchased and the commodity's price, and such a curve can therefore be called an *average revenue* curve. Every unit of the commodity has to be sold on the market at the same price: if the producer's total receipts were divided by his total sales, his average revenue per unit of output, which will obviously be the same thing as its price, would be arrived at.

But just as economists distinguish between average and marginal cost, so a distinction can be drawn between average and marginal revenue. If average revenue is equal to the total receipts from the sale of a commodity divided by the total number of units of the commodity sold, then *marginal revenue* is equal to the *change* in total receipts brought about by a change of one unit in the total number of units of the commodity which are sold.

At first sight it may seem that, as all units of a commodity are sold at the same price, marginal revenue (as so defined) must be the same thing as the price at which the marginal unit is sold, and therefore the same thing as average revenue. But this is not necessarily so. The essential point about the falling demand curve (i.e. one sloping downwards from left to right) is that in order to sell more of a commodity the price (*of all units*) has to be reduced; the marginal revenue from one unit of output is therefore the price at which it is sold *minus* the fall in revenue from all the other units of output which the sellers have to offer at a price lower than before in order to persuade the market to absorb this extra, marginal unit. Given a stable demand curve of the usual, downward-sloping type, marginal revenue must always be *less* than price; it may even be negative.

Consider the example shown numerically in Table 10.1 and diagrammatically in Fig. 10A. In order to increase sales, the price

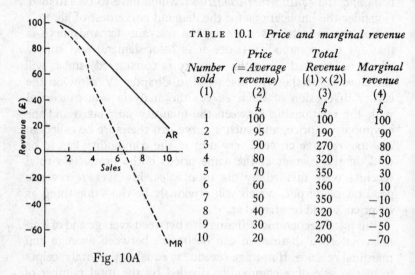

TABLE 10.1 *Price and marginal revenue*

Number sold (1)	Price (=Average revenue) (2) £	Total Revenue [(1)×(2)] (3) £	Marginal revenue (4) £
1	100	100	100
2	95	190	90
3	90	270	80
4	80	320	50
5	70	350	30
6	60	360	10
7	50	350	−10
8	40	320	−30
9	30	270	−50
10	20	200	−70

Fig. 10A

of the commodity has to be progressively reduced. As a result, the total revenue rises as sales increase up to the sixth unit, although it increases less and less rapidly as the market price is reduced. After the sixth unit total revenue actually declines, since the expansion of sales is insufficient to offset the decline in price necessary to secure it (i.e. elasticity of demand falls below unity); as a result, marginal revenue becomes negative.

Wherever the demand curve is falling then, as it usually is for the output of an industry as a whole, a distinction must be drawn between *average* revenue, or price (the *average* receipts per unit at each level of output) and *marginal* revenue (the addition to total receipts resulting from the last unit produced).

3   INDUSTRY AND FIRM: EQUILIBRIUM CONDITIONS

The second context in which the distinction between firm and industry is important is that of the conditions necessary for equilibrium. It will be remembered that, in economics, by equilibrium is meant a situation in which there exists no tendency towards change. For an industry, then, equilibrium means a situation in which there is no tendency for new firms to enter it or for existing firms to leave it; for a firm, it means that the entrepreneur has no incentive either to increase or to reduce his output. Under what conditions will such equilibrium situations be achieved?

Consider first the industry, which on this occasion presents the easier problem. In an earlier chapter the concept of 'normal' profit was introduced, by which was meant the rate of reward which the entrepreneur concerned could expect to earn in any industry open to him. Now, entrepreneurs will be attracted *into* an industry if the average rate of profit being earned in it is above this normal level, and they will tend to move *out* of an industry if they are earning in it less than this normal level. Equilibrium, for the industry, means that firms are neither moving in nor moving out; it means, therefore, that the level of profits in it is neither above nor below the normal level, and hence is equal to it.

When will this normal level of profit be attained? The average amount received by entrepreneurs per unit of output is given by the average revenue or price curve – the demand curve discussed at some length in Chapter IV. The amount paid out by entrepreneurs per unit of output *including the normal profit due to them in respect of their own contribution* is given by the average cost curve discussed in Chapter VIII. It follows, therefore, that entrepreneurs are receiving normal profits, no more and no less, when average cost equals average revenue, or price. If average cost is *above* price, then they are earning something less than normal profit per unit; if average cost is *below* price, then they are earning excess (i.e. above normal) profit. For any industry open to possible new entrants to be in equilibrium, average cost must equal average revenue.

Turn now to the firm. The basic assumption in all economic analysis is that each person is seeking to maximise his economic well-being and acts rationally towards that end. It follows that the entrepreneur must be assumed to seek the maximum profit from his firm. So long as a firm is in existence at all, the entrepreneur will produce the output which brings in the greatest profit or the smallest loss. When is this situation reached? Here the two concepts of marginal revenue and marginal cost must be brought together. Marginal revenue is the addition to total receipts arising from the last unit of output; marginal cost is the addition to total cost which it incurs for the entrepreneur. Now, if by increasing his output an entrepreneur can add more

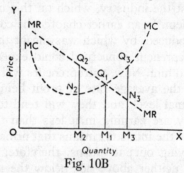

Fig. 10B

to his total receipts than he adds to his total cost, obviously he is increasing his total profit. If he adds more to cost than to receipts, he is reducing his total profit. He will *maximise* his profits, then, when marginal cost *equals* marginal revenue.

The example shown in Fig. 10B illustrates this graphically. Let the curve *MR* represent the marginal revenue brought in by each unit of output and *MC* the addition to total cost made by each unit. The entrepreneur's profits will be maximised at output OM_1, where the curves intersect and marginal revenue equals marginal cost. At any smaller output, say OM_2, it will be possible to increase total profit, since the extra cost involved in expanding output (M_2N_2) is smaller than the extra receipts which the extra output would earn (M_2Q_2). At any larger output, say OM_3, the extra receipts (M_3N_3) are smaller than the extra costs (M_3Q_3). At output OM_1, where the curves intersect, the entrepreneur adds just enough to his revenue to cover the marginal cost of production and his own normal profit.

For full equilibrium in an industry, then, it is necessary to have (a) the number of firms in the industry constant and (b) the output of each firm constant. For (a) the necessary condition is that the profits made by entrepreneurs should be at the normal level, which means that average cost must equal average revenue, or price, at the ruling level of output. For (b) the necessary condition is that each entrepreneur is making the maximum profit possible, which means that marginal cost must equal marginal revenue at the ruling level of output. In full equilibrium, therefore, each firm will be producing that output at which average cost equals average revenue *and* marginal cost equals marginal revenue.

One last word of warning should perhaps be added. The fact that a producer is maximising his profits does not mean that his output is at an optimum from an economic point of view. The optimum output is that at which the inputs are combined in the most efficient way – i.e. the output at which average cost of production is at its lowest point. This output *may* be that which yields the producer maximum profit (i.e. marginal cost may equal marginal revenue at the point of minimum average cost); as the succeeding chapter shows, however, this occurs only in the special and limiting case of perfect competition.

FURTHER READING

J. DOWNIE *The competitive process*

E. MANSFIELD *Micro-economics* Ch. 14

R. TURVEY *Demand and supply* Allen & Unwin, London 1971

CHAPTER XI

Price under Perfect Competition

1 WHAT IS PERFECT COMPETITION?

As a starting-point for the explanation of the process whereby the exchange value of a commodity is determined, it is convenient to postulate a hypothetical situation called perfect competition. No one suggests that such a situation has ever existed for other than a few exceptional commodities; the hypothesis is used merely as a simple framework in which the essential factors are analysed before moving closer towards the infinitely more complex situation which exists in the real world. Many subjects learnt at school (algebra, for example) will have only limited *direct* usefulness in later life, but that by no means implies that the study of them is useless. The important thing is that they help people to think in a careful and systematic way when faced with a particular type of problem, and in this way may contribute a great deal to their work in later years. So it is with the concept of perfect competition. It is most unlikely that perfect competition will ever be seen in the real world, but, nevertheless, through its study it is possible to acquire a system of approach which in due course will help a great deal in tackling the more complex situations which are in fact encountered in the real world.

This state of perfect competition, then, is a purely hypothetical one. To the economist, it implies the absence of monopoly power − i.e. the absence of any power on the part of any individual firm or consumer to influence market prices. In it certain things are assumed about each of the two groups of persons involved in economic exchange − producers and consumers. So far as the supply side is concerned, it is assumed, first, that there is a large number of sellers competing with one another – sufficiently large a number, that is, for each seller to be contributing an infinitely small part of the total supply, and hence to be unable to affect the market price significantly by changes in his output. Secondly, it is assumed that each producer (being a very small element in total production) has a perfectly elastic supply of the factors of production; he can increase his output, in other words, without driving up the level of wages, rent or interest currently prevailing in the industry. Thirdly, it is assumed that there are no restrictions on the free entry of firms into the industry or their movement out of it. Finally, each producer is assumed to be aware of the rate of profit being made by every other producer.

So far as the demand side is concerned, it is assumed again that the number of consumers is so large that no single buyer is able to perceptibly influence the market price by altering the scale of his purchases. Secondly, all buyers are assumed to have perfect knowledge of the price being asked for the commodity concerned in every part of the market, and it is supposed that neither transport costs nor inertia prevent them from taking advantage of any divergence in price which might develop in different parts of the market. Finally, buyers are assumed to have no preference as between the various producers of the commodity – that is, that there are no differences, actual or imaginary, between the product of one firm in the industry and that of any other firm in the industry.

This is a formidable collection of assumptions – so much so that it is worth repeating that their purpose is solely to put on one side, for the moment, the large number of subsidiary influences which usually operate, and to expose the basic forces common to all markets. To attempt an analysis of the highly complex markets of the real world, where these simplifying assumptions do not hold, without first clarifying the essential features of a simplified situation would be attempting the impossible; it would be setting out on roller-skates without first mastering the trick of walking.

2   THE DEMAND CURVE UNDER PERFECT
COMPETITION

Consider the demand curve facing the individual firm in this hypothetical situation of perfect competition; it will be convenient to refer to this as the *sales curve* so as to prevent confusion with the demand curve for the commodity facing the industry as a whole. Since the firm's product will be identical (by definition) with that of the rest of the industry, it might seem that its sales curve will be the same as that facing the industry as a whole – i.e. downward-sloping, as in Fig. 10A. This is not the case, however, as will become clear by recalling the assumptions of the situation of perfect competition. By hypothesis, each firm is producing so small a part of the industry's total sales that no change in its output can perceptibly influence price. Whatever its output, therefore, the individual firm sells at the (given) market price, so that its sales curve is a horizontal line drawn through the market price, *OP*, as in Fig. 11A, and extending over the whole range of its possible output.

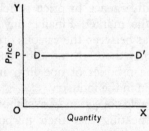

Fig. 11A

Can a separate marginal revenue curve be drawn in this case? Obviously it cannot; if each unit is sold at a constant price, each one must add exactly the same amount to total receipts as every other unit. Here there is only price to consider; there is no adjustment necessary because of the price-reduction enforced by increased sales, because no price-reduction is involved. For the firm in perfect competition, then, average revenue, or price, and marginal revenue coincide.

It may seem rather odd that each firm in an industry should face a horizontal (i.e. perfectly elastic) sales curve while the firms collectively face a falling demand curve. How can the addition of a large number of horizontal curves result in the industry's falling curve ? The answer is that the individual sales curves facing each firm cannot legitimately be added up. Each of them is drawn up on the assumption that the rest of the industry maintains a constant output, so that any expansion by an individual firm will not result in any significant movement along the output axis of the industry's demand curve. If *all* firms expand, of course, there is naturally a perceptible movement along the industry's output axis and the market price will fall. But for any firm in isolation, market price can be taken as determined by forces entirely outside its control.

3 MARKET EQUILIBRIUM UNDER PERFECT COMPETITION

The various strands can now be pulled together in order to see the full pattern of perfectly competitive equilibrium. It has been established that each firm faces a perfectly elastic (i.e. horizontal) sales curve, such as that shown as *DD'* in Fig.11A, and that with such a sales curve average revenue and marginal revenue coincide. The condition for equilibrium in the industry is that average cost must equal average revenue, while for equilibrium of the firm marginal cost must equal marginal revenue. But average revenue and marginal revenue coincide under perfect competition. The equilibrium conditions therefore require that, at the ruling output, average cost and marginal cost should *both* equal average revenue, or price, and must therefore be equal to one another. It follows that the equilibrium situation for each individual firm must be of the kind shown in Fig. 11B(i) – output settling at that point where the sales curve is tangential to the average cost curve, and where the average cost curve is at its lowest point. The corresponding position for the industry as a whole will be that shown in Fig. 11B(ii), where the scale of the output axis *OX* will of course be very much smaller than in Fig. 11B(i). Output will settle at the point where the market demand curve DD' intersects the industry's long-run supply curve SS'. The industry's output will therefore be ON and price OP.

Why should this rather special combination of features necessarily be involved in the equilibrium position of each individual firm? Consider it in two parts: first, *why* should output settle at the point of minimum average cost?; second, *why* should the sales curve be a tangent to the average cost curve at that particular level of output? The answer to the first question is that, as has been established, equilibrium requires that both average and marginal cost should equal price and therefore one another;

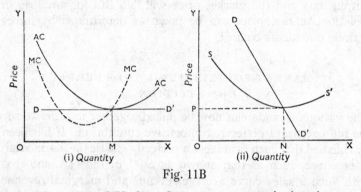

(i) Quantity   (ii) Quantity

Fig. 11B

but with a normal U-shaped cost curve, marginal and average cost can be equal only at the lowest point of the average cost curve. So long as marginal cost is *below* average cost each extra unit of output is costing less than the average for output as a whole, and overall average cost must be falling. So long as marginal cost is *above* average cost, the average (on the same kind of reasoning) must be rising. When marginal cost equals average cost, the average must be neither rising nor falling – i.e. it must have reached its lowest point and not yet started to rise again.

Turn to the second question: why should the sales curve just touch the average cost curve at this minimum point, thereby forming a tangent to it? The reason is that the equilibrium conditions require price (average revenue, equal in this case to marginal revenue) to be equal to both marginal and average cost. It is only at this point, where average and marginal cost are themselves equal, that the single price can be equal to both average and marginal cost. Hence it is only if the sales curve touches the average cost curve at this particular point that full equilibrium, of both firm and industry, can be attained.

This can be seen if other cases are considered in which this special combination of requirements is not achieved. In Fig. 11C the horizontal sales curve is above the point of minimum cost. If the firm produces output OM_1 it will itself be in equilibrium, because marginal cost equals marginal revenue at that point and its profits are maximised. But at that output its average revenue (M_1Q_1) will be in excess of its average cost (M_1N_1) and it will therefore be earning more than normal profits; new firms will

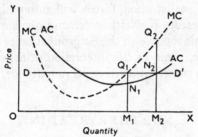

Fig. 11C

be attracted into the industry by these excess profits, so that the industry will not be in equilibrium. (As new firms come in, total supply will expand and the market price will fall, so that the individual firm's sales curve will fall until it touches the average cost curve at its lowest point and profits are back to normal.) Conversely, if it produced OM_2 average cost and average revenue would be equal, profits would be normal and the industry would be in equilibrium. But the firm would not be maximising its profits; at output OM_2 the marginal cost of production (M_2Q_2) would be in excess of the marginal revenue brought in (M_2N_2) and the firm would be reducing its total profit with every unit it produced after OM_1.

Whatever other situation is postulated, then, either the industry or the firm will be in a state of disequilibrium, and price will continue to change. Only when price is equal to both marginal and (minimum) average cost will both the individual firm *and* the industry as a whole be in a state of complete balance. In all this, of course, it is assumed that the forces of adjustment – changes in output or the movement of firms – are given time to work themselves out, although the analysis could easily be conducted in terms of short-run and long-run cost curves if it was desired to allow for the differences introduced by the existence of time-lags.

So a fundamental conclusion of the theory of value is arrived at: *given conditions of perfect competition, the price of a commodity tends to equality with its marginal cost of production.* As has been seen, price will also be equal to the minimum average cost of production. If for any reason the equality of price and marginal cost is disturbed, forces will automatically be brought into play to restore it. Neither demand nor supply can be said to have a dominant role in the determination of price, therefore; price is the outcome of the interaction of demand and supply, each making a contribution of equal importance.

FURTHER READING

E. MANSFIELD *Micro-economics* Ch. 8
A. M. LEVENSON and B. S. SOLON *Outline of price theory* Ch. 9
J. HADAR *Elementary theory of economic behaviour* Chs. 5–6

CHAPTER XII

Price under Monopoly

1   THE NATURE OF MONOPOLY

IN the previous chapter a hypothetical situation was discussed in which the number of competing producers of a commodity was so large that no single producer was able to exert a perceptible influence on the market price through variations in his output. Logically the opposite extreme of *monopoly* can be conceived of – a situation in which a single producer controls the entire output of a certain commodity. Like the concept of perfect competition, monopoly is easier to define theoretically than to identify in practice. A great deal turns, as before, on the definition of a commodity. In a sense, every producer has a monopoly of tutes which is required for a product to become a separate commodity rather than one of a number of types, or brands, of a commodity. In a sense, every producer has a monopoly of his own product provided there is even the smallest difference, actual or imaginary, between the goods he sells and those sold by his rivals; on the other hand, the existence of monopoly could be denied altogether on the grounds that a substitute of some kind exists for every product under the sun, as indeed it does.

In economic analysis the use of the word monopoly lies between these two extremes. Each brand of chocolate, or motorcars, or cigarettes, is not treated as a separate commodity, and therefore their producers are not treated as monopolists. On the other hand, a product such as coal is treated as a separate commodity even though gas and electricity and oil are to some degree substitutes; hence the National Coal Board, having the sole right to produce and supply coal in Britain, is generally treated as a monopoly.

Just as a flexible, commonsense attitude is adopted in deciding when a product is or is not a separate commodity, so a reasonable attitude is adopted towards the extent of control over total output required before a producer is regarded as a monopolist. To say that a firm does not have a monopoly because it produces only 95 per cent, and not 100 per cent, of the total supply of a commodity would clearly be unrealistic. Rather, a producer would be said to have a monopoly of a commodity if he controls such a large share of total output as to be able to exercise decisive control over the supply and price of the commodity through variations in his output.

The essential point about monopoly, then, is that *there ceases to be a distinction between the firm and the industry*. A firm which has a monopoly position in any market *is* the industry so far as equilibrium analysis is concerned. By definition, no other producers can exert any perceptible influence on total supply or on price, whatever the level of profits enjoyed by the monopolist. So far as equilibrium is concerned, it is only the firm which requires analysis; so long as the firm is in equilibrium, then of necessity the industry is in equilibrium.

2 SOURCES OF MONOPOLY POWER

A firm – or group of firms operating under some common direction – may acquire and retain a dominant position in the market for a commodity by various means. A common source of monopoly power in history has been the control of one or more factors of production. In particular, the ownership of deposits of *raw materials* may give an unchallengeable position to a firm in producing a commodity for which those raw materials are essential. In the long run, a position built up on this advantage is likely to be undermined by either the exhaustion of the deposits involved or the development of alternative natural or synthetic materials.

A second important type of factor promoting a monopoly position is that of *legal restriction* on the entry of potential competitors into an industry. In Britain, for example, many fields of activity are closed to private firms, and the sole right of operation is conferred by statute on one enterprise – the Central Electricity Generating Board, National Coal Board and the Post Office are familiar examples. More commonly, the law of *patents* can be invoked by a firm to secure the sole right of manufacture of a new product or use of a new process. Finally, *tariffs*, or taxes on imports, may be used to prevent foreign producers from competing with a domestic firm, or the same result may be attained by import restrictions of a quantitative kind.

Thirdly, competition may be prevented by *financial* factors. Highly capitalistic industries, such as the manufacture of iron and steel, require enormous outlays on capital equipment before production can be carried out on the level necessary to compete with an established firm; as a result, potential competitors may find it virtually impossible to enter the industry. In other industries, a firm may have acquired such goodwill in a market that new entrants could break into the market only through an expensive advertising campaign.

Finally, a monopoly position may be built up through various devices specifically designed to prevent competition. An existing producer may deliberately sell a commodity at a *loss* in order to drive competitors with smaller reserves into bankruptcy. A trade union may pursue a *closed shop* policy – i.e. adopt measures designed to ensure that employment in a factory is confined to its members – with exactly the same end in view. Until recent years, another common practice was for producers to form themselves into a *trade association* of one form or another, and enforce restrictions on full competition through collective measures. For example, a mutinous entrepreneur might be brought to heel by a closing up of his channels of supply or of sales, since the association as a whole could threaten suppliers or retailers with a complete stoppage of orders or deliveries unless their measures were enforced. By the Restrictive Trade Practices Act of 1956, however, such *collective* resale price maintenance (as distinct from the enforcement of a 'recommended' resale price by an *individual* producer acting alone) was declared illegal in Britain.

3   MONOPOLY EQUILIBRIUM

Having seen how monopoly power may originate, it is necessary
to consider what the exercise of that power may mean in terms
of the equilibrium price and output in the market for a monopolist's product. As was mentioned above, the analysis is relatively
simple, since by definition the condition for equilibrium in the
market as a whole becomes identical with the equilibrium condition for the (single) firm. For the firm, equilibrium is attained
when profits are maximised, and the possession of monopoly
power makes no difference whatever to this rule. The peculiarity

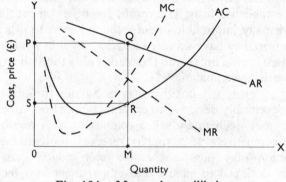

Fig. 12A   Monopoly equilibrium

introduced into the analysis by monopoly power is not that the
requirements for equilibrium are affected; it is that there are
no additional requirements which must be met for full equilibrium of the *industry* to be attained, as there are under perfect
competition. The rule is simply that the monopolist will maximise his profit, and the previous reasoning, by which it was
established that profits are maximised when marginal cost and
marginal revenue are equal, remains perfectly valid.

Monopoly equilibrium, therefore, implies a situation such as
that shown in Fig. 12A. As the monopolist supplies the whole
market, the demand (or average revenue) curve facing him will
be that for the commodity as a whole, and hence will usually
be downward-sloping; the distinction between sales curve and

demand curve disappears. The monopolist will maximise his profit at that output which brings marginal revenue into equality with marginal cost (*OM* in the diagram). Over and above the 'normal' profit which is an element in the average cost curve, he will receive on each unit of output excess, or monopoly, profits equal to the difference between average cost and price (the area *RSPQ* in the diagram therefore represents the monopolist's total *excess* profit).

So far the argument has been conducted with reference to a single unified market throughout which the monopolist charges a single price. Precisely similar considerations apply to what is called a *discriminating* monopoly − that is, a situation in which a monopolist is able to break his market into two or more separate and isolated sections in which separate prices can be charged. A Harley Street specialist may charge two different fees for rendering an identical service to two different men, if he thinks one can afford to pay more than the other; firms have been known to sell at one price in the home market and a different price in the export market; the British Electricity Boards supply a single product − electricity − at different prices to industrial users on the one hand and domestic consumers on the other. In such cases a monopolist seeking to maximise profits will sell in each section of the market that output which brings the marginal revenue from each section into equality with the marginal cost of his total output. If the elasticity of demand for his product differs considerably between the different sections of his market, then the prices he will charge will also differ considerably, since the greater the elasticity of a demand curve the closer does marginal revenue come to price at any output. As was noted earlier, an elasticity of demand greater than unity means that total expenditure on the commodity increases as price falls, so that marginal revenue (the *change* in total expenditure) will be positive and may approach the level of the price itself. Elasticity *below* unity means that total expenditure falls as price decreases; hence marginal revenue, being negative, is much below price. The monopolist will be producing only that output which makes marginal cost equal to marginal revenue, so that the more rapidly marginal revenue falls (i.e. the less elastic the demand) the smaller the monopolist's output, and therefore the higher the market price.

An example of such a situation is provided in Fig. 12B. Suppose that the curves shown in Figs. 12B(i) and (ii) represent the average and marginal revenue respectively in the monopolist's two separate markets. The first is clearly a market with a small but inelastic demand, whereas in the second the demand is greater but more elastic. The curves TAR and TMR in Fig. 12B(iii) represent the total average and marginal revenue from the two markets combined; they are obtained, of course, by adding the curves in Figs. 12B(i) and (ii) across horizontally. If the monopolist's marginal cost is now plotted, its intersection

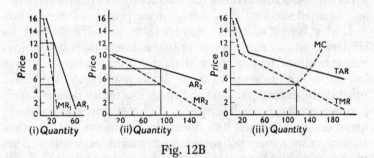

Fig. 12B

with the total marginal revenue curve fixes his total output − in this case 115. At this output marginal cost is £5, and he will therefore sell that quantity in each separate market which brings in a marginal revenue of £5 in each case. It will be seen that this means that he will sell 25 in the first market (at a price of £12) and 90 in the second (at a price of about £7·75). If his total output were anything other than 115, marginal cost and marginal revenue would not be equal and his profits could therefore not be maximised. If he divided his sales between the two markets in any other way, he would gain less additional revenue from the market in which sales increased than he would sacrifice in the market where sales diminished.

This illustration of the important role which elasticity of demand plays in the allocation of sales between separate markets helps to bring out one of the two main features of the price and output policy of a monopolist. This is that a monopolist will never expand output beyond a point at which elasticity of demand falls close to unity. An elasticity of unity implies that total outlay is unaffected by a reduction in price, and this means that marginal revenue (the change in total outlay) is zero. Since the producer must incur *some* marginal cost by expanding output, his profits will be reduced if he has no additional revenue to offset marginal cost. Hence a monopolistic agricultural organisation, for example, might prefer to destroy some of its crops rather than sell them in a market. If the demand for the crop is inelastic, the sale of this marginal element in the market might result in a *negative* marginal revenue and thus profits would be bound to fall, even if the crops destroyed had no marginal cost whatever.

The second main feature of monopoly equilibrium is that, in comparison with *perfect* competition, price will usually be higher and output will usually be lower. Under perfect competition, as the last chapter showed, output will settle at that point where price is equal to marginal cost. The monopolist produces that output at which *marginal revenue* is equal to marginal cost. As the demand curve for any normal commodity is downward-sloping, marginal revenue will always be to the left of average revenue, or price (i.e. at any output marginal revenue will always be lower than price). It follows, then, that the marginal revenue curve will cut the marginal cost curve to the left of the point at which the price curve cuts it – i.e. at a point where output is lower. The monopolist makes his excess profits, in other words, by holding down output and holding up price, and he is not prevented from doing this (as he would be under perfect competition) by a movement of firms into the industry under the attraction of the abnormally high level of profits prevailing there.

An illustration of this is provided by Fig. 12C, where the market demand curve is given by *AR* and the corresponding marginal revenue curve is *MR*. If the industry is a perfectly competitive one, the curve *SS'* can be taken to represent its long-run supply curve. The analysis of the previous chapter has established that equilibrium will be achieved when each firm in the industry is operating at the point of minimum average cost, where price equals marginal cost. Hence output will be *OM* and price *OP*. If the industry consists of a single monopolist, however, *SS'* becomes his average cost curve and his output will be determined by his marginal cost curve *MC*. Where this intersects the marginal revenue curve, his profits will be maximised; since profit-maximisation is assumed to be his sole objective, this will be his equilibrium point. Hence the monopolist's output in this case will be *OM'* (lower than the competitive output) and his price will be *OP'* (higher than the competitive price).

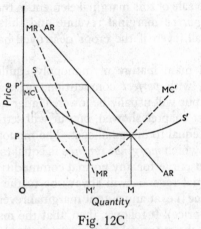

Fig. 12C

Two qualifications must immediately be made to this conclusion, however. First, it rests on the assumption that the level of costs is the same under monopoly and under competition. This may not be so. A monopolist, by concentrating production under single control, may gain considerable economies of large-scale production. As a result, the monopolist's marginal cost curve may be considerably lower than that prevailing under competition, so that price may be lower and output higher under monopoly, despite the presence of excess monopoly profits. This is not so improbable as might be thought at first sight. In the supply of gas or electricity, for example, the market is usually a limited geographical area; frequently one modern generating plant can easily supply the entire market. It would obviously be wasteful, and therefore costly, if the market were served by rival generators, with rival pipes and cables in the same streets, all operating at much below their full cápacity. The same is true of railway systems; the idea of duplicating expensive permanent ways and operating staff has only to be considered to be seen to be absurdly wasteful. Monopoly and excessively high prices, therefore, are by no means synonymous.

The second qualification is that when monopoly is compared unfavourably with competition, it is *perfect* competition with which the comparison is being made, and perfect competition seldom, if ever, exists in reality. The more appropriate comparison in reality is between monopoly and the imperfect form of competition which is usually the practical alternative. As will be found in the next chapter, imperfect competition frequently involves a good deal of waste and inefficiency (especially in matters such as product differentiation and competitive advertisement) which might not be experienced with a monopoly. This strengthens the possibility, then, that monopoly costs (including selling as well as production costs) may be lower than those prevailing under the kind of competition actually experienced.

Nevertheless, the fact remains that the existence of monopoly power (whether in the form of pure monopoly or as an element in the half-competitive, half-monopolistic world examined in the next chapter) has a restrictive effect on output, tending to result in higher prices to the consumer and higher profits for the producer than would otherwise prevail. This is particularly the case when demand is relatively inelastic, so that marginal revenue falls rapidly; the steeper the demand curve, the further to the left will be the point at which the marginal cost and revenue curves intersect; this means that a monopolist's output would be smaller, and his price higher, than would be the case under competition despite a substantial reduction of cost which might be secured through the monopoly organisation. Hence the problem of monopoly policy cannot be ignored in an economy where monopolistic elements exist to any significant degree.

4 MONOPOLY AND PUBLIC POLICY

There has been a growing realisation during the present century of the dangers of monopoly, and especially of the possible exploitation of the consumer through restricted output and high prices, and the undue concentration of economic power in a small number of private individuals, which may result from a monopoly position. There can be little doubt that these dangers are real, although it must be remembered that the analysis of monopolistic prices rests (as always in economic theory) on the assumption that entrepreneurs invariably act so as to maximise their profits. If this assumption does not hold – and this may frequently be the case in reality – then the conclusion that price will usually be higher under monopoly than under competition will have to be qualified.

Assuming, however, that other things being equal a monopolist does usually seek to maximise his profits, how can the exercise of monopolistic power, harmful as it is to the consumer, be restricted? In the first place, the monopolist's power is always limited by the existence of substitutes, to which consumers may turn if prices are set too high. In other words, substitutes will increase the elasticity of the demand curve facing the monopolist, and it has already been seen that the gap between monopoly price and competitive price will always be smaller the greater is the elasticity of demand. Even if no close substitutes are produced in the same country, a monopolist must always be careful to keep his price below the point at which it is possible to import similar products from abroad and market them at a competitive price.

Secondly, a monopolist may not charge the high price which maximises his profit for fear of stimulating *rival producers* to enter his market in order to share in his high profit. A monopoly position resting, for example, on the high costs of entry into the industry may be only a qualified one; competitors may not be prepared to incur the high costs of setting up in the industry so long as the rate of profit in it is only a little above the normal level, but they may reconsider their judgement if the profits being earned by the monopolist become very high indeed and present a strong temptation.

Thirdly, a monopolist may be content to earn something less than the maximum rate of profit open to him in the hope of *extending the market* and so increasing his long-run profits. He may deliberately hold down the price of his product in the belief that, by accepting lower profits in the short run, the growth of the demand for his product will be encouraged; a relatively low rate of profit on a large output in the long run may attract him more than a high rate of profit on the small output indicated by existing demand conditions.

For all these reasons, then, the *existence* of monopoly powers cannot necessarily be taken to imply the full *exercise* of these powers. In many cases, the loss suffered by the consumer as the result of a moderate use of monopoly power may be more than offset by the gain he enjoys because of the lower costs – production and selling costs – brought about by the concentration of output in a single enterprise, or a small group of enterprises operating in association with one another.

Nevertheless, in many – and probably most – cases the consumer suffers to a greater or lesser degree from the existence of monopoly, despite all these qualifications and limitations of the monopolist's power. When the abuses of monopoly become substantial, it may be thought that only intervention on the part of the government can ensure adequate protection for the consumer. Such intervention may take the form of a complete transfer of the control of an industry out of private hands, or at least a direct control over the industry's price and output policy. For example, the relatively high capital costs incurred in the production and supply of gas and electricity made it inevitable, from an early stage in the history of these industries in Britain, that a single producer would operate on a monopolistic basis in each area. The wastes involved in duplicating or triplicating gas works and pipe systems in an area which could be adequately served by a single producer (and which would *have* to be served by a single producer if the potential economies of large-scale output were to be realised), would be obvious to even the bitterest opponent of monopoly. Hence, the supply of gas and water was either taken over by local government authorities themselves or was conducted by private corporations having the sole right of operation in each area but restricted fairly severely in their powers to raise prices or to increase their profits. Subsequently, of course, the economies gained from a consolidation of the industries into single units operating on a nation-wide basis have been thought sufficient to justify their nationalisation. For similar reasons, in most countries postal services are provided by an agency of the government itself.

The operation of an industry by a government or some semi-governmental body, however, is not always considered a desirable development; this may be because of political considerations, or because of technical reasons which suggest that a particular industry is not conducive to efficient management by an official body. In such cases, other means of restraining or eliminating monopoly powers have to be adopted. Practice varies widely from country to country in this respect. In the United States, for example, a vigorous anti-monopoly campaign has been conducted for many years through the processes of the law. Specific monopolistic practices, and particular forms of company organisation which are considered to be means of securing monopoly power, have been declared by statute to be illegal, and an energetic branch of the government has been charged with the discovery and prosecution of breaches of the law. Although it is impossible to measure the degree of success enjoyed by measures of this kind (after all, even the extent of monopoly itself cannot be measured, let alone the influence of public policy upon it) it seems likely that it has exercised a salutary effect in discouraging producers from trying to build up monopoly positions.

In Great Britain the attitude towards monopoly has been rather different until recent years, the tendency being to avoid general condemnation of particular practices or forms of organisation. The reason for this has been partly the belief that there are few legal restrictions which a competent company lawyer cannot invent some means of surmounting, but mainly the conviction that practices which may be undesirable in some cases may be perfectly defensible in others. It had been thought better to consider each industry separately, therefore, and to legislate when necessary on an *ad hoc* basis.

A significant departure from this policy occurred in 1948 with the establishment of a Monopolies Commission charged with the consideration of practices and policies being pursued in industries referred to it for examination by the appropriate government department. In its reports after each investigation, the Commission was required to indicate practices which it considered to be contrary to the public interest, and the government were given powers to declare such practices to be illegal. A far-reaching development of this policy occurred in 1956 with the passage of the Restrictive Trade Practices Act, under which various practices of a monopolistic nature were declared to be illegal unless firms adopting them could satisfy a Restrictive Practices Court that they are *not* contrary to the public interest in their particular case. Each industry has to register these designated practices within a specified time with a Registrar appointed for the purpose and to either obtain approval of them from the Court or abandon them within that specified period. Yet another development occurred in 1965 when the functions of the Monopolies Commission were extended to include the scrutiny of proposed mergers between firms and the prohibition of such mergers if they appeared likely to create an unacceptable degree of monopoly power.

It is exceedingly difficult, and in any case probably too soon, to judge the efficacy of this policy. It is fairly certain, however, that its degree of success will depend heavily on the extent to which the existence of this legal machinery and examination induces the general body of entrepreneurs to abandon monopolistic practices (or abstain from their adoption), rather than on the number of successful prosecutions conducted with its aid. All statutory law depends, in the last resort, on the general acceptance of it by the overwhelming majority; a law which the bulk of the population regards as a bad law cannot succeed or survive in a democratic society. This is true of the law relating to monopoly; it will attain its end only if it expresses and reflects a general belief amongst entrepreneurs themselves that monopoly is in general undesirable, and is something from which in the long run they, like society as a whole, can only suffer.

FURTHER READING

E. MANSFIELD *Micro-economics* Ch. 9

J. HADAR *Elementary theory of consumer behaviour* Ch. 7

A. M. LEVENSON and B. S. SOLON *Outline of price theory* Ch. 10

A. BEACHAM and N. J. CUNNINGHAM *Economics of industrial organisation* Ch. 6

C. K. ROWLEY *Anti-trust and economic efficiency* Macmillan, London 1973

M. A. UTTON *Industrial concentration* Penguin Books, London 1970

CHAPTER XIII

Price under
Imperfect Competition

1 THE NATURE OF IMPERFECT COMPETITION

T H E two preceding chapters have been concerned with the analysis of the forces determining price under certain extreme and hypothetical circumstances, that of perfect competition on the one hand and of pure monopoly on the other. It is almost impossible to discover a single commodity in the actual world which is exchanged under conditions of perfect competition, and equally difficult to discover instances of pure monopoly. As frequently happens in other connections, the reality is to be found somewhere between the two extremes; the vast majority of markets display characteristics of both monopoly and competition, the monopoly element tending to dominate in some, that of competition in others. Such situations, where neither pure monopoly nor perfect competition prevails, economists call *imperfect competition*.

How can this mixture of competition and monopoly arise? Usually it is caused by factors operating on both the supply side and the demand side of the market mechanism. On the supply side, perfect competition postulates an infinitely large number of producers, each unable to influence the market price perceptibly, while pure monopoly requires a single seller free from the potential competition of rival producers. In reality there are usually several producers of the same commodity but not an infinite number of them, with the result that each producer *can* exert a significant influence on total supply through changes in his own output, and can therefore influence price perceptibly;

at the same time, some degree of competition exists, so that the equilibrium of the industry, as well as of the individual firm, has to be taken into account.

On the demand side, elements of both competition and monopoly are found because of the existence of different brands, or types, of any given commodity; these possess individual characteristics but are nevertheless close substitutes for one another. Perfect competition rests on the assumption that consumers regard the products of the various firms in an industry as identical in all respects; in the real world, through advertisement and branding, the consumers of most commodities are led to believe (rightly or wrongly) that Company A's lightbulbs are a different product from Company B's lightbulbs, even though the two brands may actually be physically identical. Pure monopoly, on the other hand, postulates that there is no close substitute for Company C's product, whereas the products of Companies D and E are usually fairly close substitutes. The modern economy is therefore one of part monopoly and part competition; each producer has, in a sense, a monopoly of his own product (Company A, obviously, is the sole supplier of 'A Brand' lightbulbs) but each is facing the competition of other brands of the same product which consumers regard as fairly close substitutes.

The prevalence of imperfect competition in real life is indicated by the widespread use of competitive advertisement (or, more generally, 'selling devices' – free gift vouchers, competitions, 'surprise' presents in cornflake packets, and all the rest of it) in order to attract customers. Such phenomena could not occur under either perfect competition or pure monopoly. The seller under perfect competition could gain nothing from competitive selling campaigns, since by definition his product is identical with that of the large number of competing producers; any benefits resulting from the campaign would be felt no more by the firm undertaking it than by any of his rivals, so that the procedure would be pointless. The pure monopolist, on the other hand, has no need of advertisement; he is the sole supplier of his product and there are no rivals to be beaten through these various selling techniques. Of necessity, then, the existence of competitive advertisement and product differentiation in an industry connotes imperfect competition; since these things are absent from singularly few industries, it is clear that in considering imperfect competition the analysis is coming fairly close to the real world at last.

2 MARKET EQUILIBRIUM

As imperfect competition combines features of both monopoly and perfect competition, it is not surprising that the analysis of market equilibrium under imperfect competition indicates that it involves elements of both monopolistic and competitive equilibrium. From the monopoly analysis is taken the falling sales curve facing the individual firm; unlike the producer under perfect competition, the entrepreneur operating under imperfect competition faces a range of market prices rather than a single price determined for him by forces outside his control. If he raises his price, some of his customers will turn to rival brands which they consider to be fairly close substitutes and which they will prefer now that his product has become relatively expensive. On the other hand, he will not lose *all* his customers, since some will still retain a preference for his particular brand of commodity despite its relatively high price.

One important factor in this context may be the existence of transport costs. Customers may prefer the product of a nearby supplier to otherwise identical products being sold some distance away; they may prefer to pay a price for it which is somewhat higher than that charged for rival products rather than incur the expense, or effort, of removing their custom elsewhere. They may be undeterrred by an increase in the relative price of a product, also, by the intangible but powerful force of goodwill; customers become attached to a particular seller through habit, or tradition, or through personal and social relationships with the producer.

For any of these reasons, then, a producer under imperfect competition would not lose all of his customers by raising price in comparison with his competitors, as he would under perfect competition. Conversely, by reducing price he would attract some, but not all, buyers who were previously customers of his rivals. The firm in imperfect competition, then, shares with the monopolist the phenomenon of a falling sales curve for its product, and does not face the horizontal sales curve characteristic of the firm operating under conditions of perfect competition.

Unlike the situation under monopoly, however, market equilibrium under imperfect competition involves a consideration of the conditions for equilibrium of the *industry* as well as of the individual firm. The monopolist is untroubled by the concept of equilibrium of the industry; the monopolistic firm *is* the industry, and so long as it is itself in equilibrium that is an end of the matter. In this respect, however, the situation of imperfect competition is similar to that of perfect competition. For a long-run market equilibrium, it is not enough that each individual producer should be in equilibrium; firms are free to enter (or leave) an industry if the profits being made in it are higher (or lower) than the normal level for the economy as a whole, and the industry will be in full equilibrium only when the number of firms in it is showing no tendency to change. (If there is *not* complete freedom of entry into the industry, of course, firms may persistently enjoy super-normal profits and the term *monopolistic competition* is often used to describe situations of this kind. However, there is no need at this stage to attempt to deal with every possible type of situation which could arise in practice.)

Equilibrium under imperfect competition, then, requires the same double set of conditions as under perfect competition − i.e. equilibrium of the firm *and* equilibrium of the industry. As has been seen for both perfect competition and for monopoly, the firm can be in equilibrium only when its profits are maximised, and, as before, this occurs when marginal cost and marginal revenue are equal. The condition for equilibrium of the industry is also exactly the same as under perfect competition − that is, that the prevailing profit-level equals the normal level for all the entrepreneurs concerned, a situation which is established only when average cost and average revenue are equal. Unlike the perfectly competitive situation, however, marginal revenue and average revenue (price) are not identical under imperfect competition, because the monopoly elements in the situation give

the individual firm a falling sales curve rather than a horizontal
one.

The situation in which the two sets of equilibrium conditions
will be realised is illustrated in Fig. 13A. At output *OM*, the
equilibrium of the firm is secured by the equality of marginal
cost and marginal revenue, while the equilibrium of the industry
is assured by the equality of average cost and average revenue.
But why should *both* equalities occur so conveniently at the
same level of output in this way? The answer to this question
is simply that both equalities can occur *only* when the two average curves – *AC* and *AR* – are tangential to one another as they

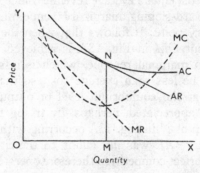

Fig. 13A

are at the point *N*. The fact that *AR* (the sales curve) is a tangent
of *AC* at *N means* that the slopes of the two curves are equal
at that point. At any point to the left of *N* the curve *AC* is
steeper than *AR*; this means that marginal cost must be smaller
than marginal revenue – it is pulling the *average* cost down more
rapidly than marginal revenue is pulling down average revenue.
At any point to the *right* of *N* the curve *AC* is less steep than
AR; this means that marginal cost must be greater than marginal
revenue – it is pulling the *average* cost down less rapidly than
marginal revenue is pulling down average revenue. Hence, at
the point *N* where the slopes of the average cost and average
revenue curves are equal, marginal cost and marginal revenue
must be equal. It is at the point where the average revenue,
or sales, curve makes a tangent with the average cost curve – and

only at this point – that the necessary dual equilibrium conditions are fulfilled.

Two points of contrast between this situation and that prevailing under perfect competition are worth noting. First, price under imperfect competition will be equal to average cost and will therefore be *greater* than marginal cost; under perfect competition, price tends to equality with marginal cost. Second, and more important, the output at which a firm will be in equilibrium under imperfect competition will be smaller than that at which average costs are at a minimum. The output of the firm settles at the point where marginal cost equals marginal revenue and where average cost equals average revenue. Since the firm's sales curve is downward-sloping, marginal revenue must be less than average at every point. It follows that when the dual equality, shown at output *OM* in Fig. 13A is achieved, marginal cost (being equal to marginal revenue, which is less than average revenue) must be less than average cost, so that average cost is still falling at the equilibrium level of output. (This point is most easily appreciated, perhaps, by trying to imagine the tangency shown at *N* in Fig. 13A occurring with a falling sales curve if the curve *AR* was *not* falling to the right of *N*.) The firm under imperfect competition therefore operates permanently at less than optimum output, since the optimum level of output is that at which goods are produced at the lowest average cost of production.

There is one point of contrast between the equilibrium position under imperfect competition and that under monopoly. The monopolist maximises his profits at a level above the normal for the whole economy, and the more inelastic the demand facing him the greater will be the excess of monopoly profit over normal profits. Under imperfect competition profits are not abnormal; as long as new firms can move into the industry, they will prevent abnormal profits from continuing, while firms will leave the industry if profits fall below the normal level.

3   THE SIGNIFICANCE OF IMPERFECTLY
COMPETITIVE EQUILIBRIUM

This analysis brings out clearly the sort of situation which will tend to prevail in an industry characterised by imperfect competition. Each firm will be earning only normal profit, but each will be operating at a level of output which is too small to permit the full exploitation of the economies of large-scale production. In the industry as a whole, there will be too many separate firms producing individual brands of the product, and as a result each will have some degree of unused capacity.

It would follow from this that imperfect competition has substantial wastes necessarily associated with it. On the one hand there are the direct and obvious wastes of competitive advertisement and other 'selling' measures. Firms expend resources – labour, raw materials, etc. – in an attempt to influence consumers away from rival products and towards their own, although all the products may be identical in all important respects. As all firms will be indulging in this selling process, the competing efforts are bound to cancel themselves out to a large extent, so that no one benefits ultimately except the persons making a living from sales promotion. Even if it is not entirely wasted through this mutual cancelling-out, the expenditure of resources in this way can benefit one producer only by damaging another, so that no net benefit can be gained by producers as a whole. The consumer suffers in all this, of course, because the price of the product concerned will have to be high enough to cover these selling costs; society as a whole suffers through the frittering-away in this way of productive resources which could be used to more useful purpose in the creation of wealth.

Not *all* advertisement can be condemned as being wasteful and socially undesirable, however. Selling techniques which are educative have a necessary role in a dynamic and developing world; they may inform the consumer of the existence of substitutes, new uses for commodities, or prices in different parts of the market, thus helping him to gain the maximum satisfaction from his limited income. Indeed, it is difficult to conceive of new products ever being successfully marketed if producers were unable to bring them to the notice of consumers, and stimulate their taste for them, through all the channels of modern salesmanship. In such circumstances, selling costs are just as necessary an element in total production costs as are those of labour or capital. But only a limited proportion of present-day advertisement is of this strictly informative kind; the greater part is clearly competitive — designed to capture business from rival producers through exploitation of the psychological susceptibilities of the consuming public, rather than through lower prices or higher quality.

The second type of waste and inefficiency incurred as a result of imperfect competition is less obvious to the public eye but probably of far greater absolute magnitude. This is the waste implicit in the existence of too many firms in each industry, all operating at less than their optimum output; the analysis has shown that this is an inevitable consequence of imperfect competition. Society as a whole is bound to suffer if production is carried on at an average cost higher than the minimum which is technically necessary. If the number of competing producers were reduced and the same output supplied by firms operating at optimum capacity, average production costs would be lowered, which means that resources would be set free to add further to the wealth of society. Wherever monopolistic elements exist, in the form of pure monopoly or of imperfect competition, costs of production will be above the minimum possible and society as a whole will be poorer than it need be.

Having said all this, two important qualifications must be made. The first point is that the important thing for consumer satisfaction is that consumers should have what they want, not what someone else (however benevolent and knowledgeable) thinks they *should* want. The ideal towards which society should try to work, from a purely technical point of view, may be that of a perfectly competitive world where producers, all operating at minimum average cost, supply identical products; it may be, however, that the majority of consumers prefer the sort of world in which any given product is supplied in a large number of brands, each having (or believed to have) its own special characteristics. It has to be remembered that the practice of branding products has a good deal to be said for it from a consumer's point of view. It is much *easier* to ask for a packet of X soap or a bar of Y's chocolate, and to be certain from experience of the exact nature of the product which will be obtained, than to choose from a large array of un-named varieties of an infinite range of quality and composition differing from shop to shop, which would be the closest approximation to perfect competition which society could ever hope to attain. It is convenient to be able to rely on paying the same price for any given brand wherever it is bought. Above all, the human race derives satisfaction from *variety* as such, and many people would sooner have a selection of Ford cars and Jaguar cars and Fiat cars and so on – and pay rather more for them – than be reduced to the drab uniformity of a cheaper People's Car for all. In other words, the costs of advertisement, and even of excess capacity, *may* be costs which consumers as a whole are prepared to pay in order to obtain the choice and variety associated with a world of imperfect competition. The words 'perfect' and 'imperfect' are used by economists in a purely technical sense to describe the degree of competition, not the world which emerges from it. It is by no means certain that most people would *like* a world of perfect competition even if they could have it.

But how much variety do people want, and how much are they willing to pay for it? Are they deliberately *made* to want variety through the slick techniques of modern salesmanship? Is the gain from branding really sufficient to justify the costs which it involves? These are questions which are hardly open to objective analysis; in the last resort the consumer must choose for himself, and the task of the economist is to indicate what is involved in the choice rather than to presume to make it.

There is a second qualification to any general condemnation of the wastefulness of imperfect competition. It will be recalled that in the previous chapter a warning was expressed against an uncritical acceptance of the view that price is necessarily higher in monopolistic conditions than it would be if perfect competition prevailed; the monopolist may be able to secure economies of scale which result in a lower price to the consumer than could be secured in any other way. A similar warning is applicable to the case of imperfect competition. In the real world it may be that, if economies of large-scale production are substantial, the entire needs of the market for a commodity can best be met by a relatively small number of firms each producing a large output. If an industry consisted of a great many small firms, so that something approaching perfect competition existed, none of the firms might be producing enough to obtain full economies of scale. The gains to the consumer from a higher degree of competition might thus be more than offset by his loss in having to pay a price sufficient to cover unnecessarily high costs of production. In a complicated world, therefore, it is unwise to conclude that a situation in which competition is imperfect is *ipso facto* undesirable from a social point of view.

FURTHER READING

E. MANSFIELD *Micro-economics* Chs. 10–11

J. HADAR *Elementary theory of economic behaviour* Ch. 8

A. M. LEVENSON and B. S. SOLON *Outline of price theory* Ch. 11

K. LANCASTER *Introduction to modern micro-economics* Ch. 6

CHAPTER XIV

The Price Mechanism

1 THE ALLOCATION OF RESOURCES

OCCASIONALLY men are encountered who have organised and managed enormous factories, employing perhaps ten thousand people, in the consistently successful production of some particular commodity. Such people are regarded as being of outstanding administrative ability, as indeed they are; it is an immensely difficult task to maintain an efficient co-ordination of thousands of different people making the various parts of a commodity at different speeds, different times and often different places. Every refrigerator, or motor-car, or television set that comes off the assembly lines of a modern factory is in itself a miracle of administrative as well as technical ability.

It is an extraordinary thing, then, that the vastly more complex economic system as a whole continues year after year to meet an infinite number of demands for an infinite number of commodities with the incredibly high degree of efficiency which has come to be accepted as commonplace. If the daily paper fails to appear through the letter-box one morning people are very surprised, whereas they are not in the least concerned when it *does* arrive as usual, although this is a much more astonishing event. Consider, for example, the co-ordination of effort which lies behind the simple fact of the delivery of a morning newspaper. Trees have been grown and felled in Canada or Scandinavia; they have been processed into woodpulp and transported across thousands of miles of sea; the pulp has been turned into newsprint in paper-mills; the news has been collected via an intricate network of national and international communications; type has been set up and the news printed with machinery manufactured in a hundred different engineering factories; road and rail services of great complexity have been used to bring the newspaper to the door of the consumer. And this is a highly simplified account of a process no more complicated than a hundred thousand others which continue, day after day, in order that when a person asks for marbles or beans or hairpins or razor blades or anything else in his local shop the goods he wants will in fact be there.

If organising the manufacture of a single commodity in a single factory is a respectable administrative feat, therefore, the intelligent co-ordination of an economy comprising, in the case of Britain, a working force of some 26 million people must involve a fantastic degree of organisational ability. Yet, in an economy such as that of the United Kingdom no single person acts as a co-ordinator and controller – which is just as well, since the task would be far beyond the range of human ability. But how can the economic system function without the perpetual chaos that would result, for example, if a single railway system tried to operate with no one in the signal box? The answer is that *price* does for the economic system exactly what the signalman does for the railway system. It is through the *price mechanism,* as it is called, that the co-ordination of activity in the whole economic system is achieved. The analytical system built up in the preceding chapters can throw a good deal of light on how this is done. It will be easiest if the process is first outlined within the framework of something approaching perfect competition; in the following section the picture will be modified to allow for some of the imperfections found in the real world.

The theory of demand indicates how the consumption of wealth is guided and influenced through the medium of price. The total consumption possible for each individual is determined, in the first place, by the operation of price. Each consumer has a certain income in the form of a specific sum of money becoming available to him every week, or every month, or every year. The price of a commodity is the amount of money which he has to hand over in order to obtain possession of it. The total volume of goods and services which he can consume is therefore determined for him; he can go on consuming until all his income has been spent. More important, the price mechanism allows him to distribute his expenditure amongst those goods and services which he believes will give him the maximum possible satisfaction. The earlier analysis has shown that by arranging his expenditure so that the marginal utility he derives from each commodity is everywhere in the same ratio to price, the consumer will obtain the greatest possible amount of satisfaction. From the consumption side, therefore, the price system limits the total amount which any individual can consume, but at the same time leaves him complete freedom of choice so far as the pattern of his expenditure is concerned. (Although, as was noted in the previous chapter, that choice may be influenced by advertisement and other techniques of sales promotion.)

The theory of production helps to explain how the preferences of consumers as between different commodities are transmitted to producers and thus influence the flow of the factors of production to each industry. Consumers will be willing to pay different prices for different quantities of a commodity; entrepreneurs can therefore estimate the marginal revenue to be derived from various levels of output. Given the technological conditions governing production and the prices of the various factors of production, entrepreneurs will be able to calculate marginal cost at various levels of output. Marginal revenue and marginal cost will together determine how much of each commodity will be produced by each entrepreneur. The analysis of Part V will show how the prices of the various factors of production are determined; these, taken in conjunction with the proportions in which the various factors are combined in each enterprise, determine the distribution of total income.

So the complete picture takes shape; total income, through the price system, determines total consumption; the structure of consumption and production is reflected in the pattern of relative prices, while total income is determined by the numbers of units of the various factors at work and by their respective prices. At every stage, price enters into the process as the expression of the outcome of the pressures of demand and supply in each sector. Every consumer and every producer exercises an individual choice in his use of resources, although in cases such as those discussed in the following section the government also intervenes. Through the price system the decisions of both consumers and producers are brought together in such a way that the factors of production are attracted into the uses in which they can best meet the needs of consumers.

2 OPTIMUM ALLOCATION

In the hypothetical world of perfect competition, which, fortunately or unfortunately, is far removed from the world of reality, the free operation of the price mechanism would not only coordinate all the infinite number of economic activities going on at any moment, but would do so in the ideal way. It will ultimately secure the *optimum* allocation of all economic resources – that is, guide all of the factors towards their most productive uses, and hence ensure that the maximum satisfaction is being obtained by society from the resources at its disposal.

It will be remembered that under conditions of perfect competition price will everywhere tend to equality with marginal cost and every producer will operate at his point of minimum average cost. The fact that average costs are everywhere at their lowest point means that every firm is operating at peak efficiency; there is no loss anywhere because of firms operating at too low an output (and leaving unexploited some potential economies of large-scale output) or at too high an output (and incurring diminishing returns).

Not only will each firm operate at its optimum output. For the economy as a whole, the equality of marginal cost and price will ensure that productive resources are distributed between commodities in exactly the right pattern. Price, it has been seen, reflects the extra satisfaction derived by consumers from the last unit of a commodity they consume; marginal cost measures the extent to which resources are used up by the last unit of a commodity produced. If the marginal cost of a commodity exceeded its price, society would be losing more in the form of resources used up than it would be gaining in the form of extra satisfaction, and the output of the commodity would therefore be too high; if the price exceeded marginal cost, society would be receiving more in the way of satisfaction than it would be losing through the loss of resources in the process of production, and output of the commodity would be too low. Total satisfaction will always be increased if resources are switched away from industries where the extra satisfaction to consumers by their output was less than their cost, and towards industries where the extra satisfaction provided by their output exceeded their cost. Such gains would continue until marginal cost was everywhere equal to price. Under perfect competition, then, all resources would be used in the best possible way and in the best possible use.

Does this mean that in the 'competitive', free-enterprise economies existing in the real world this ideal state of affairs is actually achieved? Unfortunately it does not, so that it is impossible to draw the dogmatic conclusion that if all economic activity were determined solely through the operation of free market forces – i.e. the price mechanism – all would be for the best in the best of all possible worlds. There are three main reasons for this.

First, and most obviously, perfect competition is seldom, if ever, attained in reality, since it postulates a great many conditions which it is impossible to attain in the world as it exists. Consequently, some degree of monopoly is to be found in almost all industries. The implication of this, of course, is that price and marginal revenue cease to be equal, and since entrepreneurs operate at that output where marginal cost equals marginal revenue (which is always less than price) the result will be that marginal cost will be lower than price in an imperfectly competitive world. *How much* marginal cost will be below price will depend on the slope of the firm's sales curve (i.e. on the degree of monopoly power it enjoys), but as long as it is below price at all, resources cannot be in their optimum use. The economic welfare of society will be smaller than it would be if output were expanded until price fell to equality with marginal cost. And, as was noted in the last chapter, other direct wastages – advertisement, etc. – will occur when competition is imperfect.

The second factor is the existence of gains or losses to society as a whole which individual consumers cannot, or will not, appreciate and which therefore fail to be expressed through price. For example, the maintenance of the Armed Forces could not be left to private enterprise because no individual can measure the value of such services to society as a whole; not all parents would be willing to pay for the education of their children, because not all of them would appreciate the value of education for their own children or for future generations of society; the provision of roads in isolated areas could not be left to private initiative, because they would seldom prove to be profitable in the monetary sense.

In recent years increasing attention has been paid to the *social costs* imposed by the production of many commodities – that is, costs involved in their production which do not have to be paid for by the enterprises involved in their manufacture, nor therefore their consumers in the form of a higher price. The most important of these arise in connection with the environmental damage inflicted by many productive processes – the pollution of the atmosphere, rivers and sea, the disfigurement of the countryside, the litter of virtually indestructible containers and so on. It cannot be doubted but that these by-products of production impoverish society, but since the firms in question do not normally have to pay for them they are not counted in their costs. Hence a gap appears between utility to the consumer and marginal cost for another reason – the true cost is being under-estimated. The output of such products (and there are a great many of them) is too high and their price too low.

Over a great many fields, then, social or political considerations may be important or even dominant, and it is generally agreed that in such cases the State has the right, and even the duty, to interfere in some way with the operation of free market forces. The State may work *through* the price mechanism, if it is believed that the true benefit accruing to society as a whole (including future generations) from the consumption of a commodity is not accurately measured by the price established by ordinary market forces. For example, it may impose a tax on a commodity whose consumption is considered undesirable for some reason (e.g. a tax on motor-cars to discourage their consumption at home and encourage their export); conversely, it may subsidise commodities which it wishes to see consumed on a bigger scale (e.g. milk). Occasionally it may prohibit altogether private production and exchange of a commodity, as in the case of drugs or poisons.

Finally, the allocation of resources achieved by perfect competition would be an optimum in the true sense only if the distribution of income prevailing in the economy was the optimum distribution. It will be remembered that even if every consumer of a commodity is willing to pay the same price for it, it still cannot be said that all consumers derive equal marginal utility from it. A rich man may be satisfied with a low marginal utility from a commodity because the sacrifice implied by its price is a small one to him; a poor man may derive a high marginal utility from the same commodity at the same price. The price mechanism will allocate resources in the way that is indicated by demand; it is conceivable that, in an economy where a few are rich and the majority are poor, resources could be drawn by the pressure of demand into the production of luxury yachts and private swimming-pools when (by any reasonable standards) they would have been better employed in clearing slums and equipping hospitals.

For all these reasons, then, there exists in most economies some degree of State intervention designed to correct the distortions introduced into economic activity by imperfections of competition or the maldistribution of income, or to make provision for needs of a social, strategic or political nature. How far such intervention should proceed is largely a question of personal judgement (expressed through the appropriate political machinery). Society as a whole must arrive at its own conclusions concerning, first, the relative efficiencies of private and public enterprise in the achievement of purely economic ends, and, secondly, the relative importance in the use of resources of economic and non-economic considerations. In almost every society it is widely accepted that only the State can effectively direct resources to the achievement of ends such as defence and law and order; in a few countries the State has assumed control of all economic activity to the exclusion of private enterprise. In most countries, the position is somewhere in between – i.e. they have 'mixed' economies, as they are called. The relative strength of private and public control in the mixture, of course, is a question for political decision, because ends rather than means are involved, and in such decisions the economist has the right to be heard as an ordinary citizen but no more.

3   CHANGES IN SUPPLY AND DEMAND

In view of the fact that most present-day economies are 'mixed', in the sense that resources are allocated partly by the decisions of private individuals and enterprises and partly by government intervention of one form or another, it is useful to consider the way in which adjustments occur in both the private and public sectors. This section will be concerned with the private sector – that is, with the adjustments carried out through the operation of a free market.

Assuming that the private sector is characterised by some degree of competition, suppose that an increase occurs in the supply of a commodity, as the result of an expansion in an industry or of some technical development enabling a greater output from existing capacity, without any corresponding change in the demand for the commodity. If the extra output is to be sold in the market, price will normally need to be reduced; the law of diminishing utility suggests that consumers derive a smaller marginal utility from a commodity as its total supply is increased so that they will be willing to buy extra units only if its price falls. If the increased output is due to expanded capacity rather than a reduction in costs, the fall in price will drive profits in the industry below the normal level; firms will move out of the industry, and both supply and price will gradually revert to their original level. Thus, in Fig. 14A(i) if with no change in technological conditions (i.e. an unchanged supply curve $S_1 S_1'$) output is raised from OM to OM', price will be driven down from MP to $M'P'$; at this price, the industry as a whole will be suffering losses equal to $P'QRS$, and under the pressure of these losses output will be driven back again to *OM*. If costs have been reduced through some technological improvement, however, the fall in price will continue until it becomes equal to the new (lower) level of average cost. When this point is reached, output will cease to expand and the market will rest in its new equilibrium position. This is shown in Fig. 14A(i) by the downward shift in the supply curve to S_2S_2'; if output remained constant, price would now be well in excess of average cost and abnormal profits would appear. Under the spur of this existing producers would increase their output, or new firms would be attracted into the industry until the new equilibrium output OM' was achieved and price settled at $M'P'$.

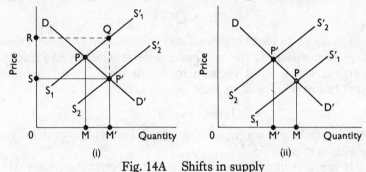

Fig. 14A   Shifts in supply

A numerical example may be helpful in the analysis of a situation of this kind. Suppose the weekly demand schedule for a product is defined by

$$Q_d = 100 - 5P$$

where Q_d is the quantity purchased at the price P in £s. This suggests that if price rose to £20 the demand would fall to zero while if price were, say, £15 the demand would amount to $100 - 75 = 25$ a week. Similarly, suppose the supply schedule is defined by

$$Q_s = 10P - 50$$

which suggests, in turn, that at prices below £5 supply is zero (negative supplies can be neglected as having no meaning in this context).

Equilibrium in the market implies that the quantity demanded at any price is equal to the quantity being supplied at that price – i.e. that

$$Q_d = Q_s$$

and, thus, $\qquad 100 - 5P = 10P - 50.$

Solving this equation for P gives a value of £10 and inserting this value for P into either the demand or the supply equation yields a value of 50 for equilibrium weekly output.

Suppose now that, with unchanged demand conditions, technological change transforms the supply schedule into

$$Q_s = 7P - 8$$

which suggests that both fixed and variable costs of production have been reduced: the minimum price at which production is worthwhile has been reduced to a little over £1.14. The new equilibrium price will be given by

$$100 - 5P = 7P - 8$$

which yields an equilibrium price of £9 and an equilibrium weekly output of 55.

If supply contracts for any reason, the opposite sequence will occur. The commodity will have become scarcer in relation to others and consumers, warned of this by the rise in its market price, will be encouraged to reduce their consumption of it. If the scarcity is due to some fundamental technical change (i.e. a rise in the cost of production) price will continue to rise until it equals the increased average cost, and output will contract until this point is reached. Thus, in Fig. 14A(ii) the supply curve shifts upwards to $S_2S_2{}'$, so that for any output in excess of OM' average cost is above price and losses will be experienced in the industry until output is driven back to that point and market price is forced up from MP to $M'P'$. If costs have not risen, on the other hand, producers will be encouraged to enter the industry by the rise of price above average cost and the consequent emergence of excess profits. As new firms come in, price will be driven down again to its original level and the previous equilibrium will be restored.

In this process of adjustment to changed conditions of supply, two points are worthy of note. First, the analysis assumed some degree of competition – perfect or otherwise – so that it was taken that firms could enter or leave an industry in response to changed profit-levels. If no competition existed, however, adjustment could only take the form of changes in a monopolist's price and output; in general, the movement of price and output in response to any given change in supply conditions under monopoly can be expected to be smaller than if some degree of competition exists. Secondly, the process of adjustment, if allowed to operate freely, will ensure that if variations of efficiency exist amongst producers, the relatively inefficient entrepreneur will be driven out first in any movement of contraction and brought in last in an expansion. If prices fall relatively to costs, profits will turn into losses first of all amongst producers whose costs are relatively high, so that the pressure on such producers to leave the industry will be especially great. Conversely, if prices rise in relation to costs, the super-normal profits will be smallest for relatively inefficient entrepreneurs, and the incentive to expand output or to enter an industry will be comparatively weak.

With changes in demand, the sequence is similar. A rise in demand will force up prices in the short run, causing profits to increase in the industry concerned. This will indicate to producers that the commodity involved is now wanted with a greater intensity than before; existing producers will expand output under the spur of higher rates of profit, while new firms will be attracted into the industry by the same cause. If consumers' total expenditure is unchanged throughout, this increase in demand for one commodity will be paralleled by a decline in the demand for other commodities; if consumers spend more out of a fixed total on one thing, then they must spend less on others. In some other industry or industries, therefore, a precisely opposite process will be occurring; demand, prices and profits will have fallen, and producers will be using up less resources for the production of their commodities, setting those resources free for the expansion in the industry faced with an increased demand.

In the long run the consequences of the shift in demand are less clear-cut: a good deal will turn on the long-run cost conditions prevailing in the industry. The three possibilities are shown in Fig. 14B. In Fig. 14B(i) is shown the case of the constant-cost industry. The short-run increase in price from OP_1 to OP_2 stimulated by the shift in demand from D_1D_1' to D_2D_2' induces an expansion in the capacity of the industry illustrated by the shift in the supply curve from S_1S_1' to S_2S_2'; in the new equilibrium, market output will have risen to OM_3 but price (i.e. long-run average cost) will have reverted to its initial level.

Fig. 14B(ii) illustrates the situation in an industry subject

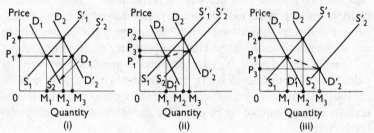

Fig. 14B   Shifts in demand

to increasing costs – i.e. where the expansion of the industry is associated with net external diseconomies of scale. The short-run increase of price and output to OP_2 and OM_2 is the same as before; the shift to the new short-run supply curve S_2S_2', however, results in somewhat higher average costs so that the final equilibrium price OP_3, while less than the short-run price OP_2, is higher than in the constant-costs case.

The final possibility is of course illustrated in Fig. 14B(iii); here the analysis deals with an industry experiencing decreasing average costs due to net external economies as expansion proceeds. The short-run price OP_2 falls back as capacity expands from S_1S_1' to S_2S_2', not only to the initial level OP_1 but to the new, lower level OP_3. Clearly, then, the long-run impact of a shift in demand is critically dependent on the long-run cost conditions prevailing in the industry concerned.

An important aspect of the adjustment of the economic system to changes in demand and supply is the role played by elasticity in allocating the burden of the adjustment process between price, on the one hand, and output on the other. Generally, the smaller the elasticity of supply in comparison with that of the demand for the product, the greater will be the impact of any given shift in demand on market price, and the smaller the corresponding adjustment in the quantity sold; conversely, a similar shift when demand is inelastic in comparison with supply will have a relatively large effect on the volume of sales and a small effect on price. Fig. 14C provides examples of this. In Fig. 14C(i) demand is relatively elastic and supply inelastic; hence the drop in demand, shown by the shift of the demand curve from D_1D_1' to D_2D_2' reduces output and consumption relatively little – from OM to OM' – but price falls significantly, from OP to OP'. In Fig. 14C(ii) the opposite situation is portrayed – demand is inelastic in comparison with supply – and a similar shift in demand has little effect on price but the change in sales – from OM and OM' – is considerable. The difference in the adjustment process is best exemplified in the real world by a comparison between the effects on price of shifts in the demand for manufactured goods, on the one hand, and primary products – i.e. agricultural and mining products – on the other. For physical reasons the output of primary products is not easily adjusted, nor can they always be stored if it is desired to hold back current production from the market. Hence their supply tends to be

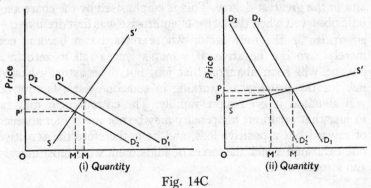

Fig. 14C

highly inelastic, even in comparison with a demand which is often inelastic also; as a result, their prices tend to be unstable and subject to wide fluctuations from time to time. Changes in the demand for manufactures, on the other hand, usually have a much smaller effect on their prices; supply being relatively elastic, it is able to respond fairly quickly to changes in demand and so moderate the movement of market prices.

Through shifts in demand and supply, then, the economic system is constantly adjusting itself to changes in the relative scarcity of different commodities, changes which can occur through alterations in either the supply conditions of a commodity or the strength of the public's desire for it. It will have been noticed that a crucial role in the adjustment process is played by profits. It is because of a rise or fall in the rate of profit that plans are put into operation for the increase or reduction of output. The rewards of other factors of production (labour, land, etc.) are also liable to fluctuate in response to changes in demand, encouraging those factors to move out of uses for which they are wanted less urgently than before and into uses where supply is unduly small and more factors of production are required. But since it is the entrepreneur who performs the function of engaging and organising the other factors, it is through *profits* that the impulses arising from changed demand or supply conditions are first transmitted. In the modern world where wages, rent and interest commitments are not easily varied (for reasons discussed at a later stage), a change in price affects profits first and in the greatest degree. This is emphasised by the characteristic observed when the factor of enterprise was first discussed – enterprise is the only factor whose reward can become not merely zero but negative. If a man's wages fall to zero in a job, he will soon abandon that job, but if he actually has to pay for the privilege of working in someone else's factory he will abandon it even more rapidly. The entrepreneur may be in just that position; his penalty may be not merely an absence of reward but a positive loss, and he is therefore the sensitive point through which the forces of adjustment work most quickly and strongly.

4 TAXATION AND RATIONING

The methods by which the State can influence the use of economic resources are difficult to describe briefly precisely because they are numerous and may be based on considerations outside the range of purely economic reasoning. In its use of resources which it employs directly, for example – in the Civil Service or Armed Forces – the State is not impelled by the motive of maximising economic gain, which is the motive force economic analysis has to assume at work in privately-owned enterprises. It is motivated by concern for the social welfare of the people, or for the safety of the country, or even in some cases by the aim of maintaining or increasing its physical power over its citizens. Motives of this sort cannot be handled by economic analysis; the economist can simply say that resources used for such purposes are lost to the direct creation of wealth, and that the responsibility of the government is to try to balance out (by some criteria) the gain accruing in social and political welfare and any loss suffered in economic welfare.

Much the same is true of other means by which the State intervenes in normal economic activity in the pursuit of political ends. Tariffs may be imposed on imports, for example, in order to protect an industry (such as agriculture) the prosperity of which is considered essential on strategic or social grounds. The State may control the use of raw materials or labour in order to favour defence production, exports, or the development of particular regions. Here again the problem is one of having to balance a political or social gain against an economic loss, and such questions are ultimately matters for individual human judgement rather than scientific analysis of the kind which economists seek to employ.

A more extensive form of government intervention, however (at least in peace-time), is the manipulation of market prices through internal taxation or subsidies, and, to a much lesser extent, the control of demand through rationing. In the former case the effects (although not, of course, the motives) are amenable to economic analysis because the adjustment occurs through the medium of the market price. The imposition of a tax can be treated as an increase in costs of production, while a subsidy can be treated as a reduction in the cost of production. As was established at an early stage, the total revenue brought in by a tax on a commodity (and, conversely, the total amount expended in the form of subsidy payments) will vary with the elasticity of demand for the product. With taxation, the consumption of a commodity will be much affected by the imposition of a tax if its demand over the relevant price range is comparatively elastic, and the revenue brought in will be small; the output and consumption of a commodity with an inelastic demand will be little affected by an indirect tax, and the total tax revenue will be relatively large. The effects of a subsidy are similar so far as consumption and output are concerned, being greater the more elastic the demand; it follows that total subsidy payments will be larger the more elastic is demand.

Will the price of a commodity change to the same extent as a change in the tax or subsidy associated with it ? This depends on two sets of forces. On the demand side, the elasticity of demand, and hence the slope of the marginal revenue curve, will determine the extent to which output will fall (and price rise) as the result of the imposition of a tax; the price must rise until marginal revenue and the new level of marginal cost are again brought into equality. In general, the more elastic the demand for a product, the less will price increase (and the more output will fall) as the result of an indirect tax. There are two limiting cases; where elasticity of demand is zero, the full tax will be added on to price and output will be unaffected and the tax will be borne wholly by the producer, while if demand elasticity is infinite output will be reduced to zero (although such a combination of events is obviously inconceivable in the real world).

Secondly, the effects of a tax on price will depend on the conditions of supply. If a commodity is produced under conditions of increasing costs, the long-run increase in price caused by the tax will be offset to some extent by the lower costs of production as output falls. Conversely, if decreasing costs prevail, price will tend to rise by more than the tax, since average costs of production will increase with falling output. The effects of a subsidy can be analysed in a similar way, because a subsidy is merely a negative tax.

An illustration is provided by Fig. 14D. Here a tax, RT, is levied on every unit of the product sold. The supply curve is therefore shifted bodily up by the same amount, from SS' to S_1S_1', output falls from OM to OM' and price rises from OP to OP'. This increase in price, however ($PP' = RS$) is smaller than the tax levied; the difference, ST, is in effect absorbed into the lower average cost at which output is now produced. Generalising all this, it can in fact be shown that the part of

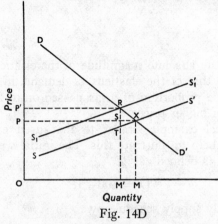

Fig. 14D

an indirect tax passed on in the form of a higher price will bear the same relationship to the remainder of the tax as does the absolute magnitude of the elasticity of supply to that of the elasticity of demand at the point concerned. In terms of Fig. 14D, in other words, RS/ST is equal to the elasticity of supply at X divided by the elasticity of demand at X.

This is not too difficult to prove. The ratio of the increase in the price to the consumer (RS) to the reduction in the return to the producer (ST) is obviously RS/ST. Now considering the original price, P, the elasticity of demand ($\Delta Q/Q \div \Delta P/P$) is given by $SX/OM \div RS/XM$; that is,

$$e_d = \frac{SX}{OM} \cdot \frac{XM}{RS}$$

and
$$RS = \frac{SX \cdot XM}{OM} \cdot \frac{1}{e_d} .$$

Similarly, elasticity of supply at price P was given by

$$e_s = \frac{SX}{OM} \cdot \frac{XM}{ST}$$

and
$$ST = \frac{SX \cdot XM}{OM} \cdot \frac{1}{e_s} .$$

Hence
$$RS/ST = \frac{1}{e_d} \Big/ \frac{1}{e_s}$$

$$= e_s/e_d .$$

The greater the absolute magnitude of the elasticity of supply in relation to that of the elasticity of demand, in other words, the greater the proportion of a tax passed on to the consumer in the form of higher prices.

A numerical example similar to that used earlier in this chapter may help to illustrate this. The initial weekly demand for a product is defined as

$$Q_d = 100 - 5P$$

and the weekly supply schedule by

$$Q_s = 11P - 60 .$$

The initial equilibrium price can thus be calculated to be £10 and weekly output 50.

Suppose that a Value Added Tax of 10 per cent is now levied on the product: if the price charged to the consumer is again denoted by P then the price received by the supplier must be $P/1 \cdot 10$ – that is, a supplier's price of £10 becomes a market price of £11 after the imposition of tax. Hence market equilibrium is defined by

$$Q_d = Q_s$$

i.e.
$$100 - 5P = 11\left(\frac{P}{1 \cdot 10}\right) - 60$$

so that market price becomes about £10·67 and weekly sales fall to about 47. The seller's price must therefore be £9·70 on which a tax of £0·97 is paid: of this £0·67 is passed on in the form of a higher price and £0·30 is the reduction in the seller's price in comparison with the initial situation.

Consider now the demand and supply elasticities. A rise of £0·67 has caused a fall of 3 in weekly purchases: elasticity of demand (at the initial price of £10) was thus

$$\frac{-3}{0·67} \cdot \frac{10}{50} = -0·9 \text{ (approximately)}.$$

Similarly, a fall of £0·30 in the seller's price has caused a fall of 3 in weekly output, so that elasticity of supply is

$$\frac{-3}{-0·30} \cdot \frac{10}{50} = 2.$$

The ratio of the magnitudes of these elasticities (2 : 0·9) is equal to the distribution of the tax between buyer and seller (0·67 : 0·30).

Taxation, positive or negative, is a means whereby production and consumption are influenced through price. Rationing is an attempt to achieve a similar end by regulating the demand at any given price. If a commodity is in short supply (as it usually will be if rationing is considered necessary) the supply curve will have shifted to the left, and price would normally be driven up. The effect of rationing is to cause a similar shift to the left of the demand curve, preventing or moderating the rise in prices. In this way the shortage does not result in the relatively poor members of the community being pushed out of the market by the relatively rich, as might happen if the forces of demand and supply were allowed to work unchecked. In wartime conditions, when the commodities in short supply may be essential to the health and strength of the community, it may be expedient to share out the shortage, so to speak, through rationing in order to ensure that everyone, and not just the fortunate members of society who can afford high prices, obtains an amount necessary for his or her health.

The situation is shown in a simplified way in Fig. 14E. For

some reason the supply schedule of the product concerned has shifted back from $S_1S'_1$ to $S_2S'_2$; the natural result of this would be a rise in market price from OP_1 to OP_2. If the government wished to prevent this price increase, ration coupons or licenses could be issued – without which the purchase of the commodity would be illegal – to the total amount of OQ_3 shown by the vertical line Q_3R. This intersects the new supply schedule $S_2S'_2$ at a point such that the quantity OQ_3 will be forthcoming at the old price OP_1.

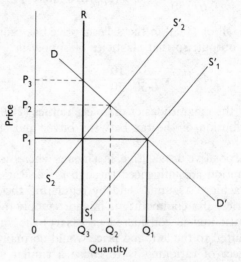

Fig. 14E   The rationing situation

In normal times, however, rationing has several disadvantages. One is that a substantial amount of labour and other resources may be required for its administration – including the prevention of 'black market' prices rising to the level OP_3 in Fig. 14E – and such resources would probably add more to the wealth of society if they were employed in productive uses. Secondly, by arbitrarily limiting the consumption of everyone, the principle of maximising satisfaction through free choice is contravened. I might prefer more bacon and less sugar than the rationing system allows me, while another person might prefer less bacon and more sugar. Given a free choice each consumer would spend his money appropriately and get the most satisfaction out of his limited income. If rationing is imposed, consumers are prevented from achieving their optimum patterns of consumption, unless they indulge in the (usually) illegal and inefficient process of bartering or selling ration coupons. Thirdly, by preventing a shortage from having its normal effect of a rise in price, rationing impedes the normal forces of adjustment – high profits, stimulating higher output and new entrants to the industry. It will be noted in Fig. 14E that the imposition of rationing and price control has had the effect of choking off output Q_3Q_2 which the 'natural' price increase would have stimulated. In special situations (such as wartime or other crisis periods) this process of adjustment may be impossible, or able to work only very slowly, so that a rise in price would not serve this useful purpose. In normal times, however, this consideration is an important one which is not lightly disregarded. Unless it is unavoidable, measures to deal with a shortage should not have the effect of preventing its disappearance.

In the light of the analysis of consumer behaviour, then, it can be concluded that if a government seeks to protect or favour a particular section of the community, it is generally better to do so through an adjustment to the *incomes* of the section concerned; interference with the *price* of a commodity has the effect of dispersing the benefit or burden indiscriminately amongst all consumers, and of compromising the exercise of free choice. This is not to say that in particular cases the influencing of market prices cannot be justified; for example, the government may wish to increase the consumption of milk by children, or discourage the consumption of harmful commodities, and direct intervention in the market for those particular commodities may be necessary to attain this end. Each case has to be considered on its own particular merits. But it will usually be found that the use of indirect taxation – i.e. the taxation of particular commodities – has to be justified on the grounds that if the government raised *all* the revenue required through direct taxation (i.e. taxes on persons or enterprises, rather than commodities) there would be a possibility of serious ill-effects on incentives.

FURTHER READING

E. MANSFIELD *Micro-economics* Ch. 15
J. HADAR *Elementary theory of consumer behaviour* Ch. 14
K. LANCASTER *Introduction to modern micro-economics* Chs. 9–10
D. M. WINCH *Analytical welfare economics* Penguin Books, London 1971, Chs. 1–7

PART V

THE THEORY OF INCOME DISTRIBUTION

CHAPTER XV

Wages

1 THE CONCEPT OF MARGINAL PRODUCTIVITY

So far the analysis has been concerned with the forces which determine the price or value of different commodities. Now it is necessary to turn to the question of the way in which the value of the output of enterprises producing these commodities is shared out between the various factors of production which are involved in that output. It has been noted earlier that the total proceeds from the sale of commodities are used to pay the wages (using this term to include salaries) of labour, the rent of land, and interest on capital; whatever is left after these costs have been met constitutes the reward for the factor of enterprise – i.e. profits. In what way are these various shares determined? It will be convenient to leave the discussion of interest on one side for the moment, since it is a purely monetary phenomenon and can be fully understood only after the examination of the monetary system in Part VI.

The previous analysis has shown that supply and demand together determine the prices of goods; similarly, they determine the prices paid for productive inputs – i.e. wages, rent, interest and profits – and the same type of analysis can be used to explain the way in which this occurs. The consumer, in maximising his welfare, seeks to bring the relative marginal utilities of all the products available to him into the same ratio as their relative prices. The outcome depends on demand, based on the desire of consumers for a product, and supply, based on the cost of producing it.

In principle, exactly the same is true of productive inputs used by entrepreneurs assumed to be seeking to maximise profit. Their demand is based on the benefit entrepreneurs believe they can derive from the use of those inputs in the productive process — benefit expressed in terms of additional revenue or profit rather than utility. Their supply is dependent on the costs necessary to bring forth the necessary quantities on to the market. In a competitive market, the interplay of demand and supply tends to bring the price of any product into equality with its marginal utility; similarly, in a competitive market the interplay of demand and supply tends to bring the price of a productive input into equality with its marginal productivity.

Three warnings need to be sounded immediately in connection with even this most general statement. First, just as the marginal utility of a commodity to a consumer may prove to be different from what it was expected to be, so the marginal productivity of an input is frequently known only within a wide range of error. The statement of general principles of behaviour should under no circumstances be taken to imply precision and certainty in reality. Secondly, the equality of price and marginal revenue can be postulated only in the special limiting case of perfect competition; similarly, in the real world of monopolistic elements the relationship between price and marginal productivity must inevitably be qualified and complicated. Finally, just as the analysis of the consumer maximising utility ignores irrational and non-economic forces operating in the real world, so the concept of an entrepreneur carefully balancing marginal productivity against cost is an over-simplification. If anything, non-economic influences are more prominent in the markets for factors of production than in the markets for commodities. The marginal productivity analysis, in other words, provides a very general framework for describing the forces at work in factor-price determination but certainly not a precise and detailed map of reality.

2   THE DEMAND FOR LABOUR

Having stated the marginal productivity concept in general terms, it is now necessary to examine the determination of the prices of individual inputs. It is convenient to begin with the input known as labour and its price, wages, if for no other reason than that wages constitute the most important single form of income in a modern community; in 1974, income from employment accounted for something over 67 per cent of the gross national product of the United Kingdom.

Labour must be regarded, of course, as a very special agent in production, since (unlike land and capital) it is inseparable from the personality of its supplier. No producer employs labour in his factory or office; he employs men and women. Although people sometimes speak of 'hands' in an enterprise, human beings are a good deal more than mere hands. When land or capital are left unused, for example, there is merely waste; but when men and women are unemployed there is more than just waste involved – there are all the moral and social evils associated with unemployment. Although economists must for many purposes treat human labour as merely one of several factors contributing to production, it is important to remember that men cannot be regarded as a special kind of machine to be put to work and nothing more. The concentration on the productive activities of human beings, which is called labour, should not be taken to imply a belief that this is the only aspect of human economic activity with which the economist need be concerned. It is equally important to remember that wages are more than simply an element in cost, or the price of a factor; they are also the main form of income for the great majority of the population. As a result, many macro-economic considerations apply to the general level of money wages and these are left over until Part VII below. For the moment the discussion will be confined to the basic economic influences bearing on the price of labour relative to that of other productive inputs – and even then it has to be again emphasised that the conclusions established by formal economic analysis will have to be modified subsequently in order to take account of the social and political factors which play an important part in the real world.

What then constitutes the demand curve for labour? In the case of commodities it was possible to relate the quantity purchased to the utility derived by consumers from the commodity concerned. The people who purchase labour, however – i.e. the entrepreneurs who pay for the services of workers in their enterprises – derive no direct utility from the labour with which they are supplied. Labour is wanted by them not for itself but for its contribution to the production of the goods they are supplying. The utility of a unit of labour to the entrepreneur is represented by the value of the output which that labour can produce. If a certain man can produce in, say, a week's work goods from the sale of which the entrepreneur will receive revenues greater than the wages he has to pay out (after meeting any variable other costs involved) then that man's labour will be purchased; on the other hand, if the man cannot add as much to the value of output as he has to be paid in wages, then the entrepreneur will not find it worth his while to employ him.

The analysis of the demand for labour can be conducted with the aid of the techniques already used to examine the demand for and supply of commodities. Let QQ' in Fig. 15A(i) represent the isoquant along which a particular entrepreneur is operating at a given level of production; here it is more convenient to think of this curve as recording a given output in terms of its market *value* rather than its physical quantity. Assuming for the sake of simplicity that capital and labour are the only variable factors of production, the relative price of labour – i.e. its current wage-rate in relation to the current cost of capital – is shown by the price line P_1A_1, and at this level of wages the entrepreneur will employ a quantity OL_1 of labour. Now, if the wage-rate falls, all other things remaining equal, so that the price line moves over to P_2A_2, the amount of labour employed will rise to OL_2; similarly, it will rise to OL_3 if the wage-rate falls further and the price line moves to P_3A_3. (The analogy with the settler of Chapter II purchasing different types of fencing material is obvious.) By simple aggregation, it is now possible to derive the demand curve for labour by the industry as a whole, such as DD' in Fig. 15A(ii), relating the number employed to the level of wages. In effect, this is a curve of the *marginal revenue product* of labour, since an additional unit of labour will be employed only if the addition it makes to the market value of output – the value of its marginal productivity – is sufficient to cover its wage-cost. If wages were *below* marginal revenue product, on the other hand, entrepreneurs would compete for labour at any given wage-rate (since each unit would add more to revenue than to cost); as a result, the demand curve would shift upwards until marginal revenue product was brought into equality with the wage-rate.

In Fig. 15A(ii) the demand curve for labour is shown as sloping downwards from left to right. Why is this? The answer lies partly in the law of diminishing returns. The curve (like all demand curves) is drawn on the assumption that other things remain equal; in this case it is assumed that the amounts of the other factors employed in the industry are unchanged, as well

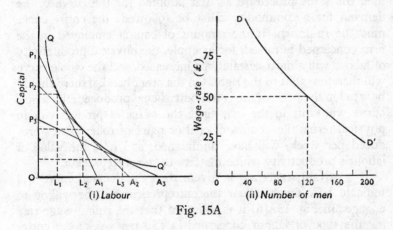

Fig. 15A

as the state of demand for the product, and of technological knowledge. It has been seen that if increasing amounts of a factor (of constant quality) are applied to a constant amount of another factor, or group of factors, the extra physical product resulting must progressively diminish. Hence the curve of the marginal *physical* product of labour will be falling as the amount of labour employed increases (although it may first of all rise to a maximum point in the early stages, of course).

A second reason for the downward slope of the labour productivity curve is that for the industry as a whole (and for the individual entrepreneur if competition is imperfect) the addition to total revenue derived from each unit of output will decline as output rises, because the price of the commodity will need to be reduced if an increased output is to be sold. The *marginal revenue* derived from each unit of output after the first, as was shown in Part IV, is bound to be less than price and is also bound to fall as output expands. What matters to entrepreneurs, of course, is not the *price* at which labour's product is sold but the *additional revenue* which it brings in. Labour will be employed only if its wage does not exceed this latter amount, which progressively diminishes as more labour is employed even if the physical productivity of labour is constant.

If the assumption of other things being equal is removed, then the same procedure as that adopted for the curve of the demand for a commodity must be followed: the entire curve must be re-drawn. If the amount of capital employed in the firm concerned is raised, for example, the physical productivity of labour will almost certainly be increased, and the whole curve will therefore shift to the right. On the other hand, if there should be a fall in the price of the commodity being produced, the whole curve will shift to the left, since the *value* of productivity in physical terms (i.e. tonnes of coal or pairs of roller skates produced per week) will have diminished, and it is the value of labour's productivity which matters to the entrepreneur.

If a certain wage-rate is given, then the demand curve will indicate how much labour the entrepreneur will be willing to engage. In Fig. 15A(ii) it is assumed that the ruling wage-rate for the type of labour concerned is £50 per week; the entrepreneur, of course, will have to pay *all* units of labour at the same rate, whatever their marginal productivity, just as a consumer obtains all units of a commodity at the current market price, whatever the level of marginal utility he derives from them. The curve shows that at this wage-level, 120 men will be employed. If entrepreneurs employed fewer than this, they would not be maximising their profit, because each man engaged is still adding more to the value of output than entrepreneurs would need to pay him in wages; if entrepreneurs employed more than 120 they would again fail to maximise profits, since they would be paying every man after the 120th more in wages than he was adding to the value of total output.

3   THE SUPPLY OF LABOUR: POPULATION

The nature of the demand for labour being understood, it is now necessary to consider the forces governing supply. Of necessity the discussion here must be much more discursive, since the expression 'supply of labour' covers two rather different concepts. First, it may refer to the *potential* supply of labour and thus be concerned with the size of the total population of a country and its geographical and occupational distribution. Secondly, it may refer to the *actual* supply of labour and be concerned with the number of units of labour (man-hours or man-weeks) which any given group of people are in fact willing to offer employers at different levels of wages or salaries.

To begin at the beginning, what determines the total size of the population of any country at any time?

If a nineteenth-century economist had been asked this question his answer would probably have been influenced by the arguments put forward with great force in 1798 by an English clergyman, Thomas Robert Malthus. The essence of these arguments was that population tends to expand to – and beyond – the limits imposed by the means of subsistence available, so that positive checks on population growth such as wars and disease were necessary (unless people themselves corrected this tendency for population to expand with undue rapidity) to confine the numbers of humanity within the limits imposed by the available food supply. Implicit in this argument was the belief that a rise in the standard of living would stimulate an increase in the size of the total population, while a fall would have the reverse effect.

History has shown that this distinctly pessimistic view of the economic destiny of the human race is not well founded. Britain, for example, has a population at the present time which is roughly five times as big as it was at the time when Malthus wrote; yet that vastly increased population is living at a much higher standard of subsistence than was the common lot in 1800. The reason is that Britain has been able to obtain supplies of food from countries all over the world which were little more than undeveloped colonies – and certainly not major food exporters – when Malthus was considering the problem of feeding Britain's population. Not only have new lands been exploited; agricultural methods and equipment have undergone tremendous development in the past century and these have raised agricultural productivity to levels which would have seemed inconceivable to earlier generations. At the same time, a tendency has emerged for people to have smaller rather than larger families as their standard of living rises (largely because the burden of raising children rises with it).

Does this experience mean that from an economic point of view society can be indifferent to the possibility of over-population? This would be far from the truth; economists conceive of an *optimum* population – that population which, given the amounts of land, capital and enterprise available to a community, is such as to maximise output per head in that community. So long as the average output per head is rising as population increases, then the community is *under*-populated; if average output falls when population increases, the country is *over*-populated. The optimum cannot be thought of as some absolute number; it is closely related to the available supplies of the other factors of production and will change from time to time as the effective supply of the other factors changes.

Bearing in mind these considerations, it is clear that vast areas of the globe – especially in India and China, but perhaps also in certain parts of Eastern and Western Europe – are over-populated, in this sense that average output would rise if the amount of other factors was raised in relation to the amount of labour. This could be done, *either* by reducing the size of the population, holding the supply of other factors constant, *or* by increasing the amounts of the other factors which are combined with the existing labour force.

In some countries, on the other hand, fears have been expressed that a very different prospect is faced – i.e. that of a declining population – and this has caused serious concern. Why is this? Surely a smaller population would mean that there would be more wealth available, and therefore a higher standard of life, for each individual? Unfortunately the matter is not as simple as that. A declining population gives rise to a number of difficulties. The first, and most obvious, is that a fall in the size of the population will raise average output per head only if the country was over-populated (in this economic sense) in the first place, which is by no means always certain. Secondly, a falling population implies an increase in the average age of the community; since the birth-rate is lower than the death-rate, the older age-groups tend to become a relatively larger element in the population. This ageing can have serious effects. Since older people are generally less adaptable than the young, the economy may become less able to absorb the constant change and adjustment involved in technological development. Further, mobility of labour is likely to decrease; shifts of labour from a declining to a growing industry are effected mainly through a cessation of recruitment to the one and increased recruitment to the other, and this process will inevitably be hampered if the number of young people entering employment is diminishing.

A third disadvantage of a declining population is that the smaller size of the market and of the labour supply may result in the loss of the gains which, as was mentioned earlier, normally arise from large-scale production. (The rapid economic development in Britain during the eighteenth and nineteenth centuries was only made possible by the rise in the country's population.) Fourthly, a population in which the 'active' age-groups (i.e. people of working age) were becoming proportionately less important, and the retired or dependent section becoming more important, would be faced with a serious burden of welfare services. The provision of pensions, health services, homes for the aged and so on ultimately depends on the productive capacity of the employed population. If the number of old people was increasing while the size of the occupied population was diminishing, greater demands would be falling on the output of a smaller number of producers. Certainly the burden of taxation to finance these social services would bear increasingly on the active members of the community, and this might seriously discourage them in their efforts.

For all these reasons a declining population could be a matter for some concern, but this is certainly not to say that it could not also bring important advantages. If the population was initially in excess of the optimum for the country concerned, naturally the wealth available per head would increase if population fell. In a country like Britain, where a large population is crowded into a relatively small area, a reduction of numbers would provide an opportunity for removing over-crowding of houses, towns, schools and the countryside as a whole. It might also help Britain's foreign trade position, since a smaller demand for food and raw materials (which Britain imports from other countries on a large scale) could be wholly reflected in a reduction of imports, home output being unchanged. In this way the proportionate reduction in imports might be much greater than that in the population. For example, consumers in the United Kingdom spend at the present time something of the order of £8 500 million a year on food, of which roughly £3 000 million is imported. If the demand for food fell by 20 per cent, so that total requirements fell to £6 800 million a year, but home food production was unchanged, Britain's import needs would fall to £1 300 million a year. A fall of 20 per cent in the demand for food would therefore cause a fall of about 60 per cent in import needs.

In all this discussion, of course, only the economic aspects have been touched on. Population changes have significance from the strategic, environmental and political points of view; since 'population' means human beings, the subject also has fundamental moral and social aspects. In discussing these matters the economist can claim no special authority or knowledge, but obviously these considerations must not be overlooked.

4   THE POPULATION OF THE UNITED KINGDOM

It will be instructive now to examine briefly the characteristics of the British population. The trend of the total population of the United Kingdom in the past century may be seen from Table 15·1. Between 1851 and 1911, the total rose rapidly – its decennial increase averaged between 11 and 14 per cent (i.e. 1·1 to 1·4 per cent per annum). After 1911, however, the rate of growth showed a marked decline to a decennial average of somewhat less than 5 per cent, and in the past twenty years it has remained constant at about this level. The main factors at work in this rapid increase in the second half of the nineteenth century and the slower increase in the first half of the present century have been the birth- and death-rates; on balance the net movement of people into and out of the United Kingdom reduced its population by about 4 million during the period 1871–1931, while during 1931–61 there was a net inflow of only around 20 000 people immigrating into the United Kingdom. The death-rate has continuously declined (from an annual rate of 22 per 1 000 total population at the beginning of the 1870s to about 12.0 per 1 00 at the present time) although its decline in recent years has been less rapid than in the nineteenth century, contributing to a minor degree to the recent slowing down of the

TABLE 15·1   *Population of the UK, 1851–1971*
(millions)

1851	22·3	1931	46·0
1871	27·4	1951	50·2
1891	34·3	1961	52·7
1911	42·1	1971	55·5

Source: *Annual Abstract of Statistics, 1974* (HMSO, London, 1974), Table 6.

expansion in total population. The decline in the birth-rate has been of much greater influence – it fell from 35 per 1 000 in the early 1870s to a little over 16 per 1 000 in the early 1930s, and in recent years has been running at about the same figure.

The probable future trend of population in the United Kingdom is a matter of some dispute. If the birth- and death-rates continue at their present level, then the population would continue to grow at about 5–6 per cent every ten years. A Royal Commission on population reporting in 1949 estimated that the population of Great Britain would be somewhere in the range of 41–57 million by the end of the present century, according to which assumptions were made concerning future movements in birth- and death-rates. Recent population experience, however, has led to drastic revisions in these forecasts. The official British demographers are now inclined to believe that the population of the United Kingdom will grow steadily to a total of about 66 million by the end of the present century.

The change in the *age and sex structure* of the British population during the present century may be seen from Table 15.2.

TABLE 15.2   *Age and sex structure of the population of the United Kingdom, 1901–71*

	1901		1971	
Age-group (years)	*000s*	*% of total*	*000s*	*% of total*
0–14	12 422	32·5	13 388	24·1
15–29	10 808	28·3	11 679	21·0
30–44	7 492	19·6	9 759	17·6
45–59	4 639	12·1	10 177	18·3
60–74	2 345	6·1	7 918	14·3
75 +	531	1·4	2 594	4·7
Total	38 237	100·0	55 515	100·0
Of which Males	18 492	48·4	26 952	48·5
Females	19 745	51·6	28 563	51·5

Source: *Annual Abstract of Statistics, 1962,* Tables 6–8, *Annual Abstract of Statistics, 1974,* Table 8

It will be noted that there are more females than males in the British population, and the numerical superiority of the former has persisted throughout the present century, despite the fact that year by year considerably more boys than girls are born.

This latter phenomenon probably owes something to 'artificial' causes; two world wars have inevitably taken a heavy toll of men serving in the Armed Forces. The most important reason why the number of females continues to exceed that of males, however, is the tendency for women to live longer than men;

at the present time the average newly-born child in Britain has a life expectancy of 69 years if it is male but 75 years if it is female. (The male's greater exposure to occupational strains and hazards is no doubt an element in this, but the much higher rate of infantile mortality amongst boys indicates that the main cause is a purely physiological one.)

The age distribution is of greater economic significance. The ageing of the British population during the present century can be seen from Table 15·2. In 1901, nearly 61 per cent of the population was under the age of 30, whereas by 1971 this proportion had fallen to a little above 45 per cent; conversely, the over-sixties accounted for 75 of every 1 000 in 1901 but 190 of every 1 000 in 1971. The significance of such a trend has been discussed at some length in the previous section; it is, of course, the inevitable consequence of a falling birth-rate combined with a falling death-rate.

TABLE 15.3 *Geographical distribution of the population of the United Kingdom, 1911–71*

Region	1911		1971	
	000s	*% of total*	*000s*	*% of total*
South-East and East	12 932	30·7	18 900	34·0
South-West	2 688	6·4	3 781	6·8
Midlands	5 525	13·1	8 500	15·3
North and North-West	12 503	29·7	14 838	26·8
Scotland	4 760	11·3	5 229	9·4
Wales	2 421	5·8	2 731	4·9
Northern Ireland	1 251	3·0	1 536	2·8
Total	42 080	100·0	55 515	100·0

Source: *Annual Abstract of Statistics, 1974* (HMSO, London, 1974), Table 6.

The *geographical* distribution of the population is shown in Table 15·3. The most interesting feature of this table is the shift in the distribution of the population away from what may be called the extremities of the United Kingdom – Scotland and the North of England, Wales and Northern Ireland – and towards the 'central' area covered by London, the East and South-East of England and the Midlands. This 'central' area accounted in 1911 for just about 44 per cent of the total population; fifty years later the proportion was around 50 per cent. This movement reflects to some extent the increasing urbanisation of the British population, and the continuous drift of population away from rural areas. At the present time, indeed, about a third of the total British population is to be found in the seven great conurbations of Greater London, West Midlands, West Yorkshire, South-East Lancashire, Merseyside, Tyneside and Clydeside.

The shift in the geographical distribution of the population, of course, is closely connected with its redistribution amongst different industries in response to changes in the structure of the economy. The marked changes which have occurred in the *occupational distribution* of the British population in the past century may be seen from Table 15·4, which refers to the occupied population of England and Wales. The decline of some traditional occupations – especially agriculture and the textile industries – is especially striking. In 1851 these two industries accounted for something of the order of 44 per cent of the total working population; by 1971 the proportion had fallen to only 8 per cent. This is a very large part of the explanation of the relative decline of the numerical importance of Scotland and the North, Wales and Northern Ireland, since these areas were especially dependent on agriculture and/or the textile trades.

Offsetting this decline is the growth of the proportion of the population engaged in industries which now play a dominant role in the British economy – and in particular the engineering trades and metal manufacturing. More people are also now engaged in what could be called the administration of output, in the realms of wholesale and retail distribution and financial and commercial services generally. The increasing importance of the government, central and local, as an employer is also brought out by the occupational statistics. These changes have constituted the 'pull' for population which was being pushed out of its native regions by the decline of older industries.

The United Kingdom, then, has a population which has more than doubled itself in the past century and which continues

TABLE 15.4   *Distribution of the occupied population of England and Wales, 1851–1971 (% of total)*

Industry	1851	1901	1971
Agriculture and fishing	21·4	8·5	2·8
Mining and quarrying	3·9	5·5	1·6
Manufacturing	34·6	31·3	35·3
Of which:			
Textiles and clothing	*22·2*	*14·1*	*5·0*
Metals, machinery, etc.	*6·1*	*9·1*	*18·1*
Other manufacturing	*6·3*	*8·1*	*12·2*
Building, decorating, contracting	5·0	7·1	6·8
Transport and communication	5·4	9·7	6·4
Central and Local Government	1·5	2·6	5·9
Commerce, finance and distribution	5·3	9·0	29·2
Personal service	14·6	14·6	8·2
Other	8·3	11·7	3·8
Total	100·0	100·0	100·0

Source: Adapted from data given by E. A. G. Robinson, *Economic Journal*, Vol. LXIV, No. 255, September 1954, p. 459, Table III and *Annual Abstract of Statistics, 1972*, Table 146.

to grow. Its density of population per square mile, in fact, is one of the highest in the world amongst countries of any comparable size – 589 compared with 231 in France, 404 in Italy, 56 in the United States and a mere 5 in Canada. It is a population which is ageing, however, and Britain therefore faces all the problems which that implies. Furthermore, the British population is highly urbanised and highly industrialised, and is therefore dependent for a large part of its food on supplies from abroad. That, too, as will be seen at a later stage, raises immensely important and difficult problems.

5   THE MOBILITY OF LABOUR

For an economy it is not only the size and efficiency of the labour force which matter; it is also important that labour should be used where it is most needed, and that its distribution should change smoothly in response to developments in the pattern of production and demand. This raises the question of the extent to which the labour force has the quality of *mobility* – the power to move from one place to another, or one industry to another, whenever such movement is called for.

Mobility is of two kinds. First there is geographic, or *lateral,* mobility – the movement from one area to another. Generally, such movement is hampered by a number of factors. Human beings tend to develop an affection for their own neighbourhoods and to build up social relationships in their area through clubs, societies, unions and churches; naturally they are reluctant to move to different neighbourhoods where they will need to start rebuilding these relationships anew. The costs and inconvenience of movement constitute further obstacles, especially in connection with the buying and selling of houses. Parents are reluctant to disrupt the education of children by moving them from one school to another. Again, people are often unaware of opportunities existing outside their own district. Most often of all, sheer inertia militates against movement. And, as was mentioned in an earlier section, all these factors operate the more strongly in a population whose average age is rising. Resistance to change tends to increase in direct proportion to age; a population in which the relatively young are a diminishing fraction will be less capable of dynamic adjustment than one in which the relative size of the higher age-groups is diminishing. When the mobility of labour as between different *countries* is considered, of course, the obstacles become greater and more numerous. Language pro-

blems arise; differences may exist in working conditions and
social security systems; the costs of movement are much greater.

Experience shows clearly enough how important such
obstacles have proved in practice. In the depression conditions
of the 1930s enormous numbers of men in the particularly badly-
hit regions of Britain (the 'depressed areas') remained unemployed for years despite the fact that, towards the end of the
depression at any rate, their chances of getting a job would have
been considerably improved if they had moved to the recovering
regions of the London area or the Midlands. Similarly, in most
post-war years unemployment levels in Scotland and Northern
Ireland have almost invariably been at least twice as high as
in Britain generally despite, more often than not, the existence
of plenty of unfilled vacancies in the central regions of Britain.

Britain has also provided an illustration of the difficulties,
physical and psychological, attached to the international movement of labour. During 1959–61, net immigration into the United
Kingdom rose to between 90 000 and 100 000 a year – a large
movement, but scarcely overwhelming in relation to a population
of nearly 53 million experiencing a natural increase of some
300 000 a year. Nevertheless, the problems alleged to be raised
by this inflow were adjudged serious enough for the government
of the day to abandon the long-cherished principle of free entry
into the United Kingdom for any Commonwealth citizen in order
to acquire powers of control over the rate of immigration.

The second type of mobility can be termed occupational, or
vertical, mobility – the movement of people from one industry
or trade to another. The specialisation of labour sometimes
means that a man cannot use his training and experience in
more than a limited range of industries. Certain occupations
can be pursued in a large number of industries, of course, so
that people practising them in a declining industry can transfer
to an expanding industry without too much difficulty – typists,
accountants or lorry-drivers, for example, can carry on their jobs
in a very wide range of industries. One of the advantages of
extreme division of labour, however, is precisely that it permits
the use of people trained, in a short time, to perform very skilfully
an extremely limited range of operations – the machine-minder

working with a machine repeating the same process many times a minute, or the person performing an operation of half-a-dozen movements on a steadily-moving assembly belt. Restriction of skill and training within such narrow limits can present serious problems if the firm or industry concerned is a declining one and if the expanding firms are calling for labour with different or more general skills.

The hindrances to vertical mobility may also be deliberately imposed by society itself. Trade unions and professional associations frequently impose restrictions on entry with the aim of preventing too much competition for jobs, so holding up the level of wages or salaries. High costs of apprenticeship or education (in terms of time as well as money) may prevent people from entering an occupation for which they are well suited. Movement from one social class to another – which is frequently involved in movement from one occupation to another – is difficult, and achieved by only a small fraction of the population.

Although geographic and occupational mobility can be distinguished in this way in principle, in practice, of course, the two may work together. In many instances, industries are heavily concentrated in particular regions – the reasons for this are touched on in the following chapter – so that the decline of a particular industry may be synonymous with the decline of a whole region. The people concerned may be hindered in their movement by *both* the orientation of their skill and experience to a specialised industry now in decline *and* the lack of alternative employment opportunities in their own region. Hence the appalling problem presented by the depressed areas in the 1930s and the industrial diversification policy of post-war years referred to in the next chapter.

A high degree of labour mobility is obviously desirable for an economy which seeks to reap the benefits of a progressive technology or to sell in world markets where the pattern of demand is never stable. How, then, can mobility be increased? Lateral mobility can be encouraged by an efficient and comprehensive system of employment exchanges, by government grants to assist in training and resettlement or to meet costs of movement, and by a stock of houses which leaves some margin for movement. In Britain, government policy has operated in most of these ways for some considerable time now. Yet the innate human revulsion from the uprooting of house and home remains, and all experience indicates that people are reluctant to move even when faced with the prospect of prolonged unemployment in their own area. Direction of labour under statutory powers is one remedy, but it is one which is generally agreed to be incompatible with the democratic way of life and unacceptable for any but the most desperate situations, such as that of war.

Another remedy is to move industry to the worker, rather than *vice versa,* the location of industry being influenced by a group of official weapons ranging from financial inducements to building controls. Such a policy has its advantages, not the least of which being the avoidance of wastage of physical and non-physical social capital – houses, schools and the intangibles which go to make a living, virile community – which has been involved in the past through the decline and depopulation of whole areas. It has its dangers, too, of course; for many industries there is a limit to the extent to which their location can be altered without an intolerable rise in production costs. So far as international labour mobility is concerned, recent British experience shows only too clearly that its functioning may call not only for the appropriate material provisions – houses, welfare services and so on – but for a degree of social tolerance and understanding which is greater than that likely to be forthcoming.

On the occupational side, a good deal of progress has unquestionably been made in countries such as Britain through the opening of educational opportunities to all classes of the community, irrespective of means. It would be too much to say that complete equality of educational opportunity now exists in Britain, but certainly there is considerably more opportunity for the children of relatively poor parents to train for and enter skilled trades and professions than was the case even a generation previously. Restrictions imposed by trade unions and professional associations still exist, and hence prevent complete freedom of entry, while movement between social classes can never be an easy process. The strength of each of these factors is gradually declining, but simultaneously the increasing pace of technical change is rendering the need for occupational mobility more urgent. The traditional assumption that a man will probably remain in the same type of job throughout his working life is becoming not only unrealistic but positively dangerous, and it is certain that the provision and use of industrial re-training facilities will have to become far more widespread in the final quarter of the century than they were previously.

6 WORK AND LEISURE

The preceding sections have been concerned with one aspect of the supply of labour – the influences governing the size and distribution, geographic and occupational, of the total population. Now the second aspect of labour supply must be considered: given the total *number* of the potential labour force in a given area, how much labour will actually be offered for sale, so to speak, at any given wage-rate in any given industry? What governs the decision of any individual to work more or fewer hours – or not at all?

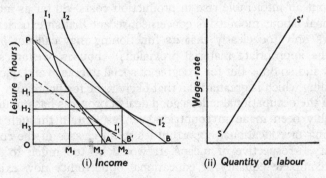

Fig. 15B

The decision can be analysed in exactly the same way as that in which the demand for commodities was analysed. In this case the individual is in effect sacrificing hours of leisure for the income derived from the labour he is able to perform in them, the wage-rate being the price of this income in terms of leisure foregone, and *vice versa*. The indifference curves in

Fig 15B(i) therefore show the combinations of leisure and income (both measured over a given interval, say a week) which give him equal satisfaction. The price line embodies the current wage-rate; the smaller its slope, the higher the wage-rate – i.e. the greater the income sacrificed for each extra hour of leisure taken (or earned for each hour sacrificed). In the initial situation the wage-rate is given by PA, and at this level of wages the individual concerned will take OH_1 hours of leisure (i.e. he will work PH_1 hours a week) and earn a weekly income of OM_1. If the wage-rate now rises, leisure becomes more expensive; when the price line moves to PB, the individual will reduce his leisure to OH_2 hours (i.e. he will work an extra H_1H_2 hours) and increase his income to OM_2.

By continuing in this way, and aggregating the results for all individuals in the market, the supply curve of labour for the industry can be constructed. An example is given by SS' in Fig. 15B(ii). This is a 'normal' – i.e. upward-sloping – supply curve; the higher the wage-rate, the more the labour forthcoming will be. An increase in the wage might encourage the existing labour force to work longer hours, and will also draw into the firm or industry men who were previously employed elsewhere and who are attracted by the higher wages. For the economy as a whole, of course, the total labour supply cannot be increased in this second way, but higher wages might attract into employment people who were previously not seeking employment – married women, for example, or retired people.

Like changes in the demand for an individual commodity, however, these changes in the number of hours of labour offered at different wage-rates embody both a substitution effect and an income effect. In Fig. 15B(i) the former was measured by the movement in the *slope* of the price line from PA to PB, whereas the latter is reflected in the movement from one indifference curve $I_1I_1{}'$ to a higher curve $I_2I_2{}'$. If the income effect is excluded by drawing the price line corresponding to the new wage-rate as a tangent to the first indifference curve – as is done with PB' in Fig. 15B(i) – it is possible to discover what the substitution effect of the change in the wage-rate would have been if there had been no simultaneous income effect. It will be seen that the hours worked would have increased *more* than H_1H_2 – by H_1H_3 in fact – showing that the higher income attained by the individual was partly taken out in the form of increased leisure in relation to the leisure which would have been taken at that wage-rate if income had not also been raised.

In this instance, the income effect, while moderating the substitution effect, was not strong enough to entirely offset it – more hours were in fact worked at the higher wage than before. It is by no means inconceivable, however, that the income effect should be so strong as to *more* than offset the substitution effect. If wages rise, a man can now earn any given income by working fewer hours. If he aims at maintaining a certain standard of living (requiring a given income per week or month) rather than obtaining the *maximum* possible income, the rise in wages will mean that he will be able to enjoy his 'target' standard of living with fewer hours of work, so that the supply of labour will be reduced rather than increased. In effect, the wage increase has made the worker better off and he proceeds to use his extra wealth to buy more leisure – e.g. longer week-ends or a mid-week afternoon – just as the income effect of a fall in the price of bread is seen in a reduction of the consumption of bread and an increase in the consumption of higher-quality foods. Conversely, a fall in wage-rates may mean that *more* labour is supplied than before, as workers attempt to maintain their incomes.

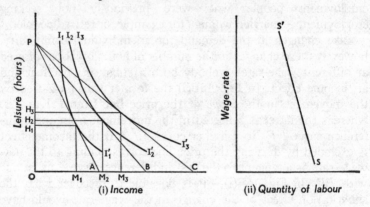

Fig. 15C

An example is given in Fig. 15C. The shape of the indifference curves in Fig. 15C(i) is such that as the wage-rate rises – i.e. the price line moves from *PA* to *PB* and then to *PC* – the amount of leisure which the individual chooses to take rises from OH_1 to OH_2 and then OH_3. The derived supply curve of labour would thus be a backward-sloping one like SS' in Fig. 15C(ii). For simplicity this is shown as sloping backwards throughout its length, but such a curve is not likely to exist in reality; a curve sloping back over *part* of its length, however, is perfectly conceivable. For any single firm or industry, the income effect is unlikely to be dominant; it would probably be more than offset by the inflow of labour from other industries stimulated by higher wages (or vice versa). For the economy as a whole, however, or for industries which do not easily attract outside recruits (the coal-mining industry may be an example), the income effect may be important. Indeed, it is a feature of advanced economies that the working hours of labour tend to fall; high productivity brings high wages and living-standards – and also a demand for increased leisure in which to enjoy them.

7 THE DETERMINATION OF WAGES UNDER COMPETITION

Bringing together the demand and supply curves, the way in which the level of wages is determined in any industry can be seen. In Fig. 15D is shown a demand curve DD', relating the marginal revenue product of labour to the numbers employed; this indicates how much the employers are willing to pay for different amounts of labour. The supply curve, SS', shows the amounts of labour which will be forthcoming at various wage-rates. If wages are competitively determined – that is, assuming away for a moment the possible influence of trade unions, government wage legislation, etc. – the wage-rate will tend to settle at *OP*, because only at this wage is the demand for labour in the industry equal to the amount of labour being offered (i.e. *OM* units). If the wage was above this level, the demand would be insufficient to absorb the total amount of labour being offered at that wage; unemployment would result, until the competition

for jobs forced the wage down again. If the wage were below
this level the supply of labour would fall below the demand at
that wage; the pressure of competition amongst employers to
obtain labour would eventually force wages up to the equilibrium
point. All this assumes that wages are determined solely by the
free play of competitive forces; in the real world, of course,
this is by no means always true, and the process of wage determination is consequently a good deal more complex.

In a situation of perfect competition the individual firm (being
an infinitely small component of the industry) would be faced
with the current market price for the labour used in the industry,

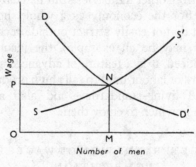

Fig. 15D

and would be unable to influence the level of wages by increasing
or diminishing its demand for labour. The supply curve of labour
to the firm would therefore be a horizontal line through the market
wage-rate. For the industry as a whole, however, a shift in the
demand curve for labour will significantly influence the level of
wages, the exact degree of movement in wages in response to
a change in demand depending on the elasticity of the labour
supply curve.

Two other points are of some importance. First, an individual
firm, or even an industry, can usually treat its wage level as
independent of the demand for its product. If wages in that
industry are increased, the income, and therefore the expenditure
of its workers, will rise. The workers in a particular industry,
however, are unlikely to form a considerable element in the mar-

ket for the commodity it produces, and the impact of a wage increase on the market demand curve facing the industry concerned will probably be insignificant. For the economy as a whole, however, the position is different. A *general* wage increase is almost bound to be followed by an increase in demand generally, so that demand as a whole cannot be considered to be independent of costs of production. As will be seen in Part VII, this fact has important implications for policy measures aimed at securing stability of the general price level and of employment.

The second point relates to the relationship between wages and the productivity of labour. So far these have been treated as if they were quite separate, with productivity as one of the independent variables determining wages. In many cases, however, the position may be reversed, and wages may influence productivity. If a low level of wages means a low standard of living, with inadequate housing, education and nutrition, it may well result in a low standard of efficiency amongst the labour force. Many employers would propound the principle of the *economy of high wages,* meaning by this that if a man is well paid, so that he enjoys a high standard of living, his working efficiency will be raised and with it his productivity. It may sometimes be necessary, therefore, to break this vicious circle of low productivity resulting in low wages which in turn cause low productivity. It seems that a realisation of this fact underlay the attempts at government intervention in wage determination in Britain early in the present century. And it is important to remember that it is no mere coincidence that the labour force of the United States is at once the highest-paid and the most productive in the world; American wages are high because productivity is high, but the high productivity in turn owes something to the high wages.

Summing up then, it is obviously of considerable importance that a clear distinction should be maintained between wages and labour-costs per unit of output; while the worker is primarily concerned with the total wages or salary he receives, the employer is interested primarily in the cost of the labour involved in making each unit of output. The two things are not necessarily correlated. For example, if in one factory men are paid £50 a week and each produces an average of 250 units of output a week, while in another producing the same commodity men are paid £40 a week and each produces an average of only 160 units, the labour costs per unit are obviously lower in the first factory than in the second, despite the higher level of wages prevailing in it. The fact that the level of wages in a country are very high by no means implies that the commodities produced in that country are more expensive than those produced elsewhere; if this were so, indeed, it would be impossible to explain the success of United States exporters in world markets.

8   RELATIVE WAGE-LEVELS

If wage-rates are determined by the interaction of the supply of labour and its marginal revenue product, it might reasonably be expected that they would tend towards equality, labour moving into highly paid industries and moving out of low-paid industries until relatively little variation of reward remained. Admittedly, some degree of inequality would always be expected, since some people have greater innate mental or physical ability than others, and therefore have a higher productivity. Most of the variations *within* any given occupation could certainly be explained on some such grounds.

This factor could not explain the wide differences which exist between different occupations, however — there is no special reason why all the men of innate ability should cram into one or two occupations and desert all the rest. Yet such differences do exist; in the Britain of 1975, for example, an agricultural labourer would consider himself lucky to earn £2 000 a year, an experienced worker in the engineering trades would expect at least £3 000 a year, while the average doctor would be disappointed to receive much less than £7 000 a year. To some extent such differences in annual earnings may be due to differences in hours of work — i.e. in the number of labour-units supplied by an individual — but this would not go far in explaining the inequalities of earnings which exist. What are the causes of these differences?

First, the wage-rate may not be synonymous with the actual

value of payments for labour. On the one hand, labour may receive certain rewards not included in the wage-rate; the coal-miner receives concessionary coal, the farm worker obtains milk, meat or eggs, the transport worker is allowed free travel, the civil servant has valuable pension rights, and so on. On the other hand, the worker may have *deductions* to make from his wages – to buy tools or uniform necessary in his work, or to compensate for expenses of travel or training and education which someone, if not he himself, has incurred on his behalf.

Secondly, the nature of the employment has to be taken into account. A high wage may be necessary not so much because of high productivity but in order to compensate a worker for bad working conditions. The work may be dangerous or unhealthy (like coal mining) or dirty and unpleasant (like sewerage disposal), or the employment may be insecure because of seasonal or other fluctuations in demand and output. Another factor is that a job may involve a high degree of responsibility meriting special reward, or may involve a long and expensive period of training. This latter factor may be especially important in maintaining a scarcity (relative to the prevailing demand) of people possessing 'professional' skills – lawyers, engineers, architects, etc. Conversely, a man may willingly accept a relatively low wage because of the attractiveness of the work; it may have high social esteem, which he values; or it may provide an opportunity for the able few (amongst whom almost everyone automatically includes himself) to earn an extremely high income – barristers as a whole are not well paid, but many enter the profession despite this fact because of the fabulous earnings of a small minority of the profession.

Thirdly, a group of advantages or disadvantages may be associated with the general environment within which the employment is situated. Certain geographic areas are widely regarded as being more pleasant to work and live in than others; the opportunity for wives or children to obtain employment varies from place to place and may be an important consideration for a family; rents are generally lower in the country than in large towns; housing accommodation may be easier to obtain in one area than in another. All these factors can enter into the mind of a worker when balancing up the attractiveness of different occupations.

It is closer to the truth, then, to say that labour looks at the *net advantages* of different occupations, rather than to imagine that money wage-rates are the sole attraction for labour. Analytically, all these other factors enter into the shape and position of the supply curve. For two industries, offering identical wages but possessing different degrees of non-monetary advantages, there would be separate supply curves, the industry possessing the greater net advantage from the point of view of labour having a supply curve further to the right than the other.

Having introduced all these complications, it still does not follow that in the real world labour moves from industry to industry until the net advantage from employment has been brought to the same level in all. There are the influences of trade union and government intervention which may prevent the forces of competition from fully working themselves out; more will be said of these in succeeding sections. There is also the pressure of convention; certain wage differentials, as they are called, have existed for many years and have become established in the minds of both workers and employers as necessary and normal. Thirdly, there is the influence of public opinion; certain occupations, such as teaching or medicine, are regarded as being of special responsibility and in some rather vague sense *entitled* to a relatively high reward. Most important of all, there are the hindrances to mobility, both between areas and between occupations, which were described in Section 4. The effect of all these influences is to break the total labour force into 'non-competing groups', and by restrictions on the free movement of labour to prevent the equalisation of the net advantages accruing from different occupations. It is mainly because of this that there is still substantial truth in the generalisation that the occupations which are most attractive, in all senses, are also the most lucrative.

9   THE ROLE OF TRADE UNIONS

So far the determination of wages has been discussed solely in terms of the forces which would operate in a competitive world.

In real life, however, the forces of competition are not allowed to function with complete freedom (although in the long run they are bound to determine the broad trend of wages), and a major factor in this context is the power and influence of trade unions. The basic aim of a trade union is that of strengthening the bargaining power of workers in relation to that of employers, so as to ensure that the worker obtains his fair share of the product to which he contributes and that he is given decent conditions of work. Without some kind of association with his fellow-workers, the individual employee is almost invariably in a weak bargaining position in comparison with the employer. To the average entrepreneur, the question of whether he employs one more worker or not is seldom of any great importance; to the worker concerned, however, it is frequently a matter of infinite importance, since (unlike his employer) he seldom has reserves on which he can live in idleness rather than accept what he considers to be an unfair bargain.

Theoretically, the forces of competition (as the analysis has shown) will ensure that labour is paid a wage equal to the value of its marginal product; the question of unfair bargains does not appear to arise. In practice there is no guarantee that labour will receive the full value of its marginal product. First, it is seldom possible to calculate what the value of labour's marginal product actually is, except within fairly wide limits; when output rises with an expanded labour force it is generally extremely difficult to say how much of the extra output is attributable to labour, how much to the capital used, or how much to the entrepreneur's own ability. Secondly, it has already been observed that the flow of labour from industry to industry is restricted by a great many factors, so that great inequalities of marginal product and earnings may persist. (In any case, if *all* employers paid their workers less than their marginal product, even complete mobility would be insufficient to rectify the situation.) The precise level of wages in any industry, therefore, is a matter for bargaining between employer and worker, and the fundamental aim of trade unionism is to ensure that workers bargain collectively and on terms of at least equal strength with the employer. In many cases it has succeeded so well in this task that the bargaining strength of a large trade union is considerably greater than that of an individual employer, so that employers also resort to conducting wage negotiations through a collective organisation.

How can a union succeed in obtaining higher wages for its members than could be secured by an individual worker ? Essentially it does this through an actual or threatened restriction of the supply of labour – by shifting the supply curve to the left. Occasionally it may do this by imposing limitations on the numbers entering the industry (laying down apprenticeship requirements, or restricting new entrants to sons or daughters of its own members) or by restricting the amount of labour supplied by workers in the industry (by limiting their hours of work, or their rate of physical output). The power of the trade union lies fundamentally, however, in its ability to reduce the supply of labour to zero (so far as its own members are concerned, at least) by calling a strike. In all these measures, of course, the extent of the union's power will depend on the proportion of an industry's labour force which is included in its membership, on the degree of determination and discipline of its members, on the extent of its financial reserves and on the ability of its leaders.

However powerful a union may be, theoretically there are definite limits to the extent to which it can increase the wages of its members. In the first place, although the precise value of labour's marginal product may not be known, a point will be reached when it will be quite clear to an employer that at the current wage it is simply not worth his while to employ labour if wages rise further. If the union persists in pursuing wage demands past that point, unemployment is bound to occur and the union will be forced to moderate its demands. (At the same time, the possible stimulus to productivity of high wages, noted at an earlier stage, should be borne in mind in this context.)

A second, and closely related, factor is the *elasticity of substitution* existing in the industry – i.e. the ease with which other factors can be substituted for labour in the production of the commodity concerned. As wages increase, the entrepreneur may find it has become profitable to employ less labour and more land or capital, because the latter factors have become relatively cheaper. Much will depend, in turn, on the elasticity of supply of these alternative factors to the industry. If the capital employed is of a highly specialised nature, for example, it may not be possible to obtain more of it without considerable delay or without causing a substantial rise in its price. The greater the elasticity of substitution in the industry, of course, the more limited are the powers of the union to secure higher wages.

Finally, much will depend on the elasticity of demand for the product in question. If the demand which an entrepreneur faces is highly inelastic, he will be able to pass on the higher wages to the consuming public in the form of higher prices without seriously damaging his sales; his resistance to union pressure will therefore be relatively slight. Conversely, an entrepreneur facing a highly elastic demand knows that an increase in price will seriously reduce his sales, so that higher costs can only be sustained at the expense of correspondingly reduced profits; hence he will not easily accede to wage demands. However strong a union may be, therefore, in principle a point must be reached after which higher wages will be secured only at the price of significant unemployment amongst its members; no responsible union leader would willingly incur the risk of that.

All this is theoretically valid; in the very long run, and in relation to *real* wages, it is also sound enough as an explanation of the forces at work in practice. As a commentary on the course of *money* wages in recent years, however, it is a good deal less than wholly realistic. The position of immense political and industrial strength which the trade union movement has built for itself in modern Britain (and perhaps most other industrial countries), together with a market situation in which overall demand has more often than not been pressing on the available supplies of goods and services, have seriously qualified the realism of the assumption – implicitly underlying the theoretical analysis – that demand and supply curves are independent. If an entrepreneur encounters a claim for higher wages in the knowledge that it is, after all, only one element in a much wider and more or less recurrent process of wage increases throughout the economy, his attitude towards it is naturally profoundly influenced by that knowledge. *General* increases in wages inevitably mean general rises in market demand, including that for his own product. He will therefore tend to absorb the higher labour cost without too much concern, confident in the expectation that in a buoyant market the higher costs can simply be passed on to the consumer in the form of higher prices.

Not unnaturally, the trade unions in such a situation listen with a good deal of scepticism, on their part, to prophecies of dangerously reduced profit-margins as a result of higher labour costs; profit-margins, like labour costs, can also be passed on to the consumer through higher prices in a buoyant market. Hence the danger of the cost-price spiral to which reference was made earlier, especially for a country seeking to sell goods in foreign markets in competition with countries having a less pronounced upward drift of wages and prices; this is an issue which will receive more attention in a later chapter. In the long run, obviously no one benefits (and all may well suffer) from increases in monetary incomes having no foundation in real terms. Once the spiral starts, however, no individual section of the community is likely to conceive the arrest of the spiral to be its own special responsibility.

10   STATE INTERVENTION IN WAGE-DETERMINATION IN BRITAIN

The general policy of modern British governments has been that the process of wage bargaining is best left to the individual unions and employers concerned, and until recently legislation had been restricted to defining the powers and legal position of trade unions. Two main types of exception to this broad statement have to be made, however, because governments have intervened in wage-determination in two main ways. First, legislative intervention has been adopted in particular industries where (*a*) trade unions have been unable to develop and attain reasonable strength, or (*b*) a dispute has proved insoluble through the existing conciliation machinery. Secondly, governments have become more and more involved in trying to regulate the *general* trend of money wages – a matter discussed more fully in Chapter XXVIII below.

Under the first heading, government action in Britain dates back to the *Trade Boards Act* of 1909. This Act empowered the Board of Trade to create machinery in four 'sweated' trades to decide upon and maintain a minimum wage. In these trades a great deal of female and juvenile labour was employed at extremely low wages and frequently under appalling conditions; partly because of the character of the labour force, and partly because of the small-scale and scattered nature of the trades concerned, virtually no trade union organisation had developed which could correct these features. These trades constituted classic examples of the vicious 'low productivity – hence low wages – hence low productivity' spiral mentioned previously.

The effect of the institution of minimum wages was not primarily to cause a reduction in employment, but to increase the efficiency of labour; this resulted partly from the improved diet and living conditions made possible by the higher wages, and partly from the fact that employers were forced to use the more expensive labour supply more effectively. The number of industries covered by the Trade Board system was gradually increased, and in 1945 the Wages Councils Act continued, and somewhat extended, the provision of the earlier Acts, the Boards being given the new title of *Wages Councils*. Together with those created by other legislation for agriculture and the catering industry these statutory councils now establish minimum wages for about one-third of the employed population of the United Kingdom.

Under the second heading, the government in Britain has a long tradition of providing means for the settlement of industrial disputes which still remain after the normal processes of negotiation have been exhausted. If both parties to a dispute so desire, the Advisory Conciliation and Arbitration Service is able to appoint independent arbitrators or arbitration tribunals; these hear both sides of the case and announce a final decision. Although there is at present no compulsion on either party to accept this decision, few unions or employers would persist in refusing to accept it. Apart from positive arbitration, the Department of Employment has facilities for carrying out further negotiation and discussion between the disputing parties which can be tried before a strike or lock-out is declared.

The powers of the government, then, are still confined to fixing minimum wages, or intervening in disputes, in particular industries only. There is strictly speaking no official wages policy in Britain in the sense of a systematic control over the relative levels of pay in different industries or occupations. The wage *structure* is still theoretically the outcome of a large number of independent and unrelated wage agreements in various industries.

Since 1970 two major inroads have been made into this position, although the success of either is not easy to assess. First, a statutory framework was created for the control of all incomes and prices – not only wages – in an attempt to control inflation. These measures will be outlined in Chapter XXVIII below. Secondly, a fundamental departure from past practice was made by the *Industrial Relations Act* of 1971 in which the powers and conduct of trade unions were brought within a legislative framework. This Act provided for the registration of trade unions and for the definition of what were and what were not 'fair' industrial practices in pursuit of wage claims or in other disputes with employers; equally it provided for sanctions under the criminal law for anyone adopting 'unfair' practices in industrial disputes and made trade unions financially responsible for breaches of contract induced by its officials if the agreed procedures for negotiations and settlement of disputes had not been observed. The Act became the subject of acute controversy between those who saw it as a belated attempt to make a new power in the realm – official or unofficial trade unionism – subject to the ordinary laws of contract and, on the other hand, those who regarded any attempt to impose a legislative framework on the processes of industrial relations as being both futile and inherently repressive. Both measures were finally abandoned with the accession of a Labour government in 1974.

FURTHER READING

E. MANSFIELD *Micro-economics* Ch. 13
K. LANCASTER *Introduction to modern micro-economics* Ch. 8
J. E. KING *Labour economics* Macmillan, London 1972
A. M. LEVENSON and B. S. SOLON *Outline of price theory* Ch. 12
L. C. HUNTER and D. J. ROBERTSON *Economics of wages and labour* Macmillan, London 1969, Parts I–III
B. J. McCORMICK *Wages* Penguin Books, London 1969

CHAPTER XVI

Rent

1 RENT AS A PAYMENT FOR LAND

IN its usual sense, the word 'rent' means the payment made by a person for the privilege of using for a period of time an asset belonging to someone else. A person pays rent for the use of someone else's house or farm; equally, people 'rent' a car or cooker or television set. In economics the word originally related only to the income received from the ownership of land; in recent years the word has also come to have a special technical meaning in economics, and this will be discussed in the next section.

Considering the first, and simpler, definition of rent as the income received from the ownership of land, it is obvious that it is more limited in extent than when the word is used conversationally. When people speak of the rent of a house they certainly refer to a payment for the use of the land on which the house is built; the greater part of the payment, however, represents a fee for the use of the resources locked up in the building itself — i.e. a payment for the use of *capital*. Similarly, the rent of a television set has nothing to do with land; it is in fact a payment for the use of the capital which the owner has invested in the set. Even in the case of a farm, the rent that a tenant farmer pays to his landlord is only partly a payment for the 'natural and indestructible powers' of the soil; part of it is a return on the capital embodied in the farm in such things as farm buildings, fences and the drainage system. In economic analysis care must be taken to use the word rent *only* for the income received from the ownership of land, even though in practice it is frequently impossible to determine how much of a payment usually called rent is in fact rent in this technical sense of the word and how much is interest on capital.

How is the rent of land determined? The familiar demand-and-supply analysis can answer this question exactly as it did in the problem of wages. Considering the supply side first, it is obvious that the concept of a supply curve is hardly appropriate for land as a whole, as opposed to particular types of land. A supply curve connects the different amounts of a commodity or factor forthcoming and the prices which have to be offered to obtain those amounts. But the total supply of land does *not* vary, except within extremely narrow limits, and another feature of land, of course, is that it has *no* cost of production. (The implications of these peculiarities of the overall supply of land are examined at some length in a later section.) If a supply curve is to be drawn up, then, it can only refer to the amounts of land used in particular activities – such as wheat-growing or sheep-rearing, or building. If the rent offered for, say, pasture-land is increased, landlords will withdraw their land from arable farmers and lease it to sheep-rearers. Conversely, if only a low price is offered for pasture-land, landlords will prefer to lease their land to builders or wheat-growers who can offer a higher price for it. A supply curve for land in specified uses is therefore a perfectly valid and helpful concept.

Its derivation follows the familiar lines. Let the curves in Fig. 16A(i) represent the indifference map of a landowner who has 50 acres of land which he can either keep for his own personal use or rent out to farmers. If the current annual rent offered for agricultural land in his area is £40 an acre the price line is *PA*, and he will rent out 20 acres; if the level of rents rises to £60 an acre, he will rent out 30 acres, and so on. The income effect is unlikely to be very great here; as the landowner becomes richer he may want to retain a little more land for his own use than he would otherwise have done, but this aspect is unlikely to be important in comparison with the substitution effect. Hence a supply curve, like *SS'* in Fig. 16A(ii), can be drawn up by aggregating the amount of land offered by all landowners at different levels of rent.

On the demand side no special difficulty arises. Each unit

of land put to productive use is capable of adding a certain sum to the total sales receipts of the entrepreneur employing it; this sum is the value of its marginal productivity. The amount which an entrepreneur will be willing to pay for any given unit of land will be determined by its marginal productivity, so that the demand curve for land will be a productivity curve similar to the labour demand curve. Like the latter, the demand curve for land will be downward-sloping, and for two reasons – diminishing returns (i.e. falling *physical* marginal productivity)

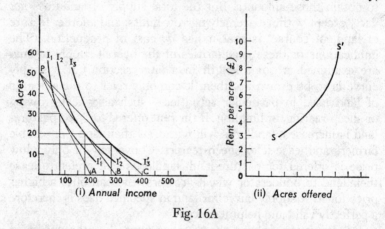

Fig. 16A

and the smaller *value* of any given physical product as total supply increases and market price is reduced.

By constructing demand and supply curves on the same axes, the determination of the rent paid for land in any particular use can be analysed in the familiar way. The level of rent may be affected by a shift in the demand curve or in the supply curve. The former could occur as the result of, for example, a change in market demand for the commodity concerned, while the latter might be caused by a change in the earnings of land in other uses, which would naturally affect the amount of land offered to the given industry in response to any specified rent.

The general picture is thus clear enough: the determination of the price of land will display the same characteristics as the determination of wages or the price of any other input. Rather special considerations apply to the supply of land, however, and it is to these that the following sections will turn.

2   THE SUPPLY OF LAND

When land is spoken of in economics, rather more is meant than when the word is used in ordinary conversation. Land in the sense of a physical area of the earth's surface is naturally the major element involved, because this area is an indispensable element in the production of foodstuffs and raw materials. The responsiveness of land to attempts at such production varies widely from one region to another, and this has important consequences for the pattern of economic life in various regions.

Other elements in the nature and quality of the earth's surface are of considerable importance, however. Physical environments vary in their degree of suitability for economic activity; *climatic conditions*, for example, may not be conducive to high productivity in agricultural or, indeed, industrial pursuits, while on the other hand they may constitute a region's major asset, as in the case of tourist centres. Again, the *position* of land may be good or bad, in that it may be accessible or inaccessible to other trading areas, or international shipping routes, or major markets. The *superficial nature* of land is important; mountainous country is more difficult and expensive to develop than flat country in which communications are easily established.

A third set of factors is involved in what land may *contain* below its surface. The distribution of mineral wealth throughout the world has played an important part in economic progress, and will continue to do so. What is important in this context is not merely the actual quantity of mineral wealth which land may contain but the ease with which it can be extracted. Many coal seams in Britain are becoming exhausted, for example, not in the sense that all the coal has been taken out of the ground but in the sense that the coal which remains is too inaccessible or thinly dispersed to justify the costs of mining it. Under this heading could also be included the potentialities of different areas of land for the supply of *power*; mountainous country may score in this respect even though it is less valuable in other ways.

Indeed, paradoxical as it may seem, 'land' from the point of view of the economist may include the sea, inasmuch as the extraction of fish (or natural gas) from the sea is a form of economic activity which displays many of the characteristics of agriculture or mining.

Bearing in mind all these aspects of land from the economic point of view, it will readily be appreciated that it is difficult to distinguish in practice between those qualities of a particular area of land which are natural to or inherent in it and those which have been given to it through the application of human resources. One field may be more fertile than another not because it is in some sense an inherently better piece of land but because it has been ditched and drained more efficiently, or because more fertiliser has been used on it. At any moment of time these two contributory factors in the yield of land – the natural element and the added element – are always inextricably tangled up with one another, so that in practice it is usually impossible to attribute some of the yield to the one element and the remainder to the other.

Nevertheless it is easy to distinguish between them *in theory*, since they are distinct concepts. It is important that this distinction be drawn in economic analysis, because it is only the first type of quality – the natural, inherent attributes of the soil – which arises from land itself. The qualities added to it originate from labour or capital, and must be treated as products of those inputs. Having made this distinction it is possible to discuss the characteristics of land as an economic factor; there are two which are peculiar to land and this justifies the treatment of land in economic analysis as a separate factor of production.

The first of these is that, unlike the other three factors, land is *fixed in supply*. A small amount of land may be reclaimed each year from the sea, or lost to it through erosion, but the net change involved is so small that it can be neglected. This apart, the total area of land available to mankind as a whole is a fixed quantity, although the total amount actually in use may vary from time to time. The *effective* amount of land – that is, the amount measured in terms of productive capacity – may also vary, as the fertility of land is exhausted through unwise cultivation or increased through technical development; in the 1920s and 1930s, for example, a large area of the Tennessee Valley of the United States was first reduced by inefficient cropping and erosion to a dust-bowl, and then restored to a high degree of fertility by scientific culture, irrigation and afforestation. But those qualities of land which are independent of human activity – its position, climate and whatever innate qualities exist which can be neither destroyed nor increased by any human agency – are fixed in supply. It was because of this characteristic that the law of diminishing returns, discussed earlier in Chapter VI, was first formulated in connection with land.

The second peculiarity of land is that it has no *cost of production*, another feature not shared by other factors. To produce labour certain costs have first to be incurred – the rearing, educating and training of human beings. Capital and enterprise also have a cost of production which has to be incurred if those factors are to be brought forth. But land has no such cost for society as a whole; the fixed quantity was given to mankind by its Creator, and no one ever needed to expend wealth or effort to bring it forth. An individual using someone else's land has to pay for it, of course; it has a cost *to him*. But this would be only a transfer between individuals, and society as a whole has incurred no costs. (All this refers only to the innate qualities of land; the qualities added by human effort naturally have a cost of production.) It follows that it is always profitable to use land, however small the return it brings; because its cost to society is zero, the return must be greater than the cost, and hence there must be a social gain. This characteristic of land, like its fixity of supply, has given rise to the concept which has subsequently been extended to other factors – in this instance, the concept of *rent* as a surplus.

3 RENT AS A SURPLUS

So far the determination of rent has been treated, like that of wages, as a special case of the general theory of competitive price developed in Part IV. If it is attempted to extend the argument to cover the determination of the rent of land as a whole (as opposed to land employed in a particular use) a serious difficulty is encountered. In the case of factors other than land a supply curve for the factor as a whole can be conceived of, a curve which embodies the relationship between the average price offered for the factor and the total quantity of it supplied. If the general level of wages falls so low that it is below that necessary to maintain a bare level of subsistence, the total amount of labour available will fall as the population is reduced through starvation; if the rate of interest falls, the amount of capital offered will diminish, and so on. All the factors except land have a cost of production, in some sense, and the supply will contract if the price of the factor falls below this cost. The cost of production of labour, or enterprise, is the effort and training required if a day-old baby is to be developed into a potential worker; the cost of production of capital is the sacrifice of the immediate command over wealth which must be incurred if it is to be used to bring in an income over the future. But land has no cost of production; it is a free gift of nature which no one has ever sacrificed anything to produce. Further, as has also just been noted, the total supply of land is fixed within narrow limits; no matter how high or how low its price may be, its quantity is unchanged, precisely because there is no *necessary supply price* which must be paid to bring forth a supply of land.

Because of these unique characteristics it follows that for all land taken together rent is a *surplus*, in the sense that it corresponds to no effort or sacrifice incurred in supply and requiring a reward. If wages or profits or interest fall to zero the supply of the corresponding factors would dry up, so that these payments obviously perform a necessary function. But rent has no such function; it is entirely a surplus corresponding to, and compensating, no cost of production. As was remarked in the previous section, this led to the development of the concept of *economic rent*; that is, the word 'rent' in this special economic sense is used to describe a payment over and above the necessary supply price of a factor.

If rent is defined in this way, it will be apparent that rent can be received by any factor, not only land. For the total factor supply, only the payment for land is wholly economic rent and nothing else, because land is the only factor having no cost of production at all. But in the case of factors supplied to any particular industry, any or all of them may receive some rent. It was pointed out in Chapter V that the *real* cost of a commodity is the sacrifice of the alternative uses of the factors used up in its production. A parallel concept can be supplied to factors of production themselves. Before an entrepreneur can obtain the use of any factor he must offer it at least as much as it could earn in the most suitable alternative employment open to it. This sum of money, its 'best earnings elsewhere', is the necessary supply price of that factor to the industry; it is usually referred to as its *transfer cost*. The reward paid to a factor must be at least equal to its transfer cost, otherwise (by definition) it will move into some other occupation; any amount paid to a factor in excess of this transfer cost is a surplus – i.e. it is economic rent. The surplus, or rent, is the difference between the actual earnings of a factor and its necessary supply price, or transfer cost.

In any particular industry, then, economic rent may be received by labour, enterprise or capital as well as by land. For example, suppose that a successful barrister earns £10 000 a year, and that if he ceased to practise law the most lucrative alternative employment he could obtain would be that of, say, a civil servant at £6 000 a year. So long as he earns more than £6 000 at the Bar, therefore, he will be content to remain a barrister; he will abandon the profession only if his earnings fall below £6 000. His transfer cost, in other words, is £6 000. But everything he earns in excess of this is rent, since he would remain in that occupation even without this extra reward. Similarly, a salesman in the washing-machine industry, Mr X, may earn £5 000 a year because he has a special flair for selling washing-machines; if he moved into any other industry he might earn no more than, say, £800 a year. The difference between £800 and £5 000 a year is economic rent, sometimes referred to, in this context, as a *rent of ability*. This expression is used because earnings far in excess of transfer cost can arise only if the factors concerned possess some special qualities which are not reproducible. For example, if Mr X had no special ability setting him apart from all other salesmen, two possibilities would immediately arise. Either *all* salesmen would be earning £5 000 a year in other industries, or they would move into the washing-machine industry, since, being as able as X, they would want to share in the high income X was making. In the former case X's transfer cost would be £5 000, since he presumably could also earn this sum elsewhere, being of the same ability as other salesmen; in the latter case, X's earnings would be driven down by the competition of the salesmen attracted into the industry. In either event the gap between actual earnings and transfer cost would be destroyed, and the economic rent would disappear.

It is difficult to conceive of economic rent arising from the ownership of capital, because (unlike innate human ability) any special features of capital assets resulting in unusually high earnings can in general be reproduced in other capital assets. If a sudden increase in the demand for houses to rent results in a high yield on the capital invested in such houses, other houses (in normal times) would be built with capital diverted from other uses; this switch of capital would continue until *either* the high rents disappeared *or* the interest paid to capital in other uses rose into equality with the level prevailing in the house-renting industry. However, it is possible to conceive of capital receiving rent in exceptional cases. For example, the revenue derived over a period of years from exhibiting the original Stephenson 'Rocket' to the general public would certainly be far in excess of either its original cost of production or the cost of building an exact replica. This excess would be in the nature of economic rent.

It is clear, then, that the concept of economic rent is one of very wide application – one capable of application, indeed, to *any* input whose supply curve in any occupation is of less than infinite elasticity. Consider the situation illustrated in Fig. 16B, where market forces have resulted in a price of OP and a supply of OM: it is immaterial for present purposes whether the demand and supply functions relate to a productive input or a physical product. Since the supply schedule SS' is upward-sloping – i.e. has less than infinite elasticity – every unit supplied except the last (at point M) is receiving a price (OP) in excess of that strictly necessary to obtain it. For example, the unit corresponding to the point M' would be forthcoming at a price $M'Q$; in fact it receives a price $M'N'$ so that the difference, QN', is a payment over and above its necessary supply price – that is, it is economic rent. By similar reasoning, *all* of the area *SPN* out of the total payment *OPNM* (i.e. *OM* units at a price of *NM* each) is economic rent – it represents revenue received by the suppliers of the input or commodity which is in excess of that strictly necessary to bring forth that supply.

A similar kind of argument could be advanced in relation to the area *DPN* under the demand schedule. This represents

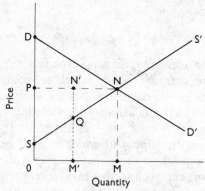

Fig. 16B Economic rent and consumers' surplus

payments which the purchasers of the input or commodity *would* have been willing to make in order to obtain it had it not in fact been obtainable at the price *OP*. This area is a kind of consumers' rent – or, as it is more usually called, a *consumers' surplus*. It is a representation of the benefit derived by consumers from the ability to buy at the market price something which they would have been prepared to pay a higher price for if necessary.

The concept of economic rent has important theoretical, if not practical, implications for taxation policy. If wages, profits or interest are taxed beyond a certain degree it is possible that serious effects may be felt on the supply of factors and hence on production: workers may be unwilling to work long hours, entrepreneurs may be less inclined to assume risks for the sake of large profits, investors may be reluctant to lend money. But the taxation of economic rent, by definition, could have no influence on incentives or effort, since it is an unnecessary payment so far as factor-supply is concerned. Unfortunately it is extremely difficult to distinguish in practice between economic rent and other forms of income, although the attempts to tax the market value of land whose value appreciates because of, for example, housing developments around it constitute an illustration of the transfer of economic rent from private landowners to society as a whole.

4   QUASI-RENT

Considering the elasticity of supply of factors of production, there are at one extreme factors which are completely fixed in supply, and at the other extreme factors, such as ordinary unskilled labour, which are in fairly elastic supply so far as any individual industry is concerned. Between these extremes can be found factors the supply of which is fixed in the short run but which is responsive to demand changes after the lapse of time. In the short run such factors may receive rewards considerably in excess of their supply price, and if this happens they can be said to earn economic rent. The difference between them and the resources discussed in the preceding section − land and other factors possessing some peculiar, innate qualities of economic value − is that the rent they earn is essentially temporary; the passage of time is bound to remove the causes leading to their excess earnings. For this reason the surplus payment received by these factors is known as *quasi-rent*.

An example will indicate how and why quasi-rent can arise. When free dental treatment first became available in the United Kingdom as a result of the introduction of the National Health Service, the demand for the services of qualified dentists was greatly increased. As there was in existence only a limited number of people with the requisite qualifications, the result was a substantial increase in the earnings of this specialised form of labour, and the people concerned found themselves earning considerably more than they could have obtained in any alternative occupation open to them – i.e. their earnings exceeded their transfer cost. After the lapse of a time sufficient to train the new entrants attracted to the dental profession by these high earnings, however, the supply of labour to the industry increased and the earnings of dentists returned to a more normal level. The surplus earnings enjoyed between the initial rise in demand and the full adjustment of the labour supply to the new conditions could be called quasi-rent.

Similarly, an increase in the demand for a product will generally cause a rise in its price, and hence in the profits of enterprises producing it. If the capital equipment involved in its production is to some degree specialised, as it frequently is, it will be some time before extra equipment can be manufactured and installed in order to meet the increased demand, and until the capacity of the industry has been fully adjusted the owners of existing enterprises will be earning unusually high profits. The excess of these profits over the necessary supply price of the equipment concerned is a quasi-rent.

Like pure economic rent, therefore, quasi-rent is a surplus over and above the necessary supply price of a factor which arises out of some special quality or ability of the factor concerned. Unlike pure economic rent, quasi-rent is essentially temporary; the qualities or abilities which give rise to it *can* be increased in supply, but only after the lapse of a period of time during which quasi-rent is earned.

From the concept of a payment for the use of land or other natural agents, then, rent has developed an extended significance in economics. The word is now used *either* (in its original sense) to mean the income derived from the ownership of land, *or* to mean any income paid to a factor which exceeds its necessary supply price, or transfer cost. In the latter sense, the modified form of 'quasi-rent' is employed, in reference to rents of a temporary nature arising only from a time-lag in the supply of factors to changed conditions of demand. It is most important, of course, that the sense in which the word 'rent' is being used should always be made clear.

5   SITES AND INDUSTRIAL LOCATION

One important quality of land, as has been noted, is its geographical position, apart altogether from its fertility. For this reason, a piece of land may have a value out of all proportion to its agricultural potentialities. A hectare of land in London's West End is worth much more than hundreds of hectares of first-class farming land; this is because for some purposes a hectare of poor land in Piccadilly is worth ten thousand good hectares in Cumberland.

Site values may be derived, as in that instance, from the favourable position of the land in relation to potential demand. They may originate in the relative *isolation* of land, if residential building is involved. Most important of all, however, is that different areas have widely different values as sites upon which production can be carried on. Hence it is necessary to analyse the various factors which influence the value of land as an *industrial* site. Why is it that one piece of land will command a high price as a site while another, of equal or greater agricultural value, will command only a low price? Why, in other words, are industrial costs higher in one location than in another?

Probably the most important factors historically which have led industry to particular areas are those of *power* supplies and *raw materials*. The woollen industry, for example, one of Britain's oldest industries, was originally dependent on water power (i.e. before the application of the steam engine) and as a result it tended to be carried on in relatively hilly areas (such as the West Riding) where fast-flowing streams were available. Similarly, when steam power become widely adopted, manufacturing industry was attracted to regions such as the North of England and South Wales where ample coal supplies were available.

The importance of raw materials is self-evident. For industries concerned with the *extraction* of these materials, such as coal, slate and metal ores, one area will obviously have advantages over another. Such industries can be located only in areas where the minerals are deposited in the quantity and geological conditions necessary for their extraction to be worthwhile. For industries *using* raw materials, the advantages of some areas over others may be equally compelling. 'Heavy' industries, such as the manufacture of iron and steel, consume large quantities of coal and mineral ores, and it is advantageous for such industries to be operating close to the supplies of these materials; to transport them from the area in which they are mined to another area where they are used in production would add considerably to production costs. During the great development of these industries in Britain during the eighteenth and nineteenth centuries, therefore, the coalfields of the country became also centres of manufacturing industry. The industries consuming large quantities of iron and steel, such as shipbuilding and engineering, are in their turn attracted to the areas in which iron and steel are produced. Nowadays, when large quantities of raw materials are imported into Britain from abroad many industries find it advantageous to operate near *ports*; flour milling, for example, takes place predominantly at the ports where foreign wheat is imported, since the wheat can be taken directly into granaries from the holds of ships with a minimum of expensive handling operations.

On the other hand, there is a similar saving of transport charges if industries are close to the major *markets* for the finished product; these may not be, and usually are not, the same areas as those from which the raw materials are drawn. For an industry making goods sold to consumers rather than to other producers, it will be advantageous to be located near the great centres of population; London attracted many of the new industries making consumer goods (for example, electrical goods and furniture) during the 1920s and 1930s mainly for this reason. Hence an industry may be pulled towards different areas – one where its raw materials are to be found and another where its market lies. The outcome will depend on the nature of the product. If the raw materials used up are bulky and the finished product relatively cheap to transport (as is the case with the 'heavy' industries) the industry will tend to locate itself close to raw material supplies. If the final product is more expensive to transport, because of its bulk, its fragile nature or the need for rapid delivery, the market will exercise the greater pull – as with biscuits, or electrical goods, or bread. For industries whose product *cannot* be transported – service trades, for example, such as hotels, laundries, garages, or professional services – the locality of the market will entirely determine the localisation of the industry.

These are all factors which may attract an industry to a particular area in the first instance. When an industry has established itself in a certain area, however, cumulative forces may be set up which tend to retain it in that area. *Subsidiary trades* may establish themselves around an industry in a particular area, so increasing the cost advantages of that area for a firm setting up in the industry – marine engineering has grown up especially near centres of shipbuilding such as the Clyde, and firms specialising in the manufacture of textile machinery have been drawn towards Lancashire, where their major customers are established. This may extend to institutions specialising in the handling of an industry's raw materials or finished product, such as the Liverpool Cotton Exchange for the Lancashire cotton industry or the Bradford firms specialising in dyeing and finishing for the Yorkshire woollen industry.

Again, an area in which an industry becomes concentrated tends to develop a skilled *labour supply* with special knowledge of that industry, so that a new firm would find there a pool of skilled labour which it would be unlikely to find elsewhere. (On the other hand, in times of acute labour shortage, a firm might be attracted to an area where a labour supply is easy to obtain because there was no industry there previously.)

It is easy to see how these factors tend to be cumulative in effect. Once an industry is established, subsidiary or specialised trades are set up in the area, increasing the cost advantage of the area for that industry. The growth of a skilled labour force accustomed to the industry operates in the same way. Hence an industry may be attracted to an area by its acquired advantages long after the 'natural' forces which attracted the industry initially have ceased to operate. The town of High Wycombe became the centre of the furniture industry, for example, primarily because it was close to the beech trees of the Chilterns which originally supplied the industry with its main raw material. The industry no longer relies on local wood, but the area still attracts new firms because it contains specialists in furniture machinery and processing, a labour force traditionally skilled in furniture making and schools and technical colleges paying special regard to training for the furniture industry.

Although these are the major forces affecting the location of industry in different areas, other factors may operate in particular cases. High in the list of these would certainly come the facilities for transport and communication which an area enjoys: easy access to the motorway network or express rail services are vitally important to practically any industry. Good *harbour facilities* are obviously of vital importance to shipbuilding and repairing trades; the qualities of the local *water supply* and the peculiarities of the local *climate* are reputed to have determined the specialisation of Burton in brewing and Lancashire in spinning; a low *rent* may attract industries to relatively undeveloped areas; occasionally, the local availability of *capital* may attract an industry – a well-known aircraft company initially established itself in Yorkshire in the 1930s, for example, because a local landowner was prepared to put capital into the venture in an attempt to relieve unemployment amongst the people of his area. All these factors may contribute to making the costs of production in a particular industry lower in one area than another. On the other hand, the owner of a firm may be drawn to a locality for purely personal reasons of a non-economic, and even irrational, nature.

The advantages to an industry of a high degree of specialisation within an area are obvious enough. Unfortunately, the experience of the depression of the 1930s made clear that such specialisation also had grave social dangers. As was stressed in the discussion of labour mobility in the previous chapter, an undue dependence by a community on a limited range of industry can result in widespread poverty and hardship if that industry encounters bad times. If industry is diversified, a depression in one may be offset by prosperity in another, and the area as a whole will not be unduly affected. In one-industry areas there is no alternative employment if depression hits that industry, and the whole region is seriously affected.

Mainly because of this danger, government policy in Britain since 1945 has favoured the diversification of industry, especially in areas which before the war were dependent on one or two basic industries and were especially hit by the depression of the 1930s. Under the *Distribution of Industry Act* of 1945 these 'development' areas, as they are called, received special treatment. The government was empowered to build factories or to promote trading estates in them so as to attract firms to those areas as tenants; it could give financial assistance to such firms, and in the days of controls over building and raw materials such firms tended to be favoured in precedence to those operating outside the development areas. Under various *Town and Country Planning Acts* of 1943, 1947 and 1955 power has been given to local government authorities, acting with the advice of the central government, to control the development of land throughout the country so as to prevent further industrial building in areas in which it is considered that industrial development has proceeded far enough. By the mid-1950s many of the original 'development' areas had ceased to present special problems, whereas other, less clearly defined areas were beginning to experience difficulties which, while less extensive than had been the case in the old development areas, were nevertheless serious enough in intensity. An attempt to make policy more flexible was made by the *Distribution of Industry (Industrial Finance) Act* of 1958, which empowered the government to give financial assistance to firms moving into areas scheduled from time to time on the basis of having had a minimum rate of 4 per cent unemployment for a year.

It was soon apparent that such a policy operated too slowly – by the time an area had experienced substantial unemployment for a whole year and a firm had then managed to satisfy the authorities that financial assistance was justified, the original problem of the area might well have ceased to be soluble. Recessions tend to become increasingly intractable the more they are prolonged. Furthermore, increasing stress came to be laid on the existence of *under*-employment in certain regions rather than unemployment – that is, a situation in which the proportion of the adult population actually entering the labour force was well below the national average. Here, it was felt, were potentialities for economic growth which were not being exploited primarily because of the lack of suitable employment opportunities. Hence a clear shift in emphasis occurred in official policy. The *Local Employment Act* of 1960, which repealed the previous legislation, embodied most of the powers contained in the 1945 and 1958 Acts, including the ability to give assistance to areas named from time to time in the light of current conditions, rather than to a rigidly defined list. Most important, it enabled the government to act in areas where there is a *special danger* of high unemployment, and does not require the authorities to wait until an area has necessarily *experienced* such unemployment before acting. Finally, from 1966 onwards, a system of cash grants for new industrial investment in plant and machinery was introduced in place of the previous system of granting investment allowances to be set against tax liability. The value of these grants can be substantially increased if the investment occurs in certain *Special Development Areas* (e.g. communities heavily dependent on collieries which are no longer viable) where the economic and social problems of technological change are particularly acute. The government also has powers to give other forms of assistance to firms being established or expanded in such areas – loans and grants for specific projects, the building of factories for sale or renting on advantageous terms and so on.

The problem in all these attempts to avoid the dangers of undue concentration and specialisation is that the forces attracting industry to particular areas are often powerful. If state intervention is necessary to induce an industry to locate itself in some area other than that it would itself have chosen, the implication is that as a result the industry will be located in areas where its costs of production are higher than they would otherwise have been. For goods which the community itself consumes, this higher cost represents the price of a better balance in the distribution of industry, and can be borne as such. For industries facing foreign competition in home or export markets, however, the extra cost is more serious; foreigners will see no reason why they should pay for improvements in British industrial distribution, and will naturally exploit their cost advantage. The crucial problem here, then, is to reconcile the need for a balanced distribution of industry with that for the highest possible level of industrial efficiency.

FURTHER READING

A. BEACHAM and N. J. CUNNINGHAM *Economics of industrial organisation* Ch. 4

R. TURVEY *The economics of real property* Allen and Unwin, London 1957, Chs. 2–5

J. ROBINSON *The economics of imperfect competition* Macmillan, London 1948, Ch. 8

R. S. EDWARDS and H. TOWNSEND *Business enterprise* Macmillan, London 1958, Chs. 6, 16 and 17

CHAPTER XVII

Profit

1   PROFIT AS AN ACCOUNTING SURPLUS

LIKE the word 'rent', the expression 'profit' is one which is used in ordinary conversation a good deal more widely and loosely than in economic analysis. Many people would say that profit is the difference between the price at which a commodity is sold and the cost of the labour and raw materials used up in its production. A moment's consideration will show that the sum arrived at in this way would be considerably more than the rewards of the factor of enterprise, which is the meaning of the word profit in economics. It would include a certain amount which entrepreneurs would need to set aside for the *depreciation* of the capital employed; as was noted in Chapter VIII, a certain amount of capital consumption occurs in almost all production, and a deduction must be made from gross receipts merely to maintain capital intact.

A second deduction which has to be made is that of *interest* on the capital employed. Apart from the need to maintain capital intact, a payment must be made to the lenders of the funds with which capital was purchased to compensate them for sacrificing the control of their wealth over the period during which it is used in production. It may be that an entrepreneur has employed his own capital in the business; if this is so, part of the apparent profit received by him is in fact interest on his capital, even though a separate deduction under this heading is not actually made.

Thirdly, some of the accounting profit may really be *wages* for the labour performed in management. In a public joint-stock company, managers are usually paid officials whose salaries are shown as an element of cost in exactly the same way as the wages of operatives. If an entrepreneur carries out management duties himself, however, a separate payment may not be made to him on this account; nevertheless, an element in gross profits in the accounting sense will need to be deducted as wages of management. A farmer's net income, for example, may constitute not only profits but also sums received by him as wages in respect of the labour he (and probably his wife) has supplied during the period. If he owns his own farm another part of his net income may represent the rent of the land which he owns and, so to speak, puts at his own disposal for the purpose of agricultural production.

Consider, for example, a small shopkeeper who has invested his own savings in his shop and the capital to stock it. He employs one assistant and his sales in a certain year amount to £60 000, the purchase price of these from the wholesalers amounting to £54 000. After allowing for his other costs (rates, lighting, heating, etc.) his profit margin might appear to be:

Gross sales	£60 000
Cost of goods	£54 000
Gross profit	£6 000
Less: Wages of assistant	−£1 500
Other costs	− £800
Net profit	£3 700

The figure of £3 700 would, however, be a distinct over-statement of his real profit in the economic sense. From this total must be subtracted, first, an allowance for the labour which the shopkeeper himself has presumably put into the business during the year – at least the equivalent of the cost of his assistant. Secondly, allowance must be made for the annual cost of his premises: in fact he owns them, but if he did not an annual rent would have been payable (or obtainable from another tenant). Finally, some allowance should be made for the cost of the working capital locked up in the business – say 10 per cent per annum on an average working capital of £5 000. Hence the appropriate calculations might have run:

Apparent net profit	£3 700
Less: Cost of own labour	−£1 500
Rent and depreciation of premises	−£ 800
Interest on capital	−£ 500
True profit	£ 900

True profit, then, is the sum remaining from the value of output after payments (actual or imputed) have been made in respect of the land, labour and capital employed in production – including any of these inputs supplied by the entrepreneur himself – and after a deduction has been made for capital depreciation. It is this which is the reward paid to the entrepreneur as such; it is completely distinct from any reward he may obtain in respect of functions he may discharge as a supplier of labour, land or capital.

2 PROFIT AS A COST

Defined in this way, profit could still be regarded as a surplus, since it is the sum left over from the sale of output after the factors of land, labour and capital have received their share of the product. It is a residual in the sense that the rewards of the other factors are determined in advance, whereas profit fluctuates according to the proceeds of current production. Unlike the other factor-prices, it may even be negative; the entrepreneur may find that at the end of an accounting period his economic activity has actually left him poorer than when he began.

Yet profit is still a cost of production from the economist's point of view. It is a cost because it is necessary to call forth a supply of the factor of enterprise, which is as necessary to the production of wealth as any other factor. To be exact, an entrepreneur is induced to undertake production because of the profit he *expects* to receive; the profit he actually receives cannot influence his decision since it emerges only after the event. In practice, however, the expectations of profit which entrepreneurs hold are bound to be strongly influenced by the profits they have actually received in the past from similar production efforts. Hence, profit can be treated as the cost of enterprise, even though it is the *expectation* of profit which is the operative element.

True profit is a cost of production because a price has to be paid to ensure a supply of entrepreneurs. As was noted in the previous chapter, profit, like all other factor incomes, may include an element of economic rent or quasi-rent; nevertheless, there will always be a minimum price necessary if the factor of enterprise is to be supplied. If profits fall to an unduly low level, men who would otherwise have fulfilled the functions of the entrepreneur will instead seek employment as workers, managerial or otherwise, or be content to live on any income they can obtain from the ownership of land or capital. But profit fluctuates much more than the payment to any other factor, both from one industry to another and from one time to another; since it can be negative in some cases there may be no limit to its fluctuation in either direction. Why is this?

3   THE BEARING OF UNCERTAINTY

In Chapter II it was stated that the special role of the entrepreneur in an economy was that of undertaking the responsibility for bringing the other factors together to form a productive unit, and of bearing the uncertainty inevitable in such a process in a changing and unstable world. The supplier of labour, or land, or capital, at least knows in advance the reward which will be obtained during the term of the contract under which these factors are engaged. This is not to say that the owners of these factors run no risk whatever. The owner of capital may discover that a borrower is a fraud who proceeds to dishonour his contract to repay the capital; the landowner may be ruined by flood or earthquake; the worker may lose his job and suffer prolonged unemployment. But these risks, of dishonesty, natural calamity or economic depression (like those of war, or personal violence, or disease), are risks which are shared to some degree or other by all members of society. The entrepreneur, whether a single person or a group of ten thousand shareholders is involved, cannot rely on some guaranteed level of earnings; he has to sustain the special uncertainties of changes in fashion, or technological development, or misjudgement of the market — all the thousand and one factors which may falsify expectations regarding the volume of sales of a product, the price it will obtain or the costs it will involve.

In a free and dynamic economy these factors are bound to operate. Demand is certain to jump unexpectedly from one product to another, unless consumers are forcibly deprived of their right to exercise a free choice; new inventions will render machinery and methods obsolete and relatively wasteful, unless technological advance is somehow brought to a standstill; errors of judgement will surely occur unless men are suddenly endowed with a capacity for predicting the future accurately. Production in anticipation of demand must always involve uncertainties, and if production is to be carried on at all someone must be willing to shoulder them. *Someone* must undertake the task of anticipating the way in which demand, innovation and consumer taste are going to change in the future and take the chance involved in developing a new product or process. Not only must a 'best guess' be made in these matters; it has also to be backed with resources which may be lost if the guess turns out to be a bad one. The suppliers of labour, land and capital have to be paid their reward whatever the outcome; if the price eventually obtained for a product is insufficient to meet these rewards, then the entrepreneur must make up the deficiency from his own resources. The placing of one's own wealth in peril of loss is not a prospect which would appeal to many people unless there was some compensating hope of gain. Profit is the reward which induces people to assume the special and vital role of the entrepreneur.

It is the existence of uncertainty, then, which lies at the root of profit. If the world relapsed into a static state in which neither demand nor costs of production could conceivably change, uncertainty would vanish from the economic scene, and with it would vanish the necessity for profit. In the real world, of course, uncertainty is always present. Various undesirable eventualities (losses through fire, or theft, or tempest, for example) occur in society as a whole with such regularity that insurance companies are prepared, for an appropriate fee, to relieve individuals of the possibility of loss implicit in them; to the extent that these eventualities can be insured against, of course, the entrepreneur can treat the insurance premium as a cost of production, like any other cost, and profit will not be required to induce entrepreneurs to face such risks. But there will always remain the possibility of eventualities – fluctuations in demand or technological developments, for example – which do not occur with sufficient regularity to enable insurance companies to indemnify entrepreneurs against them. And the insurance companies themselves will always be bearing the residual uncertainty, so to speak, involved in the contingencies for which they *do* provide cover; their calculations of the probability of death or fire may be completely upset by a plague or wave of arson, so that they in turn will require profit to compensate *them* for taking this chance.

It follows that the rate of profit necessary to induce an adequate supply of entrepreneurship – the 'normal profit' included as an element in the cost curve – will vary from industry to industry according as the degree of uncertainty varies. Some commodities (most foodstuffs, for example) have a stable demand curve over long periods of time, while the possibility of sudden and drastic changes in the method of their production is not especially great. In such industries a relatively low rate of profit could be expected to prevail. By contrast, a brand-new product has an unknown future; it may be a resounding success but it may also be a dismal failure. A particularly high rate of expected profit may be necessary to induce people to risk resources in such a venture. Wherever the uncertainties attached to producing goods are especially great, profits will have to be high if entrepreneurs are to come forward, whether the uncertainty arises from the nature of the product, the method of production, the time-lag between committing resources and recovering them through the sale of output, or from the prevailing environment.

4 PROFITS AND THE ALLOCATION OF RESOURCES

The way in which the price mechanism allocates resources to different uses in a competitive economy was described in Chapter XIV. The rather special role of profits in this process justifies particular stress, however. After all, it is the entrepreneur who takes the initiative in a competitive society. It is he who has to decide what shall be produced and in what quantity, how much labour, land and capital shall be used and in what proportions. Since profit is the element which determines the action of entrepreneurs, it follows that it has a vitally important function in the allocation of resources.

It is through changes in the rate of profit that the competitive impulse is first felt. If the output of a certain commodity is greater than the consumer thinks desirable (i.e. the utility derived from it is low in relation to the scarce resources absorbed in its production), the price at which it will sell in the market will fall. Since the entrepreneur has to pay the agreed rewards to land, labour and capital whatever the price at which the product sells, profits will inevitably be small; if price falls far enough, profits may be replaced by losses. In this way the entrepreneur is warned that he is not employing resources in a manner which will render the maximum possible satisfaction to the community, and he will be forced to use the resources at his command in a different way or go out of production altogether.

Conversely, an entrepreneur who uses resources so as to cater for a novel and relatively strong want felt by the community will obtain a high price for his product, and will therefore enjoy high profits. This will encourage him to increase his production and add even further to his profits; entrepreneurs will also be encouraged to move resources from less profitable industries into this high-profit industry. Through fluctuations in the level of profits, then, the community expresses its judgement that more resources should be used in some directions and fewer resources in others, and the entrepreneurs concerned are stimulated or discouraged accordingly.

Profit not only acts as a guide to the industries in which entrepreneurs should expand or contract output. It also provides a means whereby the more efficient entrepreneurs are enabled to draw resources away from the less efficient. At any given market price, a highly successful entrepreneur, who will have, by definition, relatively low costs of production, will be enjoying a high rate of profit. He will therefore have an incentive to obtain more factors of production in order to expand output, and will be prepared to offer slightly higher wages, rent and interest so as to obtain them. The inefficient entrepreneur, by contrast, will have been making only a minimum rate of profit, and even this will disappear as factor-prices are bid up by his competitors; eventually his profit disappears completely and he is forced out of business, setting free the resources he was previously using for employment by more efficient producers.

In this way, then, profit does more than merely ensure that an adequate supply of the factor of enterprise is forthcoming. In a perfectly competitive world it provides to entrepreneurs a compelling indicator as to the kind and quantity of commodities which the community considers they should produce with the available factors of production. Bearing in mind the basic assumption that consumers set out to distribute their expenditure so as to maximise the satisfaction they obtain, it follows that by means of relative profit-levels resources are distributed amongst different industries in such a manner as to maximise the satisfaction which a society derives from the scarce resources at its disposal. Furthermore, the function of profit is to weed out the inefficient entrepreneurs and ensure that production is carried on under the direction of the entrepreneurs whose relative efficiency is highest.

All this, however, presupposes the existence of a perfectly competitive world, and, as was established at an earlier stage, the real world is far from perfectly competitive. The picture must be modified, therefore, to allow for the existence of monopoly.

5   MONOPOLY PROFITS

It was concluded earlier that under imperfect competition price would be higher than it would be if the commodity was produced under conditions of perfect competition. This was not because the producers were making relatively high profits, however; when equilibrium prevails in an imperfectly competitive industry, all entrepreneurs are earning the normal profits appropriate to their ability. Price is unduly high because there are too many firms producing at a rather low level of output, and at some point on the average cost curve which is above the possible minimum. Under imperfect competition, prices are high because costs are high; the evil of the situation is not especially high profit-margins but the waste of unused capacity. (It will be remembered that the question of whether the advantages of imperfect competition are sufficient to outweigh this evil is one of personal opinion rather than one of objective analysis.)

In monopoly situations, however, different considerations apply. Because of his controlling position in total production, a monopolist is able to hold price above average cost; price is high not only because production is carried on at a relatively high-cost level (which it usually will be, of course) but also because the producer is making exceptional profit out of his monopoly power.

How can such excessive profits be reconciled with the considerations determining the nature and functions of profit which have just been discussed? The answer can only be that the excess, or supra-normal, profits received by a monopolist are a form of economic rent, in its sense of a surplus over and above transfer cost. It has already been established that economic rent can be enjoyed by any factor having some quality which cannot be increased in supply. The monopolist obviously has such a quality – he has the ability, derived from natural or artificial factors, to restrict the supply of a commodity and hence to obtain a high price for it. Previously economic rent was conceived of as arising from innate and non-producible qualities, or, in the case of quasi-rent, from the physical impossibility of increasing the supply of a certain factor in the short run. In principle there is no difference between, on the one hand, rent arising from a scarcity due to the physical impossibility of increasing the supply of a rent-earning quality, and, on the other hand, rent arising from the natural or artificial limitations which constitute the foundation of monopoly power. If the monopoly position is a permanent one, the entrepreneur's profits in excess of the normal level are a form of pure economic rent; if the monopoly power is temporary (such as one arising from patent rights during a specific period of time) then the excess is a quasi-rent.

What are the implications of monopoly profit for the allocation of resources? Cbviously it can no longer be concluded from the existence of a high level of profits in the actual world that the industry involved is one in which an unusually large element of uncertainty prevails, or that the entrepreneur concerned has exceptional ability. The high profits may be a reflection of some degree of monopoly power which permits an entrepreneur to reap an economic rent at the expense of the consumer. Nor can profits always be relied upon to stimulate entrepreneurs to make the optimum use of society's scarce resources. A monopolist, as the analysis has shown, does not carry production to that point at which average costs are equal to price. High profit will not lead to higher production because the monopolist himself is already operating at the output which gives him maximum profit, while the presence of monopoly power means that other entrepreneurs are not able to move into the industry in order to share in the high profits prevailing in it. If monopolies exist in the economy (as they do in the real world) then the profit mechanism will not lead to the optimum distribution of resources; output will be too low, profits will be unnecessarily high, and the consumer will be deprived of the full benefit of the wealth-producing powers of his society.

FURTHER READING

c. j. hawkins and d. w. pearce *Capital investment appraisal* Macmillan, London 1971

b. s. keirstead *An essay in the theory of profits and income distribution* Blackwell, Oxford 1953

d. m. lamberton *The theory of profit* Blackwell, Oxford 1965, Chs. 1–4

p. j. d. wiles *Price, cost and output* Blackwell, Oxford 1961, Ch. 11

CHAPTER XVIII

The National Income

1 MEASURING THE NATIONAL INCOME

THE journey through the elementary analysis of the functioning of the economic system is now well advanced. It has been seen that economic activity is aimed at the satisfaction of as many of society's infinite wants as possible from the limited resources at its disposal; that consumers distribute their expenditure so as to derive the greatest benefit from their income; that resources are combined so as to meet the demands of consumers; that the value of a product in relation to other products is determined by the interaction of demand and supply; and finally the analysis has shown how the value of every product is shared between wages, rent, interest (to which the discussion will have to return later), and profits.

If all this is brought together the concept of the *national income* is arrived at — that is, the total flow of wealth produced, distributed and consumed by the economy as a whole. Just as an individual can arrive at a figure for his total income by adding up everything he has received from work or property during a given period, so a nation as a whole can add up all the incomes of its citizens over a period and arrive at its *national* income.

How can this be done in fact? It is known that every penny of every price is someone's income, and that income can arise ultimately only from the production of something; hence it follows that the total income received by society as a whole during, say, a year can be conceived of as a circular flow comparable to the flow of water around the cooling system of a car. A highly simplified picture of this flow is given in Fig. 18A. Consider first the box labelled 'Enterprises' which represents all those activities devoted to the production of goods and services within the country. From here incomes are paid out in the form of wages, salaries, rent, dividends and interest to the households – i.e. society looked at in its role of groups of spenders rather than producers. A meter inserted at this point would measure Gross National Income (GNY); the significance of the word 'Gross' is explained a little later. From the households income flows out again as expenditure – including expenditure on capital goods by householders in their capacity as owners of productive enterprises – and a meter inserted at this point between households and the market in which goods are sold would measure Gross National Expenditure (GNE) at market prices. Finally, the proceeds of these purchases of capital and consumer goods flow on and back to the enterprises which produced them; a meter inserted between the market and the enterprise sector would thus record Gross Domestic Product (GDP) at 'factor cost' – a term explained below.

It follows from all this, then, that the national income of any country for any year can be calculated either by adding up the value of all *sales* of finished goods and services, or by adding up the values of all types of *production*, or by adding up the *incomes* received by all individuals or organisations. These three things – total expenditure, total production and total income – are really the same thing looked at from different angles. In practice, all three methods of measuring the national income are employed; since there are gaps of varying degrees of importance in the statistics available under each heading, the three methods check and supplement each other.

It may be helpful to indicate broadly the way in which the official statisticians set about the task of compiling their national income estimates, which in Britain are published every year. The first method is that of estimating total expenditure on finished products. The total amounts spent on *consumer goods* are estimated from statistics relating to the annual sales of wholesalers and retailers. A basic source of such data is the Census of Distribution which is carried out periodically; for this census, every shop makes a return showing (amongst other things) the total value of its sales. For the intervening years the statisticians rely on data supplied by a smaller number of shops which are

regarded as a representative sample. To these estimates of purchases of goods has to be added the estimated expenditure on
personal services of all kinds, such as entertainment, repairs,
professional services and domestic help. Then the amount spent
on *capital goods* has to be added. As such goods are purchased
mainly by companies, the major sources of data here are company

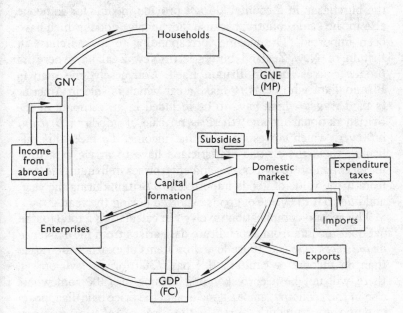

Fig. 18A The national income flow

balance sheets, tax returns, and the Census of Production (briefly
described below); from these can be calculated the amount spent
on fixed assets (plant, buildings, vehicles, etc.) and on stocks
of raw materials and finished or semi-finished goods.

The calculation of total expenditure, however, is not entirely
a straightforward affair even in principle (the statistical problems
of estimation, of course, are very considerable). Certain pitfalls
have to be avoided, and in the process of avoiding them the
published national income estimates become somewhat compli-

cated. It is obvious that in calculating a country's national income *via* estimates of total expenditure, only purchases which provide income for someone else in the community should be included, while care should be taken to see that no such purchases are excluded. This is a little trickier than might be supposed at first sight because of two complications. The first is *foreign trade*. An effect of the existence of such trade is that some of the purchases in a country do *not* provide income for someone else in the same country, because they involve goods which have been imported. The income corresponding to my purchase in Britain of New Zealand butter is in New Zealand, where its producer lives, not in Britain itself. Conversely, the man in Birmingham who helps to make a car which is sold in America is paid wages which have to be included in an estimate of the British national income; there is no sale of goods *in Britain,* however, which corresponds to that income. To meet this difficulty, then, the British statisticians have to arrive at a total for all expenditure by persons and enterprises in Britain, *subtract* from it the value of goods imported into Britain during the year, and *add* to it the value of goods exported during the year.

The second complication involved in calculating a total for the national income from expenditure data arises from the existence of *indirect taxes* (i.e. those levied on items of expenditure rather than on income or capital). If I pay £300 for a television set, there will not be a corresponding income of £300 somewhere else in the economy, since a good deal of the price paid disappears into the government's purse in the form of taxation receipts. Conversely, when a mother buys a pint of milk for her small daughter the income received for that milk is considerably more than the price she pays because the government pays part of the farmer's price for milk in the form of a *subsidy,* which is a kind of negative indirect tax. If the estimate of total expenditure is to be used to measure the incomes actually received as a result of current production, then, statisticians have to take the basic estimate of total expenditure, *subtract* the value of indirect taxes and *add* the value of subsidies. When they do this it is said that they are measuring the national income at *factor cost* (i.e. at what the various factors of production were actually paid for it); if they do not make this adjustment they are measuring at *market prices*.

The second method of measurement of the national income is the addition of the values of the goods and services produced by all the enterprises in the economy – i.e. the estimate of the value of total *production*. For almost all of industry, such estimates are based on the Census of Production; returns for this are made by all industrial establishments in the United Kingdom every five years and by a fairly large sample in every year. These returns provide a great deal of information about the productive activities of the enterprises; in particular, they state the value of the goods produced by them during the year concerned. For industries not covered by the Census of Production, estimates are based primarily on statistical material covering the amounts paid in wages, salaries, rent and interest in such industries, together with balance-sheet and tax data bearing on the profits made by the firms concerned. As has been established, the payments made to factors of production plus the residual sum going to profits (or minus any losses) must equal the values of the goods produced.

As in the expenditure method of calculating the national income, care has to be taken to avoid possible errors of principle in totalling the value of current production. Once again there are two major considerations. The first is that *double-counting* must be avoided – that is, the total must not include the value of both goods *and* the value of raw materials, etc., used up in their production. For example, assume that a refrigerator sold for £100 embodies steel worth £20. If the statisticians added up the gross value of the production of steel and refrigerators, the £20 worth of steel would be counted twice – once as part of the output of the steel industry and again when it is included in the value of the output of refrigerators. To avoid this error, the output measured for each industry is not its gross output – i.e. the full sales-value of the goods produced – but its net value, or the 'value added' by each industry – i.e. the market value of the output *minus* any raw materials or semi-finished goods purchased from other producers.

The second point about production totals is similar to this.

Just as the statisticians must avoid including in the value of output goods or materials already counted in the output of some other producer, so they should avoid including any *capital* consumed. It was noted in Chapter VIII that when capital depreciates, or wears out, in the course of production (as it almost invariably does), the extent of that depreciation has to be subtracted from the value of output to arrive at a true figure for current production; unless this is done, a certain amount of capital consumption is included in what purports to be a figure for current creation of wealth. In measuring the national *income*, then, the consumption of *capital* involved in its production during the period concerned should be subtracted. As was explained in Chapter VIII, this is an extremely difficult task statistically, but an attempt is nevertheless made nowadays to measure capital consumption in the United Kingdom; this important matter is discussed further in Section 3 below. If this deduction is not made from the value of production, the resulting national total is called the *gross national product*: only when a deduction *is* made for capital depreciation can the term national income be correctly applied to the estimate.

The third and final method by which the national income may be estimated is that of totalling all *incomes* received by persons and organisations in the country. Such a total can be derived from data collected annually for the purposes of tax assessment in respect of both persons and companies. To this must be added the incomes received by official agencies of one kind or another which carry on productive activities – public corporations, such as the BBC and the Post Office, nationalised industries and trading branches of the central and local government.

Once again, however, a complication has to be dealt with. As was emphasised earlier, the national income represents the value of the wealth produced by a community over a certain period. The total of incomes should therefore include only those receipts which are directly related to the production of goods – i.e. only factor-rewards. In a modern economy, however, the state frequently attempts to make the distribution of incomes more even by taking income from the relatively rich in the form of taxation and handing it over to the relatively needy in the form of what are called *transfer payments* – for example, children's allowances, old-age pensions and other social security grants. These payments enter into the incomes of a good many people in the community. But if the statisticians included them in the income total for national income purposes they would be falling into the old trap of double-counting. If a man earns £3 000 a year as a coal-miner and pays £600 a year in taxation, which is transferred to someone else as a pension, the total amount of wealth *produced* by both the miner and the pensioner is only £3 000, since the pensioner is producing nothing. The government has decided that of the £3 000-worth of wealth produced by the coal-miner, the miner should dispose of £2 400-worth and the pensioner £600-worth. But if the statisticians simply added both incomes together they would arrive at a total of £3 600, which overstates the true value of current production; the transfer income has been included in both the original income from which it was taxed *and* the income of the person to whom it was transferred. To correct the income total, all transfer incomes must be subtracted; only incomes directly related to current production of goods and services must be counted in.

These are the three methods, then, by which an estimate of the total national income may be attempted, and some (by no means all) of the complications involved in them. In theory, the three approaches should lead to identical totals; if they do not it can only be as a result of imperfections and gaps in the statistical data. In fact, the art of compiling such estimates has now reached a sufficiently high degree of perfection to enable a reasonably accurate total to be arrived at each year. It will be instructive to consider briefly the estimates of national income and expenditure in the United Kingdom for the year 1973.

2   NATIONAL INCOME ACCOUNTS

Each year the official estimates of the national income and gross national product of the United Kingdom are published in a Blue Book called *National Income and Expenditure*. The Blue Book contains a large number of tables giving various items in considerable detail; the present discussion need only be concerned with the basic table; this will be sufficient to indicate the kind of information which can be obtained from the annual estimates.

The most comprehensive table is that of the gross national product and national income, since this brings every item together and gives a picture of the economy as a whole. For 1973 the estimates were those shown in Table 18·1; the preceding discussion will have explained the nature of most items in the table. Five features of the income side of the table call for brief comment. The first is the item 'income from self-employment', which represents the incomes of people such as farmers, shop-keepers and small-business proprietors who receive a 'mixed' income from both work and property. As it is never possible to separate out the various elements of their income – how much is wages, how much a reward for entrepreneurship, etc. – only the total is shown. Secondly, the item 'interest' does not appear; the reason for this is that the profits shown are those *before* payments of interest and dividends, so that to include a separate item 'interest' would involve double-counting. Thirdly, the word 'rent' is used in national income accounting in the usual sense of income from real property. It is impossible, of course, to calculate receipts of pure economic rent or quasi-rent. Fourthly, there appears a mysterious item 'stock appreciation', which refers to the change in the value of stocks of goods arising not from a change in their quantity, or volume, but from movements in the prices of the goods involved. Any profit made from a rise in the value of a given stock of commodities will be included in the item 'profits' (just as will be sums required to make good the depreciation of capital), but since it corresponds to no increase in the current production of wealth, and to no item of expenditure, such value-changes have to be excluded from the total of current national income (just as capital depreciation must be). Finally, any income received from the ownership of property in other countries is part of a nation's disposable income and will have been used for its current or capital expenditure; hence it is added in by the item 'income from abroad'.

From a table of this kind a great deal more than simply the total of the gross national product can be learnt. On the expendi-

TABLE 18.1 *Gross National Product of the United Kingdom 1973.* (£ million)*

Expenditure		Income	
At market prices:	£		£
Consumers' expenditure	44 855	Income from employment	42 890
Public authorities' current expenditure on goods and services	13 270	Income from self-employment	6 244
		Profits	10 670
Gross domestic capital formation	14 445	Rent	4 894
		Unidentified errors	589
Total domestic expenditure	72 570	Total domestic income	65 287
Plus exports	21 542	*Less* stock appreciation	−3 111
Less imports	−22 291	*Plus* income from abroad	1 095
Gross national expenditure	71 821		
At factor cost:			
Plus subsidies	1 456		
Less indirect taxes	−10 006		
Gross national product at factor cost	63 271	National income and depreciation	63 271
Less capital consumption	−7 012	*Less* provision for capital depreciation	−7 012
National Income	56 259	National Income	56 259

* Based on *National Income and Expenditure* 1963-1974 (HMSO, London, 1974), Table 1.

ture side is shown the broad pattern of the way in which the community is *disposing* of its income – how much is being spent on personal expenditure, how much the government is spending on goods and services and how much is being set aside for addition to the stock of capital goods – a particularly important question discussed in the next section. From the income side is seen the relative importance of the main factor-rewards; what proportion of the total product is paid to labour, what proportion to profits, etc. The relative importance in year-to-year changes in total incomes of wages, rent and profits can be discovered, thus throwing a good deal of light on the underlying forces at work in a period of rising or falling incomes and demand.

Other tables published annually proceed to break down these aggregates into more detail. For this purpose the economy is divided into six sectors – persons, companies, public corporations, local government authorities, the central government, and a 'rest-of-the-world' sector showing transactions with other countries. Separate tables then set out the different sources of the incomes of each sector and the various ways in which those incomes are disposed of. An especially useful group of tables, for example, show in detail the values of the contributions made to the national product by the different sectors of the economy; Table 18.2 presents a summary of this information for 1973. Similarly, the personal income and expenditure table shows the relative importance of wages, salaries, transfer payments and dividends in total personal income, and changes in these components; on the expenditure side it shows how much of this total is spent, how much paid in direct taxation and how much is saved.

A full appreciation of the wealth of information to be gleaned from a set of national income accounts can be obtained *only by looking carefully through an actual set of accounts*; there is no fuller or clearer guide to the characteristics and development of an economy. They will provide an answer to a great many questions. How rapidly is the national income expanding ? How does the rate of increase compare with that of other countries ? How much of the total income is being set aside to add to capital ? How does the size of this share compare with previous years or other economies ? How important a role does the government play in the consumption of total income ? How important are undistributed profits and personal savings as sources of finance for investment ? Are any significant changes occurring in the pattern of consumer expenditure ? The list is almost endless. A later section will use the national income accounts to throw some light on the important question of the distribution of the national income.

TABLE 18.2 *Gross Domestic Product of the UK by industry of origin, 1973*

	Value of output in £ million	% of Total
Agriculture, Forestry and Fishing	2 166	3·2
Mining and Quarrying	872	1·3
Manufacturing industry:		
Chemicals	1 734	
Metal Manufacture	1 589	
Engineering	5 140	
Vehicles	2 332	
Other metal products incl. shipbuilding	1 758	
Textiles, leather and clothing	2 121	
Food, drink and tobacco	2 327	
Other	3 957	
	20 956	31·2
Construction	4 580	6·8
Gas, electricity and water	1 957	2·9
Transport and communication	5 465	8·1
Distribution	6 794	10·1
Finance, commerce and other services	12 800	19·0
Public administration and defence	4 266	6·4
Public health and education	3 726	5·5
Ownership of dwellings	3 668	5·5
	67 250	100·0

Source: *National Income and Expenditure* 1963-1973 (HMSO, London, 1974), Table 18. The items of stock appreciation and residual error have not been included in the total. The division of the total for manufacturing industry is based on estimates made by the author.

3 CAPITAL FORMATION AND CONSUMPTION

Standards of living vary tremendously amongst the different societies in the modern world, and the primary cause of this, of course, is that the productive capacities of different countries are widely different. Why should one set of people be able to produce more wealth per head than another ? A good many factors can be mentioned in explanation, such as differences in the skill and strength of the labour forces, or in the natural resources available, and the contrasting social and political histories of various races. But pride of place in such an explanation would invariably be given to the fact that the amounts of capital with which different societies are equipped vary tremendously. One coal miner produces more coal than another. There may be many reasons for this; but in practice the main reason may well be that one is winning coal with a pick while the other has power-operated cutting and loading machinery to help him. In almost all productive processes machinery can carry out operations at an infinitely greater speed, and for a longer continuous period, than the strongest and most skilful labourer.

If the use of large amounts of capital is the major road to high productivity, why have not all countries acquired as much capital to assist their labour force as have the highly developed economies? To answer this question it is necessary to appreciate what is involved in the acquisition by a community of capital equipment – *capital formation* as it is called. By definition, capital goods are such as to yield their full benefit only over a considerable period after their construction. If resources are devoted to the production of such goods it is therefore necessary for a community to resign itself to sacrificing for a time the satisfaction it could have enjoyed immediately if the resources had produced consumer goods rather than capital.

Consider a simple example. Crusoe, on his island, had a limited amount of corn. Without the slightest danger of over-eating he could have eaten the lot in the first few months. Instead, he set some aside and planted it. In order to provide the seed for planting, he had to cut down his rate of consumption, which was not pleasant; but in the fullness of time he had his reward in the form of a good crop. The situation is essentially the same in a complex economy; if labour and other resources are used to add to the stock of capital, then the society must sacrifice the consumer goods those resources *could* have produced and which it could have enjoyed immediately. If there are unused (unemployed) resources which are put to work on capital formation – road building, or constructing factories – a society can add to its capital without reducing its consumption; even here, however, the element of sacrifice is present, since the society is still foregoing the consumer goods which those unemployed resources could have produced if society had chosen to employ them differently.

This is the crucial factor in raising the productivity of what are nowadays called under-developed countries. Present needs and satisfactions – i.e. current consumption – must be to some extent denied if capital is to be produced. But if a country is very poor it may be *impossible* to deny present needs; there is little point in providing people with capital if, in the process, they all die of starvation. This is a compelling consideration for countries possessing a democratic system of government, at any rate. If a government regards the welfare of its citizens as secondary to the greater glory of the State, however – and is in a position to disregard the feeling of its citizens – the economic development of a country may be pressed forward at an accelerated pace by holding down present consumption by brute force and disregarding whatever human suffering may follow as a consequence. Hence, a high rate of capital accumulation was achieved in the Soviet Union during the 1920s and 1930s through deliberately incurring the cost of appalling hardship and outright starvation on a vast scale. The different standards of values accepted in most Western countries, and their different political systems, of course, make policies of this kind impossible for them.

Most countries must attain a certain standard of wealth, therefore, before they can feel themselves in a position to set aside resources for capital formation; yet in many cases a standard of production sufficiently high for this can only be attained *after* they have acquired more capital. This vicious circle can be broken only by outside help from richer countries. If a wealthy country gives or lends wealth to a poorer country, then the latter can devote this aid to capital formation without reducing its level of consumption. For example, India, say, can carry out a programme of irrigation works only by using labour previously at work producing food. Without that food many of its people would starve, so Britain and other countries lend to

India the food with which the population can be fed while the capital construction is under way. When it is finished, India's food output will rise significantly – certainly by more than enough to repay the loan over a period of years.

A distinction has to be made, however, between *maintaining* the community's capital stock and *adding* to that stock. In the previous section it was argued that production uses up capital just as it uses up labour and raw materials, and unless resources are set aside to replace this used-up capital the community will be consuming more than it is currently producing. If it continues to do this, of course, it will eventually find its wealth-producing capacity seriously reduced, and it will be substantially poorer as a result. Now, if the capital stock is large it may be a long time before this using-up process seriously affects production; the maintenance of a house may be neglected for years before the rain pours through the roof in sufficient quantities to make life really uncomfortable. If there is a compelling enough reason, then, a community may for a number of years consume more than it is really producing, through the expedient of not using resources for the maintenance of capital but using them, instead, to produce goods which are immediately consumed. During a war, for example, when the outcome of the year or two years ahead is the vital consideration and the more distant future can be left to look after itself, the maximum contribution to the war effort will be secured by using on war production resources which should have been devoted to maintaining the nation's capital intact. In due course all this neglect of capital will need to be made good, and this will then involve a greater sacrifice of current consumption than would otherwise have been necessary. But the assumption is that in the meantime the war will have been won, and that is the vital consideration. That is partly why the British public had to endure rationing and shortages long after the Second World War; Britain had to make good the capital depreciation which had occurred throughout the war years.

Just as economists distinguish between gross and net output to allow for the real but usually unseen element of capital consumption in the course of production, so they distinguish between gross capital formation (or *gross investment,* as it is often called) and net capital formation (or *net investment*). The total use of resources in making capital goods is gross investment. Some of this investment, however, is merely replacing the capital the economy is currently using up (i.e. depreciation) and is not *adding* to its capital at all. Only by deducting this element from total investment is it possible to get a true indication of the amount by which the stock of capital has been *increased*; this amount is called net investment. It is the rate of net investment which indicates how rapidly a community is adding to its productive capacity.

Reference has already been made on more than one occasion to the fact that in practice it is very difficult to measure the extent to which capital has been worn out over a particular period, especially if an allowance is made (as it certainly should be) for the intangible process of obsolescence and if the estimates are complicated by changes occurring contemporaneously in the general level of prices. (The replacement of a machine purchased five years previously may require considerably more than its original cost if the prices of capital goods have risen in the meantime.) An indication of the differences between gross and net output in the United Kingdom in recent years, however, is given by the following estimates presented in the 1974 Blue Book on National Income and Expenditure (in £million):

TABLE 18.3   *Capital consumption in the UK*

	Gross National Product	*Capital Consumption*	*Net National Product (National Income)*
1967	35 233	3 355	31 878
1968	37 668	3 653	34 015
1969	39 679	3 969	35 710
1970	43 537	4 518	39 019
1971	48 957	5 173	43 784
1972	54 903	5 941	48 962
1973	63 271	7 012	56 259

It will be seen that the correction necessary to allow for depreciation – about 10 per cent of gross output – is by no means an insignificant item.

An important point to remember is that one element of capital comprises claims on other countries – claims in the form of either foreign currencies (or gold, which will purchase them) or the ownership of physical assets (mines, plantations, factories, etc.) in foreign countries. Adding to such claims constitutes investment, just as much as adding to the stock of plant and machinery at home. Investment may therefore be *domestic* (adding to capital within the country) or *foreign* (adding to claims on other countries). This latter type of investment has been of special importance in the history of the United Kingdom.

It is clear from what has been said that a high rate of investment is a necessary condition for increasing economic strength; at the same time, it involves the sacrifice of present consumption, which is never a pleasant experience. How is this conflict between future wealth and present enjoyment resolved? In a country such as Britain, where capital is owned by both the State and private individuals, it is the outcome of decisions taken by both sets of people. The government (including nationalised industries) decides how much should be set aside for the increase of socially owned capital; the owners of private businesses decide how much they will add to their capital, guided largely by the price of capital in relation to the wealth they expect it to bring in (a process which will receive a good deal of discussion at a later stage). These decisions concerning investment play a crucial role in determining the overall level of prices and employment, and this too will need to be investigated in detail later on.

4   NATIONAL INCOME AND WELFARE

The national income estimates produced annually should never be accepted too slavishly, precisely because they *are* estimates; of necessity they are frequently based on inadequate or untrustworthy data. Apart from the statistical difficulties of estimation, however, there are important theoretical reasons why changes from year to year in the estimated national income cannot always be taken as implying corresponding changes in the economic welfare of a society. The first and most important point is that, at least in the context of macro-economics, economic analysis (which includes national income accounting) can take account in practice only of transactions which are normally carried out through the medium of money. A change may occur in the nominal value of the national income, therefore, simply because some activity which was previously carried on without the use of money has become a monetary transaction, even though there has been no change in the actual supply of goods and services becoming available. For example, the services of housewives are not included in the national income because they are not paid for; if housewives suddenly decided to have their washing done in laundries rather than do it themselves at home, the value of the output of the laundry industry (and therefore the estimated national income) would increase, although there might well be no increase in the total real value of the personal services being rendered in the economy as a whole.

A second point is closely related to this. Since national income is measured by current monetary values, a rise or fall in the general price level will cause the national income total to rise or fall, even if there has been no change in its real value. For example, between 1938 and 1973 the national income of the United Kingdom rose from £4 816 million to £56 259 million – an increase of nearly 1 000 per cent. Does this mean that the British public were eleven times as well off in 1973 as they had been in 1938? Obviously it does not, since a large part of this rise was due solely to the rise in the general price level, rather than in the supply of goods and services available. In fact, statistics of price movements indicate that in real terms – that is, excluding changes due solely to those in the general price level – the national income of the United Kingdom rose by only about 112 per cent between 1938 and 1973.

Thirdly, the total of the national income must always be interpreted with reference to the general economic environment in which it was produced. A rise in the national income might be accompanied by an even greater rise in population, so that the *per capita* income, and by implication the average standard of living, would have fallen rather than risen. For this reason, the rise of 112 per cent in the national income of Britain between 1938 and 1973 was associated with an increase of only about 80 per cent in real national income *per head*. Again, the national income of a country may rise during wartime, but the switch of resources to war purposes (which may contribute to social or political well-being but can hardly add to economic welfare) may mean that living standards have been reduced. Another possibility is that a higher national income may be the result of inadvisedly long hours of work, or the employment of house-wives in industry to the detriment of family life, or of dictatorial powers of industrial conscription and direction of labour. Yet another – of increasing concern – is that increased output may be associated with environmental deterioration whose adverse effects on social welfare (if they could be measured) more than offset the positive effects of increased physical wealth. The exhaustion of natural resources raises similarly difficult and important issues. Without rejecting completely the usefulness of national income estimates as an important indicator of social welfare, then, it is clear that many other factors should ideally be taken into consideration in association with them.

Finally, the absolute amount of the national income has to be considered in conjunction with its distribution, a subject which merits separate discussion. Here it is sufficient to observe that a rise or fall in the national income does not necessarily imply a rise or fall in *everyone's* income. If a rise in national income is associated with a redistribution of income in favour of the rich, it may be that the poorest members of the community are even poorer than before. *Some* people are better off than before, but the welfare lost by the poor may be greater than the increase in the welfare of the rich; hence economic welfare as a whole may be reduced. It is seldom possible to say dogmatically that economic welfare has increased or decreased, because the incomes of some people may have moved in an opposite direction to those of everyone else. As it is impossible to measure the welfare of different people on some objective scale, it can never be quite certain that the gains more than offset the losses, and *vice versa*.

Despite all these qualifications, the estimate of total national income per head of the population remains the best single indicator of the wealth-producing powers of a country and of changes in its standard of life. The qualifications discussed above imply that such estimates should be interpreted with caution; this is especially true if a comparison is being made over a period in which prices, conditions of work, income distribution or other major features have undergone significant changes.

5 THE DISTRIBUTION OF THE NATIONAL INCOME

So far this Part has been concerned primarily with the distribution of the national income between the four factors of production. The analysis has shown that in a perfectly competitive world the wealth produced in an economy would be shared by the various factors in accordance with their marginal productivity. Price tends to equal marginal cost under perfect competition; this means that the value of all commodities would be equal to the value of the marginal product of all the factors employed. That value, in turn, would be paid out in wages, rent, etc. in accordance with the marginal productivities of the factors concerned. Since the real world is not a perfectly competitive world, there is not perfect knowledge or perfect mobility. Marginal productivity is seldom capable of precise measurement; obstacles exist to the free movement of factors which would equalise marginal productivity in all sectors; monopoly powers are exploited and rents obtained; trade unions and associations bring uneven bargaining pressures to bear.

It would be futile to attempt to embody all these complex and frequently immeasurable forces in one comprehensive analytical structure in the hope of explaining the actual world from *a priori* reasoning. It is necessary, therefore, to resort to empirical investigation to discover what is the actual distribution of the national product between factors. By studying changes in that distribution something may be learnt concerning the forces which are influencing it.

The national income accounts can throw a good deal of light here, and Table 18.4 presents data compiled from them. As was mentioned earlier, interest is not shown as a separate item in the national income table, but is included in profits. Movements in the relative shares of wages, profits and rent, however, can be traced fairly easily. (In Table 18.4 income from self-employment has been combined with employment income, since the wages element is probably predominant; income from abroad has been combined with profits and interest for similar reasons.) It will be seen that between 1938 and 1973 the estimates suggest a

TABLE 18.4 *Distribution of UK Gross National Product between factors, 1938–1973*

Source of income	£ million		% of total	
	1938	*1973*	*1938*	*1973*
Employment and self-employment	3 669	49 134	70·9	77·7
Profits and interest*	1 036	9 243	20·0	14·6
Rent	470	4 894	9·1	7·7
Total	5 175	63 271	100·0	100·0

* Less stock appreciation but including income from abroad and residual error.

Source: *National Income and Expenditure*, 1955 and 1974.

marked shift in the distribution of the national product in favour of labour and against rent-receivers; the share of profits and interest fell even more in the same period. Does this mean that the marginal productivity of labour has increased in relation to that of capital? It is unlikely that an explanation in these analytical terms would be a correct one. The major influences have almost certainly been the increased bargaining power of labour, and government intervention to hold down the level of rents. Labour's bargaining position undoubtedly improved between these years; 1938 was a year in which about 13 per cent of the insured labour force was unemployed (so that the supply of labour was plentiful in relation to the demand for it), while 1973 was a year in which unemployment accounted for less than 3 per cent of the insured labour force. For many years rents had been held down by the various Rent Restriction Acts passed by a succession of governments; as a result, the total of rent payments increased by only about 940 per cent over a period in which the nominal value of the national income rose by more than 1 100 per cent.

Another aspect of the sharing of the national income is that of the distribution amongst persons, rather than factors. The ultimate purpose of the production of wealth, after all, is its consumption by people, rather than by the theoretical conception 'factors of production', and payments in respect of more than a factor of production are often included in the income of a single individual. How has the distribution of income as between rich and poor altered? From the fact that the share of labour has increased it might be inferred that the relatively poor section of the community had benefited at the expense of the well-to-do, but this would not be absolutely certain.

To obtain a fairly reliable picture of what has happened in recent years, reference can be made to the personal income tables in the national income Blue Book; the relevant data are summarised in Table 18.5. The incomes which matter are those remaining after payment of income tax, since it is this *disposable income* which is a reflection of the wealth-consuming power of different sections of the community.

TABLE 18.5 *Distribution of personal incomes after tax in the UK, 1938–1971*.*

Income Range (£)	(% of total) 1938		1971	
	No. of Incomes	Amount of Incomes	No. of Incomes	Amount of Incomes
– 499	96·4†	79·0	21·1†	30·0†
500– 999	2·4	8·0	25·9	12·0
1 000–1 999	0·8	5·0	40·0	35·9
2 000 +	0·4	8·0	13·0	22·1
Total	100·0	100·0	100·0	100·0

* Based on *National Income and Expenditure,* 1956 (HMSO, London, 1956), Table 28 and *Annual Abstract of Statistics No 111* (HMSO, London, 1971), Table 337.
† Partly estimated.

An examination of the data in Table 18.5 will bring home the significant change which has occurred in the distribution of disposable personal income in the United Kingdom since 1938. In that year about 96 per cent of the persons in receipt of separate incomes commanded, after payment of tax, less than £500 a year, and together received only 79 per cent of the total disposable personal income in the economy. By contrast, about 8 per cent of disposable income was received by a small number of persons, numbering less than 0·5 per cent of the total number, whose income exceeded £2 000 a year. This marked disparity between the relative size of income groups in terms of numbers, and their relative shares of total disposable income, indicated a fairly pronounced inequality in the distribution of income. By 1971 this inequality had been much reduced. Only 20 per cent of income recipients possessed a disposable income of less than £500 a year and accounted for 30 per cent of total disposable income. Persons in receipt of disposable incomes exceeding £2 000 accounted for about 13 per cent of the total numbers and only about 22 per cent of total disposable income. The share of disposable income going to the middle section of the income group had risen (from 13 per cent in 1938 to 48 per cent in 1971) while the importance of the lowest range of incomes had fallen correspondingly. The general rise in money wages and prices between 1938 and 1971, of course, is a major cause of the decline in the size of the amounts received by persons in the very lowest income-group; that a redistribution, as well as a general lifting, of incomes has occurred, however, is evident from the very marked increase in the proportion of the total population now classified in the highest income-range.

Two questions are raised. First, why does a substantial, if reduced, degree of inequality persist? Second, what forces have been responsible for its reduction in the last thirty years or so? The answer to the first question is relatively straightforward. Theoretically, inequality of personal incomes could arise *either* through differences of productivity within factor groups, *or* through an unequal ownership of factors by persons. Some inequality undoubtedly arises from the first cause; some men are naturally more able than others, some land is more fertile than the rest. It is difficult to believe, however, that there are many people whose productivity is so exceptional that they can earn incomes which even after tax were four or five times greater than the average for the community as a whole. Hence the main cause of inequality of personal incomes must be the concentration of the ownership of property – land and capital – in the hands of a relatively small number of people. It seems fairly safe to conclude from the statistics available that in recent years about two-thirds of the property in Great Britain has been owned by a tenth or less of the adult population.

How has this come about? The main cause has certainly been the *inheritance* of property. Factors ranging from a capacity for hard work and thrift to sheer good luck (if nothing less admirable) have enabled a small number of persons to bequeath substantial sums to their descendants. Then, by investing their inheritances, the beneficiaries in turn have been able to leave even larger accumulations to their descendants – the larger the amount invested the greater the income it will bring in, and hence the more rapidly can the accumulation increase. Furthermore, the inequality of property tends to lead to inequality of earning-power. A man with capital can afford expensive training and education, or to become an entrepreneur; people of equal innate ability may be able to do neither because of their lack of capital. The unequal earning-power accentuates the inequality of property-ownership, and so the process continues in snowball fashion.

Turning to the second question of the causes behind the *reduction* of the inequality, it should be noted that the inequality of opportunity just referred to has been much lessened by the widening of educational facilities in recent years. It is no longer true to say that a university education, or a protracted course of technical training, requires wealthy parents or exceptional self-sacrifice and powers of endurance. It remains true to say, however, that a person will seldom be able in practice to adopt the role of an entrepreneur without substantial capital to invest in his own enterprise.

Nevertheless, the dominant factor at work has been that of progressive taxation – that is, a system under which large incomes or estates are taxed at a rate which is proportionately much higher than that levied on small incomes and estates. For example, in 1938 and 1971 a person with an income of less than £250 before tax would have paid, on average, considerably less than 1 per cent of his income in income tax. In 1971, a person with an annual income of £15 000 would have paid away an average of about 47 per cent of it in the form of tax, compared with 49 per cent in 1938. Similarly, the proportion of an estate taken by the British Exchequer in the form of death duties increases rapidly as the size of the estate increases, and this rate of progression of death duties has become more and more pronounced in recent years. Furthermore, in very recent years the British tax system has at last recognised that the appreciation of capital values is as much a source of wealth as the receipt of income flows, and a capital-gains tax has been introduced to take account of this. Its long-term effects remain to be seen, but it must work in at least the same direction as a system of progressive taxation on incomes.

It should be noted that the role of the state in the redistribution of income is not confined to the process of revenue collection. In its expenditure, too, the modern British government redistributes income by spending large sums on social services of all kinds which tend to favour the relatively poor rather than the rich. Expenditures of this kind have become increasingly important in recent years. Between 1938 and 1973, the expenditure of British government authorities on goods and services (largely, but by no means wholly, social services), subsidies and grants to persons, such as pensions and unemployment benefits, rose from £736 million to £15 004 million – or from 15 to 27 per cent of the national income. It would be true to say, nevertheless, that the main way in which the modern state attempts to reduce inequality of income distribution is by a system of progressive taxation of income and property.

How far should this process continue? Should the state continue to increase the progressiveness of taxation until it is impossible for anyone in the community to retain a disposable income which is more than, say, 50 per cent greater than the national average, or to bequeath any significant capital to his descendants? On this type of question, as has been seen, the economist is not competent to pronounce. There is no way of comparing the utility enjoyed by different persons; hence it is impossible to discover by any objective test if the community as a whole is better off or worse off than before as a result of a further redistribution of income. This is an issue of politics or ethics, not economics.

Certain considerations of an economic character, however, must never be forgotten. It may be that the redistribution of income or property after a certain point will begin to have serious effects on incentives to work and save. An entrepreneur who is not allowed to retain more than a small fraction of the profits he makes may decide that, considering the risks of loss he runs and the mental strain he is under, the game is not worth the candle. A man forbidden to bequeath his capital to his son may prefer to relax his efforts and live on his capital, rather than leave it for the tax-gatherers. Innovation and risk-taking may decline and decay; capital accumulation may become unfashionable. The results of all this *may* be that the dynamic pulse of an economy will weaken, so that the national product will cease to grow as rapidly as it might otherwise have done. The process of stagnation may be slow and gradual, but it will be none the less real for that. If all this occurs, the protagonists of the poor and weak may find that they have done harm rather than good, that they have stupified, if not killed, the goose that lays the golden eggs. It is better to have 5 per cent of £100 than 10 per cent of £40; the lower income-groups might be better off with a small share of a high and expanding national income than with a large share of a low and static income.

But many would dispute that such results would follow from any likely degree of redistribution. They would argue that a large element of existing profits, rent and interest is really rent in the sense of an economic surplus. Entrepreneurs, they would argue, would go on being entrepreneurs even if profits were a tenth of their current level; capitalists would still lend at $\frac{1}{4}$ per cent per annum, because there is nothing else they can do with their capital. Further, the ill-effects on production following from the impoverishment of the rich might be more than offset by the good effects of giving better conditions, education and opportunities to the relatively poor.

The argument is incapable of dogmatic resolution. Perhaps few economic problems of the time are more pressing than that of discovering the correct solution. Is there a point at which redistribution of income so saps the vitality of the capitalistic, or private property, system that the gains in equality are more than offset by the losses caused by disincentive effects on production? If there is such a point, has the United Kingdom reached it? If it is reached, is the price of further equality too high? Or is equality as such sufficiently desirable to compensate for losses in the absolute value of output? The discussion is moving into a realm where the questions are easy to pose, and where there are many of them; society as a whole, rather than the economist individually, will have to grope its way to what it conceives to be the truth in these fundamental issues.

FURTHER READING

T. F. DERNBURG and D. M. McDOUGALL *Macro-economics* McGraw-Hill, New York 1960, Chs. 2–4

W. BECKERMAN *An introduction to national income analysis* Weidenfeld and Nicolson, London 1968, Chs. 1–4

D. C. ROWAN *Output, inflation and growth* Macmillan, London 1968, Chs. 3–4

C. BLYTH *The use of economic statistics* Allen & Unwin, London 1960, Chs. 4–5

R. MAURICE (ed.) *National accounts statistics* HMSO, London 1968, Chs. 1–5

CHAPTER XIX

Public Finance

1 THE ROLE OF GOVERNMENT

THE analysis of the preceding chapters has been concerned primarily with the use of resources by individuals and productive enterprises, be they privately-owned companies or public corporations of various types. As may be seen from Table 18.1 of the previous chapter, however, nearly 20 per cent of domestic expenditure at market prices in the United Kingdom at the present time in fact originates with the current expenditure of public authorities – i.e. central and local government – and these account for nearly as high a proportion of domestic capital formation. Altogether, then, public authorities currently dispose of a fifth of the resources absorbed within the British economy, which represents a very large element of total demand to which the analysis of the previous chapters has only a limited and qualified application. It is thus necessary to examine briefly the main features of the acquisition and disposal of resources by the government sector – the subject of public finance.

The primary aims of the private use of resources are easily defined: consumers seek to maximise the welfare of themselves and their families, while enterprises seek to maximise their profits. These, at least, are the assumptions on which economic analysis rests. The aims of government in the modern economy are less easily defined, however; at least four conceptually distinct functions of public finance can be listed. The first may be called the *provision of essential public services*, the oldest and simplest of government functions. The services in question are those which relate to the existence of the State itself and which cannot, of their nature, be performed by any other agency – the upkeep of the head of state, of the legislature, or of the courts of justice, the maintenance of law and order within the state and the provision of facilities for defence and diplomatic representation to safeguard its interests from external dangers and discharge its international responsibilities.

The second main function – much more varied in the extensiveness of its interpretation from country to country – is the encouragement or control of *particular sectors* of the economy for strategic, social or economic reasons. The role of government may be indirect, as in the case of support to various types of activities through subsidies, or to particular industries through financial assistance or advisory services of various kinds. Or it may be direct, as in the case of industries which are partly or wholly government-operated – the postal service is an almost universal example. How far it is expedient, or possible, to extend this function of government, directly or indirectly, is of course a highly controversial matter in which political rather than economic considerations tend to dominate.

A third function which has become of increasing importance during the present century is the application of *social policy*. This will involve both the revenue side – i.e. the level of taxation and its distribution amongst different sections of the community – as well as the expenditure of governments on what are generally called social services – education, health and so on. As was made clear in an earlier chapter, it is only in the perfect competition of pure theory that the unregulated forces of the market will result in the maximisation of welfare in a society, and then only if the distribution of income is assumed to be the optimum one. In reality the wide inequalities and hardships of industrial societies have generated public pressure forcing governments to moderate the distribution of wealth to some degree or other. Precisely how far this function should be carried is, again, an essentially political issue.

Finally, modern governments have assumed responsibility for the *overall state of the economy* – i.e. for the maintenance of a high and stable level of employment, for the encouragement of the maximum rate of growth in the economy's productive capacity over the years, and the preservation of solvency in its external trading relationships. Once again this involves both revenue and expenditure – i.e. the resources which government takes out of the purses of its citizens year by year by taxation, the resources it puts back into their hands through its expenditures, and the relationship between these two flows. More will be heard of this particular aspect of public finance after the discussion of macro-economics and international economics in Parts VII and VIII.

It will be appreciated that while these various functions can be distinguished from one another in principle it is by no means always easy to determine the precise aim of a particular measure in practice. Taxation used to finance essential services will obviously play a part in the income-redistribution aspect of social policy, while subsidies originally introduced as a social measure (as were the British agricultural subsidies) may come in time to play an important part in the encouragement of a particular economic sector. This multiplicity of purpose will become evident from a brief study of the major features of British public finance at the present time.

2   CENTRAL GOVERNMENT EXPENDITURE

What might be called the house-keeping account of the central government – the Budget – is normally presented to the legislature once a year. It constitutes the plans of the government of the day for its expenditure during the year ahead and its proposals for the financing of them. There is more than one way of presenting this account; for present purposes the form adopted in the national income accounts – and summarised in Table 19.1 – is the most convenient. In actual practice the expenditure plans of the various government departments (the Estimates) are drawn up and presented to the legislature first; the Chancellor of the Exchequer draws up his taxation proposals only after the expenditure plans are finalised – unlike the ordinary household which, being usually unable to determine its own income, has to fit expenditure to income rather than *vice versa*. It will therefore be logical to examine the expenditure side of the account first.

Government expenditure is itself capable of more than one classification, but an essential distinction for the economist is that between current expenditure – i.e. recurrent in nature and not resulting in the acquisition of assets – and capital expenditure. Current expenditure in turn can be subdivided. The most important category, as will be seen, is that on goods and services; this means that the expenditure absorbs productive resources directly. The major item here, of course, is that of *defence*, military and civil; the resources absorbed consist mainly of the services of men and women in the Armed Forces or providing personal service to them, at home or abroad, the provision of accommodation, food and clothing for the Forces, and the development and manufacture of armaments. The second big item is *health*, which involves primarily the staffing, equipment and operation of the National Health Service. Other expenditure under this heading covers the costs of civil service departments not attributable to particular services, of central police services and courts of law, employment services and so on.

The second major category of expenditure consists of subsidies, by which are meant payments to permit the sale of certain products at less than their full cost of production. Most important at one time were the *agricultural* subsidies, most of which were deficiency payments to British farmers on products sold on the home market for something less than the guaranteed prices negotiated annually between government and farmers as part of the official agricultural policy. Originally introduced during the Second World War as a means of holding down the cost of living (i.e. as an act of social policy), until recently these were an important element in a broader policy of assisting British farmers to survive in the face of low-cost imports from overseas producers. With Britain's entry into the EEC, however, they are destined to be replaced by import levies as the main method of agricultural support (see Chapter XXXII below). Other subsidies include the central government's share of the losses sustained by local government authorities in renting municipal housing at less than its full cost (obviously part of social policy) and the operating losses of the railway system (designed to assist a particular sector of the economy).

The third major category of expenditure consists of direct monetary grants to persons, all of which fall under the heading of social policy. Some of these, such as *National Insurance benefits* (mainly retirement pensions, unemployment and sickness benefits) are by way of being contractual payments, corresponding to contributions under the national insurance scheme, and payable only to persons qualified to receive them by virtue of such contributions. Others, like supplementary benefit payments, family allowances or scholarships, have no such contributory requirements: they are financed from the proceeds of taxation generally. (The National Health Service, also, is financed from general taxation and is available to all without any kind of contributory qualification; part of the contributions collected compulsorily under the National Insurance scheme is nevertheless earmarked for the health service.)

There are two other large items of expenditure. Interest on the *national debt* represents the quarterly or bi-annual payments on the outstanding accumulation of borrowings by the government in previous years; more will be said about the national debt in a later section of this chapter. *Grants to local authorities* will be discussed in the section devoted to local government finance.

The various items of capital expenditure are largely self-explanatory. Less than a fifth of the total constitutes expenditure on *direct capital formation* by the government itself in spheres for which it has responsibility – especially offices and other buildings, the maintenance and expansion of the road system, new hospitals and clinics for the health service, and military installations of all kinds under the defence programme. The major form of capital expenditure by the central government is in fact indirect – the granting of loans to nationalised industries and local government authorities to finance *their* capital formation. Other important capital transactions involve the country's external financial relationships – the movement in foreign exchange reserves and deposits in international monetary institutions. These items will be more easily understood after the discussion of international currency matters in Part VIII below.

3 CENTRAL GOVERNMENT REVENUE

Like its expenditure, the government's receipts may be either current in nature – i.e. flows which recur year by year – or capi-

TABLE 19.1 *Central government* revenue and expenditure, 1973 (£ million)*

Revenue		Expenditure	
A. CURRENT ACCOUNT			
1. Taxes on income:		6. Goods and services:	
(a) Income tax	6 929	(a) Defence	3 322
(b) Surtax	342	(b) Health	2 497
(c) Corporation tax	1 872	(c) Other	1 834
	9 143		7 653
2. Taxes on expenditure:		7. Subsidies:	
(a) Tobacco	1 100	(a) Agriculture and food	287
(b) Value added tax	2 023	(b) Other	1 064
(c) Oil and petrol	1 620		
(d) Beer, wines, spirits	978		1 351
(e) Import duties	434		
(f) Other Customs and Excise	302	8. Grants to persons:	
		(a) National Insurance benefits	3 927
Total Customs and Excise	6 457	(b) Supplementary benefits	705
		(c) Family allowances	360
(g) Motor vehicles	518	(d) Education grants	469
(h) Selective Employment Tax	132	(e) Other	539
(i) Other	282		
			6 000
	7 389	9. National Debt Interest	1 801
		10. Grants to local government authorities	4 099
3. National Insurance and Health contributions	3 873	11. Other	347
4. Trading income and rents	113	Total current expenditure	21 251
5. Interest and dividends, etc.	1 686	12. Current surplus	953
Total	22 204	Total	22 204

B. CAPITAL ACCOUNT

12. Current surplus	953	17. Capital expenditure:			
13. Taxes on capital	797		(a) Research	29	
14. Currency issue	544		(b) Roads	293	
15. Other receipts	−241		(c) Health	253	
16. Borrowing:			(d) Defence	46	
(a) National Savings	144		(e) Other	196	
(b) Other	1 695			——	
				817	
				——	
		18. Loans to overseas governments		62	
		19. Investment grants		641	
		20. Loans and grants to local authorities		1 260	
		21. Loans and grants to public corporations		803	
		22. Other		526	
Total	4 109	Total		4 109	

* Including National Insurance Funds

Source: *National Income and Expenditure*, 1963–1973 (HMSO, London, 1974), Tables 39–40.

tal items of a once-for-all kind. The bulk of its current receipts, of course, is provided by taxes of various sorts, taxes being compulsory levies on the citizens of a country which correspond to no product or service, given in return. In turn, taxes are most conveniently classified according as to whether they are related to the current income of the taxpayer concerned, or to his capital wealth, or to the purchase of goods and services subject to expenditure taxes.

The first category, income taxes, are straightforward in principle. In British fiscal practice, all individuals whose annual income exceeds a specified minimum are required to pay taxes on their net income for each year. Persons, of course, have various allowances – for dependants, insurance premiums, interest charges on house-mortgages and so on; after deducting these from taxable income tax is levied at progressively increasing rates on successive bands of income. For example, in 1973–74 a tax of 30 per cent was levied on the first £5 000 of income remaining after the deduction of allowances, a rate of 40 per cent on the next £1 000 and so on until a rate of 75 per cent was levied on income in excess of £20 000 after allowances. An additional tax of 15 per cent, known as the 'investment income surcharge' was also levied on investment income in excess of £2 000 a year. *Surtax* was an additional tax levied at an increasing rate on persons in receipt of incomes in excess of a specified level but this was abolished after the 1972–73 fiscal year when the progressive income tax system described above came into operation. Taken overall, then, the British income-tax system is a highly progressive one – that is, the amount of income taken in taxation not only increases as incomes rise but increases more rapidly than income itself. *Corporation tax* is levied only on companies; it is nowadays calculated as a flat rate on the annual profits of an enterprise after payment of charges such as loan interest.

At the present time, taxes on capital (shown as a capital receipt in the lower half of the table) form a relatively minor element in the British tax structure. Until quite recent years the only operative taxes of this kind were death duties, levied at a progressive rate on estates passing on the death of their owner. In 1962, however, a far-reaching departure was made with the introduction of a short-term capital gains tax. Until then, a person whose wealth increased through a rise in the capital value of his property escaped tax liability altogether on this increment (death duties apart, of course) unless he was continuously making such capital gains in the course of his ordinary business, as would be the case with a successful stockbroker. The tax introduced in 1962 in effect brought such gains into the income-tax net, provided the assets on which they were made were bought and sold within six months (or three years in the case of land). It was generally believed that for various reasons the effect of this tax would not be very great in revenue terms as it was then formulated. In the 1965 Budget, however, the 'short-term' element was removed and the tax was extended to all capital gains except those arising on certain assets such as owner-occupied houses or life insurance policies.

The second category, *taxes on expenditure,* is equal in importance with income tax in terms of the total revenue brought into the Exchequer. The three groups, tobacco, oil and alcoholic drinks, are together responsible for more than 50 per cent of these – all commodities with a relatively inelastic demand, of course. Purchase tax and Selective Employment Tax were abolished in 1973 and replaced by a *value-added tax,* a dual-rate duty levied on the final sales value of a very wide range of goods and services. Most of Britain's import duties were originally applied in order to discourage the consumption of imported goods, but nevertheless bring in useful revenue also.

The item of *national insurance and health contributions* cannot be easily classified as either inside or outside the tax category. Nominally, they are payments into a fund which entitle the contributor to draw them out again at specified times in the form of a pension or other benefits. They are not at first sight consistent with the definition of a tax as a levy in return for which no corresponding benefit is given. In practice, however, the continued rise in the general price level has led to periodic increases in the level of pensions and other benefits – virtually on political grounds – so that the connection between a person's accumulated payments into the insurance fund over the past and his entitlement to benefits has become an exceedingly tenuous one. Like a tax, also, these contributions are compulsory for all employed or self-employed persons.

The other revenues of a current nature are small in magnitude in comparison with the proceeds of taxation. *Trading income and rents* comprise mainly the rents received from government-owned land and buildings. *Interest and dividends* comprise receipts on loans made by the government to local authorities and nationalised industries on which, of course, the borrowers are required to pay interest.

How are the government's capital expenditures financed? In the first place, with any *surplus* remaining from its sources of current revenue after all current expenditures have been met. (If a *deficit* were experienced on current operations, of course, this item would move over to the other side of the table and would join the list of capital items requiring finance.) Secondly, revenues arising from taxes on capital wealth (i.e. death duties) or capital gains are included. Thirdly, any receipts from the additions to the *currency issue* can be added in. The whole question of currency is explored in the next two chapters; it is sufficient for the moment to say that if the government instructs the Bank of England to increase the volume of its notes in circulation, the Bank in effect hands them over to the government in return for securities – promises to pay at some future date – so that the government has an extra sum of money with which to finance expenditures. (Once again, *a reduction* in the note issue would in effect shift this item over to the other side of the table.) Finally, the government may have *miscellaneous capital receipts* from time to time – capital grants from foreign governments, sales of surplus stores, disposal of holdings in industrial firms, etc.

Having added up all these receipts and compared the total with that for its capital outgoings, then, the government is left with an overall surplus – if capital receipts, including the current surplus, exceed capital expenditures – or an overall deficit if the opposite is the case. How this surplus is used, or deficit filled, is a question to which the discussion must now turn.

4   THE NATIONAL DEBT

As a general rule, an individual household or firm must limit expenditure to its current income except to the extent to which borrowing is possible and desirable. The scope for the latter is usually somewhat restricted by the need – on both sides – to ensure that the service of any debt (i.e. its periodic interest charges and eventual repayment) will be matched by a higher income on the borrower's side from which to meet it. A government, however, is in a different position. It has the ability to create money, since it possesses a monopoly of note-issuing powers (a matter investigated in the next chapter). This has two implications. In the first place it is able to finance its expenditure, if it wishes, by creating new money, a possibility not legally open to any other member of society. Secondly, and following from this, its debts are widely acceptable by potential lenders; given the power to create money, the government need never be *unable* to meet its obligations – at least to its own citizens – so that its credit-standing is extremely high and its borrowing-powers enormous.

The government therefore has three separate ways of financing its domestic expenditures, leaving aside the possibility of free gifts or grants it may receive from foreign governments. First, it can use the proceeds of the various types of taxation described in the previous section. Secondly, it can create new money. Thirdly, it can borrow by means of an expansion of the National Debt. The extent to which the last method has been used in the United Kingdom from time to time may be judged from the fact that in 1974 its accumulated national debt amounted to about £40 000 million. This consists of promises to repay specified amounts at some date – specified or otherwise – in the future, and, almost always, to pay agreed sums by way of interest periodically in the meantime. About £1 500 million represented borrowing from abroad, the interest and principal sum of which is payable in foreign currencies. About an eighth of the remainder (the 'internal debt') comprised very short-term borrowings (the 'floating debt') mainly from the banking system; about two-thirds consisted of longer-term securities repayable after anything from a year to twenty-five years, or, indeed, at any date the government should choose. As will be seen from Table 19.1, the annual interest charge on this debt is a formidable item in the annual budget.

In presenting a budget, then, a Chancellor does not have a simple problem of merely balancing receipts with expenditures. His problem, given a programme of expenditure to which the government is committed, is to decide *how* the resources necessary for that programme are to be obtained. If taxation is levied, the resources can be assumed to be taken away mainly from current expenditure; if borrowing is used, the proceeds will probably come mainly from funds which would otherwise have been available to finance capital formation; if currency creation is used, the distribution of the sacrifice of resources will depend on the effects which such credit creation will have on prices and production generally. The position may be further complicated by the existence of unemployed or under-employed resources in the economy; the use of resources by the government in such circumstances may involve no sacrifice of consumption or investment, but may in fact prevent the *wastage* of those resources through unemployment. Exactly parallel considerations apply, of course, when a Chancellor faces a situation in which prospective receipts, at prevailing tax rates, exceed prospective government expenditure. He can seize the opportunity to reduce taxation and thus prevent the emergence of the potential surplus; on the other hand, he can budget for a surplus which will be used either to *reduce* the volume of currency or to redeem part of the outstanding national debt.

These are highly complex matters which will become clearer after the discussion of macro-economics in Part VII. For the moment the essential point to remember is that the size and structure of the revenue side of the budget is in no sense determined merely by the need of a government to finance its own expenditure. It has direct and significant effects on the use of resources by the rest of the economy, both individuals and enterprises, so that it is the prevailing state and needs of the *economy as a whole* which must guide the Chancellor in his decisions concerning the size and nature of the receipts he proposes to obtain in the year ahead.

5   LOCAL GOVERNMENT FINANCE

Around a third of the expenditure of the government sector in the United Kingdom at the present time is carried out by local government authorities; the main agencies in this are the County Councils although the District Councils have responsibility in some minor expenditure matters. In general, the local government authorities are left with responsibility for functions of an essentially local, rather than national, character, although even here they have to operate within limits and upon standards laid down by central government departments with varying degrees of precision.

The main features of the revenue and expenditure of this branch of government in the United Kingdom are shown in Table 19.2. Taking expenditure first, the division into current and

TABLE 19.2   *Local government authorities revenue and expenditure, 1973 (£ million)*

Revenue		Expenditure	
A. CURRENT ACCOUNT			
1. Grants from central government		6. Goods and services:	
(a) Non-specific	3 563	(a) Education	2 764
(b) Housing	178	(b) Roads	363
(c) Roads	1	(c) Health	615
(d) Police	271	(d) Police	524
(e) Other	84	(e) Sewerage and refuse	361
		(f) Other	990
	4 099		5 617
2. Rates	2 617	7. Housing subsidies	309
3. Rents	1 398	8. Scholarships	209
4. Trading income	154	9. School meals and milk, etc	42
5. Interest, etc.	138	10. Debt interest	1 403
		Total current expenditure	7 580
		11. Surplus	826
Total	8 406	Total	8 406
B. CAPITAL ACCOUNT			
11. Current surplus	826	15. Capital formation:	
12. Capital grants from central government	240	(a) Housing	956
		(b) Education	521
13. Loans from central government	1 020	(c) Roads	344
		(d) Sewerage	284
14. Other borrowing	1 153	(e) Water	108
		(f) Other	542
			2 755
		16. Capital grants to persons	162
		17. House purchase loans	322
Total	3 239	Total	3 239

Source : *National Income and Expenditure,* 1963–1973 (HMSO, London, 1974), Tables 43–4.

capital is again useful. It will be seen that by far and away the most important single item of current expenditure is that on *education,* principally the salaries of teachers and other school staff, the maintenance of schools and the provision of their equipment, stationery, books and so on. Another important category of expenditure on goods and services is that on *roads,* meaning the ordinary maintenance of roads and not their construction (which would be capital formation, of course). The traditional local authority services such as public health services and the local police forces are also important items under this heading. The other large item of current expenditure is of course *debt interest*; about a third of this represents interest on loans from the central government, the remainder being interest payments on borrowings from time to time in the past in the open capital market.

More than a half of the capital expenditure of local authorities in 1973 consisted of expenditure on building new *houses* and *schools,* or in improvements to them. Capital expenditure on *roads* is relatively small, since financial responsibility for the main trunk roads in Britain rests with the central government, even though new road works may be carried out on its behalf by the local authorities themselves in the capacity of agents.

About 80 per cent of the current revenue of local authorities in Britain at the present time comprises *government grants* and *rates.* The latter is the only major source of independent revenue at the disposal of local authorities. It is derived from the levying of a fixed tax per £ on the value of land and buildings within the area of the authority concerned. (It is, therefore, a *regressive* tax, like all expenditure taxes; if two persons occupy houses of equal rateable value, the tax will represent a larger proportion of the income of the poorer of the two than of the richer − unlike income tax.) The current grants from the central government are nowadays mostly non-specific, which means that they are not related to defined expenditure items. The main purpose of these grants is to achieve something approaching *equalisation* amongst different local authorities. Hence they are proportionately larger for the authorities of thinly-populated rural areas whose rate resources are very limited than for well-to-do urban areas which can rely on a relatively large income from rates.

Unlike the central government, local authorities have no power to create money; hence they must either finance their capital expenditure from their own surplus current revenue, and such capital grants as the central government may give, or they must borrow to cover the difference. (If their surplus plus capital grants *exceeds* capital expenditure, of course, they can pay off a corresponding amount of accumulated debt.) In recent years the central government has tended to discourage local authorities from borrowing from the Exchequer and has required them to borrow in the open market (i.e. from banks and other private lenders) whenever possible. It will be seen from Table 19.2 that in 1973 local authorities as a whole nevertheless borrowed, on balance, a total of some £1 020 million from the Exchequer. Even this was insufficient to provide finance for capital expenditure in excess of their current surplus and capital grants; hence they collectively borrowed a further total of £1 153 million from private lenders. Provided that the proceeds were well used in building new schools, houses, roads, water-works and so on, there is nothing alarming about borrowing on this scale. It implies, nevertheless, that as the years go on the burden of debt interest and redemption will become an increasingly significant item in their annual budgets.

FURTHER READING

A. R. PREST *Public finance* Weidenfeld and Nicolson, London 1960

U. K. HICKS *British public finances* Oxford University Press, London 1958

R. A. MUSGRAVE *The theory of public finance* McGraw-Hill, New York 1959

PART VI

MONEY AND BANKING

CHAPTER XX

The Nature of Money
and Banking

1 WHY HAVE MONEY?

ECONOMIC life revolves around the production of goods and services and their exchange for other goods and services. Previous analysis has shown why it is beneficial for individuals and countries to specialise in the production of whatever they can make best, rather than to attempt self-sufficiency; the gains of division and specialisation of labour are too great to be ignored. Exchange is a necessary consequence; if people are not self-sufficient so far as their economic needs are concerned, they must obtain the goods they do not themselves produce by offering in exchange the commodities in the production of which they are specialising. In this way they obtain not only the gains arising from specialisation but also the gains possible through exchange itself – it was seen in Chapter III that, from a given initial income, a higher degree of satisfaction can be obtained by entering into exchange than if people consumed their own produce and nothing else.

The process of exchange is entered into in order to exchange goods for other goods. In real life, however, people seldom do this. A producer exchanges his output not for goods but for money, and when he obtains goods from other people he does it by offering *money* for them, not goods he has produced. In other words, an extra stage is introduced into the process. Instead of exchanging goods for goods (a process which is called barter) people exchange their goods for money and then exchange the money for the goods they want. This is an additional complication and one which, as will be seen later, has given rise to considerable difficulties and confusion. Why introduce such a complication?

There are three substantial advantages in conducting exchange indirectly through money, rather than directly in the form of barter. First, the process of exchange is itself immensely facilitated by using money. When goods are bartered, it is necessary for each of the two persons involved to be prepared to accept whatever the other is offering, and this is much more troublesome than it might sound. If I am a watchmaker and want to barter a watch I have made for a pair of shoes, I have to find someone who not only has shoes to offer but who is willing to exchange them for the kind of watch I make; obviously it might take me a long time to find such a person. It is easy to envisage the difficulties which would be encountered under a system of barter by a blacksmith wanting to obtain a dress for his wife, or a baker trying to obtain a bicycle.

Nor is this the end of the story. The process of exchange by barter would make impossible a world of specialisation and division of labour. If a man is one of five thousand helping to make railway locomotives in an engineering workshop, what commodity could he barter against the necessities of life? How could a policeman barter the product of his labour? What could a bus driver offer a farmer a hundred miles away so as to obtain food? Clearly, the process of barter is inconsistent with an economic system which has attained any substantial degree of specialisation, or with one in which the production taking place results in any but the simplest and commonest necessities of life.

The first and vital role played by money in economic life, therefore, is that of a *medium of exchange*. It permits the separation of exchange into the two distinct acts of buying and selling, without requiring that the seller should purchase goods from the person who buys his product, or *vice versa*. Hence producers are enabled to concentrate on finding the most suitable outlet for their goods, while buyers can concentrate on finding the cheapest market for the things they wish to purchase. Specialisation is encouraged, because people whose output is not a complete commodity but an intangible contribution to the manufacture of one in which many others are involved can be paid an amount equivalent to their share of the product, and can use this money income to purchase whatever they wish.

Another function of money is to act as a *measure of value* — that is, it serves as a unit in terms of which the relative values of different commodities can be expressed. In a barter economy it would be a difficult and time-consuming task, to say the least, to determine how many electric-light bulbs were worth *x* kilograms of raw cotton, or how many fountain pens should be exchanged for a tonne of coal. The process of establishing relative values would have to be undertaken for every act of exchange, according to whatever commodities were being offered against one another, and according to the particular persons entering into the exchange. If I am trying to barter fish for cups and saucers, for example, a great deal would turn on whether the person willing to exchange cups and saucers on these terms is or is not keen on fish.

The establishment of relative values by the process of barter would not only waste a great deal of time and effort. Under such a system the outcome of exchanges would be so uncertain that few entrepreneurs would be prepared to undertake production in advance of demand. Specialisation and large-scale manufacture require that an entrepreneur should pay out in wages, interest and rent a large part of the value of a product long before the product is sold. If the amount for which the product will be sold could not be anticipated within reasonably narrow limits, the risk involved in production would be enormous; the entrepreneur, in any case, would have little idea of how costs of production compared with probable selling price, so that there would be no means of deciding if the production of a commodity was an economic proposition.

A third, and related, function of money is that of acting as a *store of wealth*. It is difficult to envisage saving occurring under a barter system. Obviously there would be no way in which persons rendering services could set aside some of their output to meet possible emergencies in the future. Nor could anyone engaged on only one stage in the production of a commodity save part of his output, since he would be producing nothing tangible. Even when a person actually produced a complete commodity the difficulties would be overwhelming. Most commodities deteriorate fairly rapidly, either physically or in value, as a result of long storage; even if storage were possible, the practice of storing commodities for years on end would involve obvious disadvantages – imagine a coal-miner attempting to save enough coal to keep him in his old age, for example. Yet if wealth cannot be set aside, or can be accumulated only with great difficulty, how can future contingencies be provided for, or capital formation undertaken so as to raise productivity? The use of money disposes of these difficulties; instead of having to store physical commodities, a producer can set aside sums of money which can be used in the future for whatever purposes he chooses. Without money, debts could be incurred only in terms of specific commodities; the modern system of financing capital accumulation from funds derived from a large number of different people and institutions would be impossible.

It is clear, then, that many of the essential characteristics of a highly developed economic system – division of labour, large-scale production in advance of demand, widespread exchange, and the accumulation of capital – are intimately linked with the use of money. Indeed, without money to facilitate exchange, production and saving, it would be impossible for an economy to develop beyond the primitive level which survives in communities still conducting their economic affairs on a barter basis.

2   REQUIREMENTS FOR AN EFFICIENT MONEY

Money can be defined only in terms of its functions. By that is meant that *anything* is money which serves as a means of exchange, a measure of value, and a store of wealth. Money is as money does. Put more formally, if the word *liquidity* is defined as the ability to turn wealth into any form without loss or delay, then money can be said to be *anything which confers complete liquidity on its holder*. This means that to be money a commodity must be generally acceptable in exchange for goods or services of any kind and for the settlement of debts.

The precise substance which is used as money, or its shape and size, is a matter of convenience and convention; all that really matters is that it should confer complete liquidity.

In the course of history an extraordinary variety of substances and commodities has been used as money by different communities and at different times. Among them are shells, animal teeth, particular types of stones, cattle and all kinds of metal; in post-war Germany, cigarettes were widely used as an accepted medium of exchange. In recent centuries the use of gold and silver was adopted by most Western countries until their replacement by paper money in the present century. The only quality which all these things have shared in common has been that they commanded the *confidence* of the community in which they were used. That is the only essential requirement if something is to fulfil the functions of money; the community must have confidence in it as a means of exchange and of settling debts. If that confidence is lost, then no commodity, be it stamped with every conceivable mark by the monetary authorities, can survive as money. History is full of examples of monetary units which were once perfectly acceptable and stable but which have been forced into disuse because for one reason or another the general public lost confidence in them. So long as a person believes that he can obtain goods in return for the commodity used as money, he will be perfectly willing to accept money, whatever its form, in return for his own goods and services. If doubt arises, however, as to the possibility of disposing of money for goods of roughly the same value as those against which it was accepted, people will be unwilling to part with goods and services for it and hence it will cease to be money.

There are other, less important, qualities which are desirable in a money material. It should be fairly *portable*; lead money for example would be inconvenient because of its great weight. Similarly, it should be *homogeneous*: that is, one unit of it should be identical with any other unit. If this were not so, people would almost certainly place a greater value on some units than on others, and there would be a tendency for different prices to be demanded when different units of money were being tendered in exchange. Thirdly, it should be *divisible*, so that it can be used in convenient units. Again, it must be *durable*, so that its quality does not deteriorate with keeping. People would be reluctant to use, say, cows as money because of the risk that a cow might die before it could be used for a purchase.

Gold and silver possess these incidental qualities to such a marked degree that for many centuries they were regarded as the only form of money worth consideration. They are durable and homogeneous metals, and their value is high in relation to their weight; further, their annual output from mines is small in relation to the total stock in existence, so that unsettling fluctuations in the total supply of them were unlikely. These and other incidentals are matters of convenience, however, rather than essential to the nature of money. Many materials have in fact been used as money for considerable periods of time despite their marked inconvenience in many respects; the people of the Pacific island of Uap, for example, have for centuries used as money enormous stones of such weight that their physical transport is a matter of extreme difficulty.

Nowadays paper money has replaced gold and silver in most highly developed economies. Such money has all the good qualities of gold and silver, and in addition has two which the precious metals do not possess; it costs virtually nothing to produce, and its total supply is completely within the control of the State. How the use of paper money originally developed is a matter which will be considered in the following section.

3   THE NATURE OF BANK CREDIT

When the word 'money' is used in ordinary conversation people have in mind the notes and coin handled in everyday transactions. These things *are* money, of course, but in a modern economy something like nine-tenths of all transactions carried out – by businesses and government agencies, as well as by private persons – are effected not with the use of notes and coin but through *bank credit*. What exactly is bank credit, and how is it that it has come to be the most important means of carrying out exchanges in the modern economy?

So far as Britain is concerned, the history of bank notes and bank credit can be said to have begun in the seventeenth century. Because of the insecurity generated by the Civil War, the habit grew up amongst the wealthy of depositing their valuable assets (especially gold plate) with goldsmiths; the latter were men accustomed to handling such things, were equipped with vaults and strongrooms and were generally regarded as being people of integrity. When these assets were deposited, the goldsmiths naturally gave the person concerned a receipt indicating the value of the assets held by them on behalf of the depositor, and embodying an undertaking to hand the assets back to their owner when required.

During this period, gold coins were the most important form of money in circulation, and gold plate could be handed into the Royal Mint for melting down and conversion into coins of the currently-required gold content. If people who had deposited gold plate with a goldsmith required money to pay debts, therefore, they would frequently present their receipt to the goldsmith concerned, have plate minted into coins and pass the coins over to the creditor. Before long it became obvious that a lot of trouble and expense would be saved if the debtors, instead of reclaiming and minting their gold plate, simply handed the goldsmith's receipt over to the creditor, endorsing it to the effect that ownership of the wealth involved had now passed from the debtor to the creditor. Provided he had confidence in the honesty and reliability of the goldsmith, the creditor would find it just as satisfactory to have payment in gold held safely in the goldsmith's vault as in the form of gold coin. Indeed, more often than not this procedure was more convenient for both creditor and debtor.

At this stage, then, the bank note which is nowadays familiar was beginning to emerge. The goldsmith's *receipt* (not the gold for which it was a receipt) was being accepted in payment of debts, so that it had become a form of money. It will be noted that the factor of confidence was a vital element – the goldsmith's receipt was accepted only if creditors had confidence in his solvency and honesty. Given this confidence, the receipts might pass from hand to hand in settlement of debts, without anyone at any stage actually presenting the receipt and demanding the gold plate in respect of which it was originally issued. Fairly soon the goldsmiths realised that it would be more convenient for all concerned if the receipts were issued for fixed sums – £50, £100, and so on – so that they would be more easily used for settling transactions of different amounts. This brought the receipts even closer to the modern bank note.

So far, however, *credit* had not really entered into the picture, except in the sense that the goldsmith's 'credit', or business standing, was an important factor determining the acceptability of his receipts. But each one of his receipts was still backed by gold in his vaults, and (assuming his honesty) every one could have been honoured simultaneously. In a sense, it was still the gold which was circulating, the receipts being used merely as a convenient way of handing it over. Before long, however, the goldsmith realised that his receipts were passing from hand to hand, and only occasionally did anyone actually come to him demanding the repayment of gold in exchange for the receipt – either because the depositor concerned was of an unusually suspicious temperament or, more probably, because he needed to mint the plate into coins of relatively small denominations for transactions (such as wage payments) for which the use of the gold receipts was unsuitable. It followed, therefore, that goldsmiths could issue notes to customers considerably in excess of the value of the gold in their possession, *provided* that they always had sufficient gold in their vaults to meet any demands likely to be expressed for it. In order to issue these excess notes, the goldsmiths simply adopted the role of moneylenders. There are always people wanting to borrow money for one thing or another and willing to pay interest on their borrowings. The fact that the notes lent by the goldsmiths had (unlike their original notes) no gold 'backing' was of little consequence. All the notes were identical, and circulated on equal terms with one another.

This is a crucial point, so it is worth looking into it in a little more detail. Suppose that the acceptance of gold receipts or certificates has become so widespread that only one person in ten will actually insist that the receipt should be honoured and the gold handed over. If a goldsmith has accepted gold to the value of £1 000 for safe keeping, then he is only likely to be asked to repay £100 of it at any one time. Knowing this, he lends out £9 000 in the form of gold receipts bearing his signature, duly receiving a rate of interest from the borrowers. Receipts bearing his signature are now circulating to the tune of £10 000. As and when they come into the hands of one of the mistrustful 10 per cent who prefer to see gold rather than a mere receipt, he has the £1 000 in gold in his vaults to meet their demands. Since on average only 10 per cent of the £10 000-worth of his receipts will be coming in for conversion into gold, £1 000 will be sufficient to meet all likely claims. The mistrustful one will go away with his £1 000-worth of gold. In due course, however, he will spend it, and it will pass into the hands of one of the majority who prefer to keep their wealth in the goldsmith's vaults; so the £1 000-worth of gold comes back to the goldsmith, ready for the next customer from the suspicious 10-per-cent group. And so it can go on, the majority passing their wealth to one another in the form of the goldsmith's receipts, and the goldsmith earning an income from the loans he has made. It is important to note that the 90 per cent majority are *not* leaving their wealth idle, any more than the minority; they are simply effecting their exchanges through the medium of the goldsmith's receipts rather than through gold coin.

Once again *confidence* is of the essence in the whole business. The majority are content to accept the gold receipts in return for goods they have sold only because they are confident that the gold is obtainable from the goldsmith and that other people, in turn, will be prepared to accept the receipt from *them* in exchange for goods. If for any reason that confidence is lost, then no one will be prepared to accept the goldsmith's receipt (no longer believing that the goldsmith is willing or able to honour it); everyone will try to obtain gold from the goldsmith in return for receipts which they can no longer use to settle debts. If the goldsmith has in fact issued receipts in excess of his holdings of gold, then someone is going to be disappointed and the goldsmith goes out of business, unless the latter can persuade all his debtors to repay their borrowings immediately in gold. The fundamental difference between the use of gold receipts in this stage of development and the preceding stage is that receipts (or notes) for which there is no corresponding deposit of gold in the goldsmith's vaults are now in circulation. In the earlier stage it was the gold itself which was being used to settle transactions; the receipts were simply the means by which the transference of gold from person to person was effected. In the second stage it is goldsmith's *credit* which is being used to settle the majority of the exchanges. So long as confidence is maintained in the goldsmith's receipts, then his credit can be used to settle debts just as well as gold; hence it is money.

The goldsmiths have now more or less disappeared, and their place has been taken by banks so far as the business of credit-creation is concerned. Apart from this, the version of events just given is applicable to the situation at the present time. Nowadays the reserve, or backing, underlying credit consists of Bank of England notes, rather than of gold – more will be said about this development in the next chapter – and the receipts of the goldsmiths have been replaced by cheques. The latter change is a refinement of considerable convenience, but nothing more. The goldsmith's receipt was a promise to repay a certain amount of gold; when it was endorsed by the original depositor, the benefit of the promise was in effect transferred to a third party. Fundamentally, a cheque is exactly the same; it is a request to a bank to transfer to a stated person a certain amount of the bank's indebtedness to the depositor. It is more convenient than notes because the exact sum involved can be written on it, so that transactions can be settled precisely.

Otherwise, a modern bank is following the same procedure as the goldsmiths of the seventeenth century. It has a basic reserve of cash which is acceptable as money to everyone. From experience, it knows that only a small proportion of its depositors will use *in the form of cash* the wealth deposited with it; the majority will instead transfer claims on it to their creditors (written in the form of cheques) which the creditors, in turn, will be prepared to accept and transfer in payment of *their* debts. So long as the bank has enough reserves to meet the needs of the minority who will want to draw out their wealth in cash or, more important, to satisfy any reserve requirements specified for them by the authorities, it can give credit to customers far in excess of its actual cash reserves. The bank credit used to settle the vast majority of transactions occurring in the economy is of this kind; it rests on a small cash reserve and the confidence of the general public in the banking system. In December 1974 the total indebtedness of the British banking system amounted to well over £100 000 million; the banks actually held £1 440 million in cash.

4 BANK CREDIT AS MONEY

Since the modern banking system could honour at any one time only a small fraction of its total indebtedness, can a cheque, which transfers this indebtedness from one person to another, be called 'money'? It has been seen that money is anything which performs the functions of money − anything, that is, which is generally acceptable in settlement of a debt. Since the majority of transactions are in fact carried out through bank credit − that is, by cheque − clearly bank debt *must* be money. The fact that, if all the creditors of a bank rushed in at the same time to demand the repayment of their deposits in cash, the vast majority would be refused is quite irrelevant. Given confidence in the banks, the public do *not all* demand cash at the same time; only a small proportion of bank debt is ever required to be changed into cash, and the banks keep sufficient for the purpose. For most people, the transfer to a creditor of the debt which a bank owes them is a method of settling transactions which is as effective as, and considerably more convenient than, the use of notes and coin. Admittedly the confidence of the public in the banking system is absolutely vital, and without it bank credit would be worthless. But this is true of *any* form of money; if the British public were suddenly assailed by doubts as to their ability to purchase goods with pound notes, no one would accept any more pound notes and the Bank of England pound note would cease to be money.

The total supply of money in Britain at the present time, then, exists in a number of forms. First, coins made largely of copper and silver; secondly, notes of various denominations issued by the Bank of England and a small number issued by banks in Scotland and Northern Ireland; finally, the deposits (or indebtedness to customers) of the commercial banking system. In December 1974 the actual amounts of these various components were as follows (in £ million):

Coins	415
Bank of England notes	5 631
Other notes	279
Total notes and coin	6 325
Less bank holdings	−1 142
Notes and coin with public	5 183
Commercial bank deposits	35 154
	40 337

Of these only Bank of England notes are *legal tender* in unlimited amounts, while coins are legal tender up to £2; by legal tender is meant a form of currency which the law requires creditors to accept in settlement of a debt. A bank cheque is not legal tender, and a creditor could obtain legal enforcement of a demand to be paid in Bank of England notes. In practice, as has been stated, bank cheques are generally accepted by creditors, and commercial bank credit in fact constitutes far and away the most important element in the total money supply.

One last point is of great importance. In ordinary conversation the word 'money' is frequently used when it is *income* which is really meant: people say that a man earns a lot of money, or has little money to live on. But money and income are two entirely separate and distinct concepts, and confusion will result if the terms are treated as interchangeable. Money is a definite *stock* of notes, coin and bank deposits existing at a particular moment of time; income is a *flow of wealth* accruing to a person or institution over a period of time. For example, a man may have a high income but hold little money, preferring to spend his income rapidly, or to hold his savings in some form other than money. The quantity of money and the level of incomes may thus move in opposite directions; between 1968 and 1969 for example, the national product of the United Kingdom (i.e. the level of incomes) rose by about 6 per cent, while the total stock of money in existence actually fell slightly, at least on one basis of measurement. The fact that incomes are usually (although not invariably) paid in the form of money should not be allowed to obscure the important distinction between the two things; electric current is conducted through wires, but this does not mean that electricity and wire are interchangeable concepts.

FURTHER READING

W. T. NEWLYN *Theory of money* 2nd edn., Oxford University Press, London 1971, Chs. 1–3

A. B. CRAMP *Monetary management* Allen and Unwin, London 1971, Ch. 1

D. C. ROWAN *Output, inflation and growth* Chs. 14–15

T. SCITOVSKY *Money and the balance of payments* Unwin, London 1969, Chs. 1–2

CHAPTER XXI

The British Banking System

1 HISTORICAL DEVELOPMENT

IN the previous chapter a brief account was given of how gold-smiths had developed the business of note-issue up to the end of the seventeenth century. So profitable was this pursuit that the goldsmiths (and other tradespeople who saw the possibilities of issuing notes against their own capital reserves) began to concentrate on this side of their business to the neglect of their original functions until ultimately they became full-time bankers, inviting deposits from outside sources. The Bank of England, which was to play an especially important role in the development of British banking, was formed in 1694; it was conducted as a commercial bank like any other, but in return for a loan to the government of the day it received the unique privilege of a charter of incorporation. This meant that the Bank became a joint-stock company, able to combine the resources of a large number of shareholders, whereas no other bank was able to operate on a joint-stock basis until 1826. For more than a century, therefore, the Bank of England had access to considerably greater resources than any other bank, and inevitably acquired a dominant position in the British banking system. So strong was its relative position, in fact, that the private banks soon came to regard the notes issued by the Bank of England as substitutes for a gold reserve.

The ability of banks to issue notes in excess of their reserves unhappily constituted a standing temptation for them to overdo the process and issue far more notes than was advisable. As a result, the eighteenth and early nineteenth centuries were characterised by periodic banking crises. One bank would be found unable to honour its commitment to convert its notes into gold on demand: the news of this would cause panic amongst the depositors not only of the bank involved but also amongst those of other private banks. When these 'runs' on the banks developed (i.e. when everyone holding bank notes rushed to the bank of issue demanding conversion into gold) it was inevitably found that the total commitments of any bank could not all be honoured simultaneously; bank-collapses on a wide scale frequently resulted and these often provoked depression in industries connected, in the role of lender or borrower, with the banks involved.

Two major consequences gradually followed from these periodic crises. First, a succession of legislative measures, together with the natural reactions of the banks themselves to these unhappy experiences, resulted in a strengthening of the private banks through amalgamations. More important still, the policy of these private banks underwent a fundamental change; the emphasis was placed to an increasing degree on the financing of specific commercial transactions by means of credit, while the issue of notes became less and less important. Secondly, the Bank of England, as the bank which possessed greatest resources (by virtue of being a joint-stock organisation rather than a mere partnership) and which had closest relations with the government, came more and more to play the part of the hub of the banking system. When banking crises occurred, the Bank of England frequently lent reserves in the form of notes or gold bullion to banks which were under pressure, allowing the latter to honour their obligations and so stemming the tide of panic before the entire banking system collapsed. On the occasions when the reserves of the Bank of England had become exhausted in this process, the government of the day suspended convertibility of Bank of England notes – that is, it relieved the Bank of the liability to redeem its notes in gold on demand – and declared the Bank's notes to be legal tender. As the government could then authorise the Bank to issue notes in unlimited quantities, there was no danger of any bank being unable to repay depositors in legal tender; hence the crises subsided.

These two tendencies culminated in the *Bank Charter Act*

of 1844 which established the Bank of England as the Central Bank of the United Kingdom, and gave to the British banking system the essential features which have continued to the present day. Under the 1844 Act, the Bank of England was given the sole right to issue notes, except that private banks already having an issue of notes were allowed to retain (but not increase or transfer) it. The remainder of the banking system was therefore forced to gradually abandon the practice of issuing notes, and great impetus was given to the previous trend towards deposit banking – i.e. the acceptance of funds deposited by the general public and the extension of credit to specific persons or for the purchase of relatively liquid assets. The broad structure of the Bank of England has since undergone no change from that provided for in the 1844 Act. Although it was not foreseen by the framers of the Bank Charter Act, the special position given by it to the Bank proved to be incompatible with the pursuit of ordinary banking business in competition with the other banks, and by the end of the nineteenth century the Bank of England had ceased to carry out any substantial amount of business for members of the general public.

The composition of the remainder of the British banking system has been much less stable. During the second half of the nineteenth century, and during the first two decades of the twentieth, a continuous process of amalgamation between banks was experienced, so that by the 1920s British commercial banking was highly concentrated in a small number of very large banks. This remained the position for nearly forty years, so that an influential committee on the working of the British monetary system (the Radcliffe Committee) was able to report in 1959 that nearly all the domestic banking business of Britain was in the hands of eleven banks. Even this small number was much reduced in the years immediately following by further amalgamations within the group. The 1960s, however, witnessed an enormous growth of banking institutions outside this small circle – a growth stimulated partly by official restrictions on the large established banks and partly by a disinclination towards genuine competition amongst those banks engendered by their forty years' dominance of the system.

The inherent structure of the British banking system remains, however, substantially unchanged in comparison with that of the 1920s.

At its centre stands the Bank of England, which controls and guides the system and which has ceased to conduct any substantial amount of ordinary commercial banking. Around it is a relatively small number of large commercial banks, carrying on business with the general public but no longer issuing their own notes. How the two parts of the system are linked together, and the functions which each perform, will be explored in the following sections.

2   THE BANK OF ENGLAND

From this brief survey of the historical development of the British banking system, four special features of the Bank of England can be seen, and these correspond with the four functions of the Bank in the present-day monetary system of the United Kingdom. First, it is responsible for the *issue of notes*, of which it now has a monopoly. Until 1844, as has been seen, notes could be issued by any bank. The Bank Charter Act provided, however, that the Bank of England should be divided into two parts one of which, the Issue Department, was responsible for issuing notes and given the sole right of further new issues. During the war of 1914–18 the Treasury itself issued notes, but in 1928 these notes were withdrawn and the entire note-issue was left in the hands of the Bank of England. At the present time, then, the only notes in circulation are those of the Bank of England except for the small issues of certain banks in Scotland and Northern Ireland (which are, in any case, required to hold a Bank of England note in their vaults for every note they themselves issue).

Until 1931, and except for occasional periods of crisis when convertibility was suspended, the Bank of England was required to convert its notes into gold on demand at a rate laid down by statute. Just as an ordinary bank has to maintain a certain reserve to meet demands for repayment of deposits in cash, so the Bank of England needed to hold sufficient gold reserves to enable it to meet its obligation to convert its notes into gold at any time. Since 1931, however, this obligation has been removed from it, and the note issue is entirely a *fiduciary* one – that is, there is no 'backing' of gold or anything else into which its notes can be converted. Since public confidence in the Bank is complete, however, this in no way affects the acceptability of the Bank's notes, and no one needs to convert them into some more acceptable form of money. Under the provisions of various Currency and Bank Notes Acts since 1928, the Treasury has complete control over the volume of the notes issued by the Bank, and can give the Bank authority to increase or reduce its note issue to any extent, subject to more or less formal parliamentary approval of increases over a specified limit which are maintained for more than two years.

The 1844 Act required the Bank to publish a weekly return in respect of each Department, showing the position as at the close of business on each Wednesday. Taking the return for 28 February 1974 as an example, the position of the Issue Department was as follows:

(£ million)

Assets		Liabilities	
Government debt	11·0	Notes issued:	
Other government		In circulation	4 573·4
securities	3 512·6	In Banking	
Other securities	1 076·4	Department	26·6
	4 600·0		4 600·0

The 'liabilities' side of this return needs little explanation, since the only liabilities of the Issue Department are the notes it has issued. Historically, these were liabilities in the sense that the Bank could be called on to exchange them for gold at a fixed rate; this is no longer the case, but the traditional form of balance-sheet accounting has been retained, presumably from sheer reluctance to change. The 'assets' side is a similar archaic survival. When the Bank was obliged to redeem notes in gold on demand it was required to show that it had assets to offset this liability, so as to demonstrate its ability to honour its obligations. Nowadays, with the exception of a small amount of coin and bullion retained in the interests of tradition and administrative convenience, the only assets which the Bank holds are securities – i.e. promises by a borrower to repay a sum of money on a specified or unspecified date and to pay a certain rate of interest in the meantime. Since the overwhelming majority of these are debts of the British government which could be repaid only in the form of Bank of England notes, they have little real significance as any kind of 'backing' for the note issue. (As was indicated in Chapter XIX, an increase in the note issue is in effect immediately lent to the government in return for IOUs. A reduction in the note issue would involve the government in repaying the corresponding amount of IOUs.) In fact, the whole system of accounting adopted by the Issue Department in its weekly return owes everything to historical tradition and nothing whatever to logic.

The second major feature of the Bank's development was its special relationship with the Government (it owed its origin to a loan to the Government) and it now acts as the *Government's bank*. It is the Government's agent in the handling of tax revenue, payments of interest on the national debt, raising and repayment of loans, etc. For this purpose the Bank maintains what are called *public deposits*, which are the bank accounts of the major revenue-collecting and spending departments. All government receipts are paid into these accounts and all government payments are made from them. The Bank of England is to the Government, then, what a commercial bank is to a private individual.

The third factor of the Bank's history was its emergence as the *bankers' bank*. From an early stage the London private banks began to keep part of their reserves in the form of a deposit at the Bank of England, treating these deposits and their Bank of England notes as cash equally with gold. The Bank has continued to perform this role. The big British deposit banks now hold an account at the Bank of England –

this group of accounts being called *bankers' deposits* – and use these accounts to settle indebtedness amongst themselves. Thus, if at the end of a day's business the customers of Lloyds Bank on balance owe the customers of the National Westminster £1 million, Lloyds will settle this debt by writing a cheque to the value of £1 million on its Bank of England account and handing it to the National Westminster; the Bank of England will then transfer £1 million from Lloyds deposit to the National Westminster deposit.

Until 1960, the only deposits maintained at the Bank of England by the commercial banks were of this normal, routine kind used for the clearing of interbank debts. Largely as the outcome of the report in 1959 of a Committee set up to enquire into the working of the British monetary system, however – the Radcliffe Report referred to earlier – the Bank of England was given power to call for *special deposits* from the commercial banks in Great Britain. These differ from normal commercial bank deposits at the Bank of England in two ways. First, they are *compulsory*: notice is given that a certain percentage of their total deposit accounts must be maintained by the commercial banks at the Bank of England after a certain date, and this instruction is mandatory. Secondly, special deposits are *not* at the free disposal of the banks lodging them; subject to the cash-reserve requirements mentioned in the previous chapter, the commercial banks are able to use their normal deposits at the Bank of England at any time and as they wish, but special deposits can be drawn upon only when the Bank of England gives permission for this to be done. The operation and functions of these special deposits are explained in Chapter XXIV below.

Bearing in mind the second and third functions of the Bank of England, it will be instructive to examine the weekly return of the other section of the Bank, the Banking Department; again the return for 28 February 1974 is taken as an example.

Consider first the 'Liabilities' side of the statement. The two small items 'Capital' and 'Reserves' deserve brief explanation. The 'Capital' refers to the amounts subscribed by the original stockholders of the Bank, and therefore legally due to them in

the event of its winding-up; the second item 'Reserves' represents the undistributed profits of the Bank, which are also in
law the property of the Bank's stockholders. Until 1946 the
Bank was a purely private corporation owned by its own
stockholders (although for a great many years the pursuit of
profit had ceased to be the aim of its policy), so that these items
had some theoretical significance. Under the Bank of England
(Nationalisation) Act of 1946, however, the ownership of the
Bank was vested entirely in the State, so that these items no
longer have any real meaning.

(£ million)

Assets		Liabilities	
Government securities	1 645·2	Capital	14·6
Other securities:		Reserves	130·3
Discounts and		Public deposits	81·7
advances	155·0	Bankers' deposits:	
Securities	84·1	Normal	249·9
Notes	26·6	Special	1 367·7
Coin	0·3		
Cheques in course of		Total	1 617·6
collection	66·0	Other deposits	170·9
Premises	37·9		
	2 015·1		2 015·1

The next two items, 'Public deposits' and 'Bankers' deposits',
have already been discussed; they correspond with the Bank's
functions of government bank and bankers' bank respectively.
The final item 'Other deposits', comprises the accounts of
customers other than the British Government and banks –
mainly Commonwealth governments and banks and some
foreign central banks. Some old-established business houses
still possess accounts at the Bank of England, these dating
from the period in which the Bank still competed with private
banks for commercial business; they are not important in
magnitude.

On the assets side – every banker must acquire an asset
against each liability, since the sums deposited with him (his

liabilities) must be put to some use – the first and easily most important item is 'Government securities', or debts of the British Government on which the Bank receives interest. The second item 'Other securities' is divided into 'Discounts and advances' and 'Other'. The former refers to bills discounted for, and short-term loans made to, the institutions comprising the *money market*; the nature of this item will become clearer in the next chapter, in which the operation of the money market is considered. The item 'Other securities' comprises securities of bodies other than the British government – particularly securities issued by Commonwealth and foreign governments and certain agencies set up with the participation of the Bank for the purpose of helping to finance development in British industry. The item 'Notes' corresponds with the item 'Notes in the Banking Department' in the return of the Issue Department; together with the item 'Coin', this indicates the reserve held by the Bank to meet demands from the general public (especially the commercial banks) for cash in exchange for deposits. In the past, when the Bank was required to convert its notes or deposits into gold on demand, the size of the Bank's cash (i.e. gold) reserve was a matter of considerable importance. Nowadays the Bank has no obligation to convert its notes or deposits into anything (except new Bank of England notes), so that the cash holdings of the Banking Department have little more than administrative significance.

The three functions of the Bank reflected in the weekly returns of both departments, then, are those of controlling the note issue, acting as the government's banker and as the bankers' bank. The combination of these functions gives the Bank peculiar strength in fulfilling its fourth, and most important function – that of controlling the monetary and banking system as a whole. How it carries out this function will be described in a later chapter.

3   THE BRITISH COMMERCIAL BANKS

It was seen from the brief summary of the history of British banking that during the nineteenth century there occurred a process of amalgamation amongst the hundreds of private banks which had sprung up all over the country. This proceeded so far that by the late 1950s 95 per cent or more of the ordinary banking business of the country was carried out by the eleven banks which belonged to the London Clearing House, the

TABLE 21.1   *Deposits held by main constituents of the UK banking system*

£ million

	Dec 1962	Dec 1974
Deposit banks		
1. London clearing banks	7 903	25 511
2. Scottish clearing banks	843	2 458
3. N. Ireland and other banks	215	1 677
	8 961	29 646
1. Accepting houses, etc.	663	16 231
2. British overseas and Commonwealth banks	1 134	14 406
3. American banks	454	28 733
4. Foreign banks	362	10 364
5. Other overseas banks	366	10 160
	2 979	109 540
Secondary bank deposits as % of total	24·9	72·9

Source: Bank of England *Quarterly Bulletin,* Vol. IV, No. 4, December 1964, Tables 10–16 and Vol. 15, No. 1, March 1975, Table 8.

nature of which will be explained shortly. During the 1960s, however, a remarkable transformation took place in the British banking system, the magnitude of which may be seen from Table 21.1. What had been called 'secondary' banking institutions launched a vigorous and effective expansion into some (although not all) of the activities previously substantially monopolised by the clearing banks. From holding about a quarter of total deposits in the country, these so-called 'secondary' banks were accounting within a decade for more than two-thirds.

There are, however, differences of a rather fundamental kind between these two categories of bank. In order to explain these – and thus to explain the dramatic transformation which occurred in the 1960s – it will be convenient to examine the assets and liabilities of each category in turn.

4   THE DEPOSIT BANKS

By the end of 1970 there were 15 banks officially classified as 'deposit' banks in the United Kingdom, the group being over-whelmingly dominated in terms of size by the four great clearing banks of Barclays, Lloyds, Midland and National Westminster. This group retains the traditional functions developed by the evolving commercial banking system over the late nineteenth and early twentieth centuries. What are these? First, the deposit banks undertake the safe-keeping of cash deposited with them by their customers. Secondly, the possession of these cash reserves enables them to expand credit in the way described earlier – that is, the banks incur debts which they know from experience will be passed from person to person by means of cheques and only in a minority of cases be drawn out in cash. The modern deposit banker knows that not much more than about 5 per cent of his total debts will be used by the creditor in the form of cash; so long as he has £100 in cash in his vaults, therefore, he can safely incur liabilities to a total of anything up to £2 000. By far the greater part of this £2 000 will be used by depositors to make payments by cheque, requir-ing only a transfer from one account to another within the bank. But how does a bank incur these liabilities? If a customer deposits £100 in cash, the bank automatically incurs a liability of £100 in the shape of the depositor's account on which he can call at any time. But how can the bank incur extra liabilities amounting to £1 900 so as to bring the total to the £2 000 which the bank knows can be safely incurred with its £100 cash reserve?

The answer to this question may be found by examining the statements of assets and liabilities published each month by the deposit banks: the return for December 1974 is shown in Table 21.2.

TABLE 21.2 *Main assets and liabilities of the British deposit banks, end-1974*

	£ million	% of total
Assets		
Cash	1 436	5·6
Money at call and short notice	1 507	5·9
Bills discounted	1 051	4·1
Special deposits	618	2·4
Investments	1 481	5·8
Loans and advances	18 771	73·5
Certificates of deposit	684	2·7
Liabilities		
Current and deposit accounts	27 895	94·1
Certificates of deposit	1 751	5·9
Total	29 646	
Of which, payable in £ sterling (%)	87·4	

Source: Bank of England *Quarterly Bulletin*, Vol. 15, No. 1 March 1975, Table 8.

In a full bank balance-sheet certain other relatively minor items (capital subscribed by shareholders, value of bank premises, etc.) are also shown, but the important items are those contained in the monthly returns such as that shown in the table. The first item on the assets side is the cash reserve. This comprises the notes and coin held in the tills of the banks and their deposits at the Bank of England; since a deposit at the Bank of England, like a Bank of England note, constitutes a claim on the Central Bank, it can be treated as cash just as much as notes and coin. At one time the British banks adopted a firm convention (unlike the position in some other countries, there was never any legislation governing the matter) that their cash reserves must always equal a minimum of 8 per cent of their total liabilities. Since September 1971, however, all banks operating in the United Kingdom have become subject to official requirements governing the minimum ratio between what are called 'reserve assets' and their liabilities, balances at the Bank of England merely being one amongst a list of eligible reserve assets. This matter of the regulation of banking activities by the Bank of England is discussed at some length in Chapter XXIV below. For the moment it is sufficient to say that, subject to these official requirements, all deposit bankers will need to maintain a cash balance adequate to meet the demands for cash which their experience leads them to expect with any given level of deposits. The deposit banks of the United Kingdom now enjoy so high a degree of confidence in their solvency on the part of the general public that the appropriate level of cash reserves is a matter of administrative convenience rather than one of the preservation of confidence. The next two items appearing in the list of assets are money at call and short notice and bills discounted. Both of these involve the money market, of which more will have to be said in the following chapter. For the moment it is sufficient to say that the former item comprises loans of short duration to persons and institutions in the money market, while the latter comprises short-term securities (or acknowledgements of debt) which are bought and sold on the money market. The nature of the special deposits (at the Bank of England) has already been briefly described; more will be heard of these at a later stage. On them the banks receive interest equal to the current rate of interest on the important short-term government security known as the treasury bill. The next item, investments, consists of longer-term securities which are quoted on the Stock Exchange and can be bought and sold there. The majority of the securities held by British banks are those of the British government, although some securities issued by Commonwealth governments and by the various nationalised industries are also held. Next, and of considerable importance, comes the item *loans and advances* – loans to businesses, public corporations, or private persons – which are usually made in the form of an overdraft (the right to overdraw on an account up to an agreed maximum, interest being charged only on the amount actually used). British banks dislike making loans for a long period, so that advances made to businesses are usually in respect of working capital (raw materials, stocks of goods, etc.) and not fixed capital, which can pay for itself only after a considerable period of time.

The final item, *certificates of deposit*, would not have appeared in a list of deposit bank assets (or liabilities) before 1966. As their title implies, they are pieces of paper acknowledging that a specified sum of money (the units are seldom less than £50 000) has been deposited with a banking institution for a specified period of up to five years from their date of issue. A specified rate of interest is payable in the meantime to the owner of the certificate. They differ from an ordinary deposit in a bank primarily in the fact that they are fully *negotiable* – that is to say, they can be bought and sold freely without reference to the bank of original issue. More will be said about these in the following section concerned with the secondary banking system.

If a bank finds itself able to expand credit, then (i.e. if its reserve assets are more than adequate to sustain its existing liabilities) it can do so by acquiring any of these various assets; it can go into the money market or the Stock Exchange to buy bills, certificates of deposit or long-term securities, or it can make loans to money-market dealers, businessmen or private individuals who are wishing to raise funds for the purchase of capital goods of some sort. On either type of asset, of course, the bank earns interest. An important consideration which must always influence the decisions of deposit banks, however, is that of liquidity – which, in this context, generally means the ability to convert assets into cash. Although a certain cash reserve may be thought sufficient to meet the normal demands for cash which a banker is likely to encounter, the deposit banker has the obligation to repay all his depositors in cash on demand, or at short notice, if they should require it. Hence, in the interests of safety, a deposit banker must always be able to convert some of his other assets into cash should an unusual demand threaten to exhaust his reserves. A compromise has therefore to be struck between liquidity on the one hand and profitability on the other; for reasons which will become clear after an examination of the theory of interest, the more liquid an asset the lower the rate of interest it will earn. Advances to businesses, for example, are amongst the most lucrative of the banks' assets but are relatively illiquid; if an entrepreneur cannot repay his loan at the particular moment when a bank needs extra cash there is not much the banker can do about it. Cash, on the other hand, is perfectly liquid but brings in no revenue at all. (Hence, in the bank return shown in Table 21.2, the assets are shown in the order of their liquidity and the reverse order of their profitability.) For many years it was generally said that British banks liked to keep at least 30 per cent of their resources (the 'secondary liquidity ratio', as it was sometimes called) in the relatively liquid forms of cash, money at call and short notice and bills, because both of the latter items could be turned into cash fairly rapidly and without significant loss.

Attempts to exercise control over the banking system through this conventional ratio proved ineffective for several reasons, however, and reliance is now placed on the reserve-asset ratio mentioned previously and to be discussed further in Chapter XXIV. Even so it remains a fact of life for the deposit banker that most of his liabilities are short-term and a second line of defence, in the form of an adequate stock of easily realisable assets, is as much a necessity to guard against the unexpected as is the cash reserve to guard against the foreseen.

It is necessary now to turn from the assets of the deposit banks to their liabilities. Apart from the capital subscribed by the stockholders of a bank (and an item called 'acceptances' which is both an asset and a liability, and can be ignored as a self-balancing item), the liabilities of a deposit bank are of course primarily represented by its deposits – the amounts due to its customers. When a bank acquires an asset it must automatically incur an equal liability. If it acquires cash, the persons from whom the cash is acquired are credited with an equal amount in their deposits. If a bank makes a loan, it does so by opening or crediting a deposit in the borrower's name to the amount concerned. If it buys securities, it pays for them by crediting the seller's account with the amount of the purchase. The purchase of assets is the obverse of the creation of bank credit; one is achieved by means of the other. Bank deposits may be of two kinds. First, there are current accounts, the holders of which may use their deposits (to obtain cash or transfer them by cheque) at any time and without notice; secondly, there are deposit accounts, for the use of which notice of a week or more must normally be given to the bank, and on which (to compensate for this restriction) the depositor is paid interest. At the present time roughly one-third of the deposits in the British deposit banks are current accounts while the remainder are deposit accounts.

Reference has already been made to the other main form of deposit bank liability – the negotiable certificate of deposit. As was remarked earlier, these are identical in most essential respects with the conventional deposit account except in being freely transferable from one holder to another without the necessity of giving notice to, or writing a cheque on, the bank of issue. They were introduced as a convenient way in which favourable terms could be offered to depositors of large sums of money who were willing to make relatively long-term deposits without having to simultaneously offer equally generous terms to the bulk of existing small-scale depositors. These certificates originated with the borrowing and lending of foreign currencies but are nowadays issued in sterling. As will be seen from Table 21.2, however, the liabilities of the British deposit banks are overwhelmingly denominated in pounds sterling – which is to say that their funds are drawn almost entirely from within the United Kingdom. This is one of the several points of contrast between the deposit and secondary banks.

So far, little has been said about the complications introduced by the existence of more than one commercial bank. Although in the vast majority of cases bank deposits will be passed from person to person by means of cheques, rather than drawn out in cash, a good many of the cheques written by a depositor of one deposit bank will pass into the hands of customers of other deposit banks. The other banks, having credited their customers' accounts with the sums concerned, will then demand payment of the amounts due. The first bank will be unable to meet this demand by offering to open an account for the amount owing since the other banks will of course have no desire to hold a deposit with one of their competitors.

It was in order to deal with this problem of inter-bank indebtedness that the London Clearing House was instituted in the eighteenth century and it continues nowadays together with similar clearing houses in the main provincial cities. The representatives of the members of the London Clearing House (the 'clearing banks') meet daily for the purpose of cancelling-out debts arising between the different banks. For example, if the customers of Barclays Bank have written cheques to the value of £10 million payable to customers of the Midland Bank, while customers of the Midland have written £10 million worth of cheques to the benefit of depositors in Barclays, then the two sets of claims can be cancelled against each other and no cash at all need change hands. In general, the cheques paid out to other banks by the depositors of any given bank will usually be offset over any long period of time by cheques coming in to its depositors from other banks, since few people can go on for long disposing of more funds than they have coming in. During any one day, however, this balance will not usually occur, and, after all possible cancelling-out has been effected, each member of the clearing house will be left at the end of the day with a net balance due to other banks or owed to it by other banks. Each bank will then settle up these balances by means of cheques drawn on its account at the Bank of England.

The extensive use of the cheque as a means of payment, then, allows British deposit banks to create credit considerably in excess of the cash they hold at any given moment; they are able to rely on the fact that all but a small proportion of the debts they incur will be paid into another bank account. If the accounts concerned are in the same bank, nothing more than a mere book-keeping entry is involved; if they are in different deposit banks, the transfer will be offset over any fairly long period by corresponding transfers in the opposite direction. Does this mean that the deposit banks have unlimited powers of credit creation? Clearly it does not; there are in fact three distinct limits to the power of any single bank to expand its liabilities. First, and most important, each bank must maintain the reserve-ratio laid down by the authorities; unless its reserve assets are increased a bank will be unable to increase its total liabilities beyond a figure which is defined by this reserve ratio requirement. Secondly, each bank must keep in step with the others. If one of the big deposit banks tried to expand more rapidly than the others, most of the cheques drawn on the additional deposits credited by it would come into the hands of the other banks; hence it would persistently lose cash to the others through the settlements in the Clearing House. Thirdly, the banks have rather rigorous standards in their selection of assets and if they were unable for any reason to obtain the right types of asset in the right proportions they might feel themselves unable to add to their total liabilities, however comfortable their reserves. British deposit bankers regard the making of loans and advances, rather than the purchase of securities of various kinds, as their primary business; it is certainly their most lucrative business. They would scarcely carry this preference, however, to the point of granting overdrafts to customers who fell well below their accepted standards of credit-worthiness.

5 THE SECONDARY BANKING SYSTEM

The preceding section will have helped to distinguish the two separate activities which together constitute the role of commercial banking. First, the management of the money supply – meaning by that the creation and management of bank deposits, including the administration of the complex and wide-ranging business of the recording and clearance of cheques by which those deposits are transferred from one person to another. Secondly, the *lending* of this credit for the purposes of commerce and industry through the purchase of various types of asset and, especially, the making of loans and advances.

Now these two functions are in practice separable. The deposit (or primary) banks discussed in the previous section combine both and their distinguishing feature is that the funds they lend to individuals and enterprises under the second heading are created by themselves in the course of their role under the first heading. What have come to be called the secondary banks are those institutions (at the end of 1974 there were about 200 registered in Britain) which are authorised to carry out the second function but do not deal in the first. The operation of that part of the money supply known as bank credit is an important function, but the recording and transfer of cheques involve a great deal of administrative labour and expense which is not particularly profitable. The secondary banks – so called not because of their collective size but because they deal, at second-hand so to speak, with credit created by the deposit banks rather than by themselves – do not engage in the business of administering deposits freely transferable from person to person by cheque but seek instead to attract deposits created by these other primary sources of credit and to use them in the more remunerative kinds of lending.

It has already been recorded that the enormous expansion of this kind of banking in Britain occurred in the 1960s. There were three main reasons why this period was especially propitious for this kind of expansion. First, both the demand for and supply of loanable funds were expanding rapidly under the impact of sustained economic growth unhindered by the various restrictions which had featured the decade or so after the end of the Second World War and of the availability of large dollar balances in Europe – a matter touched on in Chapter XXXIII below. Secondly, because of the long-established pre-eminence of the deposit banks, official attempts to control the state of the economy through the monetary system were almost exclusively concentrated on the deposit banks, restricting their ability to exploit this opportunity for profitable expansion. Thirdly – and for exactly the same reason – the deposit banks had settled into a comfortable semi-monopolistic framework in which they displayed remarkably little inclination towards competition amongst themselves – either in the business of attracting deposits from the general public or in gaining lending business by offering more favourable terms than other deposit banks were currently offering.

The secondary banks were inhibited by neither official restrictions nor conventional banking attitudes. They left the important but less-profitable business of credit-creation and day-to-day cheque-handling to the deposit banks but by offering favourable terms for time deposits or on certificates of deposit mounted an aggressive campaign to attract *existing* deposit balances from conventional banks – including those in foreign countries – and then re-lending them at higher interest rates than those they themselves had to offer in order to attract deposits. As may be seen from Table 21.1, in the 1960s the business boomed. Some of the institutions concerned were old-established City houses seizing a new opportunity, such as the acceptance houses and merchant banks of the money market described in the next chapter. Others were overseas banks – especially American banks – invading the British market after the manner of Henry Ford selling cars. Others again – especially the hire-purchase houses – were new companies created for the purpose.

It is natural to ask why this rapid and profitable expansion should have fallen into the hands of this new secondary system when it was doing no more than using funds which the older deposit banks could have used in the same way – and which were in fact liabilities of the deposit banks. There are two answers. First, because of their freedom from official control until 1971 and, more important, because of the fact that their deposits were repayable only after a substantial period of notice (defined in terms of months, if not years), the secondary banks were able to use a much greater proportion of their assets in the profitable, long-term end of the banking spectrum and needed to hold very little in the relatively unprofitable form of cash and liquid assets. They were thus able to offer higher interest rates to attract deposits and still enjoy a comfortable profit-margin. Secondly, partly for the same reason and partly because of their less traditional approach to banking business, the secondary banks were willing to use their funds for purposes yielding high returns but conventionally regarded by the deposit banks as faintly disreputable activities – especially hire-purchase finance.

These characteristics may be discerned in the summary of the main assets and liabilities of the secondary banks shown in Table 21.3. The 'conventional' deposit banking assets of cash, call money, bills and investments (securities) which bring in relatively low returns, account for only 3·6 per cent of the total compared with 21 per cent for the deposit banks. Loans and advances, on the other hand, amount to over 93 per cent of the total compared with less than 74 per cent for the deposit banks. What is more, loans to financial institutions and local authorities (the providers of lucrative hire-purchase and mortgage loans respectively) accounted for 42 per cent of the advances by the secondary banks within Britain but only 13 per cent of those by the deposit banks.

The source of deposits in the secondary system are also of significance. It was noted earlier that nearly 90 per cent of the liabilities of the deposit banks was denominated in pounds sterling; for the secondary banks the proportion at the end of 1974 was less than 25 per cent. This reflects the greater inclination of the secondary system to attract funds by offering terms attractive enough to bring new funds into the country from abroad; its lending propensities are equally adventurous – at the end of 1974 nearly 50 per cent of its loans were to overseas residents compared with only 5 per cent for the deposit banks.

TABLE 21.3 *Main assets and liabilities of the British secondary banking system, end-1974*

	£ million	% of total
Assets		
Cash	4	—
Money at call and short notice	1 175	1·9
Bills discounted	653	1·1
Special deposits	303	0·5
Investments	365	0·6
Loans and advances	56 246	92·6
Certificates of deposit	1 974	3·3
Liabilities		
Current and deposit accounts	72 239	90·4
Certificates of deposit	7 655	9·6
Total	79 894	
Of which, payable in £ sterling (%)		22·3

Source: As for Table 21.2.

6 CONCLUSION

The growth of the secondary banking system was encouraged partly by its freedom from the restrictions imposed on what was regarded, until the 1960s, as 'the' banking system − i.e. the deposit banks. The anomaly could not be tolerated indefinitely: by mid-1971, loans within Britain by the secondary banks, although a much smaller *proportion* of their total advances than was the case with the deposit banks, were nevertheless approaching those of the latter in absolute magnitude. At that time, in fact, bank advances within Britain by the secondary banks accounted for well over 40 per cent of the total. Hence the system of official controls over the banking system introduced in Britain in 1971 was extended to *all* banking institutions: the unintended discrimination in favour of a major element of the banking system was ended. This matter is investigated further in Chapter XXIV.

The experience of the 1960s, however, illustrates a fundamentally important characteristic of the banking system: its inherent capacity to respond to a changing environment. Evolving from the goldsmiths, British bankers first concentrated on the issue of notes and the acquisition of assets with the proceeds. When the power of note-issue was removed, they responded by becoming deposit-creators and lenders. When this power came under official restriction the secondary banking system escaped from the restriction by separating the functions of deposit-creation and deposit-lending. The future is unlikely to differ in this respect from the past: any policy measures designed to influence and control the banking system will ignore its capacity for change only at their great peril.

FURTHER READING

R. S. SAYERS *Modern banking* 7th edn., Oxford University Press, London 1967, Chs. 1–2

E. NEVIN and E. W. DAVIS *The London clearing banks* Elek Books, London 1970, Chs. 4 and 11

J. E. WADSWORTH (ed.) *The banks and the monetary system in the U.K., 1959–1971* Methuen, London 1973, Chs. 6–7

CHAPTER XXII

The Money and
Capital Markets

1 THE BILL OF EXCHANGE

IN the preceding chapter more than one reference was made to a rather mysterious thing called the bill of exchange – it featured in the returns of both the Banking Department of the Bank of England and the commercial banks. What, then, is a bill of exchange? Essentially it is a post-dated cheque drawn not on a bank but on a particular person, and its purpose is to secure a loan for a relatively short period of time. Its function is best understood by referring back to the period of history in which its widespread use developed. It is not much more than a century since the railway system of Britain was developed. Before that time, the transport of goods from the manufacturer to the merchant purchasing them, and the disposal of them by the merchant in the market was a process which took a good deal of time. This was true even if the goods were produced and sold within Britain; the time involved was even greater if the goods were either produced or sold abroad. Hence a problem of capital was raised: if the merchant paid for the goods immediately they were produced, his capital would be locked up in them throughout the period during which they were being transported and finally sold, while if the manufacturer waited for payment until the goods were finally sold, *his* capital would be locked up for some time.

Now capital is a scarce factor of production, and neither a merchant nor a manufacturer regards the provision of capital as being part of his function. Hence a conflict of interests arises: the seller wishes to be paid as soon as he has despatched the goods, while the ideal situation from the buyer's point of view would be one in which payment could be deferred until he has resold the goods. These interests were reconciled by the bill of exchange, which passed the job of capital-provision in these trade transactions to persons or institutions specially fitted for it. The bill consisted of a statement by the merchant that he had purchased goods to a stated value from the manufacturer concerned, and of a promise by him to pay that sum in three, or six, months' time, or after whatever period the merchant expected would elapse before the goods were finally sold. When despatching the goods, the manufacturer would send the bill by post to the merchant, who would sign and return it. The manufacturer would then take it to some person or institution specialising in trade finance (more will be said about such specialists in the following section) and ask for it to be *discounted* – i.e. purchased. If the merchant's reputation was a sound one, the bill would be purchased from the manufacturer at something less than its full value (e.g. a bill for £100 might be bought for £99) and the person discounting the bill would then collect its full value from the merchant after the specified period had elapsed.

In this way, all parties were satisfied. The merchant obtained credit for long enough to enable him to sell the goods and pay for them from the proceeds; the manufacturer was able to recover, at only a small cost, the working capital (cost of labour, materials, etc.) locked up in the goods and could thus devote it to further production; the person discounting the bill profited by the difference between the price at which the bill was bought and its full value at maturity. This latter difference, expressed as a percentage of the value of the bill at maturity, was really a rate of interest on the capital advanced on the transaction – it is called the *discount rate*. A three-month bill worth £100 and bought at £99 would carry a discount rate of 4 per cent – the difference (£1) divided by the value at maturity (£100) expressed as a rate *per annum*.

Bills of this kind, arising from actual transactions involving goods, are known as *trade bills*; they are classified as inland or foreign bills according to whether the movement of goods concerned is an internal one or one which involves exports or imports. Their attractiveness as a means of raising short-term capital was so great that another type, the *finance bill*, was soon developed. This is similar to the trade bill except that goods are not involved; it is, in fact, simply a promise to pay a specified sum of money on a date in the future by a person seeking to raise capital for a short period. One important type of finance bill is the *treasury bill*; this is used by the British government on a large scale as a means of meeting an excess of expenditure over revenue. Generally, the expenditure of the government is occurring more or less evenly throughout the year, but its receipts from taxation are heavily concentrated in the final three months of the financial year. Consequently, there is a need to borrow funds for the months when expenditure exceeds revenue, and towards the end of the nineteenth century the British government hit on the idea of raising such funds by means of the type of bill which had become a familiar instrument of short-term trade credit.

The treasury bill is therefore a promise on the part of the government to pay the holder of the bill a specified sum on a date in the future. Nowadays these bills are usually 91-day bills – i.e. they are repaid 91 days after the date of issue – and are issued in denominations of £5 000 or multiples of £5 000. The treasury bills offered in the market are known as *tender* bills; the Treasury announces every week the total amount of bills which are being offered and the institutions of the money market are invited to tender (i.e. bid a price) for whatever volume they are prepared to buy. The higher the price obtained for the bills, of course, the lower the discount rate which the government is forced to pay on its borrowings, and the Treasury disposes of as many bills as possible to the highest bidders. Other treasury bills, known as *tap bills*, are issued directly to official agencies of various kinds which have idle funds they are prepared to lend to the Exchequer; the rate of discount paid on tap bills and the quantity of them issued each week are for some reason regarded by the Treasury as matters of the greatest secrecy.

During the present century the relative importance of the various types of bills of exchange has altered considerably.

Immediately before the First World War, the volume of trade bills in circulation in London was about £500 million, compared with a figure of about £16 million for tender treasury bills. By 1936 the volume of commercial bills had dwindled to less than £300 million while that of tender treasury bills had risen to nearly £600 million. In the 1960s the volume of commercial bills circulating in the London money market roughly doubled and now certainly exceeds £3 000 million; the issue of tender treasury bills, on the other hand, is currently of the order of £1 200 million. The treasury bill, once the dominant element in the market, has now been overtaken by the commerical bill once again.

What is the explanation of this development? The enormous rise in the volume of treasury bills is a reflection of the expansion in the British national debt as a whole from less than £640 million in 1900 to about £40 000 million in 1974; the government borrowing necessitated by two World Wars has been the major factor at work in this. The relative decline of the commercial bill until recent years occurred mainly as a result of the improvements in transport and in banking during the present century. The former much reduced the time-lag between production and sale, and hence the amount of capital needed to finance trade; the latter enabled businessmen to finance their transactions through the more flexible and convenient medium of bank credit. Credit 'squeezes' through the banking system and the other forces stimulating the growth of the secondary banking system – discussed in the previous chapter – have been a major factor in the reversal of this long-established decline of the commercial bill in London, and the resulting change in the character of the supply of bills to the London money market, as will be seen later, has important implications for the role of the market itself.

2 THE NATURE AND FUNCTIONS OF THE MONEY MARKET

Put briefly, the purpose of the money market is to supply capital for short periods of time and to carry the risks involved in this process; the discount rate is the reward earned by the market for performing these functions. The risks in question are of two kinds: the *trade* risk and the *monetary* risk. By the trade risk is meant the chance of loss because of the inability, or unwillingness, of the borrower to honour his obligation to repay the capital advanced. For example, if a bill is discounted, there is always the possibility that the person on whom the bill is drawn (i.e. the person promising tó pay the stated sum in 3 or 6 months' time) may prove to be bankrupt when the bill matures. If this happens, the person who has discounted the bill will claim the due amount from the person who brought the bill in for discounting – i.e. the original creditor who in effect borrowed the capital on the strength of the debtor's promise to pay. If this fails to result in the repayment of the bill, then the discounter of the bill has lost his capital. The institutions in the money market are highly specialised in their trade and make it their business to know whether a bill is a good risk or not, but whatever precautions are taken the element of risk is always present to some degree in the discounting of a commercial bill.

The monetary risk is of rather a different kind. Most institutions which discount bills do so with the aid of borrowed money (most of it being lent by the commercial banks). On these funds the institutions concerned have to pay interest, and they are usually liable to have to repay the loans at very short notice if required. They make their profits by discounting bills at a rate which is slightly higher than that which they have to pay on their own borrowings. If they should be called on to repay funds shortly after the current market rate of discount has risen (why this should happen will be seen in Chapter XXIV) one of two possibilities will be open to them. The first is that they can hold on to the bills they have discounted with the borrowed money, and repay their creditors with money borrowed elsewhere at the current (i.e. higher) rate of interest; if this procedure is adopted they may well have to pay to the new source of funds a higher rate than that which they are earning on the bills they hold, consequently suffering a loss instead of making a profit. The second possibility is that they

can repay their debts by selling the bills they have discounted –
i.e. by *re-discounting* them; if the current discount rate has
risen, however, they will obtain for the bills a lower price than
that at which they originally bought them. For example, say the
discount rate rises from 4 to 5 per cent; a 3-month bill discounted at the old rate would have been bought for approxi-
mately £99 (£1 interest for 3-month credit being roughly 4 per
cent per annum), but when re-discounted at the higher rate of
5 per cent it would fetch only £98·75, assuming it still has three
months to run. In either case, then, the institution discounting a
bill suffers a loss because of the change in market interest rates.

The main institutions in the money market specialising in
this business are four in number. First are the firms of *brokers*,
either one-man businesses or partnerships, which use their own
capital plus bank loans. Most of them act as mere agents, discounting bills or buying Certificates of Deposit offered by people
or institutions wishing to raise money and then immediately
re-selling them to an institution wishing to hold them until their
maturity. Except in a minority of cases, brokers do not command sufficient resources to hold bills for their full life of three
or six months, and act merely as intermediaries between buyers
and sellers of bills and Certificates of Deposit. The bulk of discounting properly so called is carried out by discount houses
(at the end of 1974 there were twelve of these operating in
the London market); these obtain resources from (*a*) the capital
subscribed by the partners or shareholders, (*b*) the commercial
banks and (*c*) deposits from the general public. With these resources they are able to hold a large volume of short-term assets
until they fall due for payment.

The main assets held by these institutions, and their evolving
structure, can be seen from Table 22.1. In the early 1950s it
would have been a reasonably accurate approximation to say
that the discount houses were dealers in short-term government debt – treasury bills accounting for about two-thirds of
their assets and short-term government securities (i.e. debts
repayable within five years at a maximum) for most of the
remainder. As has been noted already, however, the late 1950s
and early 1960s saw the beginning of the resurgence of the

commercial bill and by 1962 such bills accounted for about 15 per cent of the assets held by the discount houses. Eleven years later, at the end of 1974, an even greater transformation was discernible. Treasury bills and short-term government securities were accounting for less than a quarter of total assets while commercial bills had grown to be roughly twice as important. What is more, two types of asset which had been virtually non-existent ten years previously had grown to well over 20 per cent of the total. The first of these was the short-term bond issued by British local government authorities; this reflected the trend in government policy, noted in Section 5 of Chapter XIX, towards encouraging local authorities to raise their capital requirements on the open market rather than through borrowing from the central government. The second was, of course, the negotiable certificate of deposit, the development of which was briefly described in the previous chapter. Indeed, it was the willingness of the discount houses to 'make a market' in these certificates – i.e. to stand ready to re-purchase them from holders needing repayment before their formal maturity – which accounts to a substantial degree for the enormous growth in the popularity of this type of asset during the later 1960s. Any interest-bearing asset is made more attractive by the knowledge that institutions with substantial resources are standing ready to reconvert them into cash if and when the need arises.

A third set of institutions operating in the money market are the *accepting houses,* about fifteen institutions whose functions as secondary banks were mentioned in the preceding chapter. The older-established of these were the great private merchant banks – Barings, Lazards, Rothschilds and so on – which functioned in the discount market long before the concept of a secondary banking system was ever dreamed of. By virtue of long experience in trade finance, and especially international finance, these firms were – and still are – able to judge the quality of a bill and to add their own credit-standing to a bill by accepting it in return for a commission. That is, a borrower who fears that the name on a bill of exchange is not well-known, so that it would be regarded by the market as a rather

TABLE 22.1   *The London discount market, 1952-74*

	£ million			% of total 1974
	Dec. 1952	Dec. 1962	Dec. 1974	
Assets				
1. Bills of exchange:				
a. Treasury bills	702	502	729	24·1
b. Other bills	42	189	1 370	45·3
2. U K Government bonds	291	488	10	0·3
3. Local Authority bonds	n.a.	n.a.	344	11·4
4. Certificates of deposit:				
a. Sterling	—	—	395	13·1
b. U S dollars	—	—	86	2·8
5. Other	32	72	92	3·0
Liabilities (borrowed funds)				
1. Bank of England	5	8	—	—
2. Deposit banks	572	803	1 481	50·8
3. Secondary banks	340	234	1 207	41·4
4. Other sources	111	140	228	7·8

Sources: Bank of England *Statistical Abstract,* No. 1, 1970, Table 7 and
Quarterly Bulletin, Vol. 15, No. 1 March 1975, Table 7.

risky proposition, can go to an accepting house having special knowledge of the trade or country from which the bill has originated, and ask it to accept the bill. The accepting house, with its specialised knowledge, will be familiar with the bill's credit-value (or at least will have the means of investigating it) and, if it is satisfied, it will accept the bill – i.e. guarantee to pay the amount due if the person named on the bill fails to pay up at the date of maturity. Such an acceptance by a firm of standing will naturally reduce the risk attached to the bill; hence it will be discounted at a relatively low rate. Over the course of history the older accepting houses have added direct banking to these traditional functions – and been joined by newer institutions – and, as will be seen later in this chapter, have also taken on functions in the long-term capital market.

The final set of institutions are the commercial banks, which enter into the money market in three ways. First, they discount bills (the third asset in the returns shown in the previous chapter) either directly, as does a discount house, or by purchasing bills from discount houses after a part of the life of the bills has elapsed. (Nowadays all the treasury bills held by the banks are obtained through discount houses in this way.) Secondly, the banks carry on acceptance business, especially for their own customers who are naturally well known to them. Finally, they lend money to brokers and discount houses (money at call and short notice) for periods ranging from overnight to a week or ten days, the loans usually being renewed as and when they fall due for repayment. As can be seen from Table 22.1, the banks now provide well over 90 per cent of the funds used by the discount houses in their operations; most of the remainder ('Other sources') comes from direct deposits attracted from institutions or individuals by the offer of interest rates higher than those obtainable from the banking system.

It may be asked why the banks should lend all this money to discount houses, rather than discount the bills and purchase central or local government bonds themselves and so enjoy the profits otherwise made by the discount houses. So far as trade bills are concerned, the reason advanced in past years was that by leaving some bills in the hands of the market, the banks were able to acquire a liquid asset (money at call) which brought in some revenue but carried none of the commercial risks attached to trade bills; during the decline of the importance of trade bills this argument inevitably lost a great deal of its force. Treasury bills and other short-term government securities carry no such commercial risk. The risk they *do* carry, however – as do the other assets held by the discount houses – is that of fluctuation in capital value when interest rates change, a matter discussed in the next chapter. By holding such assets at second-hand, so to speak – i.e. lending funds to discount houses who then purchase them – the banking system is obtaining a lucrative outlet for funds which can be recalled at very short notice but are free of capital risk in the meantime.

Evolving from its historical function of dealing with trade bills, then, the money market now provides an outlet for short-term lending by banking institutions and, equally, a source of short-term finance for a variety of purposes. Like the secondary banking system, the discount houses can be somewhat less conservative in their lending policy; although their funds are borrowed at short term they are less open to sudden pressures than the current accounts of the deposit banks so that the finance of, say, hire-purchase transactions is more open to them. Furthermore, the discount houses provide a steady market for treasury bills and short-term government stocks, a fact which is of considerable convenience to governments inevitably faced with periodic short-term financing needs. Finally, the money market fulfills an important role as an intermediary between the commercial banks and the Bank of England; the way in which this relationship actually operates in monetary control will be described in Chapter XXIV. If this link between the Central and commercial banks were to vanish, it is by no means certain from the experience of other countries in which the money market link is absent that any other system of maintaining such a link would be as satisfactory.

3 LONG-TERM SECURITIES

It has been shown that the money market comprises a number of institutions which specialise in the provision of funds for the financing of the flow of trade, usually through the medium of the bill of exchange or similar types of security. The funds involved are essentially short-term; most bills are repaid within three months, although a small minority may run for six or nine months. Loans of this duration – say, anything up to twelve months – are sufficient for financing the provision of working capital which will be embodied in finished goods and sold on the market within a few months or a body of, say, hire-purchase transactions generating a continuous flow of repayments.

Vast amounts of capital are required for periods considerably longer than this, however. A firm wishing to build a new factory, or to replace expensive plant and machinery, will need to borrow funds unless it has sufficient reserves of its own and will hardly be in a position to undertake repayment of the loan within a few months. It may be ten or twenty years before an entrepreneur will have earned sufficient revenue from new machinery or a new factory to repay their entire cost, and he will therefore need to raise funds in a form which allows him a considerable time before repayment is necessary.

The most important means of raising long-term capital of this kind from outside sources is that of the issue of securities. A *security* is a document embodying a promise by a borrower to pay periodically a fixed or variable return to the owner of the security; often, but by no means always, it also embodies a promise to repay a fixed sum (the nominal value of the security) at or by a specified date in the future. If the return offered to the holder of the security is a fixed amount per annum (usually expressed as a percentage of the security's nominal value), the security would be called a *fixed-interest* security or a *bond*. Such a security involves the supply of capital only; it is a mere title to a debt. If the return is not fixed, but is dependent on the earning of profits, then (following the logic of Chapter XVII) the supply of entrepreneurship, as well as of capital, is involved; the security is evidence of a share in the ownership of an enterprise, and not a debt. As was pointed out in Chapter V, such securities are called *shares*.

A security, then, being a claim to a fixed income or a share in profits, is a marketable asset which can be bought and sold. By issuing securities an entrepreneur will obtain funds to purchase capital equipment; in return he incurs the obligations imposed by the terms of the security.

The institutions which deal in the purchase and sale of such securities are together known as the *capital market*. They can be divided into two groups, one (the new issue market) dealing with securities being issued for the first time, the other (the Stock Exchange) dealing in securities which have already been issued to the market and which are subsequently transferred from one owner to another.

4 THE NEW ISSUE MARKET

The main institutions of the new issue market are *issuing houses* and the firms of *underwriters*. When an enterprise is seeking to raise funds from the general public, a good deal of preparation is required either by law or by the need to attract potential lenders. A prospectus must be drawn up, indicating the nature of the company, its record of profits in recent years and its plans for the future. Advice has to be sought concerning the terms on which the money is to be raised; the borrower naturally wants to raise funds on the easiest terms possible, but if all the required capital is to be raised the public has to be sufficiently attracted. The issuing houses carry out all these tasks and all the administrative work such as that involved in advertising the issue, collecting the subscriptions and despatching securities. They are a good deal more than administrators, however; their business is to know the state of the market for new loans and to ensure the success of the issue so far as they can. They are usually paid on a commission basis for their services. Prominent amongst them are the old-established merchant banks mentioned in the previous section in connection with the acceptance business.

The underwriters provide borrowers with a form of insurance. If a borrower is anxious to ensure that he will succeed in raising the full amount of the loan he is seeking, the issuing house will arrange for the issue to be underwritten by one or more of the firms of underwriters in the market. In return for the payment of a commission, the underwriters will promise to buy a stated number of the securities at an agreed price. If the public purchases the whole issue, the underwriters will not be called on; if some of the securities are left in the hands of the issuing house, however, the underwriters will have to purchase them out of their own resources. They will subsequently sell them on the Stock Exchange, but they run the risk that the price at which they dispose of them will be lower than the price at which they took them up.

Who are the purchasers of newly issued securities? Individual investors may take up some with their personal savings, but nowadays institutions such as insurance companies, pension funds, investment trusts and industrial concerns with accumulated reserves provide the bulk of the funds entering the market. If government securities are being issued, of course, the banks may be heavy subscribers.

Certain specialised institutions in the new capital market are worth mention. *Building societies* collect deposits from the public and use most of them to finance the purchase of property by private persons and companies. Several organisations supported by the banks and insurance companies, such as the *Finance Corporation for Industry* and the *Industrial and Commercial Finance Corporation*, specialise in providing capital for concerns which are seeking sums too small to be raised by the relatively expensive process of a new issue on the market, or firms which are too new to have a sufficiently long profit record to attract the ordinary investor. The British deposit banks, as was noted earlier, are reluctant to invest in relatively illiquid industrial capital, but they do lend to businesses at short-term; such loans are frequently renewed from time to time, becoming in effect relatively long-term loans. The 'secondary' banks, by contrast, actively engage in medium-term industrial lending and in the finance of both consumer and industrial hire-purchase transactions.

5 THE STOCK EXCHANGE

Few investors would be happy about sinking resources in a company if there was no way of recovering them, short of winding-up the entire concern and selling its assets − a process which in any case could hardly be brought about by an individual investor. The Stock Exchange exists in order that issued securities may be disposed of by a sale to someone else. Suppose Mr X invests £1 000 in Company A and subsequently wishes to get his £1 000 back. He can withdraw his funds from the bonds, or shares, by selling the securities on the Stock Exchange to Mr Y; X recovers his money and Y becomes, in effect, the person who has invested £1 000 in Company A. The ability to recover funds in this way, of course, makes the placing of capital in industry a much less risky affair than it would otherwise be, and accordingly the flow of funds to industry is immensely stimulated.

The major stock exchange in Britain is that established in London; there are exchanges in several provincial cities, but they are of much less importance, and in any case all of them are modelled on the London Stock Exchange. The *brokers* are the people who transact business with the general public, taking orders and delivering securities or the proceeds of them. The *jobbers* are the people who actually deal in securities on the floor of the Exchange. They deal only with brokers, having no direct contact with the public.

When an order for the purchase or sale of securities is received by a broker, he goes into the Stock Exchange and seeks out a jobber specialising in the kind of security involved in the order. Some jobbers deal only in gilt-edged stocks (those issued by the British Government and a few other very high-grade bonds); some deal in oil shares, some in foreign government stocks, and so on. The broker will ask the jobber to quote a price for the security concerned, without disclosing whether he is proposing to buy or to sell securities. The jobber, in return, will quote two prices; a higher price at which he is willing to sell the security and a lower price at which he is willing to buy. If and when the broker obtains what he considers to be a satisfactory quotation, the deal will be closed by means of an informal but none the less binding agreement between broker and jobber.

The stock exchange year is divided into a series of periods known as 'accounts'; most of these last two weeks, but a few last three weeks. At the end of each account there occurs a 'settlement day' on which all transactions have to be concluded – i.e. the securities must be delivered and the purchase price handed over. In certain circumstances a buyer or seller wishing to postpone the final delivery of and payment for the securities can arrange with the other party for the agreement to be carried over to the next settlement day; for this privilege a special fee known by the curious titles of 'contango' or 'backwardation' must be paid. The volume of business conducted on the London Stock Exchange may be deduced from the fact that in the course of 1974 it handled over 5 million separate transactions representing a turnover of about £57 000 million.

Does the Stock Exchange perform any useful function other than that of bringing in commissions for the brokers and jobbers engaged in its business? There can be no doubt that it does, and in two respects. First, as has been seen, it greatly increases the mobility of invested funds, and so reduces the risk attached to the lending of capital. Through the Stock Exchange, any investor can buy or sell securities as he pleases, provided he is prepared to accept whatever price is currently ruling for them. Furthermore, the existence of a highly developed and specialised securities market gives an investor the opportunity of seeking expert advice and guidance on a wide range of securities; the Stock Exchange Committee's practice of requiring companies to fulfil certain conditions, such as those concerning the availability of information, before allowing the shares to be quoted on the Exchange is a further protection for the investor against fraudulent borrowers.

Secondly, through the Stock Exchange a current assessment of the value of different types of asset is constantly available. For example, if the demand for shipping shares declines, the price quoted for them on the Exchange will fall, and the fall may proceed so far that the cost of acquiring a shipping line through the purchase of securities will fall below the cost of starting a new one. In this way, the economy is given an indication that ships are in excess supply, and the use of capital in the construction of new ones will be discouraged. Conversely, an expectation that the demand for electronic goods is going to exceed the supply will cause a rise in the price of shares in companies in the electronics industry; the scarcity will be expected to increase profits and hence dividends. This rise in the price of these shares will serve as an indicator to those contemplating capital construction that the community is in need of more capacity in the electronics industry.

The possibility of changes in the price of securities gives rise to *speculation* – that is, the purchase of securities in the hope of re-selling at a profit rather than as a permanent investment. If such speculation is based on considerations of the kind just discussed – genuine assessments of the changing economic values of different types of assets – it is thoroughly useful and advantageous, since it anticipates future scarcities or surpluses of different types of capital goods and thus guides current capital formation.

Sometimes, however, speculation is more akin to gambling; dealers may buy or sell securities (i.e. they may be 'bulls' or 'bears', respectively) in anticipation of price movements whether or not they believe such movements to be well-founded and justified. Experience shows that speculation of this kind, often being based on completely irrational forces, can become so out-of-hand as to deteriorate into sheer hysteria. Security prices are driven up or down by the spread of what can only be called mob emotion, in which the optimism or pessimism of one person in itself generates similar sentiments in other people in a cumulative fashion. Under such circumstances the prices quoted for securities on the market can lose touch completely with the real value of the assets underlying them, and the resulting wild swings of prices can only damage the economy as a whole even though the more expert (or luckier) speculators succeed in achieving substantial capital gains at someone else's expense.

Like most human institutions, then, the Stock Exchange can perform services of considerable value to society but can also be abused by a minority acting in their own interests who lose their heads in the process. In the United States the experience of the great Wall Street crash of 1929 stimulated the monetary authorities of that country to acquire powers to enforce detailed regulations over the operation of stock exchanges and to control the extension of bank loans for the purpose of dealing in securities. In Britain the authorities have not attempted to acquire statutory powers of a similar kind.

Perhaps this is because the banks are satisfied that within the existing framework they could prevent excessive speculation financed with bank credit; perhaps it is because the authorities have confidence in the stability and caution of the modern generation of dealers on the London Stock Exchange.

FURTHER READING

R. S. SAYERS *Modern banking* Ch. 3

W. M. SCAMMELL *The London discount market* Elek Books, London 1965

E. V. MORGAN and W. A. THOMAS *The Stock Exchange* Elek Books, London 1962

CHAPTER XXIII

The Theory of the Rate of Interest

1 THE NATURE OF LIQUIDITY PREFERENCE

THE functions of money and the institutions which comprise the monetary system having been examined, it is now possible to return to a problem which was left on one side when the various factor-incomes were discussed in Part V – the determination of the rate of interest. Interest is the payment made to owners of capital funds which they are prepared to put at the disposal of others; but *why* has it to be paid, and what factors determine it?

The analysis can begin by considering the question: why should anyone want money? This may appear at first sight an extremely odd question to ask. Anyone knows why he wants money; it is the one thing which practically everyone would be glad to have more of. But why? If the reasons are examined a little further it will be found that people want money to buy a new car, or a holiday abroad, or a house or a thousand other things – all the material things which can help to make life more comfortable and pleasant. In other words they do not want to hold money at all – they want *to get rid of it*, to spend it on all the things they *do* want. Money as such is useless; it is the one form of wealth which can yield no satisfaction or pleasure. People cannot eat or drink or wear it; it is a barren and sterile asset. The man who *does* derive pleasure from holding money – the miser – is the exception who proves the rule; he is a man who is regarded by the community as being a little mad. Yet, as has been seen, at any moment of time there is in existence an enormous stock of money – coins, notes and bank deposits – every penny of which must be held by someone; and they cannot all be misers. Why should this huge stock of wealth be held in the sterile form of money, rather than used to purchase goods and services which can add directly to well-being?

The answer lies in the functions of money. Money, it was noted earlier, confers on its holder complete liquidity – the ability to turn wealth into any form without loss or delay. Now this quality which money possesses corresponds to the desire to possess liquidity felt in some degree by every person or institution; this psychological characteristic is usually called *liquidity preference*, meaning the relative partiality for liquid rather than illiquid assets. Liquidity preference will be felt more strongly by some people than by others, and more at some times than at others, but to some degree it is felt by everyone. What motives underlie it?

There is first the *transactions motive*. For most persons and institutions expenditure is occurring constantly – daily purchases are made in shops, cinemas and so on, while businesses have to pay out wages and raw material costs. Income, however, is received only at fixed intervals; persons are paid once a week or once a month, while businesses may receive revenues from the sale of goods, months, or even years, after incurring the first costs of production. Some cash must therefore be held to bridge this interval of time between each receipt of income, and the further apart these receipts are, the larger the balances which will be required. For example, if a man earns £70 a week and spends £10 each day, he will need to hold an average of £35 in cash – £70 at the beginning of the first day of the week and nothing at all at the end of the last day. If he earned exactly the same income and maintained exactly the same rate of expenditure but was paid monthly instead of weekly, his average cash holding would be about £150 – say £300 at the beginning of the month and nothing at the end. Similarly, a business will require larger cash balances the longer the interval is between the commencement of the production of a unit of output and its final sale. Apart from this time-interval, the transactions demand for cash will depend on the level of incomes and prices ruling in the economy. If prices and wages are suddenly doubled, for example, the average wage-earner will obviously need an average holding of cash which is roughly double the previous average, assuming that he maintains the same rate of consumption of goods and services. Given a more or less stable price-level, however, the demand for cash for transactions purposes would not be expected to oscillate much in any short period, because income-payment and expenditure habits do not change quickly. As will be noted in a later section, however, the possibility that the general price-level *may* alter substantially in the foreseeable future can be an important consideration in this context.

A second motive for holding cash is that known as the *speculative motive*. To understand this motive it is necessary to consider the relationship between current market rates of interest and the price level of securities. Consider a bond carrying a promise to pay an income of £5 a year in perpetuity. If the rate of interest payable on new securities currently being offered on the market is 5 per cent – i.e. borrowers are prepared to pay £5 a year interest for every £100 they borrow – then the price of that bond will obviously be £100, whatever its nominal value (which is usually the amount for which it was sold when it was first issued). On the other hand, if the rate of interest offered by new securities coming on to the market rises to 6 per cent (i.e. borrowers are now willing to pay £6 a year interest for a loan of £100) then the bond will be worth only $\frac{5}{6} \times 100$, or about £83. This must be so, since the bond carries an income of £5 a year, and when £6 a year can be obtained on a new security costing £100, people will be willing to pay for an income of £5 a year only a sum which makes that income equivalent to 6 per cent – i.e. £83. Conversely, if the rate of interest currently obtainable on new securities falls to 4 per cent, the price obtainable for the bond will rise to $\frac{5}{4} \times$ £100, or £125; an income of £5 per year from a security purchased at £125 is equivalent to 4 per cent, the current rate.

In other words, the price of a fixed-interest security moves inversely with the current market rate of interest. The original nominal value of a bond (the amount for which it was originally sold) has no relevance to the determination of its *current* market price. The price quoted for it on the Stock Exchange on any particular day will depend on (*a*) the income it offers and (*b*) the current market rate of interest. If the current market rate is the same as the rate prevailing when the bond was originally issued, then the price at which the bond will be quoted will be the same as its nominal value. But if the current rate of interest is different from the rate prevailing at the time of issue, the bond will now command a higher or lower price than it did then, depending on whether the rate of interest has fallen or risen since the bond was first issued. The price of securities, that is to say, is determined in exactly the same way as the valuation of capital goods discussed in Chapter VIII.

Bearing these considerations in mind, it is easy to see why the speculative demand for cash (i.e. the demand to meet the speculative motive) arises. It arises in so far as people believe that the rate of interest is going to *rise*. Assume that the current market rate of interest is 8 per cent, that a person holds an irredeemable bond – i.e. one which has no fixed date for the repayment of the principal sum – bringing in an income of £8 per annum, and that he believes that the market rate of interest will shortly rise to 10 per cent. Inevitably he will prefer to hold his wealth in the form of cash rather than a security, despite the fact that he will earn nothing on wealth held as a cash balance. His bond must have a current price of about £100 (the value of an income of £8 a year when the current rate is 8 per cent); if he is right about the rise in interest rates, its price will shortly fall to £80 (£8 a year valued at a current rate of 10 per cent). If he sells now, therefore, and buys back again *after* the rate of interest has risen, he will make a profit of about £20 (selling at £100 and buying back at £80) which will more than offset the loss of interest. The stronger the expectation that interest rates are going to rise, therefore, the greater will be the speculative demand for cash. There will almost always be *some* demand for cash under this heading, since many investors will wish to keep some of their wealth in the form of cash just *in case* interest rates rise, even though they may think this unlikely.

It may be objected that the investor could switch his capital to *any* form if he thinks interest rates may rise; why should he necessarily want to keep it in *cash*? The answer is that fluctuations in interest rates will cause inverse movements in the market value of *any* asset – such as a house, or a machine, or a piece of land – which yields a fixed income. If a house brings in a net rent of £500 a year, the value of that house (assuming a free market) will be about £5 000 if the current rate of interest is 10 per cent: this will be so because £500 on an investment of £5 000 is equal to 10 per cent. If the current rate of interest rises to 12 per cent, the value of the house will fall to about £4 200; an income of £500 a year on an investment of £4 200 is equivalent to about 12 per cent. If the owner tried to sell the house for more, no one would buy it (for investment purposes, anyway) because the yield obtainable from it would be smaller than that offered by securities currently being offered on the market. Hence, only when wealth is in the form of *cash* is it completely free from this possibility of fluctuation in capital value.

Because interest rates may rise, then, a demand will exist for cash balances on the part of people seeking to avoid capital losses on income-yielding assets. Other things being equal, the lower the level of interest-rates in relation to what is thought to be a 'normal' level the greater the possibility of a rise in the future, and hence the larger the speculative demand for cash. On the other hand, if current interest rates are high, the chance of a further rise is relatively slight, and the speculative demand for cash will be small.

There is a third motive for holding cash which is something of a mixture of the transactions and speculative motives. This is usually called the *precautionary motive*. It arises because people believe that certain personal or business contingencies may arise in the future which require cash: for example, an unexpected journey away from home, or the possibility of a bargain if it can be snapped up quickly, or an accident which involves expenditure on repairs. The wealth set aside to meet these contingencies has to be held in cash; if it was held in the form of some other asset (e.g. a security), that asset might be standing at an unfavourable price at the moment when funds are needed, so that it could be turned into cash only at a loss. Since, by definition, the contingencies which the wealth would be used to meet are urgent, it would be impossible to wait for a more favourable market before selling out.

This element in the demand for cash is similar to the transactions demand in that the balances are required to meet current expenditures; it differs from it in that the expenditures concerned are unpredictable, whereas the transactions motive is concerned with fairly regular and predictable expenditures. It is similar to the speculative demand in that it is because of the danger of fluctuations in capital value that the wealth set aside is held in the form of cash, rather than of income-yielding assets. It differs from the speculative demand in that while the speculator *anticipates* an unfavourable rise in interest rates, the precautionary balance is not wanted because a particular view is held concerning the future trend of interest rates; it arises simply because an asset may have to be sold at an unfortunate moment, and the nature of the emergency precludes the possibility of waiting for a temporary and random drop in security prices to disappear.

These three motives constitute the total demand for cash. They have nothing to do with the motives for *saving*; they are concerned only with the form in which wealth is held. Many influences may explain why a person saves a given fraction of his income; an entirely separate issue is raised, however, by the question of the *form* in which he holds his savings. Liquidity preference explains why people wish to hold some of their wealth in the form of cash balances, rather than in the form of assets which will yield utility or income.

Given these constituents of the demand for cash, a schedule, known as a liquidity preference schedule, can be drawn up; this shows the amounts of cash which the public wish to hold at different rates of interest. The graph of this schedule will probably be shaped like the curve *LP* in Fig. 23A, indicating a small demand for cash when interest rates are high and a large demand for cash when interest rates are low. In other words, the smaller the quantity of cash which is available to the public, the greater will be the reward people will have to be offered if they are to sacrifice more of their cash balances. At very low interest rates, the schedule may well become completely elastic – when interest rates become very low, the possibility of a future rise (and therefore of a capital loss) is extremely strong, and everyone will want to move out of securities and into cash before security prices start to fall.

This schedule gives the demand for money. The preceding chapters have described how the total supply of money is determined. Ignoring notes and coin (which are an unimportant element in the total) the total money supply depends on the

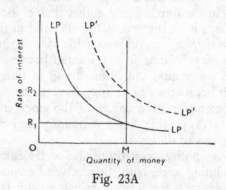

Fig. 23A

reserve assets of the banks (as influenced by the monetary authorities) and on the ratio of reserves to total deposits which the banks are permitted to adopt. The supply of money is therefore fixed at any moment, and does not fluctuate in response to changes in the rate of interest; hence it can be shown as a vertical (completely inelastic) curve as in Fig. 23A. The rate of interest will settle at the point of intersection of the two curves.

Like all demand and supply curves, both the liquidity preference schedule and the money-supply curve are liable to shifts to right or left. If the public liquidity preference suddenly increases (because of any factor which enhances the attractiveness of having wealth in the form of cash) the schedule will shift to the right: LP' in Fig. 23A. If the quantity of money remains constant, then the rate of interest will rise – in Fig. 23A it rises from R_1 to R_2. Similarly, a shift in the money-supply curve to the right (i.e. an expansion of the quantity of money) with a constant liquidity preference schedule will result in a fall in the rate of interest.

Interest, then, is the reward for parting with liquidity. Given the existing supply of money, which is fixed by the monetary authorities, a person can obtain cash only by persuading some-one who already possesses cash to exchange it for some other asset; the rate of interest is the instrument of persuasion. The more reluctant people are to give up the advantages of cash – i.e. the stronger are the forces underlying the demand for cash which have just been described – then the higher the rate of interest which will be needed to induce them to exchange cash for other assets.

2   SHORT-TERM AND LONG-TERM RATES

So far the discussion has been concerned with 'the' rate of interest; it has been assumed that there is only a single rate quoted in the market. In fact there is a whole range of interest rates covering all the different types and grades of securities. One especially important cause of differences in rates of interest is the different length of life for which securities may have to be held before their maturity – i.e. before they are repaid in cash. Normally, a short-term security will bear a lower rate of interest than a long-term security which is identical in all other respects. Why is this? The answer is that the longer the life of a security the more liable it will be to fluctuations in price, so that its liquidity is reduced. The liability to price fluctuations can best be appreciated from a simple example. Suppose the average current market rate of interest rises from 8 per cent to 10 per cent. The price of a bond with no fixed repayment date (an 'irredeemable' security) carrying an income of £8 per annum will now fall, as was noted earlier, from £100 to $\frac{8}{10} \times$ £100, or £80. Now imagine that there exists a bond similar in all respects except that it is due for repayment at £100 at the end of one year from now. If the price of *this* bond fell to £80, an enormous demand would arise for it. At the end of a year, the possessor of the bond would receive £100 as cash repayment *plus* £8 in interest, a total of £108, or £28 more than was paid for it. A gain of £28 in one year on an investment of £80 would be equivalent to a rate of interest of roughly 35 per cent – considerably more than the 10 per cent currently offered on new securities.

Everyone would therefore rush to buy such an attractive security, and its price would inevitably be driven up. In fact, its price would continue to rise until it reached just over £98. People buying it at that price would receive at the end of the year £100 in repayment *plus* £8 in interest, a total of £108 and a net gain of just less than £10. This gain, on an investment of £98, would be equivalent to 10 per cent per annum, the rate now prevailing in the market, and equilibrium would be reached.

Now consider a similar bond repayable in 10 years' time. If the price of *this* fell to £80, at the end of ten years the purchaser would have received £100 in cash repayment and £80 in interest payments – a total of £180 and a gain of £100 over the original purchase price. Ignoring compound interest for the moment, a gain of £100 over 10 years would be equivalent to an annual return of £10 on the original investment of £80 – i.e. a rate of 12·5 per cent per annum. Once again, the attractiveness of such an investment, in comparison with the ruling rate of 10 per cent on new securities, would force up its price until it reached about £90. By purchasing at this price, and receiving £180 over the security's 10-year life, the purchaser would receive a total gain of about £90, or £9·0 per annum. An annual income of £9·0 on an investment of £90 would be equivalent to 10 per cent, the rate currently prevailing in the market.

Now in this simple example the existence of compound interest was ignored, but in real life compound interest does exist. Hence the purchaser of a security must allow for the fact that annual interest payments can themselves be invested year by year. It can be shown, in fact, that for interest payments received at the end of each year the current market price, P_0, of a security will be given by the rather formidable expression

$$P_0 = \frac{I}{r}\left[1 - \frac{1}{(1+r)^n}\right] + \frac{R}{(1+r)^n}$$

where I is the annual interest payment, R the ultimate redemption value of the security, r the *current* market rate of interest and n the number of years which have to run before that final repayment takes place. Thus, in the previous example, $I = £8$, $R = £100$, $r = 0.10$ and $n = 10$. Inserting these values into the formula gives $P_0 = £87.71$. If the value of n became 20 years, all other things remaining the same, the formula would give $P_0 = £82.97$. As the value of n gets bigger, so $(1+r)^n$ will get bigger and both the expressions $1/(1+r)^n$ and $R/(1+r)^n$ will get smaller. In the limiting case, where n is very large, these two expressions approach zero and the formula reduces to

$$P_0 = I/r.$$

It can be seen, then, that securities differing only in the length of time which must pass before their maturity will fluctuate in price to different degrees as a result of any given change in the current rate of interest. In the hypothetical example just given, a rise of the rate of interest from 8 to 10 per cent reduces the price of a one-year bond to £98, that of a ten-year bond to £88 and that of an irredeemable bond (one with an infinitely long life) to £80. Long-term securities, therefore, are less liquid than short-term; there is less certainty of being able to convert them into cash without significant loss. Admittedly, a *fall* in interest rates will have precisely opposite results, and in a period when the market is predominantly of the opinion that interest rates will be lower in the future than in the present, long-term interest rates may fall *below* short-term rates. In normal times, however, there is no great degree of certainty attached to expectations about the future, and the *risk* of a given capital loss will weigh more heavily in the minds of investors than the possibility of an equal capital gain. (If it is assumed that the law of diminishing marginal utility applies to income, a reduction in a person's wealth from £100 to £90 will involve more utility than a rise from £100 to £110.)

3　OTHER RISKS AND UNCERTAINTIES

The liquidity of assets is affected by factors other than the length of their life. A debenture in a small and little-known company, for example, will not find a market as readily as one in ICI or British Leyland Motors if its holder should suddenly require to sell it. A foreign bond is subject to special risks because of the possibility of expropriation, or of the freezing of foreign funds by the government of the country concerned, factors which would drastically affect the market value of the security. Moving outside the range of securities, the liquidity of assets such as land or houses will be affected by the expense and inconvenience of selling, or the imperfection of the markets for them. A great many considerations of various kinds influence the liquidity of assets, and hence the rate of interest which will have to be offered in order to induce investors to hold them.

When assets carry a *variable* return – such as that from preference or ordinary shares of all kinds – further complications arise because they involve the factor of enterprise as well as that of capital. The purchase of an ordinary share, like that of a debenture, involves the placing of capital in a relatively illiquid form; the return on the shares must therefore include some reward for the sacrifice of liquidity. But the shareholder incurs uncertainties over and above those involved in the sacrifice of liquidity. He is not merely *lending* his wealth, as the debenture holder is; he is purchasing part of a company and thus shouldering the responsibilities of entrepreneurship. The debenture-holder is paid (and his capital ultimately repaid, if the debenture has a maturity date) whatever happens to profits. As was seen in Chapter V, however, the ordinary shareholder receives a dividend only if and in so far as profits are made. The income received on shares, then, is only *partly* interest; part of it is profit, which may be negative. If no dividend is earned on an ordinary share, the holder has not merely received nothing but has also lost the interest he could have earned if he had put his capital into a fixed-interest asset rather than shares. And as the discussion of profit showed, the earnings on ordinary shares will vary widely according to the degree of uncertainty which surrounds the outcome of the activities of different industries.

There is a corollary to all this. If the profits of a firm, or of industry generally, are expected to rise, the value of its shares will naturally rise. If the dividend paid out to shareholders by a company rises from, say, £15 per £100 share to £20 a share the market value of the share will probably rise more or less *pari passu*. In an era of rising prices, ordinary shares thus become a good inflation 'hedge' if profits rise equally with prices. A gilt-edged security yields a fixed sum in money terms; the *real* value of its yield will fall if the general price-level rises. An investor can protect himself against this loss of real income, however, by buying good ordinary shares; if prices rise, say, 10 per cent, the chances are that the dividend on the share – and thus its capital value – will also rise by about 10 per cent. In periods of actual or expected rises in prices and profits, then, the variability of the return on ordinary shares can become an advantage rather than a disadvantage. It is the fixed-interest security which carries the greater risk in such circumstances: the risk of steady erosion in *real* income.

4 THE 'NEW MONETARISM'

The consideration just referred to – the existence in recent years of a persistent tendency towards significant increases in the general price level – has been the major cause of a furious debate amongst economists concerning the nature of the demand for money. It may be as well, therefore, to summarise the nature of this debate even though it is not one which can be described as having been resolved.

The theory of the rate of interest outlined in this chapter lays primary emphasis on the relationship between the expected price level of fixed-interest securities and the demand for money. While the existence of the transactions demand for cash is certainly recognised – that is, a demand for money as a means of *spending* – the analysis concentrates on the demand for money as an *asset* – i.e. a vehicle for *holding* wealth rather than *spending* it – and, in particular, its attractiveness as an asset in comparison with fixed-interest securities.

This approach to the demand for money, associated with the work of Lord Keynes in the late 1930s, was in sharp contrast with the older approach known as the 'Quantity Theory of Money'. This theory was based on the assumption that no rational man would want to hold money except for transactions purposes – for spending, in other words – since he could put any other spare resources to profitable employment in income-earning assets of various kinds. Hence there was believed to be a fairly simple and stable relationship between the demand for money and the total amount of spending going on in the economy. The rate of interest did not enter into the demand for money: this was determined by the willingness of people to *save* at different rates of interest and of entrepreneurs to *borrow* for capital formation at different interest rates.

The Keynesian-type analysis showed this approach to be logically unsound in a world where uncertainty existed. If future interest rates were not known, it was perfectly rational for a man to hold wealth in the form of money – not for spending purposes but as an asset. As has been shown, if interest rates are liable to rise, holding wealth in the 'idle' form of money is a perfectly rational way of avoiding capital losses. The demand for transactions balances, on the other hand, was pushed somewhat into the background; if prices and incomes were relatively stable, the demand for transactions balances would similarly be stable so that changes in the total quantity of money would make their influence felt on the other element in the demand for money – the speculative demand – and thus on the rate of interest.

This implicit assumption of stability in prices and incomes, while reasonable enough in the 1920s and 1930s, has become increasingly suspect in a world where the phenomenon of inflation has in fact ceased to be a phenomenon; during the five years between 1968 and 1973, for example, the gross national product of the United Kingdom (in current prices) was rising at an average rate of more than 13 per cent per annum, which is scarcely stability by any definition. Primarily to make allowance for this, recent monetary theory (especially that associated with the name of Professor Friedman of Chicago) has led to something of a synthesis of these two approaches. Hence the somewhat misleading name given to this new approach of the 'new Quantity Theory' or 'monetarism'.

The phenomenon of inflation is incorporated into the new formulation in two ways. First, a relationship between the demand for money balances and the level of national income is specifically postulated; this takes account not only of the need for larger transactions balances to keep up with rising expenditure but also of the income-elasticity of demand for such balances in real terms. (If people want to live in bigger houses as their income rises why should they not also want the luxury of a larger bank balance?) Secondly, the rise in value of assets such as ordinary shares is specifically allowed for; put another way, the demand for cash makes explicit allowance for the fact that both money balances and fixed-interest securities impose real losses on their holders if the general price level is expected to rise. Finally, although less fundamentally, modern approaches to the demand for money take into account the possibility of people holding wealth in forms other than money on the one hand and bonds on the other — for example, ordinary shares, real physical assets or even 'human wealth' in the form of investment in the individual's own level of education or training.

Modern theory, then, treats the demand for money as a more complex affair than a simple choice between bonds on the one hand and cash on the other. Nevertheless it asserts that the relationship between the demand for money on the one hand and the factors influencing it — the expected yields on bonds and shares, the level of income, the expected rate of change of the general price-level and so on — on the other, is a reasonably stable one. Given this, it would follow that from a knowledge of these key variables the demand for money could be predicted; going one step further, if the relationship between the quantity of money and — amongst other things — the level of national income is a stable one, *control* over the money supply could lead to control over the national income.

The discussion is beginning to run into some deep issues,

one of which – the possibility of control over inflation through control over the money supply – will be further examined in Chapter XXVIII below. It must be said in conclusion, therefore, that the testing of these 'new monetarist' approaches to the demand for money has itself been the subject of acute controversy. While a good deal of statistical investigation has lent support to the approach, especially in the United States, such testing has been less successful in Britain. Further, to show that a stable relationship has existed between two things in the past is one thing; to show that one can therefore be *controlled* by the other in the future is quite another. On this crucial policy issue the debate, as remarked earlier, is still wide open.

FURTHER READING

W. T. NEWLYN *Theory of money* Ch. 5

H. G. JOHNSON *Essays in monetary economics* Allen and Unwin, London 1967, Ch. 11

H. G. JOHNSON (ed.) *Readings in British monetary economics* Oxford University press, London 1972, Part II

D. C. ROWAN *Output, inflation and growth* Ch. 11

T. SCITOVSKY *Money and the balance of payments* Chs. 4–6

CHAPTER XXIV

The Mechanism of
Monetary Policy

1 THE EVOLUTION OF MONETARY CONTROL

IN an earlier chapter it was seen that responsibility for the quantity of money in the United Kingdom, as in most highly developed economies at the present time, rests ultimately with the Central Bank as the agent of the Government itself. It is one of the main virtues of modern monetary systems that the supply of money is in principle amenable to conscious control rather than being subject to the chance influences of the mining of so-called precious metals or the discovery of deposits of stones or shells. The power to influence the supply of money in a community is a most important one – too important, in fact, to be left in the hands of anyone other than the government itself. It has been seen that the rate of interest is dependent to a large degree on the quantity of money; in examining the theory of employment, it will be found that the rate of interest and the money supply in turn play an important part in influencing the level of prices, incomes and output. The present task is to examine the way in which the authorities seek to exercise control over monetary conditions; Part VII will be concerned with the influence of monetary changes in the wider context of the economic system as a whole.

It is necessary to begin, however, with a note of caution. The message of Chapter XXI, on the British banking system, was that the institutions comprising the financial structure have shown throughout their history a remarkable capacity for evolution, not least in response to the attempts of the authorities to control their activities. The mechanism of control itself has inevitably evolved also, both in its effectiveness and in its form. Two morals follow.

First the techniques by which the authorities currently seek to assert their control over the money supply in Britain are understandable only in the light of some knowledge of this evolutionary process. The next two sections attempt to explain the powers and instruments of the Bank of England as they had operated in the present century up to 1960 and the manner in which they were supposed to achieve their effects. Section 4 describes how an attempt was made to increase the effectiveness of these techniques during the 1960s but how this, too, failed. Section 5 then sets out the 'new' system introduced in 1971.

The second moral follows logically. Just as the techniques of monetary control have evolved during the past two decades, so nothing is more certain than that they will evolve in the future. The system created in 1971 is singularly unlikely to be unchanged by 1981.

2 THE 1950S: THE TRADITIONAL ERA

Since the close of the nineteenth century the Bank of England, originally a commercial bank like any other, had come to accept the special role of Britain's Central Bank, which meant, in effect, that it had come to accept responsibility for controlling the general monetary system through its influence over the level of bank credit. To carry out this task it possessed three policy instruments which were usually operated in conjunction with one another. The first was Bank rate, the rate at which the Bank was prepared to discount or re-discount first-class bills of exchange. The Bank of England has the traditional role of *lender of last resort*; it is the one bank which will never refuse to extend credit to money-market dealers if it is called for. At the same time, it will lend only at its own price and until 1972 that price was Bank rate. The Bank had long since ceased to undertake ordinary banking business to any significant extent, but the brokers and discount houses of the money market had (and retain) the privilege of being able to take bills to the Bank of England and sell them – i.e. re-discount them – to the Bank, or, alternatively, to deposit bills as security for loans (of at least seven days' duration) on which they had to pay interest at $\frac{1}{2}$ per cent above Bank rate.

The Bank of England always sought to keep Bank rate above the current market rate of discount. For example, if bills were being discounted in the market at 3 per cent, Bank rate would be at least $3\frac{1}{2}$ per cent; this meant that a 3-month bill worth £100 would be sold to the discount houses for about £99·25 but could be sold to (re-discounted at) the Bank of England for only about £99·10. If the situation was reversed, so that Bank rate was *below* current market rates, the discount houses would be able to use their privilege of having re-discounting facilities at the Bank in order to buy bills in the market and re-sell them immediately to the Bank at a higher price; as a result, the Bank would have found itself inundated with bills.

The second weapon in the Central Bank armoury, which it still retains, is known as *open-market operations*. By this is meant simply the purchase or sale by the Bank of securities, including treasury bills, in the ordinary securities market. Such purchases or sales will have important effects. In the first place, by increasing or decreasing the demand for securities the current rate of interest will be directly influenced. More important, such operations will cause changes in the cash reserves of the commercial banks. If the Bank buys securities, the seller will receive in exchange for them a cheque drawn on the Bank of England. He will deposit this cheque with the commercial bank of which he is a customer, and the commercial bank concerned will duly present the Bank of England cheque for payment. The Bank will handle this claim just as the commercial bank handled its customer's – that is, the amount of the cheque will be added to the commercial bank's deposit at the Bank of England. The cash reserves of the commercial bank are therefore increased by the amount of the original purchase of securities. Now over this period the deposit banks followed the convention of adopting an 8 per cent cash ratio. Given a certain increase in its cash reserves, therefore, the commercial bank would have been able to expand its total deposits by roughly twelve times as much.

Conversely, if the Bank of England *sells* securities, it will receive in exchange for them a cheque drawn on the buyer's account with one of the commercial banks; the Bank will obtain payment of this cheque by reducing the commercial bank's deposit by a similar amount, and the cash reserves of the commercial bank will therefore be reduced. Once again the total deposits of the commercial bank could in principle have undergone a change which was twelve times as great as that in its cash reserves in order to maintain the 8 per cent cash ratio.

The third instrument at the disposal of the Central Bank, also retained, is that of *moral suasion*. Because of its long-established reputation as leader and controller of the banking system, any hints or suggestions that the Bank may make to the other banks are treated with great respect; they may even lead to the desired result without the adoption of any other measures. The commercial banks realise that in the last resort the Bank can always enforce its will; hence, if the Bank lets it be known that bank advances are rising too rapidly, for example, or that securities are being sold on such a scale as to damage the market in gilt-edged securities, the commercial banks may prefer to take the hint forthwith rather than wait for action to be forced on them through the use of Bank rate and open-market operations.

This moral power of the Bank of England was given a firm backing in the provisions of the Act of 1946 by which the Bank was nationalised. Clause 4, sub-clause (3) of the Act provided that

> The Bank, if they think it necessary in the public interest, may request information from and make recommendations to bankers, and may, if so authorised by the Treasury, issue directions to any banker for the purpose of securing that effect is given to any such request or recommendation.

The powers given by this clause could hardly be wider. So far as is known, no specific use has been made of them, but they must immensely strengthen the influence of any hints the Bank may give to the banking system; the commercial banks now know that the Bank of England can secure statutory enforcement of its wishes if it proves necessary.

3 THE POWERS IN ACTION

Having described the instruments which the Bank of England could employ to influence the monetary environment, it is necessary to examine the way in which they were supposed to operate. Suppose that the Bank thought it necessary to raise interest rates so as to check spending; *why* the latter should be a result of higher interest rates is a question best left over to Part VII. The Bank would probably first advise the commercial banks that in its view credit was being given too freely and too cheaply. If this advice failed to check the expansion of credit, or if the Bank considered that the situation was so serious as to justify its immediate enforcement, the other weapons would have been brought into play – Bank rate would have been raised and securities sold on the open market.

The raising of the Bank rate would usually cause an immediate rise in other short-term interest rates. The discount rate on bills would probably rise, because the discount houses would realise that should it prove necessary to re-discount bills at the Bank they would have been able to do so only at the high rate – i.e. they would have been able to sell their bills at a lower price than was previously likely. Their own discount rates would therefore be raised to cover this increased risk of loss. Further, the commercial banks conventionally maintained a fairly stable relationship between Bank rate and the rates they themselves paid to depositors and charged on loans. Thus the discount houses would have had to pay more for their loans at call and short notice, a further stimulus to the upward movement of bill rates. Businessmen would also be charged a higher rate on loans and overdrafts, and this would discourage the borrowing of money (for the purchase of new machinery and factories, for example, or for holding stocks of goods and raw materials).

At the same time, the Bank would have reinforced the increased Bank rate by the sale of securities in the open market. As has been noted, this would reduce the cash reserves of the deposit banks, and in order to maintain the 8 per cent cash ratio then prevailing the banks would have been forced to reduce their deposits by twelve times the amount of the reduction in their cash. How could they reduce their deposits? In the first place, loans to the money market would have been called in, and discount houses would have to re-discount some of their bills in order to repay their loans from the commercial banks. As the commercial banks would be trying to restrict credit, the discount houses would have been able to raise cash only by taking bills to the Bank of England for re-discount; the market would have been 'in the Bank', as it was said. The Bank of England would have made Bank rate effective, because the discount houses were being forced to re-discount bills at Bank rate, or to borrow on the security of bills at $\frac{1}{2}$ per cent above it. Again, the banks might reduce deposits by buying fewer bills and by selling some of their securities, thus causing security prices to fall and interest rates to rise. Finally, the banks might recall some advances and would certainly have been reluctant to make any new loans to borrowers. Both short-term and long-term credit would therefore have become more expensive and more difficult to obtain, so that expenditure depending on borrowed money (which covers a great deal of investment expenditure) would have been discouraged.

The tightening of credit would not have been confined to the banks and money market. The sale of securities by the banks would have been augmented by sales on the part of would-be borrowers from the banks who would have been refused accommodation and who would therefore have to sell securities if they were to obtain money. The price-level of existing securities would consequently fall, and their yields would rise. This would react in turn on the new issue market. No one would buy a new security offering a lower rate than comparable securities already obtainable on the Stock Exchange; hence the rate on current new issues would have to rise. Furthermore, issuing houses and underwriters would be less willing to sponsor new issues at a time of falling security prices; the risk involved in having part of a new issue left on their hands would naturally be more serious in a falling market than when security prices were buoyant. New capital issues would thus become more difficult to arrange as well as more expensive. Specialised credit institutions, such as hire-purchase houses and building societies, would also have to make their credit more expensive and more difficult to obtain. To attract the resources which they used to extend credit, they would have to offer higher rates so as to compete with the rates currently prevailing in the securities market; naturally their charges would have to be raised to cover this, while the volume of their business would inevitably be curtailed by the general shortage of credit.

It can be seen, then, that the impulse originating in the raising of Bank rate and the sale of securities by the Bank of England was theoretically carried to the outer fringes of the capital market and influenced the entire credit system. It is fairly easily imagined how the process could operate in the reverse direction. A fall in Bank rate would reduce the market rates on bills; security purchases by the Bank would increase the cash reserves of the banking system and encourage the banks to expand credit, making loans cheaper and easier to obtain. Security prices would rise as the banks added to their investments, and the new issue market would be stimulated.

4 THE 1960s: PLUGGING THE GAPS

In theory the control over the money supply exercised by the authorities was complete. In practice, as experienced in the 1950s, it was very much less so: periodic attempts by the government to restrain the economy through restrictions imposed on the banking system through the orthodox techniques proved conspicuously less than successful. The dissatisfaction with the state of credit control in fact led to the establishment in 1957 of a high-powered committee, known as the Radcliffe Committee, to enquire into the working of the monetary system. Like other official enquiries before it, it fell into the error of supposing that the *status quo* then prevailing was necessarily permanent and ineffective policy prescriptions inevitably followed.

The basic weakness undermining official control over the banking system, as the Committee saw it, was the growth in bank holdings of treasury bills. The argument was roughly as follows. So long as the bills held by the commercial banks had been predominantly trade bills, there was no way in which the deposit banks could resist the reduction of their cash reserves by the Bank of England through open-market operations. As has been explained, they could be re-discounted by discount houses at the Bank of England only at penal rates, and these could be increased as much as was necessary to discourage the process. If a bank re-discounted bills in the open market, on the other hand, it would get cash only at the expense of another deposit bank whose customer had bought the bill: the deposit banks *as a whole* could not increase their total cash in this way.

The previous chapter has indicated, however, that during the inter-war years the trade bill had declined, at least relatively, and the treasury bill had become a dominant element in the bill market and thus in the banks' liquid assets. This, in the view of the Committee, had introduced a fundamental change into the situation. If a bank held large stocks of treasury bills, it could add to its cash at any time by simply taking repayment of treasury bills as they matured (which could be done at any time without loss, of course, whatever the level of Bank rate) and failing to re-invest the proceeds in new treasury bills as they would otherwise have done. The Government is obliged to repay these bills at their nominal value when they fall due for repayment; it would honour this obligation by a cheque drawn on its account at the Bank of England (Public Deposits), and the Bank of England would in turn be obliged to honour the cheque by adding the appropriate amount to the account of the bank taking repayment (i.e. by transferring the sum from Public to Bankers' Deposits). Hence the deposit banks could replenish their cash by running down their treasury bills as quickly as the Bank of England reduced it through open-market operations.

There was one clear limit to this process. The commercial banks could thwart the Bank of England in this way only so long as they had sufficient treasury bills to allow them to run them off and yet retain an adequate level of liquid assets. Hence the first reaction of the authorities was to 'request' the banks in 1957 to observe a 'liquidity ratio' (i.e. cash plus call money plus bills as a percentage of deposits) of 30 — later reduced to 28 – per cent; this meant that the banks could no longer defend their cash reserves in this way. From this point on, it was argued, the banks would be unable to defeat the open-market operation policy by running down treasury bills; this would replenish one ratio (the cash ratio) but could not prevent another ratio (the liquidity ratio) from falling below the permitted minimum. A fall in cash reserves could thus have only one result: a corresponding (and intended) multiple contraction of deposits, whether through sales of securities or reduction of loans and advances. The traditional weapons of the Bank would be made effective once again. If the Bank wished to ease the credit situation, of course, it would act in the opposite direction. This, at any rate, was the theory.

As usual, things did not work out this way. The minimum ratio could become effective only if the deposit banks were operating close to it, but in practice they were usually in a situation in which their liquid assets were comfortably above 28 per cent of total deposits. Because of the enormous expansion of the British national debt in general, and of the treasury bill issue in particular, the banks were in fact holding sufficient liquid assets on most occasions to allow them to defeat the efforts of the Bank of England to reduce their cash, at least for a considerable time.

There were only two solutions to this problem. One was for the Government to reduce the treasury bill issue until the banks held no more than what they considered to be the essential minimum. Unfortunately this implied that the Government would have to either replace treasury bills with long-term securities – which market conditions by no means always permitted – or raise taxes high enough to achieve a budget surplus sufficient to redeem floating debt as well as cover capital expenditures – which was seldom politically attractive. The other solution in the opinion of the Committee was a measure amounting to a variable liquidity ratio so that the minimum requirement could be raised, whenever necessary, to the liquidity level the banks were actually experiencing at the time when action was necessary.

The authorities did not accept this recommendation but

instead, effective from 1960, introduced a new form of compulsory bank deposits at the Bank of England known as *special deposits*. The technique of the scheme was conceived as follows. Suppose that the Bank of England wished to restrict the credit-power of the deposit banks, but that the latter held sufficient treasury bills to allow them to defend their cash reserves in the way described earlier without getting below their minimum liquidity ratio. The Bank of England would then call for, say, one per cent of their deposits as special deposits. The deposit banks would not be allowed to regard these special deposits as liquid assets for the purpose of calculating their liquidity ratio: further, the Bank of England would look with extreme disfavour on any bank which sold long-term government securities in the open market in order to meet such a call for special deposits. Theoretically, therefore, the deposit banks could comply with the instruction only by handing over to the Bank the required sum from their holdings of treasury bills. The result would be a transfer of one per cent of deposits from the category of liquid assets to the category of non-liquid assets, and the liquidity ratio would fall accordingly. In theory again, the Bank of England could go on making calls of this kind until, at last, the liquid assets left to the banks would be reduced to the essential 28 per cent minimum.

In practice the system proved to be subject to two rather important weaknesses. First, the banks were able to replace treasury bills lost through the special deposit system by securing a greater *share* in the total supply outstanding in the market. They could do this, of course, by so bidding up the price which they were willing to pay for them as to make them relatively unattractive to other potential buyers. Secondly, it became clear that if the banks possess sufficient cash they could prevent their liquidity ratio from falling below the required minimum by simply acquiring other types of bill to whatever extent is necessary. Again, by bidding up the price they could obtain a larger share of a given market total; alternatively, and more importantly, they could actually increase the market supply by encouraging prospective borrowers to offer bills for discounting rather than to use the more orthodox overdraft facilities. The authorities had made the fundamental error of under-estimating the capacity of the market to provide the kind of assets which are in demand – even if long-established trends had to be reversed in the process.

Because this element of short-term elasticity in the credit system led to delays in the impact of conventional control measures – and delays at times when quick action was imperative – increasing stress was laid in the 1960s on general directives to the banks in relation to the total of their loans and advances. The authorities, in other words, 'requested' the banks to restrain their lending within some specified limit for a given period (which might be, of course, 'until further notice'). As has been pointed out, the Bank of England has statutory powers to issue such directives with mandatory force, although it never proved necessary to formally invoke those powers. This technique proved to be as unsatisfactory as all the other attempts to regain control over the banking system through *ad hoc* measures. Being concentrated on the large clearing banks it had the effect of preventing any inclination towards real competition which those banks might otherwise have experienced; if bank lending was to be officially restricted there was little point in the banks competing to attract funds from the general public and still less in competing with regard to lending terms and conditions.

More important, the official attempts to restrain lending in isolated parts of the credit system had an effect similar to that of a man compressing one part of an inflated tyre – the pressure sought outlets elsewhere and, in this case, generated the phenomenal growth in the 'secondary' banking system outside official control whose development was described in Chapter XXI. The authorities made some sporadic and rather half-hearted attempts to extend their net over these rapidly mushrooming institutions but, by the close of the 1960s, it was obvious that the time for tinkering was past and that something more far-reaching was necessary if the authorities were to regain control over a financial system whose expansion was being engendered rather than restricted by the policy techniques being employed hitherto. This finally occurred with a comprehensive revision of the methods of regulation introduced in September 1971.

5　THE 1970S: COMPETITION AND CREDIT CONTROL

The system of credit control inaugurated by the Bank of England in 1971 was distinguished by four interlocking features. First, it set out to establish a fulcrum of assets through which leverage could be exerted on the banking system and whose supply could not be regulated by the banks themselves. Second, to restore the total volume of bank credit as the variable to be controlled rather than particular uses of it such as loans and advances. Third, to make the Bank's instruments of credit control effective over all the banking system rather than merely a segment of it. Finally, to restore some degree of genuine competition in those sectors of the financial system for which semi-monopolistic attitudes and practices had become firmly entrenched – partly at any rate as a result of official attempts to control the credit system.

The first two features were incorporated in a list of assets which were officially declared to be acceptable 'reserve assets', a definition of what constituted the 'eligible liabilities' of the banking system, and what was somewhat coyly referred to as an 'agreement' that commercial banks would henceforth observe a minimum ratio of $12\frac{1}{2}$ per cent of reserve assets to eligible liabilities. Reserve assets were defined to be

a　Balances with the Bank of England;
b　Money at call;
c　UK government treasury bills;
d　Company tax reserve certificates;
e　Local authority bills;
f　Commercial bills up to a maximum of 2 per cent of eligible liabilities;
g　UK government securities maturing within one year.

This list is essentially similar to one of assets which the banks had traditionally regarded as liquid assets but there are some important differences of detail. First, the cash element covers only balances at the Bank of England (other than special deposits, of course) and excludes the notes and coin held in the tills of the deposit banks – an omission which led to a sense of unfair discrimination amongst the deposit banks, which have to carry such balances in order to conduct their business, in comparison with the secondary banks, which do not. Second, the list includes short-term government securities which would traditionally have been classified as investments, including the relatively minor item of tax reserve certificates issued to companies – in effect, short-term loans to the Government which bear interest until handed over to the Exchequer in discharge of corporation tax liabilities. Finally, and most important, the volume of commercial bills which may be counted as reserve assets was limited to 2 per cent of liabilities; the ability of the banks to create its own supply of reserve assets had at last been checked. There were no other constraints on the distribution of reserves between these different types of asset except that to ensure the smooth working of the clearing system (and of open-market operation by the Bank of England) the London clearing banks agreed to keep at least $1\frac{1}{2}$ per cent of their eligible liabilities in the form of balances at the Bank of England.

Broadly speaking, the 'eligible liabilities' of the banks consist of all their deposits denominated in pounds sterling except for deposits, other than those taken from other banks, having an original maturity of two years or more – the latter are treated as long-term loans rather than deposit liabilities. They also include the important and growing item of net issues of sterling certificates of deposit and the less important items of net liabilities in currencies other than sterling and most of the cheques in course of collection from other banks on any particular day.

The third feature of the new system was associated with its applicability to *all* banks operating in Britain. The problem of defining what is and what is not a bank is one which has baffled legislators for a great many years, but for the purposes of the reserve asset system an institution is a bank if it is registered as a bank for the purposes of the several legal rights and safeguards

which are highly desirable for any institution seeking to succeed in what would generally be called banking business – for
example, exemption from some of the requirements laid down
for institutions publicly advertising for deposits by the Protection of Depositors Act of 1963, the special treatment accorded
to banks for the purposes of income and corporation tax or
the right to issue sterling certificates of deposit.

Financial institutions inviting deposits from the public but
not wishing to register as banks were not overlooked, however
– especially the important category of the hire-purchase finance
companies. The eligible liabilities of these institutions are
defined to be all their deposits except – to avoid the obvious
possibility of double-counting – those received from banks.
The definition of reserve assets was identical with that adopted
for banks but since the finance houses, in the nature of their
business, did not normally hold many of the defined assets the
required reserve ratio was set at 10 per cent.

The fourth innovation in the revised system was a deliberate
effort to restore competition amongst the old-established
deposit banks and amongst the discount houses operating the
weekly tender for treasury bills. Until 1971 the clearing banks
had adopted an agreed single rate of interest payable on time
deposits, the rate being held at a fixed level – about 2 per
cent – below Bank rate, the minimum rate charged by the Bank
of England in its function as lender of last resort to the money
market dealers having borrowing facilities with it. Similarly,
the rates charged by the banks to borrowers in different categories had traditionally been kept in an agreed relationship to
Bank rate. The discount houses, on their side, had long adopted
the practice of agreeing amongst themselves on the price to be
offered for treasury bills at the weekly tender, thus ensuring
that one discount house did not undercut another.

Both parties were prevailed upon to abandon these restrictive
practices, the banks to determine their own borrowing and
lending rates independently of each other and the discount
houses to determine individually the prices they would offer at
the weekly tender. To emphasise this redirection of the system
towards the flexibility of competitive market forces, in 1972 the

Bank of England abandoned the long-hallowed ritual of announcing Bank rate every Thursday morning – and initiating corresponding adjustments in a whole structure of rates arbitrarily related to it. The direction of the sequence was now reversed: the Bank's *minimum lending* rate was now defined to be the average rate of discount emerging from the previous week's treasury bill tender *plus* $\frac{1}{2}$ per cent and then rounded up to the nearest $\frac{1}{4}$ per cent above. This was the intention at the time. Within three years, however, the authorities rediscovered the need to give a psychological lead to, rather than merely follow, market interest rates, and changes in the rate were again being made as deliberate acts of policy; the new minimum lending rate became the old Bank Rate by another name.

In addition to all these new arrangements, of course, the Bank of England retained all the powers it had previously possessed – the ability to indulge in the purchase or sale of securities in the open market, the moral pressure of its authority backed by the statutory power to issue directions to the banks, individually or collectively, and the right to call for special deposits from the banks which would not be eligible for inclusion in the latter's reserve assets. Taken collectively, the battery of policy instruments now possessed by the authorities – that is, Government plus the Bank of England working in collaboration with it – is certainly a formidable one. How effective can it be in practice? Theoretically the Bank can so contract or expand the money supply, and so manipulate the level of interest rates, that it can achieve almost any desired effect on the credit situation. There is a substantial degree of doubt, however, concerning the real power of monetary policy to influence the economy in practice. Put in simple terms, these doubts concern, first, the power of the Bank to regulate the volume of credit and, secondly, the importance of changes in the volume of credit as a means of influencing economic activity. The latter consideration will be left over to Chapter XXVIII.

On the first question it is clear that ultimately the Bank can contract credit to any degree it wishes, and thus raise market interest rates as high as it desires. With a contraction in its reserve assets through open-market operations and/or special deposit requirements, the commercial banking system must reduce total deposits; it has no choice in the matter. Yet the familiar warning must be sounded: the financial system has shown extraordinary resilience in the past and new institutions, assets and techniques have always developed when the need arose. Much will therefore depend on the ability of the authorities to identify and assert control over such developments as soon as they emerge. It is no simple task: just as restriction on note issue led to deposit-taking, so restrictions on deposits may generate totally new forms of credit outside the network of official control – the growth of credit cards is an obvious example.

In expanding credit, of course, the power of the Bank of England is much more seriously circumscribed. It can add to the banks' reserve assets, but there is no way by which it can compel the banks to take advantage of their increased reserves. If the banks consider the economic outlook to be so black that they are unwilling to take up securities or grant any further loans, the increased reserves will simply not be used as the basis for a further expansion of deposits. Similarly, although interest rates are bound to rise as the volume of money grows smaller, it does not follow that they can be driven down to zero by a continual expansion in the money supply. The liquidity-preference curve might become perfectly elastic at low interest rates, as it did in Fig. 23A. Security prices could rise so high (i.e., interest rates fall so low) that the market would become absolutely convinced that they were bound to fall soon. If such a view did prevail, the only effect of credit expansion would be a wholesale movement out of securities (as their price tended to rise even further under the pressure of buying by the banks) and into idle cash balances.

6   SELECTIVE CREDIT CONTROLS

Apart from the question of its power, or lack of power, monetary policy – meaning the adjustment of the overall volume and price of credit – has been criticised on the grounds that it is indiscriminate in its operation. By general credit restriction, all borrowers are discouraged, without regard to the social value of the projects for which they wish to raise funds. It makes no distinction between a local authority trying to finance house-building in a slum-clearance project and a speculative entrepreneur wishing to build a new stadium for greyhound racing; most reasonable people, however, would argue that there is a good deal of difference (in terms of social desirability) between such uses of resources.

In fact it is not strictly true to say that general credit control makes no distinction between borrowers. What monetary policy seeks to do is to expand or contract the overall volume of funds; it leaves to individual bank managers, finance houses and investors the decision as to who is to have the extra funds in a period of credit expansion and who is to be denied credit in a period of contraction. It is by no means obvious that all these individuals through whom monetary policy operates will be unaware of, or indifferent to, the need for giving priority to the projects of greatest social value. But it is undeniable that they are liable to give more attention to the profitability of a project than to its inherent social value.

Because of this, there has been a development in most Western countries of what are called selective credit controls; the authorities have acquired powers to limit or encourage the use of credit in particular, specified types of activity. The object of these powers is the assistance of sectors of the economy which for one reason or another are considered to be of critical significance – they may be of strategic importance, or a major source of exports, or especially vulnerable to damaging speculative booms.

In the United Kingdom, such controls have taken two main forms. The first is the regulation by the Government of the terms on which hire-purchase transactions may be carried out, and in particular of the proportion of the purchase price which must be supplied by the buyers as a deposit and the length of time over which the hire-purchase instalments may be spread. As hire purchase plays an important role in the sale of many durable consumer goods – for example, cars, electrical equipment and furniture – these regulatory powers can be used to affect consumer spending to a significant degree.

The second type of selective control arises from the powers of the Bank of England to issue directives to the banks, amongst which would be included the power to ask the banks to discourage or facilitate the extension of credit for specified types of activity. For example, at a time when industrial investment showed signs of recovery from an unduly depressed level in Britain the Governor of the Bank of England issued a directive to the banks suggesting that lending for the purposes of financing the purchase of real estate might now be restricted in favour of lending for industrial capital formation.

Despite the potential usefulness of these discriminating measures, some doubts have in fact been expressed about the value of such controls as permanent instruments of policy. Their impact tends to be concentrated on a narrow range of industries – especially the motor-car, electrical engineering and furniture industries – and this immediately raises questions concerning the equity of measures which bear more heavily on a small group of industries than on the remainder. It also renders the problem of rational planning for the future in such industries, liable as they are to sudden and perhaps violent changes in degree of control, an immensely difficult one. In any case it seems likely that such measures can be effective only in the short run; demand can be diverted or postponed, rather than permanently reduced, and with the passage of time it becomes increasingly difficult for the authorities to keep track of the various devices which are inevitably invented in order to circumvent the regulations, thus generating the need for a progressively more complex and extensive machinery of control to make the regulations effective. Their usefulness thus depends on their being confined to the role of occasional, emergency measures. Furthermore, experience shows that selective controls are more rapid and effective when used in conjunction with overall credit policy. Although they have proved to be of potential value, therefore, they strengthen and sharpen general monetary policy rather than replace it.

FURTHER READING

W. T. NEWLYN *Theory of money* Ch. 9

H. G. JOHNSON *Essays in monetary economics* Ch. 1

H. G. JOHNSON (ed.) *Readings in British monetary economics* Part VII

J. E. WADSWORTH (ed.) *The banks and the monetary system in the U.K., 1959–1971* Appendix 4

G. K. SHAW *An introduction to the theory of macro-economic policy* Martin Robinson, London 1971, Chs. 2–4

D. C. ROWAN *Output, inflation and growth* Ch. 16

A. D. BAIN *The control of the money supply* Penguin Books, London 1970

PART VII

MACRO-ECONOMICS

CHAPTER XXV

Aggregate Demand and Supply

1 FROM MICRO TO MACRO

THE discussion of price and production in early parts of this book was concerned with the forces governing the market price and output levels of individual products. In discussing demand the questions which the analysis sought to answer were of the form: given a certain level of income, why do consumers purchase twice as much of product A as they do of product B?; or, what is the effect on the demand for X of a change in the price of Y? Similarly, the analysis of production sought to identify the factors determining the level of output of an individual firm and thus of the industry which all such firms collectively comprise. These are important and interesting issues in the realm of micro-economics.

It is now necessary to raise the discussion to a higher level of aggregation and to attempt to answer the same type of question for the economy as a whole rather than for particular products or industries. At first sight this may seem a simple matter of adding up all the individual answers derived from micro-economic analysis for each industry in the economy and thus one which requires no special analytical equipment. In fact this is not so; the assumption that what is true for each single individual in a group is therefore true for the group as a whole is a very dangerous one and frequently quite wrong. If any individual British motorist drove along the right-hand side of a main road he would be putting himself and others to considerable risk; if *every* British motorist drove on the right, on the other hand, it would not necessarily be dangerous at all – many countries have in fact been doing it for years. Similarly, if it is postulated that the price of any individual product is doubled, certain predictions can be made about the effects on its consumption; if the prices of *all* products are doubled simultaneously, however, those predictions will certainly be falsified. Raising the level of aggregation, in other words, introduces the element of interdependence within the economic system and it will quickly become evident that rather fundamental differences are thereby introduced between micro and macro analysis.

To begin with, the two basic questions of micro-economics can be approached: these are – what determines the equilibrium output of an industry? and, what determines the equilibrium price of its product? The macro-economic equivalents are, of course, what determines the equilibrium output of the whole economy – i.e. the real national income – and what determines the equilibrium level of prices in general?

The first question is of obvious importance because, given the state of technology at any moment of time, the level of national output determines the extent to which the economy's human and physical resources are being used in some income-earning process. Now at the very outset of this book it was said that in the real world the essential problem is always that of infinite wants faced by limited resources, which are the means whereby those wants may be satisfied. It would appear to follow from this that a society could never experience any difficulty in finding suitable uses for all the productive resources at its disposal. Land, labour, capital and enterprise could be in excess supply only if the wealth of the society had become so great that all human wants had been satiated, a situation which has never yet arisen and is not even conceivable at this present time. Nevertheless, resources have been in excess supply during many periods in the past, and factors of production have been unemployed for considerable lengths of time; men and machines have been kept in enforced idleness, despite real poverty and need in the society to which they belonged. Somehow the economic machine had broken down, or at least was operating at something well below its proper capacity. Why?

One answer is that although the factors of production would be completely mobile in the theoretical world of perfect competition, in the actual world the mobility of resources is far from perfect. Because of inertia, or limited knowledge, or any one of a hundred other causes, labour and capital no longer needed in a declining industry may not be taken up immediately by industries whose output is expanding – geographical factors may hinder movement, time may be required for adaptation to the specialised requirements of the receiving industries, or the owners of factors may hope that the decline in the industry previously employing them is merely temporary. Incomplete mobility, therefore, is bound to result in some unemployment of factors in a dynamic economy, and it must be regarded as an unfortunate growing-pain which has to be borne in order to secure the benefits of improvements in technology.

Considerations of this kind can explain the unemployment of factors in a particular industry or limited group of industries. But at intervals in modern history there has occurred widespread and severe unemployment throughout the economic system as a whole, and a shift in demand from one product to another obviously cannot explain a situation of this sort. The first task of macro-economic analysis is therefore to fill this gap.

The second question has become at least equally important in recent years: what determines the level of prices of things in general and, more especially, what causes the general price level to undergo sustained movements up or down? (The concept of 'the general level of prices' is not a simple one, but the discussion of methods of measuring it is deferred until Chapter XXVII.) The movement of the price of one product in comparison with that of another is explicable readily enough in terms of shifts in demand or supply, but such shifts cannot obviously explain the phenomenon of *all* prices going upwards or downwards together. Yet precisely this phenomenon – the sustained upward movement of prices in the process known as inflation – is a worldwide one which has for years been the cause of deep concern to politicians and general public alike. Here then is the second major problem for which the special techniques of macro-economic analysis must be called in aid.

By now it will be almost an automatic reaction to any problem involving price or output to approach the analysis in terms of the interaction of demand and supply. This, if nothing else, is as true in the macro-economic context as it is in the micro-economic. The demand schedule is no longer that for some specified product, of course, but an *aggregate* demand schedule for goods and services in general; similarly, the supply curve for a particular industry must be replaced by an aggregate supply curve for all the productive enterprises in the economy as a whole. It will be convenient to begin with the latter.

2 THE AGGREGATE SUPPLY CURVE

A supply curve is a geometrical representation of the relationship between the level of output being produced and the revenue received (or at least anticipated) from that output. The earlier analysis of price determination has shown that an entrepreneur will employ inputs up to that point at which his marginal costs – the rewards to the various inputs – are just equal to marginal revenue. Unless there is a sudden and general rise in input prices, he will reduce his demand for land, labour and capital only if marginal revenue should fall – i.e. only if the demand curve for his product should shift to the left.

This familiar conclusion can be generalised and applied to the whole economy. Entrepreneurs as a whole pay out in the form of wages, rent and interest the incomes of the inputs they employ, receiving also profits as their own incomes. With a constant flow of total incomes there may occur a redistribution of inputs between one entrepreneur and another, but this will not affect the overall level of employment. These factor-costs – the sums of the incomes received in the community, or the national income – must be equalled by the total revenue derived by entrepreneurs from the sale of their products. The price of a commodity must necessarily equal the incomes – including profits or losses – derived from its production. The total revenue received by entrepreneurs, of course, is the same thing as the total expenditure on goods and services by the community as a whole.

Hence in the aggregate supply schedule AS_1 in Fig. 25A the relationship depicted is that between total market expenditure on all goods and services (= Gross National Expenditure) measured along the vertical axis and the total output of goods and services measured along the horizontal axis. Thus, if entrepreneurs collectively expect total spending in the market to amount to OE_1, this anticipated revenue will induce them to employ productive inputs sufficient to produce output OQ_1. If market spending was expected to rise to OE_2 then output would rise to OQ_2.

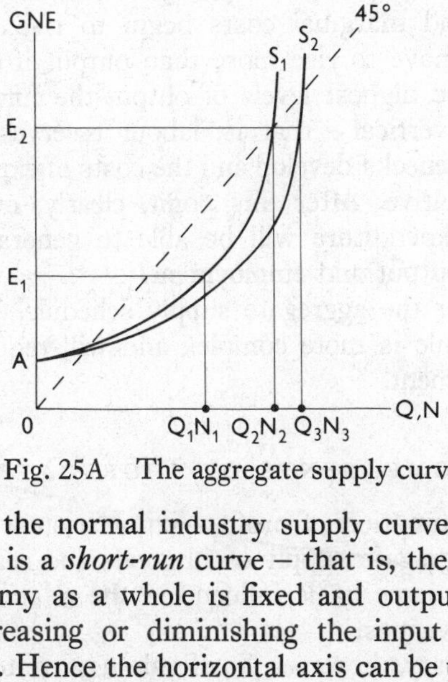

Fig. 25A   The aggregate supply curve

Now like the normal industry supply curve, this aggregate supply curve is a *short-run* curve – that is, the capital capacity of the economy as a whole is fixed and output can be varied only by increasing or diminishing the input of the variable factor labour. Hence the horizontal axis can be used to measure the number of people employed as well as the total volume of output. The output OQ_1 thus corresponds to a level of employment ON_1 and the shift in output to OQ_2 involves an increase in the number of people employed to ON_2. In the long run, of course, the curve will shift either because of changes in the capital stock or because of advances in technology. For example, an increase in the capital stock could shift the short-run curve from AS_1 to AS_2; if this happened, a level of market expenditure OE_2 would stimulate an output of OQ_3.

The short-run nature of each curve explains its general shape.

The 45 degree line in the diagram would indicate equal proportionate changes in market expenditure and output. At low output levels the slope of AS_1 is less than 45 degrees, implying
that any given rise in market spending will justify a bigger proportionate rise in output and employment. This is probable
because at low output levels the fixed capital stock will be
operating at well below its capacity and expansion can proceed
under conditions of falling unit costs. As output expands
further, however, optimum capacity is reached (after OQ_1 on
curve AS_1) and marginal costs begin to rise rapidly; hence
revenues will have to rise more than output if costs are to be
covered. At the highest levels of output the curve may closely
approach the vertical – that is, labour reserves approach exhaustion, bottlenecks develop and the costs of expanding output
become prohibitive. After this point, clearly, even very large
increases in expenditure will be able to generate little or no
expansion in output and employment.

So much for the aggregate supply schedule. The aggregate
demand schedule is more complex and will require somewhat
lengthier treatment.

3   THE COMPONENTS OF AGGREGATE DEMAND

Given the assumption of profit-maximisation it is possible to
talk of the aggregate supply of all goods and services as being
subject to the same basic influence – the relationship of costs
to expected revenues.

It is necessary, however, to divide aggregate demand into
three separate components – consumers' expenditure, investment expenditure and government expenditure – since each of
these broad groups is subject to rather special influences.
Leaving the matter of exports and imports aside for the
moment, every item of expenditure taking place in an economy
will fall under one or other of these three headings. The everyday purchases in the shops of food, clothing, tobacco, furniture,
etc. and payments for services such as entertainments, laundries
and travel, constitute consumers' expenditure; the heading
covers, in other words, all the spending which people do in

their capacity of private citizens. By *investment expenditure*, it will be remembered, is meant the construction of producers' goods such as factories, shipyards and machines. The purchase of securities, or existing assets such as houses, is sometimes spoken of as investment in ordinary conversation; the economist, however, studying the overall economic activity of society, excludes such transactions from investment because they are merely transfers from one person to another, and therefore cancel out for the economy as a whole. *Government expenditure* refers to all those purchases of goods and services by government agencies on behalf of the community, such as the provision of health and educational services, expenditures on personnel and equipment required for defence and the payment of national and local civil servants.

These three items, then, make up total domestic expenditure which, after deducting net expenditure on imports, represents the flow of spending from which factor-incomes are paid. For the United Kingdom in 1973 the orders of magnitude ($£000$ mn. at factor cost) were:

Gross national product		Consumers' expenditure		Investment		Government expenditure		Net exports
63·3	=	37·5	+	13·6	+	12·5	−	0·3

Of the third type of expenditure – i.e. that on goods and services by the Government – little need be added to what has already been said in Chapter XIX. It is an element in the total which is determined in practice mainly by political rather than economic factors; its magnitude depends on the extent of government activity, the requirements of defence, the size of the civil service, etc., while its movements from year to year are determined by current political policy. Nowadays, however, the potentialities of government expenditure as an element which can compensate for fluctuation in private expenditure are increasingly stressed, and more will be said on this subject in Chapter XXVIII. For the moment it is best regarded as an element in total expenditure which varies according to political rather than economic motives, and which, furthermore, is relatively stable from year to year. The question of exports and imports can also be left on one side for the moment since the whole subject of international trade is being left over to Part VIII. Attention can therefore be concentrated on the two main constituents of aggregate demand which are mainly economic in nature – consumers' expenditure and investment.

4 CONSUMPTION BEHAVIOUR

A great deal of this book has been devoted to the analysis of the way in which a consumer will distribute a given amount of income between all the various goods and services available to him. In considering consumer expenditure as an element in aggregate demand, however, the economist is faced with the problem of the factors determining the *total* amount which people spend, rather than the distribution of that total amongst different commodities.

The first and most obvious of these factors is the income received by a person. Most people would spend more than they do now if they had the opportunity, but their total income is a limiting factor. If a person's income rises, his purchases of goods and services will almost always increase; if his income falls, he is forced to spend less. A second factor, however, is the thriftiness of consumers; this is generally referred to as the *propensity to save* and expressed in the form of the fraction of income which is saved. The determinants of the propensity to save are numerous: examples are the attitude to future as opposed to present needs, the desire to accumulate resources to meet possible emergencies, the attraction of the interest to be earned on funds used to buy securities and the wish to provide for dependants.

The amount of a person's income is in itself an important determinant of his propensity to save. When people are so poor that they can afford only the barest necessities of life, saving is impossible; all the wealth available to them is needed to preserve life itself. As income increases, however, the more urgent wants can be satisfied; some wealth can be used in the enjoyment of commodities which make life more comfortable but which are not absolutely essential. It becomes at least *possible* for a person to save. As the standard of living rises further, the urgency of wants still unsatisfied becomes less and less, and consequently less sacrifice is involved in saving. If a person is very rich indeed, it may be difficult for him to *avoid* saving at a fairly high rate; the number of meals which a person can eat, or suits he can wear, or houses he can live in, is not easily pushed beyond a certain point. As a general conclusion, then, it can be said that as income rises the propensity to save (i.e. the fraction of income which is saved) will also rise. Put alternatively, the marginal propensity to consume (the proportion of increments of income devoted to the purchase of consumer goods) will fall as income rises; as a person becomes richer, a smaller and smaller fraction of each addition to his income will be spent. His average propensity to consume (i.e. total expenditure on consumer goods as a proportion of total income) will also fall as income rises, of course, but less rapidly than the marginal propensity to consume. This may not be true of a particular individual, of course, but will hold generally.

Data on personal consumption in the United Kingdom during recent years provide a rough illustration of these concepts. The annual averages for each three-year period were:

	Total personal incomes (Y) £ million	Total consumers' expenditure (C) £ million	C/Y	Δ C/Δ Y
1965–7	32 008	24 172	0·76	
1968–70	39 473	29 228	0·74	0·68
1971–3	54 433	39 736	0·73	0·70

The average propensity to consume, C/Y, seems to have fallen steadily from 0·76 to 0·73 while the marginal propensity to consume would appear to have remained stable at around 0·69.

It must be said immediately, however, that an immense amount of controversy has raged over the precise relationship between income and expenditure and the discussion above has done little more than state the most general of frameworks. For

example there is considerable disagreement amongst economists
as to which definition of income is most appropriate in this
context. Some would opt for current income after taxes, some
for a concept of permanent income (that is, making allowances
for receipts or shortfalls which are believed to be temporary),
while others have stressed the importance of previous peak
incomes as determining a standard of living which individuals
will seek to maintain even when their incomes decline. Again,
it is probable that the propensity to consume is influenced by
the accumulated capital wealth possessed by a person, by his
or her expectations about the future movement of prices, and
so on. A simple formulation of the propensity to consume is
sufficient for present purposes but it is obviously a highly complex concept in reality.

5   THE DETERMINANTS OF INVESTMENT

An analysis of the factors guiding entrepreneurs in their decisions concerning investment shows that this component in
aggregate demand will have no stabilising element comparable
with the influence of habit and convention which may normally
be expected to operate on consumer behaviour. As in all other
productive activity, an entrepreneur will purchase new capital
equipment only if the revenue he expects to derive from it is at
least equal to its cost of production. A sudden change in *either*
the expected profitability of an investment project, *or* in its
cost to the entrepreneur can therefore result in the abandonment of a project which was previously attractive or, conversely, in a decision to go ahead with an investment scheme
which had previously been considered to be uneconomic. How
could such sudden changes occur?

On the cost side, the main items are the cost of purchasing
or constructing the asset itself and the price paid for the funds
locked up in it. The former item, the physical costs of production, are no more likely to vary in the short run than are those
of any other commodity (although oscillations in the demand
for capital goods may sometimes have substantial effects on
their prices). More important in principle, however, are the

changes that are possible in the price of funds – i.e. the rate of interest. If an entrepreneur purchases a machine costing £1 000 and raises the funds by borrowing, he will naturally have to pay the lender the current rate of interest as a reward for sacrificing the liquidity represented by £1 000 in cash. Even if the entrepreneur uses his own funds, he still has to reckon the current rate of interest as a part of the cost; he *could* obtain a return by using the £1 000 to purchase securities rather than a machine, and this loss of interest is part of the price he pays for the machine. As was seen in Chapter XXIV, significant changes do occur in interest rates during short periods, and indeed are frequently brought about deliberately by the monetary authorities. Fluctuations in investment may well occur, therefore, because of sudden variations in its cost.

Even greater instability can be expected in the other major determinant of investment decisions – the expected revenue attributable to any given investment project, usually referred to as the *marginal efficiency of capital*. A factory or machine will go on yielding revenue, via the goods produced with its aid, for a number of years. An entrepreneur has to look a considerable distance into the future, therefore, in assessing the extra receipts which an addition to his capital equipment may bring in. Only rarely will capital goods bring in enough revenue to cover their cost within less than two or three years; many 'heavy' capital goods, such as generating stations or steel mills, may have to operate for twenty or thirty years before the revenue they earn is sufficient to cover their cost. Now a great many things can happen even in two or three years to falsify the expectations of entrepreneurs; demand may change so as to ruin the market for the product concerned, new competitors may unexpectedly enter the market, while technological developments may render obsolete overnight what currently appears to be the most modern machinery. Entrepreneurs' expectations are therefore necessarily rather vague and highly speculative. One event (a collapse of a competitor, a sudden new vogue, a temporary dip in prices, etc.) may cause a widespread revision of expectations involving new investment; changes in prevailing business views will tend to be contagious, since views of the future are largely coloured by the events of the present, and a wave of optimism or pessimism can spread rapidly throughout the business world. Above all, any increase in uncertainty about the future course of trade, or politics, or tastes, will inevitably have a dampening effect on investment decisions; an investment project once undertaken cannot be lightly abandoned, and an entrepreneur will stand to lose heavily during many years because of a single error of judgement.

On both the cost and revenue sides, then, the investment process contains a good many unstable elements; consequently, significant changes in the rate of investment expenditure can occur because of a number of possible causes. The crucial importance of expected returns, on the one hand, and interest rates on the other was examined at some length in Chapter VIII and need not be repeated here. In principle the relationship between the rate of interest and the rate of investment can be illustrated by the marginal efficiency of capital schedule shown in Fig. 25B. At any given rate of interest, say OR_1, and with any given state of entrepreneurial expectations, the rate of investment, OI_1, can be measured along he horizontal axis. If the rate of interest falls to OR_2, all other things remaining constant, the rate of investment will rise to OI_2.

The crucial significance of the phrase 'all other things re-

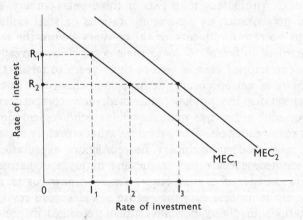

Fig. 25B   The marginal efficiency of capital

maining equal' must however be stressed and two points in particular need to be made. First, the use of a single MEC schedule in Fig. 25B is apt to give a rather misleading impression of certainty and precision in entrepreneurial expectations. This will seldom exist and in reality the schedule is liable to be shifting about as entrepreneurs become more or less optimistic. Second, the rate of investment associated with any given rate of interest is likely to be critically dependent also on the level of income and output prevailing generally in the economy. At one level of output and demand, a rate of investment of OI_1 may be generated; if the economy expands, however, profits will generally rise as demand rises and the *MEC* schedule will thus shift to, say, MEC_2, so that the interest rate OR_2 will now generate a rate of investment OI_3.

The determination of the level of investment expenditure is thus a fairly complex business. In principle, an inverse relationship can be postulated between interest rates and the rate of investment, although the elasticity of the latter in respect of the former is open to some doubt. More reliably, a positive relationship can be expected between the rate of investment and the level of output and employment.

6   AGGREGATE DEMAND AND SUPPLY

From the discussion of the two preceding sections it is possible to construct an aggregate demand schedule exactly comparable with the aggregate supply schedule of Section 2. Along the vertical axis in Fig. 25C is measured the total spending in the economy under each broad category and along the horizontal axis the level of output of goods and services and thus the level of employment in the economy. Suppose, first, that current government expenditure is assumed constant at a total represented by OG; this component of aggregate demand can therefore be represented by the horizontal line GG'. Next, suppose that investment expenditure is fixed at a minimum of OI – perhaps the total of public investment undertaken regardless of output – but rises steadily as output and employment expand along the horizontal axis; this is shown by the upward-sloping

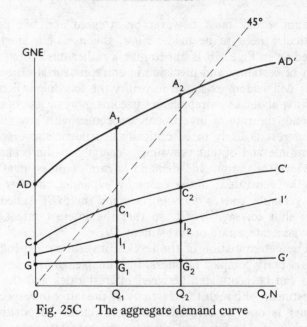

Fig. 25C   The aggregate demand curve

line II'. Finally, suppose that consumer expenditure amounts to
a minimum of OC, rises as employment (and thus income) increases but – as would be expected with a marginal propensity
to consume less than unity – rises less rapidly than income. The
curve would then be of the general shape of CC' in Fig. 25C.

The aggregate demand schedule is then obtained by simply
adding these three constituents together at each level of output
and employment. Thus, at output OQ_1 government expenditure
amounts to Q_1G_1, investment to Q_1I_1 and consumption to
Q_1C_1; adding these together gives a total of Q_1A_1; when output
rises to OQ_2 the three constituents become Q_2G_2, Q_2I_2 and
Q_2C_2, giving a total expenditure of Q_2A_2. Proceeding in this
way leads to the aggregate demand schedule AD in Fig. 25C.

It is now an easy step to bring the two schedules, aggregate
demand and aggregate supply, together on the same axes as in
Fig. 25D. The point X at which they intersect now defines the
level of output and employment at which the system as a whole
will be in equilibrium since at that point – and at that point

only – the total spending going on in the economy is just sufficient to induce entrepreneurs to maintain that level of output, and therefore of employment, which generates that level of spending. At any lower level of output, say OQ_1 in Fig. 25D, the value of demand in the market, Q_1D_1, exceeds the revenues necessary to induce that output, Q_1S_1; hence stock of goods will be declining as demand outruns output, bigger orders will

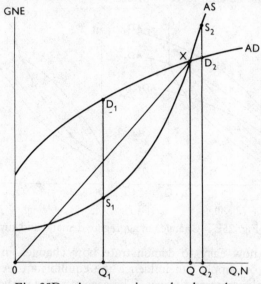

Fig. 25D   Aggregate demand and supply

be coming in from wholesalers to replace them and profits will be rising as the shortage of goods forces up prices. Hence entrepreneurs will tend to increase output and take on additional labour; the economy will move rightwards along the horizontal axis. At any level of output higher than OQ, on the other hand, the reverse will apply; aggregate spending, Q_2D_2 will be less than the costs of current output, Q_2S_2, unsold stocks will pile up and orders decline, and employment will tend to fall back. The output OQ is the only one at which there are no tendencies for employment to expand or contract; it is the equilibrium level of aggregate output.

The diagram can also reveal something about prices. At this equilibrium point, the total spending on goods and services is equal to QX; the total quantity being produced is measured by OQ. Since price is given by dividing total revenue by total quantity sold, the *general* price level is given by QX/OQ which is, of course, the slope of the line OX. The steeper this line from origin to the point of intersection of the two curves, the higher the general level of prices.

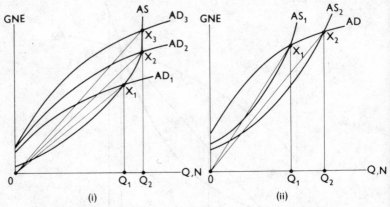

Fig. 25E   Changes in aggregate demand and supply

It is now easy to demonstrate how changes in aggregate demand or supply can influence the equilibrium levels of output, employment and prices. The case of shifts in the aggregate demand curve is shown in Fig. 25E(i). In the initial situation the aggregate demand and supply curves intersect at X_1; equilibrium output is OQ_1 and the price-level defined by the slope of OX_1. The level of aggregate demand now shifts upwards to AD_2, perhaps because of an increase in the rate of investment induced by a fall in the rate of interest or because of a rise in government expenditure. Two effects are seen; the general price-level rises, as shown by the increase of slope from OX_1 to OX_2; and total output and employment increase from OQ_1 to OQ_2. If aggregate demand now rises further to AD_3 the effects are felt only on the price-level; this is reflected in the increase in the slope of OX_2 to OX_3, but because the inelastic segment of the aggregate supply curve had already been reached, real output cannot increase beyond OQ_2. The situation is one of pure inflation: increased aggregate demand is taken out wholly in the form of a rise in prices and cannot stimulate any increase in output.

The case of a shift in the aggregate supply curve is shown in Fig. 25E(ii). The initial equilibrium output is defined by OX_1 but the aggregate supply curve then shifts to the right from AS_1 to AS_2, perhaps because of an improvement in technology or a growth in capital stock; whatever the cause, the real costs of producing any given level of output, such as OQ_1, is now reduced. With an unchanged level of aggregate demand, two effects now follow. The general price-level falls – reflected in the smaller slope of OX_2 in comparison with OX_1 – and output rises from OQ_1 to OQ_2.

The overall level of employment and the general level of prices in an economy at any moment of time, therefore, are the outcome of the interaction of quite complex considerations on the side of both demand and supply. The former involves all the varied forces governing the spending habits of consumers, entrepreneurs and government; the latter involves both the economic and technological determinants of the willingness of enterprises to produce at different levels of output and their technical capacity to do so.

7 SAVINGS AND INVESTMENT

In Sections 4 and 5 the factors governing the expenditure of consumers and of entrepreneurs have been discussed. By and large, the two sets of factors are entirely different and unrelated; the decisions of consumers in allocating income as between spending and saving will have no direct connection with those of entrepreneurs in deciding the rate of their expenditure on the maintenance of, or addition to, their stock of plant and equipment, vehicles and buildings. Despite this complete separation of saving decisions on the part of ordinary people and investment decisions on the part of entrepreneurs, however, there is an identity of a fundamental and inescapable kind between

the total amount saved in an economy during any period and the
amount invested (in its economic sense of expenditure on the
construction of capital goods) during the same period. In fact,
the amount saved and the amount invested will always be equal,
whether the level of aggregate output and prices are at their
equilibrium level or not.

This may seem a rather remarkable phenomenon – the
entirely unrelated and disconnected decisions of two separate
sets of people leading to identical results in terms of their absolute sum. On further consideration of the nature of the investing
process, however, the apparent strangeness disappears. In an
economy, the act of adding to capital consists of using a part
of current output for some purpose other than consumption.
That is what investment means – the setting aside of resources
from current consumption. Now saving is exactly the same process looked at from the other side, so to speak. If a pound's
worth of resources is devoted to adding to a society's stock of
capital goods, someone, somewhere, must own the result;
nothing can float about the economic system belonging to no
one. That someone, whoever or whatever he is, has used wealth
for the purpose of capital formation rather than for current
consumption. And that is what saving means. The amounts
that people save – in whatever form they may choose to hold
their saving – are nothing more nor less than *the monetary
equivalents of the growth in the value of the stock of capital
goods*. When people save they refrain from using all their income for consumption; but all income originates in current
production, so that the income not consumed must be offset
somewhere by *production* which has not been consumed – i.e.
which has been used to add to the stock of capital. Investment
cannot occur without saving, nor saving without investment,
any more than selling can occur without buying or lending without borrowing; they are the two sides of a single event in the
economic world.

Some elementary algebra may clarify this vitally important
fact. Let Y represent the total national income, C total consumers expenditure, I total investment and S total savings.
(Government expenditure and foreign trade are being ignored

for the moment for the reasons given earlier.) All income must arise from production, so that the value of the national income must be equal to the value of all goods produced – consumer goods and capital goods. That is,

$$Y = C + I \qquad \ldots\ldots\ldots\ldots\ldots\ldots\ldots(1)$$

Again, all income must either be consumed (spent on consumer goods) or saved; there is no other alternative. Hence

$$Y = C + S \qquad \ldots\ldots\ldots\ldots\ldots\ldots\ldots(2)$$

Since the value of the national income is the same in both equations (1) and (2), the expressions on the right-hand side of the equations must also be equal to one another – they both equal the same thing (Y) and must therefore equal one another. Hence it follows that

$$C + I = C + S \qquad \ldots\ldots\ldots\ldots\ldots\ldots(3)$$

Since consumers' expenditure (C) appears on both sides of equation (3), it can be subtracted from each side, leaving the statement that

$$I = S.$$

This merely puts in symbolic language the identity discussed in the previous paragraph. Goods produced but not consumed constitute capital formation, or investment; income received but not consumed constitutes saving. One is no more than the reflection of the other.

It is clear that the amount actually saved *must* equal the amount actually invested; what are not obvious are the implications of this equality when the relevant decisions are taken by entirely different groups of people – savers and entrepreneurs. These are only to be seen through an examination of the process of income-formation to which the discussion will turn in the next chapter.

FURTHER READING

G. ACKLEY *Macro-economic theory* Macmillan, New York 1961, Chs. 10–13

T. F. DERNBURG and D. M. McDOUGALL *Macro-economics* Chs. 5 and 7

W. BECKERMAN *An introduction to national income analysis* Ch. 6

D. C. ROWAN *Output, inflation and growth* Chs. 8–10

M. BRUCE JOHNSON *Household behaviour* Penguin Books, London 1971

CHAPTER XXVI

The Process of
Income Formation

1 THE NATURE OF THE INCOME FLOW

DEMAND must always equal supply, but the analysis of Part IV has shown that this statement is true only because a particular mechanism exists which ensures that the amount of a given commodity taken off the market by consumers is always equal to the amount put on it by producers. That mechanism is price. If prospective demand tended to exceed prospective supply, price would rise, cutting down the demand and stimulating supply. However great prospective demand might be, there is always *some* price which will be high enough to reduce it to any given level; however large prospective supply might be, there is always *some* price which will be low enough to reduce it to any given level. In any market, at any time, actual demand *must* equal supply, since for every act of sale (supply) there is a corresponding act of purchase (demand).

Now savings and investment, defined in the way outlined in the previous chapter, must necessarily always be equal; there is no means by which one can differ from the other in the way that demand and supply at a given market price may be different. Hence there is no mechanism corresponding to price which *brings* saving into equality with investment. There *is* a parallel with supply and demand, however, in that the identity of savings and investment implies repercussions on the level of *income* when the decisions underlying them change, just as repercussions are felt on market price when the supply of or demand for a single commodity changes.

To understand the nature of these repercussions, it is necessary to appreciate the interdependence of all the members of an economic system so far as their incomes are concerned. Although each individual might think that the amount he earns has no connection whatever with the amount earned by people a hundred miles away, he would deceive himself in so thinking. It is obvious that the income of a shopkeeper is closely linked with the incomes of the people living in his neighbourhood; they are his customers, and if their wages go up his trade will be brisk and his profits will consequently be raised. What is less obvious is that the wages of the customers are in turn intimately linked with the profits of the shopkeeper; when the shop prospers and profits are good the shopkeeper will buy more of the clothes, or electric irons, or books, or chocolates which his customers help to make in their factories. The coal-miner may not see any connection between his wages and the earnings of a country doctor, but it is there all the same; if the doctor has a good year he may buy a new car, which will help to stimulate the motor-manufacturer's demand for steel, which in turn will stimulate the demand for coal, and hence for coal-miners, which may tend to increase miners' wages.

What this all comes to, of course, is that the economic system is one enormous circular flow of income, with income passing from hand to hand in exchange for goods and services. *Everyone's income is someone else's expenditure.* When I buy petrol for my car the transaction represents expenditure to me but income to the garage proprietor; when the garage proprietor buys a new house it is expenditure to him but income for the builder; when the builder buys my text-book on economics for his son, it is expenditure to him but income for my publishers and me. Economically, people are utterly and inescapably dependent on one another; by altering his expenditure a person will thereby alter the income of someone else, and by changing his expenditure someone quite unknown to me may be influencing my income.

Bearing this in mind, the significance of saving and investment can be recognised. Saving is, by definition, the act of not-spending; a person who saves simply withholds part of his income from expenditure on goods and services. (He may place the funds so saved at the disposal of someone else, of course, but that is another part of the story altogether; in any case, he may not part with his savings at all.) What effect will this have on the circular flow of income? Here is some income which has come into the hands of a person and which he does not pass on to someone else through the purchase of goods. The flow of income is therefore diminished to that extent, just as a leak in a water-pipe will diminish the pressure of water flowing through the rest of the system. If the saving is achieved through a reduction in the consumption of (say) magazines, then the income of the publishers, and all those dependent on them, is reduced to the same extent. Nor is this the end of the affair. The magazine publishers, being somewhat poorer than they would have been if this saving had not taken place, are in turn forced to spend less on their own consumption of (say) cigars, so that the incomes of cigar-manufacturers are in turn diminished. So it goes on, the act of saving reverberating throughout the whole economic system in the form of reduced incomes.

An act of investment has precisely reverse effects. If a company decides to build a new factory, using either borrowed funds or their own accumulated reserves, it *adds* to the flow of income. Men are engaged in constructional work and are paid wages; raw materials or machines are purchased, adding to the revenues of their producers, and so on. These extra incomes will result in extra spending by their recipients, so that the demand for clothes, or entertainments, or food, or whatever else the incomes are spent on, is stimulated and the revenues of their producers increased. The latter, in turn, will be encouraged by the increased demand to expand production, so increasing incomes through *their* extra expenditure on wages, raw materials, etc. Once again, then, there is a chain reaction through the economy. Investment directly raises incomes through the rewards paid to factors producing the capital-goods involved, this increased income passing out again through increased expenditure.

The circular flow of income can be conceived of, then, as the passage of income from hand to hand through the production and sale of ordinary consumer goods and services. This basic income flow is *reduced* by savings, which comprise income received but not passed on again, and *increased* by investment, which represents the creation of incomes by the process of adding to the stock of capital goods. Two important questions about this income-flow remain to be answered. First, what limits, if any, are there to the changes in income which occur as a result of new acts of saving or investment? Do the repercussions go on for ever, or will they tend to die out? Secondly, why and how is the level of income affected by the equality of saving and investment? These questions will be considered in turn.

2 THE MULTIPLIER

When the company embarked on a new factory in the example just given, incomes were directly generated; for the sake of simplicity only the wages of the men engaged on building the factory need be referred to, although obviously other types of income will be involved. These wages found their way into the tills of shopkeepers selling food, or clothes, or tobacco, and thence passed to the producers of those commodities. These in turn spent more on the goods *they* wanted, and so the sequence continued. Does it go on for ever? Will an initial injection into the income flow set in motion an unending rise in incomes?

It will not, and for the reason given in the discussion of saving. If every penny of everyone's income was spent, the chain reaction *would* go on for ever, an initial injection of income passing from hand to hand *ad infinitum*. But every penny of every income is *not* spent. People save, and, as has been seen, the effect of saving is to diminish the flow of income. If people on average wish to save one-tenth of any additions to their income, an initial injection of £100 additional wages to factory-builders will result in an extra £90 spent on, say, clothing; the extra £90 received by the producers of clothing will result in an extra £81 expenditure, and so on. The wave of income will spread further and further into the economy, but with diminishing force. In this example the actual sequence will be something like this:

$$100 + 90 + 81 + 73 + 66 + 59 + 53 + 48 + 43 + 39 \ ...$$

↑
(Initial
injection)

Clearly the series will eventually tail away into nothingness. Can the situation be described more precisely than this? Is it possible to say *how much* extra income will be generated by any initial increase in spending? It is indeed possible, because it is known that the brake at work slowing down the rise in income is the propensity to save. If the proportion of any additional income people wish to put away in saving is known, it can be calculated how rapidly the extra income will vanish through the savings leak. In the example, it is known that people wish to save one-tenth of extra income; it follows that total incomes must rise by £1 000 before people's equilibrium, or 'desired' level of savings will have risen by £100. If there is an initial increase of £100 in incomes, then, this increase will be exactly offset by increased 'desired' saving only when total incomes have risen by £1 000. In the sequence given above, only the first ten items in the series of income changes originating in the initial injection of £100 are given. These actually add up to £652. If the *next* ten items were calculated and added, the total would come to about £868; if a further ten were calculated, it would be about £943. If the series were continually extended in this way, the cumulative total of the items would approach closer and closer to the sum of £1 000.

This does not mean, of course, that the total volume of *actual* savings in the economy will rise by £100 only after this process (which naturally takes time) has come to an end. Immediately investment rises by £100, saving must increase equally. The day the factory is built, its constructors are paid £100, and their income is that much greater. Until they, in turn, spend this extra income, their savings must be £100 greater − saving being the difference between income (which has risen by £100) and consumption (which is as yet unchanged). *After* they have spent part, or all, of the £100 it becomes someone else's income and (until it is passed on again through extra expenditure) forms part of someone else's saving. At any moment of time the extra saving must be equal to the extra investment. For example, suppose that the numerical sequence shown above is stopped immediately the third group have received their extra income, but before the fourth group have yet been affected (i.e. before the third group have had time to spend their additional income). The position will then be:

$$\begin{aligned}
\text{Additional incomes received} &= 100 \quad 90 \quad 81 \\
\text{Additional expenditure} &= \underline{90 \quad 81 \quad 0} \\
\text{Hence additional saving} &= 10 + 9 + 81 = 100.
\end{aligned}$$

Similarly, if the sequence were stopped just after the sixth group had received their extra incomes, the position would be:

$$\begin{aligned}
\text{Additional incomes received} &= 100 \quad 90 \quad 81 \quad 73 \quad 66 \quad 59 \\
\text{Additional expenditure} &= \underline{90 \quad 81 \quad 73 \quad 66 \quad 59 \quad 0} \\
\text{Hence additional saving} &= 10 + 9 + 8 + 7 + 7 + 59 = 100.
\end{aligned}$$

But the vital factor in these cases is that the saving being performed by the final group in the sequences is not their *equilibrium* rate of saving – it is not the saving they will perform after they have had sufficient time to adjust their expenditure to their new level of income. Hence the process of change in the overall level of incomes will continue; it will end only when *everyone* (including the final recipients in the chain of income changes) is saving and spending at his desired rate from his new level of income. Savings and investment are equal throughout; but the movement of incomes upwards or downwards, as the case may be, only comes to an end when everyone has had time to reach his *equilibrium* rate of saving (i.e. the product of his new income and his normal propensity to save).

This can be put more generally. The sequence of items in the process of income formation constitute a geometric series, since each item is found by multiplying the preceding item by a constant factor. (In this context, the constant factor is the marginal propensity to consume, which is usually represented by the letter c.) If the initial impulse of extra spending is denoted by I', then the second element in the sequence will be $c.I'$, the third $c.c.I'$ ($=c^2I'$), the fourth $c.c.c.I'$ ($=c^3I'$) and so on. If there are n elements in the whole sequence, then (n being some undefined but very large number), the sum total of the change in income, Y', will be given by

$$Y' = I' + cI' + c^2I' + c^3I' + \ldots + c^{n-1}I' \ldots (1)$$

Now multiply both sides of this equation by c; this gives

$$cY' = cI' + c^2I' + c^3I' + \ldots\ldots + c^nI' \ldots\ldots (2)$$

and subtracting the second equation from the first gives

$$Y' - cY' = I' - c^nI' \ldots\ldots\ldots\ldots\ldots\ldots\ldots\ldots\ldots\ldots (3)$$

since all the terms on the right-hand side cancel out except the initial term of the first equation and the final term of the second. Simplifying this last equation,

$$Y'(1-c) = I'(1-c^n)$$

and

$$Y' = I' \cdot \frac{1-c^n}{1-c} \ldots\ldots\ldots\ldots\ldots\ldots\ldots\ldots\ldots (4)$$

Now if c is less than one and n is a very large number, c^n will approach zero, since any fraction less than unity diminishes rapidly in magnitude as it is raised to successively higher powers. Hence the final expression becomes

$$Y' = I' \cdot \frac{1}{1-c} \cdot$$

In the numerical example quoted above, for instance, I' was £100 and c was $\frac{9}{10}$. Hence the formula indicates that the total change in incomes will be

$$£100 \times \frac{1}{1-\frac{9}{10}} = £1\,000.$$

This expression, $\dfrac{1}{1-c}$, which relates an initial change in expenditure to the total change in the general level of income which will result from it, is known as the *multiplier*.

It may be helpful if the same result is illustrated geometrically rather than by algebra. Suppose that in Fig. 26A aggregate demand is measured along the vertical axis (gross national expenditure) and national income (GNY) along the horizontal axis. Let investment be assumed constant at OI_1 initially and consumption expenditure is then added to give the aggregate demand schedule $C+I_1$. (Government spending is being ignored for the sake of simplicity.) The slope of this schedule $C + I_1$ is of course defined by the marginal propensity to consume and since this is less than unity the slope will be less than 45 degrees. In other words, the increase in consumption (measured on the vertical axis) associated with any increase in income (measured on the horizontal axis) will be less than the increase in income. By definition, gross national expenditure will equal gross national income in equilibrium, so the point of intersection between the $C + I_1$ line and the 45 degree line, X_1, defines the point at which national income will settle; since the triangle OX_1Q_1 is an isosceles triangle the two sides X_1Q_1 and OQ_1 are equal – that is, $GNE = GNY$ at that point.

Now let investment increase to OI_2 so that the aggregate demand schedule shifts up to $C + I_2$. The new equilibrium point is defined by X_2, since at this point the new level of GNE (measured by X_2Q_2) is equal to GNY (measured by OQ_2). The *change* in income, Y', is measured by X_1Z which is by definition equal to X_2Z. The change in *investment*, I', however, is equal to X_2Y; but

$$X_2Y = X_2Z - YZ$$

i.e.
$$I' = Y' - YZ$$

But YZ is the change in consumption when income rises from OQ_1 to OQ_2, i.e.

$$YZ = c . Y'$$

Hence
$$I' = Y' - cY'$$
$$= Y'(1-c)$$

and
$$Y' = I' \cdot \frac{1}{1-c}$$

which is, of course, the familiar multiplier equation.

The multiplier is clearly a most useful and important concept. Given a knowledge of the fraction of additional incomes which the public as a whole will devote to increasing its consumption, the ultimate effects on total incomes of any postulated change in expenditure can be estimated – for example, if it is known that the marginal propensity to consume is $\frac{3}{4}$, a rise of £100 million in, say, road works could be

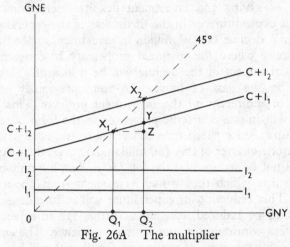

Fig. 26A   The multiplier

expected to result, other things remaining equal, in a rise of £400 million in the overall level of incomes. At the same time, it is important to remember that in real life, time-lags are liable to occur between a change in income and the full adjustment to expenditure which it will eventually cause. If my income rises today, it may be weeks or even months before I pass on the full effects of this to the rest of the economy in the form of increased expenditure. The propensity to consume in the short run, in other words, may differ substantially from that of the long run when everything has had time to work itself out. A multiplier based on long-run spending or saving propensities, therefore, can only indicate the changes in total income which will probably result from an initial change in spending after a lapse of time sufficient to allow for the full adjustment of people's expenditure to changes in their income. The change in total incomes which will occur in, say, the next month or two months may be considerably smaller than the ultimate long-run effect suggested by the multiplier.

3 INVESTMENT FLUCTUATIONS AND INCOME

It is now possible to analyse the implications of the necessary equality of saving and investment despite fluctuations in investment expenditure or in the thriftiness of the general public. Consider a decline of £50 million in investment expenditure in an economy where the marginal propensity to consume is $\frac{3}{4}$. The initial impact of the decline will be a loss of £50 million income on the part of those who were previously engaged directly or indirectly on the investment projects. This fall in income will in due course be passed on in the form of reduced expenditure; since the people concerned would have saved, on average, one-quarter of this £50 million, however, their expenditure will not be reduced by the full £50 million but only by that fraction of it which they would have spent – i.e. about £37.5 million. This reduction in expenditure will in turn cause other incomes to be reduced, causing a further fall in expenditure, the process continuing in the familiar sequence. The series of repercussions (changes of income in £ millions) will be:

$$- 50 - 37\cdot5 - 28\cdot1 - 21\cdot1 - 15\cdot8 \text{ etc.}$$

From the multiplier formula it is known that the total ultimate changes in incomes (Y') will be

$$I' \frac{1}{1-c}$$

$$= -50 \times \frac{1}{1-\frac{3}{4}}$$

$$= -50 \times \frac{1}{\frac{1}{4}}$$

$$= -200.$$

When the process has worked itself out, then, the overall level of incomes will be £200 million lower than before as a result of the fall of £50 million in investment expenditure.

The example is illustrated geometrically in Fig. 26B. Suppose that the rate of investment is initially £150 million and that the consumption function is of the form $C = 10 + 0.75 Y$; that is, consumption expenditure would amount to £10 million even in the improbable event of zero income and three-quarters of all

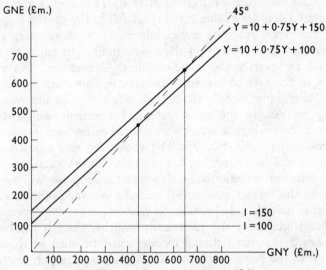

Fig. 26B   Fluctuations in the rate of investment

additions to income is spent. Hence the aggregate expenditure schedule becomes

$$Y = 10 + 0.75 Y + 150$$

and where this schedule meets the 45 degree line equilibrium national income is defined. In Fig. 26B it will be seen that this occurs at an income of £640 million. (This can be derived from the equation, of course. If $Y = 10 + 0.75Y + 150$ then $0.25Y = 160$ and $Y = 640$.)

The rate of investment falls by £50 million to £100 million and the aggregate expenditure schedule shifts down accordingly throughout its length; at the new point of intersection with the 45 degree line income has fallen to £440 million.

Naturally the equality of saving and investment has not been affected by all this. If people save on average one-quarter of marginal increments to their income, it follows that when incomes fall £200 million total saving must fall £50 million – i.e. by exactly the same amount as the change in investment. If saving and investment were equal before the change, then, they must be equal during and after it. The level of incomes has altered *because* of this equality. A fall in the rate of investment has made everyone sufficiently poorer in money terms to ensure that total savings in the new equilibrium situation are reduced by exactly the same amount. Conversely, if a rise occurs in the rate of investment, extra incomes will be generated, so enabling people to increase their equilibrium rate of saving to exactly the same extent. Investment will always generate the savings which, as was noted earlier, are the monetary counterpart of investment. The whole process of adjustment, of course, will take time, but the multiplier formula can indicate the equilibrium situation towards which the economy will move.

Given the rate of investment and the average propensity to consume, indeed, it is possible to calculate what the aggregate (national) income of the community will be, since it has been established that the national income must be such as to produce (with the given propensities to spend and save) an amount of saving equal to the rate of investment. (The *average*, rather than the *marginal*, propensity to consume is now involved, of course, since the analysis is concerned with the *total* level of income and not *changes* in the level of income.) This can most easily be seen in terms of the symbols used previously. Ignoring government expenditure and foreign trade, total income must be equal to the sum of the values of production of capital goods and consumer goods; i.e.

$$Y = I + C \text{ and } Y - C = I \quad\ldots\ldots\ldots\ldots\ldots (5)$$

It is also known that total consumer expenditure must be equal to the product of income and the average propensity to consume (C'), i.e. $C = C'(Y)$.

Substituting this expression for C in (5) gives

$$Y - C'(Y) = I$$

hence

$$Y = I \cdot \frac{1}{1 - C'}.$$

If investment expenditure equals £2 000 million and the average propensity to consume is $\frac{3}{4}$, then the total national income must be

$$£2\ 000 \text{ million} \times \frac{1}{1 - \frac{3}{4}} = £8\ 000 \text{ million}.$$

If people consume three-quarters of their income they must save one-quarter – i.e. a total of £2 000 million. Saving must equal investment.

The important point about all this, of course, is not so much the equality between saving and investment as the fluctuations in the national income which must occur as a result of this equality, assuming that variations occur in the rate of investment. If the marginal propensity to consume is a relatively large fraction, as it usually is, the value of the multiplier will be high, implying that fairly small changes in the rate of investment will have a substantial impact on the total national income. If the marginal propensity to consume is $\frac{95}{100}$, for example, the multiplier becomes 20; a change of £1 million in the rate of investment will therefore cause a change of £20 million in total incomes. Large fluctuations in income imply large fluctuations in demand and consequently in the amounts of factors of production which entrepreneurs will employ in order to meet that demand.

4 INCOME AND THE PROPENSITY TO SAVE

It was noted earlier that, in general, human beings tend to acquire fairly firm habits in the matter of saving and spending from a constant income, so that there are unlikely to be sudden and substantial changes in the propensity to consume. Nevertheless, such changes are not impossible. The growth of a 'war scare', for example, frequently leads to a rush on the part of consumers to buy up a stock of commodities which they anticipate will soon be in short supply, causing their current rate of savings to drop violently; an expectation of a fall in prices in the near future may have the opposite effect, since consumers will postpone expenditure as much as possible in order to obtain the benefit of the anticipated price reductions. Similarly, business saving may occasionally undergo sudden and substantial fluctuations; companies may change their views about the future availability of credit, for example, and place more (or less) of their current profits to reserve, while a change in the rate of tax on distributed or undistributed profits may have similar effects.

A change in the propensity to save will have effects on the national income comparable to those of a change in the rate of investment, but in the reverse direction. The level of incomes depends on (*a*) the rate of investment, and (*b*) the multiplier; a change in the propensity to save will cause the value of the multiplier to alter. If the rate of investment in an economy and the fixed element in consumption are each held constant at £100 million, a rise in the marginal propensity to save from 10 to 15 per cent will cause the multiplier to fall from 10 to about $6\frac{2}{3}$; hence the overall level of income will fall from £2 000 million to about £1 333 million. Precisely similar effects on the level of incomes will follow from a rise in the propensity to save, therefore, as from a fall in the rate of investment.

Once again the process can be illustrated geometrically. Suppose that in the first instance the consumption function of an economy is given by

$$C = 100 + 0.90\,Y.$$

Since saving is the difference between income and consumption the savings function of an economy (i.e. a statement of the amount people will *wish* to save at different income levels) will be given by

$$
\begin{aligned}
S &= Y - C \\
&= Y - (100 + 0.90\,Y) \\
&= 0.10\,Y - 100.
\end{aligned}
$$

This is the line S_1 in Fig. 26C: it shows, for example, that at an income of 1 000 equilibrium saving would be zero and at zero income people would be dis-saving 100. Where this line intersects the schedule showing the rate of investment (assumed constant at 100 in this case) the equilibrium level of income is defined. At lower levels of income *actual* saving (determined by I) exceeds *desired* saving: spending will continue to accelerate as people seek to get rid of these unwanted savings and income will rise. At higher levels of income people will be

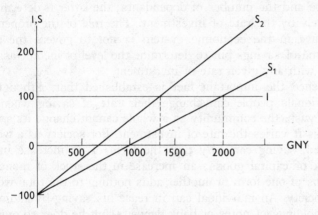

Fig. 26C   A shift in the propensity to save

seeking to save *more* than the actual saving I; hence spending will fall and the level of income will fall with it.

Now suppose the marginal propensity to save rises to 0·15; the savings function becomes

$$S = 0·15Y - 100$$

and the new savings function is given by S_2 in Fig. 26C. The new equilibrium level of income falls to around £1 333 million; the shift has not increased the amount actually saved – which is fixed by the rate of investment – but has lowered the level of aggregate income.

A change in the propensity to save cannot therefore disturb the necessary equality between the wealth actually saved in an

economy and the wealth set aside by it in the form of investment. In the example just given, the society saved 5 per cent of
its income when the national income was £2 000 million and
7·5 per cent when the national income was £1 333 million.

The *total amount* saved was the same in both cases – £100
million. In other words, there is no direct and immediate connection between the *propensity* to save and the total *amount*
saved. The former is determined by the psychological factors
discussed earlier, such as the prevailing attitude towards the
future and the number of dependants; the latter is determined
entirely by the rate of investment. The role of the propensity
to save in the economic system is not to govern the total
volume of savings but to determine the level of income associated with any given rate of investment.

Hence the important fact is established that, although as
individuals people can change their rate of saving whenever
they wish, the community as a whole cannot change its saving
unless it varies the rate of investment. For society as a whole,
indeed, saving can *only* take the form of an increase in the
stock of capital goods; an increase in the stock of monetary
claims of one form or another adds nothing to the total wealth
of society. An individual can increase his saving by adding to
his holdings of notes or bank deposits, but he does so only by
reducing the incomes (and therefore the saving) of the producers of the goods he *would* have bought had he not decided
to save more.

Does this mean that thrift, as a social characteristic, has
no economic importance? Since the total volume of saving is
fixed by the rate of investment, is it therefore unimportant
whether people save a large part of their income or not? Such
conclusions would be unsound. Although the volume of savings
is determined by investment, the propensity to save plays a
crucial role in deciding the level of money incomes in an
economy. As Chapter XXVIII will show, it often makes a great
deal of difference if a certain rate of investment results in a
high rather than a low level of total money incomes. Further,
the propensity to save, through its influence on the level of
incomes, may *indirectly* affect the rate of investment. Other

things being equal, a fall in the level of incomes will result in falling demand for consumer goods; this will usually discourage investment in the industries producing them.

This latter possibility is illustrated in Fig. 26D. Here, it will be noted, the rate of investment is not assumed to remain at some constant level but is instead assumed to be positively related to income. The initial situation is one in which equilibrium income is Y_1 and the level of investment and savings at that income is OX_1. A shift now occurs in the propensity to save so that the operative savings function becomes S_2. The

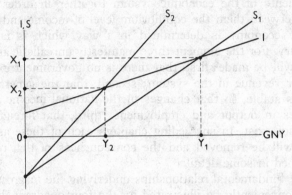

Fig. 26D   The paradox of thrift

result is not merely that the equilibrium level of income falls; because the fall in income leads to a reduced inclination on the part of entrepreneurs to invest in new capital goods, the level of investment and savings at this new level of income is lower than before, at OX_2. An increased inclination to save has had the paradoxical result of actually *diminishing* the amount saved. Hence the description 'paradox of thrift' often used in connection with this situation. It is relevant to those periods of history when, in the face of depression, governments, enterprises and individuals mistakenly embarked on 'economy' campaigns and thereby rendered depressions even deeper. Nowhere is there a more striking illustration of the 'fallacy of composition'. For an individual in economic difficulties restraint and increased thrift are usually highly desirable; when the argument is raised to the social level, however, in some circumstances precisely the reverse may well prove to be true.

5 THE MACRO SYSTEM

In the two preceding sections changes in the rate of invest-ment or the propensity to save have been rather arbitrarily assumed in order to investigate their consequences on the level of income. It is now possible, however, to bring the various ingredients of the economic system together in order to see how between them the equilibrium level of income and output in any economy is determined in a way which is far from arbitrary. For the moment three manifestly unrealistic assump-tions will be made: first, that there is no government expendi-ture or revenue in the system; second, that the general price level is stable, so that changes in the national income are real changes in output and employment; third, that foreign trade does not exist. In succeeding chapters each of these assump-tions will be removed and the consequences of that removal examined in some detail.

The fundamental relationships underlying the macro system may conveniently be illustrated by the four-quadrant diagram of Fig. 26E. The first of these relationships is that between the rate of interest, the level of income and the demand for money. Now in discussing this matter in Chapter XXIII it became clear that the demand for money contained two rather distinct elements: a demand for money as a means of exchange (the demand for active balances) and a demand for money as an asset (the demand for idle balances). These two ingredients justify the two right-hand quadrants in Fig. 26E. The bottom right-hand quadrant depicts the demand for active balances, the line L_1 showing the quantity of money (measured on the M axis) demanded at different levels of national income (measured on the Y axis); for simplicity, the relationship is assumed to be a linear one throughout. The demand for idle balances is shown by the curve L_2 in the quadrant above. Since the quantity of money available is measured along the M axis for *both* elements of the demand for money, the L_2 curve is shown as commencing at the point determined by the demand for active balances; it is the supply of money *to the right of* M_1 which constitutes the supply available for idle balances. The L_2 curve, of course, shows this demand as a relationship between the quantity available, measured along the M axis, and its price – the rate of interest – measured up the r axis.

The second fundamental relationship is that between the rate of interest and the rate of investment – the marginal efficiency

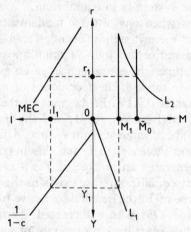

Fig. 26E   The macro system

of capital. This is illustrated by the *MEC* schedule in the top left-hand quadrant.

The third, and final, relationship is that between the rate of investment and the level of income – the multiplier. This is shown in the bottom left-hand quadrant, the multiplier line starting a little way down the Y axis to allow for the constant in the consumption function – the consumption (and hence income) which will be generated even if investment falls to zero.

All that is now needed to close, or determine, the system is the quantity of money as fixed by the monetary authorities. This is shown by the vertical line $\bar{M}_0$ in Fig. 26E, the dotted lines then tracing out the equilibrium values of all the variables in the system. The equilibrium value of national income will by Y_1. At this level of income the line L_1 reveals that a quantity of money OM_1 will be absorbed into active balances; the starting-point for the idle-balance demand schedule, L_2, will thus be M_1. From this it will be seen that the market rate of interest will settle at r_1 and at this rate the MEC schedule reveals that the rate of investment will be OI_1. The multiplier line shows that this rate of investment will generate the national income OY_1: the system is in equilibrium.

What happens when any of these fundamental relationships alters, or if the money supply changes, can be readily discovered with the aid of this four-quadrant apparatus. Fig. 26F shows as an example the consequences of an expansion in the quantity of money through the techniques of monetary policy described in Chapter XXIV. In diagram (i) the money supply has been increased from $\bar{M}_0$ to $\bar{M}_1$ and the immediate result is a fall in the rate of interest from r_1 to r_2. Under the impact of this, investment increases to I_2 and this in conjunction with the multiplier generates an income of Y_2. It is clear, however, that a state of disequilibrium now exists in the money market, since at an income of Y_2 the demand for active balances exceeds its original value OM_1; this increased demand for active balances must now react back on the rate of interest.

The second stage is shown in diagram (ii). The vertical axis of the demand for idle balances has now shifted rightwards to reflect this increased absorption of the fixed money supply. The result is a rise of the rate of interest back towards (but not of course as far as) its original level. This causes the rate of investment to fall and generates a decline in the level of income. Once again the money market is in disequilibrium; the public's holdings of active balances now exceed their requirements, given that income has fallen.

So the process continues until, by a series of adjustments, the money-market disequilibrium becomes smaller and smaller and the system ultimately reaches its new equilibrium shown in diagram (iii). The increased quantity of money will establish a new equilibrium point at which income is higher and the remaining variables are again consistent with one another. A similar sequence can be traced out by postulating a shift in the marginal efficiency of capital or in either of the elements of the demand for money; equally, a shift in the propensity to consume would be shown by a clockwise or anti-clockwise movement in the multiplier line corresponding to a fall or rise respectively in the propensity to consume.

Of course the economic system does not work in jerky, discrete steps as this description might suggest. The adjustments

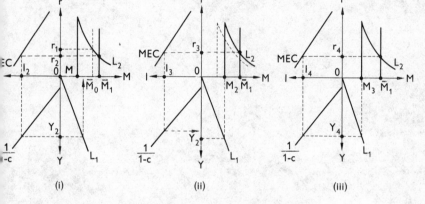

Fig. 26F   A change in the money supply

are continuous, reacting upon one another so as to prevent disequilibrium situations from attaining serious proportions. But equally the strength of the psychological factors at work in the economy should not be forgotten, which means that it is dangerous to impute undue stability or independence in the fundamental relationships underlying the analysis. The macro system is an exceedingly complex and sophisticated machine; equally it is a very high-strung affair with — as history shows — more than a faint inclination towards instability. In other words, being comprised of human beings it is prone to act like human beings.

FURTHER READING

G. ACKLEY *Macro-economic theory* Ch. 14

T. F. DERNBERG and D. M. McDOUGALL *Macro-economics* Chs. 9–12

W. BECKERMAN *An introduction to national income analysis* Ch. 7

D. C. ROWAN *Output, inflation and growth* Ch. 12

CHAPTER XXVII

Measuring the Price-level:
Index Numbers

1 THE PROBLEM OF MEASUREMENT

IN the following chapter the discussion will turn to the problem of macro-economic policy: the attempt by government, through various measures, to influence the economic system so that various aggregates approximate more closely to what are conceived to be their desirable values. Now in recent years the behaviour of the general level of prices has become a matter of paramount concern to the governments of all developed economies: why this should be so will be investigated in due course. So far rather little has been said about this concept of the general price level but since measurement is of the essence of positive economics something must now be said about the way in which some quantitative precision can be given to this rather vague concept. The present chapter is therefore something of a brief digression from the macro-economic theory which precedes and succeeds it. There is little justification in moving to a discussion of policy measures aimed at influencing the price-level, however, until something has been said about how the price-level is measured.

Now the expression 'price level' suggests an average, in some sense, of all individual prices, or at least of all the prices relevant in a particular context. The concept almost always occurs in connection with changes in prices over periods of time, when the discussion is concerned not so much with the price of one commodity relative to that of others as with the broad tendency of all prices in an absolute sense.

It is not difficult to see why it is impossible to compare *all* individual prices existing in an economy at one date with all prices existing at another. Every commodity has a price, and there are hundreds of thousands of commodities entering into exchange in any moderately developed economy; the proposition becomes even more impracticable when it is remembered that any single commodity may be produced and sold in dozens of qualities, brands and types each having a separate price. The mere task of listing all these prices would be almost impossible; recorded prices would have changed before the full list could be compiled (just as one end of the Forth Bridge is reputed to require re-painting before the painters have worked their way to the other end); it would therefore be impossible to draw up a list of all prices prevailing at a given moment.

Even if such a list could be compiled, however, it would be of little real use. The human mind is incapable of arriving at a general impression of even moderate accuracy from a collection of hundreds of thousands of different numbers varying to different degrees and possibly in different directions. Yet for many purposes it is useful, and for some it is essential, that a reliable idea should be obtained of overall movements in prices as a whole, i.e. of their direction and magnitude. The problem is solved well enough for ordinary working purposes by the application, in the particular context of price movements, of the technique of index numbers. The following section will therefore be devoted to the discussion of index numbers in general; afterwards, their application to the particular problem of price measurement will be outlined.

2   THE NATURE OF INDEX NUMBERS

Fundamentally, an *index number* is a means whereby the changes in a large number of related variables can be averaged, and the average change expressed through movements in a single number. To take a simple example, suppose there are five men whose production of different commodities in 1960 and 1975 (in physical terms) was as follows:

		Output	
Man	*Units*	*1960*	*1975*
1	Tons of coal	300	460
2	Bushels of wheat	250	220
3	Suits of clothes	60	100
4	Cwts. of bricks	30 000	30 000
5	Gallons of oil	9 000	18 000

How can the *average* growth of the output of this group over the period 1960–75 be expressed? The index number technique consists of taking as 100 the output of each man in the earlier year (the 'base-year' as it is called) and then calculating the output of each in the later year as a percentage of his output in 1960. The five figures obtained for 1975 can then be added up and the total divided by five to arrive at the average change. Thus, the calculation would be:

		Output
Man	*1960*	*1975*
1	100	153·3
2	100	88·0
3	100	166·7
4	100	100·0
5	100	200·0
Total	500	708·0
Average	100	141·6

It could then be said that, on average, this group of men produced 41·6 per cent more in 1975 than in 1960.

In this very simple example, the variables concerned (the output of five different men) were regarded as being of equal importance, so that a straightforward arithmetical average could be used to arrive at the overall index number. In many cases, however, the variables making up the group are of *un*equal importance, and allowance has to be made for this. For example, suppose that an index number of industrial production is being constructed – i.e. a single number that will represent the average change in the output of industry as a whole over a given period. If there are in the country ten different industries of varying degrees of importance, then a system of *weights* will have to be used to ensure that a movement in a big industry is given more influence in the index than a similar movement in a minor industry. These weights will have to be based on some factor which can be taken to measure the relative importance of each of the industries entering into the index. In the case of industrial production, a tolerably reliable guide to the relative importance of different industries might be the numbers of people employed in each. For example, an unweighted and a weighted index might be calculated as follows:

Industry	Output		Numbers employed in Year 1 (000's)	Output-relatives	
	Year 1	*Year 2*		*Year 1* $[(2) \times (4)]$	*Year 2* $[(3) \times (4)]$
(1)	(2)	(3)	(4)	(5)	(6)
1	100	104	2·0	200·0	208·0
2	100	103	4·5	450·0	463·5
3	100	94	1·2	120·0	112·8
4	100	110	5·8	580·0	638·0
5	100	101	3·0	300·0	303·0
6	100	82	2·1	210·0	172·2
7	100	95	0·6	60·0	57·0
8	100	99	1·0	100·0	99·0
9	100	103	1·2	120·0	123·6
10	100	106	3·1	310·0	328·6
Total	1 000	997	24·5	2 450·0	2 505·7

The unweighted index numbers would be calculated by simply dividing the totals of columns (2) and (3) by the number of variables included, i.e. 10. This would give 100 for Year 1 and 99·7 for Year 2, suggesting a slight fall in industrial production as a whole. To calculate a weighted index, however, the totals in columns (5) and (6) would be arrived at, and these would be divided by the sum of the weights used – i.e. the total of column (4). This would give index numbers of 100 for Year 1 and 102·3 for Year 2, suggesting a *rise* in overall industrial production.

The choice of the weights used in calculating an index number can be of great significance, therefore; given a certain set of changes in the variables whose overall movement is being measured, the use of two different sets of weights may well result in final index numbers which do not change even in the same direction, let alone to the same degree. Naturally this fact is of considerable practical importance.

3 THE RETAIL PRICE INDEX

Without any doubt, the index number most widely known and used in Britain is the index of retail prices, more commonly but less accurately spoken of as the cost-of-living index. Strictly speaking there is no such thing as *the* cost of living, just as there is no such thing as *the* standard of living. Conceptions of what constitutes a reasonable standard of life (which obviously must be defined before the measurement of changes in its cost can be attempted) differ widely as between one person and another, and from year to year. What is nowadays regarded as bare subsistence, previous generations would have regarded as something approaching luxury. Similarly, one man may regard two cars as an essential element in his customary standard of life and will be sensitive to changes in their price, while another man may be quite indifferent if the price of cars is doubled or trebled.

Hence, what is frequently called the cost-of-living index is really something much more limited and well-defined. It is an index number which seeks to measure the average change in the retail prices of a representative sample of the goods and services purchased by a particular section of the community.

Three main issues are therefore raised in compiling such an index. First, the section of the community which is to be covered by it; secondly, the commodities to be included; thirdly, the weights to be attached to the various commodities. There has been a series of retail price index numbers in Britain since 1892, but it will be best to confine the discussion to the ways in which the current index, which was first published in January 1963, deals with these three questions.

The first question – that of the people whose cost of living is to be measured – is open to a fairly straightforward solution. The index is compiled by government statisticians, and the government is naturally concerned with the position of the majority rather than that of small groups. Hence, the current index is based on the expenditure of households whose head had a gross income (in 1953) of up to £30 a week, but excludes households mainly dependent on pensions or national assistance of some form. This means that the expenditures involved were representative of 9 out of 10 households in the country. Although the index cannot be said to measure changes in the cost of living for every single section of the community, therefore, it certainly takes account of the prices which are important to the vast majority.

The second problem is that of selecting the commodities to be included. By carrying out a survey of the expenditure of some 3 000 households throughout the year, a mass of information about consumption patterns is obtained. As has been observed already, it would be an enormous task to collect information about the prices of every type of every individual commodity involved, especially when it is wished to compute the index every month. To make the work manageable, therefore, total expenditure by these households was classified into ten broad groups; certain commodities were taken as being representative of each group, and certain types or brands were taken as being representative of each commodity. In the current index, therefore, the prices of all commodities entering into the budget of the average household are assumed to be accurately represented by the prices of 350 individual commodities of specified type or quality. That the range of expenditure covered by this group of 350 commodities is a very wide one may be deduced from the inclusion in it not only of obvious items such as bread, milk, meat and fish but commodities such as television sets, washing-machines, ice-cream, chocolate biscuits and telephone rentals.

There remains the third problem, that of the weights to be attached to the different commodities included in the index. Obviously it would be absurd to treat a rise of, say, 10 per cent in the price of chocolate biscuits as being equal in importance to a similar change in the price of bread, which is what would happen if the index was calculated by taking an arithmetical (i.e. unweighted) average of all the separate price indices. But on what basis should different weights be allotted to the various items? The method adopted is the allocation to each item within a group, and to each group in the index, a weight which reflects the share of total household expenditure devoted to it. For example, if the average household spends three times as much on bread each week as it does on chocolate biscuits, then three times as much weight would be attached to a change in the price of bread as to a change in the price of chocolate biscuits. The survey of the expenditures of 3 000 households therefore indicates not only the commodities to be covered by the index but also the relative importance to be attached to them.

If an index is to reflect accurately changes in the cost of things actually bought by the average household (as opposed to changes in the cost of an unvarying bundle of goods) obviously it will need to be revised periodically as new items of expenditure become popular and old ones drop out, and as the relative importance of the items changes with shifts in spending habits. How far consumption patterns can change may be seen from the following comparison between the relative importance attached to the main types of commodity in the index published in Britain between 1914 and 1947, and their relative importance in the current index.

Because of these constant changes in expenditure patterns, the current retail price index departs from previous British practice in that the items included, and the weights attached

	Weights used in index numbers (%)	
	1914 index	*1975 index*
Food	60·0	*23·2*
Alcohol and tobacco	0·8	*12·8*
Housing, fuel and light	24·0	*16·1*
Clothing	12·0	*8·9*
Durable household goods	0·5	*7·0*
Services and vehicles	1·2	*20·1*
Miscellaneous goods	1·5	*11·9*
Total	100·0	*100·0*

to them, are kept under constant review in the light of a continuing investigation of household expenditure. This has the advantage of ensuring that the prices included are the prices which matter to the average modern family, and are not those of a group of commodities which have ceased to represent the prevailing pattern of expenditure. It has the disadvantage that it is difficult to see in what sense the values of the index number at two widely-separated dates can be compared, because the selection of commodities entering into the index may be quite different at the two dates. However, provided that the comparisons attempted are over, say, three or four years (during which period the selection of commodities is almost bound to be *substantially* unchanged) and not thirty or forty years, this disadvantage will be more than offset by the advantage of having the index on a realistic base.

Apart from this, there are certain dangers inherent in index numbers of this kind if they are taken (as they often are) to measure changes in the cost of the prevailing standard of living. First, it is difficult to make allowance for changes in *quality* which may offset, or more than offset, changes in price. For example, the average television set may be 20 per cent dearer in 1975 than in 1970, but if the quality of the average television set has improved between those years the cost of a given standard of television consumption may have fallen rather than risen.

Secondly, the index may not always reflect changes in *taxation* and *social services*. If indirect taxes on consumption goods are increased, prices will rise and the index will rise with it, suggesting that a given money income has a smaller real value. If *income tax* is increased, however, a similar fall occurs in the ultimate purchasing power of a given money income, but the index will give no indication of this change. Conversely, the index will suggest no increase in the real value of a given income if certain services (e.g. health services) are provided free instead of at a charge, but the standard of life associated with any given income will undoubtedly have risen.

Finally, it must be remembered that index numbers of this kind can reflect the expenditure pattern only of *broad social groups*, within which there may be individual groups undergoing different experiences. For example, the retail price level may be constant for the average household, but the average household is, of necessity, something of an abstraction. Marked changes may be occurring in the prices of commodities of especial importance to particular groups – old-age pensioners, or families with small children, or professional classes. Substantial gains or hardships may therefore be concealed in an overall average.

Nevertheless, provided it is interpreted with care, the retail price index remains a useful device. It enables a broad impression of changes in the price level of consumers' goods as a whole to be formed, and such changes may be important symptoms of the forms of economic indigestion known as inflation and deflation. The index can give a guide to government agencies as to changes in the real value of pensions and grants, while a great many wage-agreements in Britain are related to the index of retail prices, so that workers do not have to renew wage negotiations every time the purchasing power of their wages is reduced by a rise in the general price level. Finally, the index enables comparisons to be made between the real purchasing power of wages and other incomes at different dates, and hence permits an assessment of the effects of given changes in economic policy without having the issue obscured by price movements.

4 OTHER INDEX NUMBERS

For the questions with which this book is concerned, the index number of greatest importance is the retail price index discussed in the preceding section, insofar as this can be used to measure changes in the general level of prices. Other kinds of index numbers may be of at least as much interest in certain connections as the retail price index however, and it is therefore worthwhile to examine briefly some of the other index numbers which attempt to indicate changes in various types of economic phenomena and which are published regularly in Britain.

Perhaps the most widely used single set of index-numbers is that concerning real national income, either in total or per head of the population. As was mentioned in the context of national income estimates, a series of totals of the monetary value of GNP over time can give a most misleading impression if due allowance is not made for changes in prices or the total population over which that national income has to be spread. The use of index numbers can go a long way towards avoiding these dangers. For example, the statistics of gross domestic product in the United Kingdom between 1960 and 1973 were as follows:

	1960	*1973*
GDP: £000 million	22·6	62·2
GDP: Index	100	274·5
Population: million	52·4	55·9
Population: Index	100	106·7
GDP per head: Index	100	257·3
Price index: GDP	100	190·5
GDP per head at 1960 prices	100	135·1

Thus, from an initial suggestion that GDP had risen by 175 per cent between 1960 and 1973, the use of appropriate index numbers enables the calculation that in real terms GDP per head rose over that period by only 35 per cent. The difference, to say the least, is not trivial.

To a producer, changes in his costs of production will be of as much importance as changes in the market value of his product. An index number of *wage-rates* or average earnings reflects movements in one major cost element, and also indicates the development of the most important source of spending-power in the community. The construction of such an index is basically similar to that of the index of retail prices. Instead of averaging the prices of different commodities, the wage-rates or weekly earnings of different types of labour are averaged; the weights attached to the individual wage-rates are based on the numbers in each labour-group. For some purposes, and certainly for that of examining movements in total personal incomes, an index of average *earnings* rather than wage-rates may be more illuminating, since it will take account of changes arising not only from adjustments in wage *rates* but also from changes in the amounts of overtime and bonuses. Both types of index number are published monthly, not only for the country as a whole but also for important industrial groups.

Another important cost element is that of the price of raw materials, and index numbers are published every month indicating movements in the *wholesale prices* of the various types of raw material used extensively in production. Similarly, monthly index numbers are published showing changes in the prices of the *output* of important industries which supply other industries with materials or semi-finished goods, and others measure changes in the average value of the goods which are *exports* from or *imports* into the country. As will be seen in Part VIII, changes in the relative prices of exports and imports can be of enormous importance to a country, such as Britain, which maintains a high level of international trade.

Apart from all these price indicators, monthly or quarterly index numbers are published which provide an indication of changes in *quantities* rather than prices. The most important of these is the monthly *index of industrial production*. A simple example of such an index was given earlier in this chapter; the official index of industrial production in the United Kingdom is a more complex version of this. Returns are sent to the official statisticians each month by a sample of firms which are representative of major industrial groups; these indicate the level of output produced by the firms concerned in the preceding month, output being measured usually in physical terms (tonnes of steel, pairs of shoes and so on). From these data, a weighted index number is computed for each industrial group, the weight attached to the output of each firm being based on its relative importance in the group's total output. (This is discovered from an examination of the findings of the Census of Production, a survey which was briefly described in Section 1 of Chapter XVIII.) Because the index of industrial production can be computed every month, it provides an extremely important indicator of current developments in a major segment of the national economy.

Other index numbers of a quantitative nature are published monthly or quarterly covering the physical volume (as distinct from the value) of imports and exports, the level of retail sales, volume of rail traffic and a great many other economic variables. Each represents a simple and useful guide to trends in different spheres of economic activity or over the economy as a whole. All of them have to be interpreted with care, since they are subject to statistical and other weaknesses which sometimes seriously qualify their significance.

FURTHER READING

W. BECKERMAN *An introduction to national income analysis* Chs. 8–9

R. MARRIS *Economic arithmetic* Macmillan, London 1958, Chs. 8–9

F. CONWAY *Descriptive statistics* Leicester University Press, Leicester 1963, Chs. 6–8

C. BLYTH *The use of economic statistics* Ch. 3

CHAPTER XXVIII

Macro-economic Policy

1 THE ROLE OF GOVERNMENT

IT has been a characteristic of all modern societies that the responsibilities which governments have taken upon themselves – or had thrust upon them – have steadily widened in both scope and degree. Nowhere is this more clearly seen than in the context of government involvement in the economic affairs of their countries and in the steady evolution of that involvement in the course of the last century.

If a British government had been asked to define its economic responsibilities at the end of the nineteenth century, the answer would almost certainly have been confined to the matter of laws aimed at the prevention of restraint of trade – what in modern jargon might be classed as anti-monopoly legislation. Given the contemporary commitment to the doctrine of *laissez-faire* – i.e. the maximum reliance on the free play of market forces – this would have amounted to saying that the aim of government policy was the preservation, or enhancement, of the *efficiency* of the economic system.

As the nineteenth century progressed into the twentieth, however, voices were increasingly to be heard protesting at the manifest brutalities and injustices created by an unhampered competitive system, and this began to find its effect in laws governing the employment of women and children, industrial injuries, the protection of employees in sweated industries and, from the time of the famous Lloyd George budget of 1910, provision for compulsory insurance against sickness and unemployment. Increasingly, therefore, governments have had to concern themselves with the *equity* of the system.

These two areas of economic policy – efficiency and equity –

remain very much the concern of modern governments. They belong to the category of micro-economics and in earlier parts of this book they have been encountered in the contexts of monopoly control, progressive taxes and so on. As the twentieth century has proceeded, however, two major areas of macro-economic policy have become increasingly important and it is with these that this chapter is primarily concerned.

The first of these is the *stability* of the economy. Under the practical influence of the appalling wastages of the great depression during the inter-war years and the intellectual influence of the work of Keynes in the 1930s, governments have come to accept a responsibility for the avoidance of periodic disturbances of a macro-economic kind; until fairly recently this responsibility would have been defined primarily in terms of the stability of output and employment in the economy and the avoidance of depression; more recently, emphasis has shifted to the stability of prices and the avoidance of inflation. As will be seen, the two aspects of the stability criterion are closely related.

The second macro-economic policy aim which has received increasing attention is the maintenance – and, in the case of Britain, the raising – of the overall rate of *growth*. Here the government is concerned not with the efficiency, equity or stability of the economy at one point of time but with its rate of expansion over a period of years.

To these four internal aims of economic policy, two micro and two macro, has to be added a fifth policy aim of fundamental importance to an economy like that of Britain which is highly dependent on foreign trade – the maintenance of equilibrium in the *balance of payments* with the outside world. The discussion of this will be left over until the treatment of international economics in Part VIII.

The complexity of economic policy is thus clear enough. It is not merely a matter of there being several sorts of objective which a government is seeking to attain at any given moment. More important is the hard fact that more often than not these policy objectives are in conflict with one another. The pursuit of equity through sharply progressive taxation might be held to compromise the efficient allocation of time as between work and leisure; the maintenance of stability in output and employment may well make the maintenance of stability of prices more difficult; an acceleration in the internal rate of growth could compromise the state of the balance of payments; and so on. This is merely to reiterate a fundamental point made earlier: economic choices can never be stated in absolute terms but only in terms of alternatives foregone in one area in order to secure aims in another. The world of economic policy-making is a world of trade-offs, a balancing of advantages secured in one respect at the expense of losses in another.

In the last resort, therefore, policy-making under any of the five heads listed above must ultimately be a matter of politics, not economics. Economic analysis can seek to understand the alternative ways in which policy aims may be attained and, with any luck, the extent to which those aims may be achieved with the acceptance of given losses under the heading of competing aims. But economic analysis stops there; the question of whether, say, a given reduction in the inequality of the distribution of income is or is not *worth*, say, a given reduction in the rate of economic growth over the next n years is not one for which economics can provide an answer. The political decision-makers must themselves balance gains in one policy direction against losses in another according to such criteria as they can muster. The function of economics is to provide the information from which that assessment can proceed; that in itself, as it happens, is an immensely difficult task in our present state of knowledge.

2 STABILITY: MAINTAINING FULL EMPLOYMENT

The analysis of preceding chapters has established certain things about the determination of the level of output and employment in an economy at any moment of time. First, that in the short run when the state of technology and the capital stock of the economy may be assumed to be fixed within narrow limits, the level of employment will be determined by the level of output which entrepreneurs collectively are willing to produce. Second, that these decisions concerning output will depend primarily on the revenues expected to be brought in from the sale of current output and that these in turn will depend on the level of aggregate demand in the market. Third, that aggregate demand can be expected to rise as output increases, although not necessarily as rapidly, and that aggregate output will tend to approach that point at which the aggregate demand schedule intersects the aggregate supply curve. In principle, therefore, given the level of output which corresponds to full employment, government can always ensure that it is attained by so manipulating aggregate demand as to ensure that it neither exceeds nor falls short of the desired level of output. How can the government do this in practice?

The first main policy weapon is that of monetary policy. As was seen in Chapter XXIV, the Central Bank, acting under the guidance of the Treasury or other government authorities, can exert considerable influence over the availability and cost of credit, and this in turn will influence the rate of investment in the manner indicated in Chapter XXV; in so far as consumer expenditure is dependent on borrowed funds this element of aggregate demand may also be susceptible to movements upwards or downwards as the authorities believe appropriate. How effective this policy weapon is in practice is a matter open to considerable dispute. On the one hand, the evidence of history suggests that on many occasions the authorities have not enjoyed in practice the complete control over the money supply which purely theoretical considerations might impute to them; this matter has been discussed at some length in Chapter XXIV and so need not be pursued here.

Secondly, however, considerable doubts exist as to the likely effect of changes in interest rates on investment or consumer decisions even if the authorities are able to achieve such changes. For most industries, after all, capital charges are a relatively small fraction of total costs; in British manufacturing industry in 1972, for example, an annual charge of 15 per cent on capital stock would have amounted to about 12 per cent of total manufacturing costs. A rise of as much as a third, from 15 to 20 per cent, in this rate of charge would still have added something less than 4 per cent to total costs. Set against the fairly wide range of uncertainty which must inevitably be associated with entrepreneurs' expectations of future revenues, it is not surprising that the evidence suggests a rather low elasticity of investment decisions with respect to interest rates. This must be especially the case when the general price-level is steadily rising; a man who pays 10 per cent on the mortgage of a house whose value appreciates 8 per cent a year is in fact paying a *real* rate of interest of only 2 per cent per annum.

This is not to suggest that monetary policy is totally useless in the regulation of demand; both common sense and empirical evidence suggest that a change in the availability of funds, as opposed to their cost, is bound to influence investment decisions. However optimistic an entrepreneur may be, if he cannot get hold of funds to finance his project his optimism will avail him nothing. Similarly, a consumer relying on hire-purchase credit may be prepared to put up with higher interest rates (especially as he is seldom aware of the interest rate he is in fact paying) but will be forcibly restrained if he simply cannot get credit at all. The ultimate power of monetary restriction is thus beyond question; of necessity the powers of monetary *expansion*, which merely permits extra borrowing but certainly cannot compel it, are more dubious.

The main weapon employed by governments in the influencing of the level of output and employment, however, is that of fiscal policy – the use of the annual budget to influence the level of activity. The budget may achieve this end in one or all of three ways. First, as was shown in Chapter XX above, the Government's own expenditure on goods and services – such as that on defence, public administration, health services and education – is a significant element in aggregate demand, and by varying this expenditure the Government may be able to offset tendencies in private expenditure. In a period when aggregate demand shows signs of slackening, for example, the deflationary tendency could be prevented by a rise in government purchases of goods and services; conversely, in inflationary periods a reduction in government expenditure could ease the pressure of demand. This type of approach is illustrated in Fig. 28A, which shows the familiar aggregate demand schedule and the equilibrium point of intersection with the 45 degree line. Now, however, the aggregate demand schedule comprises three elements – government expenditure on goods and services, G, being added to consumption and investment expenditure. Suppose that in the initial situation aggregate demand calls forth an output, Y, which falls short of the output, $\bar{Y}$, at which the labour force would be fully employed. If government expenditure is now raised to G', all other things being equal, the aggregate demand schedule is shifted bodily upwards to $C + I + G'$ and the intersection with the 45 degree line indicates that the required level of output $\bar{Y}$ will be achieved.

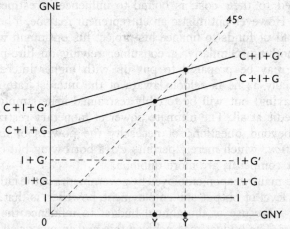

Fig. 28A	Government spending and full employment

The point may be expressed in the simple algebra of income determination. If government expenditure is denoted by G, national income is defined by

$$Y = C + I + G$$
$$= cY + I + G.$$

Hence				$$Y - cY = I + G$$

and				$$Y = \frac{I + G}{1 - c}.$$

Given a target level of Y, therefore, and assuming I and c to be fixed, the necessary level of government spending can be determined.

Once again the process is easier in theory than in practice, however; the greater part of government expenditure is determined by political considerations and is not easily varied from year to year. Defence expenditure, for example, has to be undertaken when it appears necessary rather than when it happens to be convenient from the point of view of aggregate demand; houses and schools and hospitals cannot be shelved indefinitely against the possibility that overall demand may become inadequate at some unknown future date. Similar considerations would apply to the investment expenditures of nationalised industries. In theory at any rate, these could be controlled by the Government so as to offset undesirable movements in private investment expenditure, but in practice the timing of capital investment is frequently dictated by the current needs of the industries concerned.

The second element of fiscal policy which can play a stabilising role is that of taxation. The rate of investment may be influenced to some extent by tax allowances on capital expenditure, or by a differential rate of profits tax favouring undistributed ('ploughed-back') profits in comparison with distributed profits. Consumers' expenditure may be influenced by changes in the rate of Value Added Tax or in income tax since consumers' expenditure tends to be governed by the level of *disposable* income (i.e. income after tax) rather than nominal gross income. Such changes will have an important bearing on the multiplier. Thus, let consumption be related to income after tax, and let the rate of tax be assumed to be, for the sake of simplicity, a constant proportion, t, of income; then

$$C = c(Y - tY)$$

and the income-determination equation becomes

$$Y = c(Y - tY) + I + G$$
$$= cY - ctY + I + G$$

and
$$Y - cY + ctY = I + G$$

i.e.
$$Y = \frac{I + G}{1 - c + ct}.$$

If the marginal propensity to consume is 0·8 and t is initially 10 per cent the multiplier becomes

$$\frac{1}{1-0\cdot8+0\cdot08} = 3\cdot57$$

and if $I + G = £400$ million, equilibrium national income would be about £1 430 million. Suppose that this exceeds the level necessary to generate full employment and the rate of taxation, t, is increased to 20 per cent. The multiplier would become

$$\frac{1}{1-0\cdot8+0\cdot16} = 2\cdot78$$

and the national income would tend to fall back to around £1 110 million.

It is clear, then, that both sides of the budget have a part to play in stabilisation policy and the important concept in this context is that of the overall surplus or deficit attained through the budget. In times of excess pressure on the capacity of the economy, a Chancellor of the Exchequer can 'mop up' large amounts of income by adjusting Government revenue and expenditure so as to secure a surplus of receipts over expenditures. If on balance the taxpayers of a country are paying over to the Government in the form of taxation substantially more than is being paid out by the Government through purchases of goods and services or transfer payments, the budget is obviously exerting a braking influence on the economy. When the economy is threatening to move away from the full employment position, therefore, the budget can be used in the wider context of overall economic stability, rather than in the traditional, and narrower, context of the mere raising of sufficient revenue to finance government expenditure. In times of excess pressure, a budget surplus would be desirable, since it will on balance reduce incomes and therefore demand; in the opposite situation, a budget deficit could be aimed at in order to augment the general level of incomes and so stimulate demand.

The modern budget, then, must be framed in a much wider context than was usual before 1939; in drawing it up, the Chancellor must have an eye to the overall economic situation rather than simply the current needs of the Government itself. Because of this, the budget cannot be judged on the same basis as that appropriate to the income and expenditure accounts of a private person or company. Private individuals cannot increase their own incomes by spending more than they are currently earning; if pursued for any length of time, indeed, such a course can lead only to disaster. Governments, however, are in a different position; by spending more than they are currently receiving from taxation they can play an important part in raising the overall level of incomes and thereby the output of the economy as a whole; this in turn would react back on their own income from tax receipts.

If the general level of prices could be assumed stable the discussion could be allowed to rest there; changes in the level of income would correspond to changes in the level of real output and thus of employment. Control over the target variable, the national income, would still be an exceedingly complex and difficult problem in practice but at least the variable itself would be a reasonably unambiguous concept. Unfortunately the general price level is not so well-behaved an element in the situation and a rise in national income may consist partly – or even wholly – of a change in the prices of goods and services rather than the quantity of them being produced. And that in itself is a problem to which the discussion must now turn.

3   THE PHENOMENON OF INFLATION

In the early 1960s the retail price index in Britain was typically rising by around 3 per cent a year; in the three years 1968–70 the average increase rose sharply to around $5\frac{1}{2}$ per cent a year; in the next four years it rose even further to something over 10 per cent a year. This sudden quickening in the rate of change of prices was by no means confined to the United Kingdom – it was in fact an international phenomenon – but proceeded rather further and faster in Britain than in most other countries. The problem of inflation – loosely defined to mean a sustained rise in the general price level of unacceptable magnitude – had suddenly become a major concern of macro-economic policy if not, indeed, the major one. The first question which must be posed is: *why* such concern? Why is a price level rising at 9 or 10 per cent per annum a *problem*?

The first and most extreme answer to this question is that the process of inflation (or, for that matter, its opposite – deflation) contains within itself inherent tendencies to become cumulative and for the rate of increase of prices to accelerate until the process moves out of human control and becomes hyper-inflation. The end result of this can only be a total collapse of the monetary unit of the country concerned. After some critical point a continuing rise in the general price-level – i.e. a continuing fall in the value of money – must inevitably undermine public confidence in the national currency and it has been emphasised earlier that public confidence is the one ingredient which money *must* have if it is to continue to function as money. If a situation develops which is such that money held for any length of time loses a substantial part of its real value, ultimately no one will be willing to accept money in return for goods, and this must involve the collapse of a specialised economy resting on the basis of monetary exchanges. Such a collapse of the economic system did in fact result from runaway inflation in Germany in the early 1920s and in several European countries (for example Hungary) in the years immediately after the Second World War. The social consequences of such a collapse are very far-reaching and seldom pleasant. The assertion that 'it can't happen here' is an inadequate response to such a danger.

This is admittedly the extreme case. Even without anticipating a degeneration to this type of situation, however, there are plenty of reasons why inflation is regarded as something best avoided. An obvious one is that an inflationary situation is one in which different groups in society seek to attain increases in their money incomes to compensate them for the loss of real income involved in a general rise of prices and the degree of success they attain in doing so will have little or no relationship to social justice – in other words, a rather haphazard redistribution of income occurs. Some groups are more highly organised or more aggressively led than others – or more able (or willing) to inflict hardship on the rest of the community in order to secure their ends; some producers weigh higher profit-margins more heavily against the needs of consumers than others; some incomes, of their nature, can be adjusted only after delays and with difficulty, whether they be pensions or rents or family allowances. In the jungle atmosphere engendered by an inflationary scramble it is seldom the poorest or weakest who come out on top.

Other dangers are involved. A rise in the general price level in excess of world trends may result in a country's exports being priced out of foreign markets and in a rapid rise of imports sucked in by the excess monetary demand; such a combination of events could well be a serious development for a country like the United Kingdom which is highly dependent on foreign trade. Efficiency also tends to decline in a period of rising prices; entrepreneurs have little incentive to hold down costs firmly if their profits are being boosted by rising prices. Nor are the social frictions and wastages involved in frequent re-negotiation of wage and salary agreements or other contractual arrangements to be lightly disregarded.

The social and economic dangers of the phenomenon are thus clear enough. What are its causes? In the strictly technical sense this question is easy enough to answer: in the more profound sense of identifying reliable remedies, unfortunately, it is very difficult indeed. As was noted in the discussion of aggregate demand and supply in Chapter XXV, just as the price of an individual product is the outcome of the interaction of demand and supply, so the general price level in any economy is determined by the relationship between its aggregate demand and supply functions. If the general price level is increasing, therefore, the cause must lie in a shift of one or other function or in both. The significance of the last three words cannot be overstressed.

Until relatively recently the stress in the analysis of inflation would have been on the side of the aggregate demand function. The aggregate supply curve in Fig. 28B would have been taken as more or less fixed by the state of technology, the stock of capital and so on. Inflation – that is, an upward swing in the price-line OX_1 – could be generated, therefore, only by an upward shift in the aggregate demand curve such as that from *AD* to *AD'* in Fig. 28B. The results would be the classic symptoms of inflation: a sharp rise in prices and little or no movement along the real output axis. The remedy would be equally clear – a downward shift in the aggregate demand schedule through the instruments of monetary and fiscal policy discussed in the preceding section until the price level was restored to OX_1.

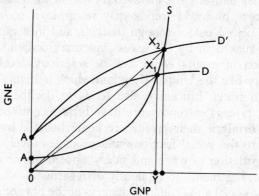

Fig. 28B Demand inflation

The experience of the 1960s showed beyond doubt, however, that this tacit assumption of stability in the aggregate supply schedule was manifestly unsound. Shifts in the schedule caused by real factors – i.e. changing technology or capital stock – are indeed unlikely to be sudden or violent. But shifts can also occur because of purely *monetary* forces – that is, changes in the prices of inputs which affect the total cost of producing any given output and therefore the total market revenue necessary to sustain that output. Upward pressure on wages is the most obvious type of influence having this effect but adjustments in profit margins or changes in raw material prices could have a similar effect.

A second tacit assumption was demolished by the same experience – that is, the assumption of independence between the two aggregate curves. As can be seen from Fig. 28C, if the aggregate demand schedule remained at *AD*, an upward shift in the aggregate supply curve caused by, say, trade union pressure for higher wages, from *AS* to *AS'*, would have resulted in a significant fall in output – and thus in employment – rather than a marked rise in prices. The new equilibrium point would be X_2, at which the price level would have risen somewhat from OX_1 to OX_2 but the main consequence would have been the fall in output from $\bar{Y}$ to Y_1. Indeed, the implicit assumption would have been that this fall in output, and the associated fall in employment, would have acted as a deterrent to the unions so that the pressure for increases in wages would have been reduced, if not eliminated altogether.

The aggregate demand curve would not in fact have remained fixed at *AD*, however. The extra money wages or profits underlying the original shift in aggregate supply would result, if granted, in additional consumer or investment expenditure. The shift in the supply curve from *AS* to *AS'*, in other words would generate a corresponding shift in the demand curve from *AD* to *AD'*; the outcome would be a marked rise in the price level, to OX_3, and little if any decline in employment. Indeed, if the authorities felt that *any* significant fall in the level of employment was politically unacceptable they might find themselves forced to adopt fiscal and/or monetary policies designed to prevent it – the aggregate demand curve would be

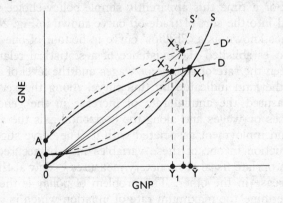

Fig. 28C   Cost inflation

pushed up even further so as to 'validate' the upward shift in the supply curve, leaving employment unchanged but the price level even higher. What, if anything, could the authorities do about it all?

4 INFLATION POLICY

So long as inflation was seen as essentially a matter of excess demand (whether that excess demand originated in, on the one hand, independent shifts in consumption, investment or government expenditure, or, on the other, was transmitted from upward movements in the supply curve) the policy trade-off involved, even if a cruel one, was relatively straightforward. With any given aggregate supply curve there must be *some* level of aggregate demand which would leave the general price-level unchanged from some previous point of time or within some defined margin of it, although the maintenance of this target price-level would inevitably involve some reduction in potential output and therefore in the level of employment. Conversely, if some defined level of employment were taken as the policy target then there would be *some* level of aggregate demand which would attain it, given the current aggregate supply curve; whatever rate of change of prices was implied by this would then have to be accepted.

For a time this apparently simple policy-choice was formalised into the sort of trade-off curve shown in Fig. 28D – sometimes known as a 'Phillips' curve in honour of one investigator who established the existence of a statistical relationship between the rate of change of wages and the level of employment of the kind indicated by this curve. Along the vertical axis is measured the annual rate of increase in the general level of prices or wages and along the horizontal axis the average level of unemployment associated with it. The curve suggests that a reduction in one of these variables may be secured – through appropriate fiscal or monetary measures – only at the cost of an increase in the other. The problem of policy is then simply to determine the maximum rate of inflation which is acceptable – say R_1 – and the level of unemployment which emerges, U_1, will then have to be generated in order to secure it. Alternatively, a target level of unemployment may be selected, say U_2, and the corresponding rate of inflation, R_2, accepted as the necessary social cost of attaining it.

Despite its attractive simplicity – which still retains for it some intellectual adherents – this hypothesis has not stood the empirical test of experience. In the late 1960s and early 1970s, in fact, an accelerating rate of inflation was associated with increasing unemployment, a combination quite the reverse of that predicted by Fig. 28D – although one which Fig. 28C shows to be quite conceivable. The inter-relationship between aggregate demand and aggregate supply proved to be even more complex than had been realised. Not only did a shift in aggregate supply react on aggregate demand in the way mentioned in the previous section; attempts to shift aggregate demand also reacted back on aggregate supply. That is to say, increases in taxation designed to reduce aggregate demand had the effect of engendering even higher wage claims as labour sought to avoid, or recover, the loss of real income which they involved.

Quite clearly the basic forces underlying the modern cost-inflation phenomenon are very much more deep-seated and fundamental than the mere technical relationship between sums of money appearing on one side of the equation as costs of production and on the other as contributors to aggregate demand. The process is essentially an argument about the distribution of income within society, with various groups seeking

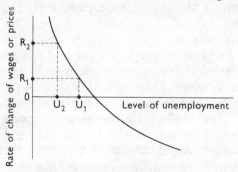

Fig. 28D   The Phillips curve

to attain or recover what are conceived by them to be appropriate and just levels of real income. The marginal productivity theory is a reasonable enough first approximation to an explanation of income distribution at the micro level – that is, of the long-run forces operating on *relative* earnings in different industries – precisely because at that level the independence of demand and supply curves is a reasonable enough assumption. At the macro level, cutting across all products and all industries, such an assumption becomes indefensible.

This is the fundamental social change which has been induced by the attainment of a continuously high level of employment in all Western economies in recent decades. Until the post-war era, the threat of unemployment was in the last resort the ultimate sanction behind the distributive mechanism at the macro level, determining the overall level of wages and profits and the relative shares enjoyed by broad groups of occupations and activities. The substantial removal of that threat – and the much-reduced consequences of such unemployment as remains – has simultaneously removed an essential ingredient in the income-distribution mechanism operating over the many decades for which Phillips was able to establish the empirical relationship embodied in Fig. 28D. This, and the associated immense growth in the power of organised labour in most sectors of the economy, underlies the contemporary problem of cost inflation. It is hardly surprising that reliance on the traditional weapons of fiscal and monetary policy has failed to come to grips with what is essentially a political and social phenomenon.

What measures *can* the authorities adopt, then, if annual changes in the price level of 8 or 9 per cent upwards – and the other wastages and frictions associated with them – are considered unacceptable? There is at this point of time no agreed answer to this question and it is no part of the function of a textbook of this kind to air contentious propositions. Two broad views may be summarised. On the one hand it is argued that the phenomenon of inflation, whatever its underlying and ultimate cause, is essentially a monetary one in the sense that continuous increases in costs, whatever their motivation, could simply not be sustained if the total stock of money were kept under strict control. If the hypothesis of a stable and predictable relationship between the stock of money and the level of income postulated in Chapter XXIII is accepted, the rise in the money value of national income from year to year cannot be greater than that permitted by the growth in the supply of active balances. Since the major cause of the growth in the stock of money in recent years has been excessive borrowing by government directly or indirectly through the banking system, the argument proceeds, the remedy lies in confining government spending, current and capital, within current receipts, restricting the growth in the money supply to the level justified only by genuine increases in real productivity and thus preventing inflationary cost increases through sheer lack of money balances with which enterprises can pay them. The efficacy of such a policy, and its probable consequences in the form of unemployment when the monetary brake is first applied, are of course matters of dispute. The evidence on the matter is, to say the least, scanty and ambiguous.

The money-stock approach to the problem of inflation is basically characteristic of those whose philosophical commitment is to the free operation of the market system and a minimising of direct government interference with it. The opposite approach to the problem is associated with those whose belief is that at the macro-economic level the market system simply cannot cope with the conflict between a state of relatively full employment on the one hand and an unrestricted system of free collective bargaining by an organised and powerful labour force on the other. As has been argued earlier, the combination of these two features destroys the independence of demand and supply schedules which is the essential ingredient of the free market system. Unless substantial levels of unemployment are to be contemplated, then, the argument runs, some restraints must be applied to the determination of money wages and prices by free collective bargaining and price-fixing by individual entrepreneurs in order to prevent the continuous and accelerating escalation of the price level. Ideally, the increases in wages and other money costs should be kept within reasonable distance of the annual growth in the real productive capacity of the economy.

The means adopted to impose these restraints – usually referred to as an 'incomes policy' – have varied in nature from country to country and time to time from purely voluntary agreements between the leaders of both sides of industry to statutory limitations on permitted increases in wages and prices administered by official prices and income boards. It must be admitted that while some temporary successes have been attained by such devices in slowing down the pace of inflation, no country has yet demonstrated that a permanent solution can be attained in this fashion. The enforcement of controls over hundreds of thousands of separate wage agreements and price decisions *without the willing consent and co-operation of the overwhelming majority* would imply a network of enforcement agencies unknown in democratic societies where governments have to survive the next general election.

Nor would a mere restriction within a given percentage increase, even if attainable, go to the root of the problem – which is, it was argued earlier, the breakdown of the traditional mechanism of income distribution in society as a whole and the failure of society to establish some systematic and workable alternative. In a dynamic economy change is inevitable and with it relativities must alter – between the demand for and productivity of different categories of worker, the prosperity and needs of different social classes or age-groups, the growth of different regions and so on. Without some flexible framework within which these adjustments can occur, distortions will inevitably develop in the economic system which ultimately impose an intolerable load on the agreed or statutory structure.

5 ECONOMIC GROWTH

If the productive capacity of an economy is maintained at or near full employment, the total output of that economy is fixed within narrow limits. If the standard of living of that economy *as a whole* is to continue to rise, therefore – and human aspirations for the standard of living have throughout history tended to outrun existing capabilities – a steady expansion of the productive potential of the economy must somehow be attained. This is possible under one or both of two heads – and they are in fact mutually connected: either the capital capacity per head of population must rise or the state of technology must be pushed forward so that increased output is derived from any given set of inputs. This is the policy aim of an increased rate of economic growth.

It should be emphasised that economic growth – the augmentation of the volume of output secured per unit of input – is not synonymous with a growth in the total volume of physical production, an assumption often made implicitly by groups deeply concerned with the quality of the human environment. Increasing productive potential permits one of two alternatives – increasing the total output of a given working population or maintaining a constant output with a reduced input of labour. Economic growth may be utilised, in other words, to secure increased leisure or better working conditions or increased education or any one of a large number of improvements in the human condition. Conventional national income accounts may therefore be a poor guide to the rate of economic growth precisely because they rely on the measurable.

It must be admitted that rather little is understood about the forces which govern the rate of growth of one country in comparison with another or of the same country over different periods of time. Complaints are frequently made that the rate of growth in the postwar British economy has been disappointingly low. Compared with other major industrial countries this is true; during the decade of the 1960s, for example, the average annual growth rate of the British economy was about 2·7 per cent, compared with about 4·7 per cent for Germany, 5·6 per cent for France, 5·7 per cent for Italy and a phenomenal 11·3 per cent for Japan. Yet judged against its own historical standards the British economy was growing at a very high rate indeed over that decade – almost certainly a record rate for any decade over which the historical statistics run. And the danger of identifying economic growth with the expansion of components in conventional national income estimates must again be emphasised. Nevertheless, official policy is to increase the British growth rate to something nearer the 4·5 per cent level averaged in Europe in recent years. How can this be done?

The first element in increased capacity – the capital stock – is fairly straightforward. The rate of new capital formation in British industry has certainly tended to be lower than that in European industrial countries and this has clearly contributed to Britain's lower growth rate – partly because the British worker has less machine-power at his elbow and partly because it is through new capital investment that the latest technology is actually transmitted to the shop floor. The remedy is clear: the allocation of a greater share of the national income to productive investment than in the past. Immediately the costs of economic growth become clear. A greater share of the national income for productive investment necessarily implies a smaller share for something else – consumers' expenditure, government expenditure or other 'non-productive' capital formation such as new hospitals or schools. Similar conflicts may be generated by the measures necessary to obtain the switch of resources into capital formation. Since investment is financed mainly from profits, the taxation system must be used to favour profits, or at least that part of profit reinvested in industry. This may very likely conflict with the equity function of the tax system or with the requirements of an incomes policy. The trade-off problem with this aim of economic policy is as inescapable as with any other.

The second element in the raising of productive potential is the improvement of technology and of output-per-unit-of-input industry by industry. Here the problems are deep, complex and very imperfectly understood. In so far as the rate of capital formation is increased progress in this direction is to some extent assured; as was just noted, new capital is usually automatically a transmitter of new technology. Over and above this, however, the rate at which advances in the industrial arts are perceived by entrepreneurs, applied by them and accepted by their labour force is a function of a vast range of psychological, social and even political factors. Change is seldom easy or pleasant; the natural human instinct is to resist it and cling to the status quo.

British management is frequently criticised for its apparent lack of enthusiasm for research and development, its inability to keep up with and adopt improved technology in the outside world and its ineptness in applying such innovations as are adopted. British labour is criticised equally often for its dedication to traditional methods and hours of work, its proneness to fierce demarcation lines between a large number of different unions represented in the same factory, and its inborne hostility to management and any suggestion emanating from it.

These criticisms are almost certainly badly overdone and even more certainly thin on empirical foundation. They are doubtless voiced in practically every industrial country, occasionally perhaps with complimentary references to how much better these things are done in Britain. But the fact that resistance to and suspicion of the forces of technological change are strong and deep-seated on both sides of industry is too plain to deny. As societies get older and richer the commitment to stability and equity tends to grow much more rapidly than the commitment to increasing wealth. It is in no sense clear that a society which gives priority to stability and the quiet life rather than to higher per capita consumption of goods and services is irrational or wrong. Equally it is clear that if a society demands additional facilities for itself – whether they be new hospitals, an improved environment or better housing or colour television and two cars in every home – which can only come from a faster rate of economic growth, it cannot simultaneously refuse to accept the costs which that increased growth inevitably imposes. The fundamental truth of all economic policy remains: no society can both eat its cake and have it.

FURTHER READING

G. ACKLEY *Macro-economic theory* Chs. 16 and 18

T. F. DERNBERG and D. M. McDOUGALL *Macro-economics* Chs. 19–21

G. K. SHAW *An introduction to the theory of macro-economic policy* Chs. 1, 5 and 6

D. C. ROWAN *Output, inflation and growth* Chs. 17 and 19–25

L. C. HUNTER and D. J. ROBERTSON *Economics of wages and labour* Chs. 20–21

PART VIII

INTERNATIONAL ECONOMICS

CHAPTER XXIX

The Significance of
International Trade

1 THE LAW OF COMPARATIVE COSTS

JUST as a modern economy is based upon internal specialisation, so the world as a whole has tended towards international specialisation as economic life has developed and expanded. Few countries aim at supplying all their needs directly from the productive activities of their own citizens. To some extent this is because self-sufficiency is seldom possible; apart from this, however, it is clear that even if it were possible it would not be to the best advantage of the countries concerned. Resources, human and material, are unevenly distributed over the face of the globe, just as talents and abilities are unevenly distributed amongst the population of any given country. Some countries are endowed with a climate favourable to agricultural production, some are not; some have vast mineral resources, others have none; some have an abundant supply of skilled labour, others suffer from a shortage of it. If resources were fully mobile, of course, they would all tend to gravitate to that region in which their combined efficiency was greatest. While factors are relatively immobile within single countries, however, their international mobility is infinitely smaller. As a result, the cost of producing any particular commodity will vary widely from one country to another, according to the supply in the different countries of the resources required in its production. Hence, it will be to the mutual advantage of all concerned that each commodity should be produced in those areas best suited to its production, and that the different areas should exchange products with one another.

International trade does not develop solely because a country is more efficient than others in the production of some commodities and less efficient in producing other commodities. If this were the sole justification of international trade, it would be impossible to explain the foreign trade of many countries which in fact export to and import from others with vastly different levels of productivity; many countries can produce *all* the commodities they consume more efficiently than any of the others with which they in fact conduct trade. Why should this be so? Why should any country import from abroad goods which it could itself produce at a lower cost?

The explanation of this phenomenon is usually formalised in what is known as the *law of comparative costs*, which states that countries will derive mutual benefit from trading with one another so long as there is some difference in their *relative* efficiencies in the production of the commodities concerned. What this means is that trade will be beneficial, despite the overall productive superiority of some countries, if it enables the more efficient countries to concentrate on the production of goods in which their superiority is especially great, importing from the rest of the world the commodities in which their productive superiority is less marked. There is here an exact analogy with the division of labour. If a man is both a first-rate musician and a first-rate motor-mechanic, it will profit him to leave the repair of his car to a professional mechanic, even though this involves the use of more time and materials than he would have used if he had done the job himself. The reason is, of course, that by devoting the time to music he can earn more than enough to pay even the relatively high cost of having his car repaired. Similarly, a country with especially great efficiency in certain types of production will earn more than enough by concentrating on those lines to repay the extra cost of importing goods which it could have made itself rather more cheaply than its foreign suppliers.

An example may help to make this clear. Consider a hypothetical world in which there are only two countries, A and B, and only two commodities which will be called loaves and machines. Taking the simplest situation first, suppose that A is able to produce 20 loaves or 5 machines with the same composite bundle of given amounts of all factors of production, and that B is able to produce with another given bundle of inputs either 18 loaves or 6 machines. Now suppose for the moment that constant costs prevail for each industry in both countries. Putting nine units of this input bundle to use, A could then produce 180 loaves or 45 machines while with ten units of its input bundle B could produce 180 loaves or 60 machines. The opportunity cost of 180 loaves is thus 60 machines in B but only 45 machines in A. Country A thus has a *comparative* advantage in the production of loaves.

These production possibilities are shown by the lines PA and PB in Fig. 29A; for each country they show the range of possibilities open, from 180 loaves and no machines in both to 45 machines and no loaves in A or 60 machines and no loaves in B. Any combination of outputs lying on the line is feasible for the country concerned but any combination on the right-hand side of it is beyond its technical reach. If no trade between countries existed, therefore, the line would denote a frontier of production limiting total output and thus total consumption.

Now suppose that trade becomes possible between the two countries and that transport costs can be neglected. If Country A wishes to consume, say, 60 loaves and use the rest of its resources to acquire machines two possibilities are now open. It can itself produce the machines, and the production-possibility line PA reveals that if it produces 60 loaves at point X_1 then it can also produce 30 machines. On the other hand it can use all its resources in the production of loaves, turning out 180, retain 60 of them and trade the remaining 120 with B against machines. What will be the outcome? Two extremes can be established. Country A may be able to extract the maximum number of machines B would be willing to part with in return for 120 loaves. Point X_3 on B's production-possibility line shows that this will be 40, since if B produced 120 loaves itself its production of machines would have to fall from the maximum of 60 to a total of 20. If trade takes place on these terms, then, the final outcome will be as follows.

	Loaves	*Machines*
A	60	40
B	120	20

Obviously, through trade A has managed to reach a combination of products beyond its own potential and B is neither worse off nor better off than if trade had not existed. Of course, the opposite may happen: B may ask, what is the minimum number of machines we need to part with in order to induce A to let us have 120 loaves? The answer will of course be 30;

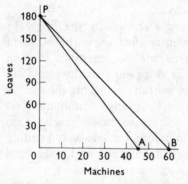

Fig. 29A   Production possibility lines

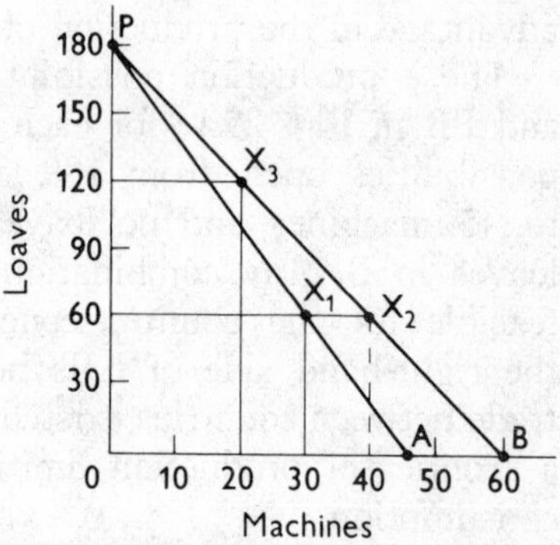

Fig. 29B   The gains from trade-constant costs

if A were offered less than this it would prefer to resort to domestic production of machines at point X_1. If it accepts 30 machines, A is neither worse off nor better off and all the benefit goes to B, which ends up with 120 loaves and 30 machines — a combination beyond its own potential internally. Needless to say, the rate of exchange — *the terms of trade* — is likely to be somewhere between these extremes and the benefits of trade will be felt by each partner.

Under conditions of constant costs, then, trade is bound to be beneficial to at least one participant — and usually to both — so long as the *comparative* costs of the products concerned differ in the two countries involved. In terms of Fig. 29B, advantage must accrue if the production-possibility lines do not coincide; given this, each country will specialise entirely on its most efficient activity and obtain other commodities solely through trade. Note that the *absolute* costs of the products are irrelevant to this conclusion: the absolute costs of both loaves and machines could be twice or three times as high in A as in B without affecting the analysis at all.

The assumption of constant costs can now be removed. This however requires an analysis of how relative prices are determined before and after trade. In the constant-cost case no problem arose: by definition relative marginal costs were constant at all levels of output and if a competitive situation is assumed relative prices could be identified with relative marginal costs. Dropping the assumption of constant costs eliminates this simplicity; relative marginal costs, and thus relative prices, will now depend on what output levels are attained for each product.

The two diagrams of Fig. 29C may help to resolve this problem. The curves $T_a T'_a$ and $T_b T'_b$ represent the production possibility curves, or *transformation* curves, in countries A and B respectively for two products X and Y. Their slopes are similar – both being concave to the origin – and indicate increasing-cost conditions. As the output of Y is expanded in either country increasing quantities of X have to be sacrificed, and *vice versa*. They are not identical, however, because comparative costs are assumed to be different in the two countries. In the absence of trade, each country will be seeking to maximise its welfare from its own production, so that if a social-indifference-curve map is superimposed on the transformation curves – the I_a and I_b curves – the point of maximum welfare will be identified. It will be that point at which the highest possible indifference curve is reached – Q_a for country A and Q_b for country B. Just as the individual consumer maximises his welfare at the point of tangency between his budget line and the highest attainable indifference curve, so a community maximises its welfare with that output defined by the tangency between the society's budget line – its transformation curve – and the highest attainable social indifference curve.

Relative prices must therefore be determined by the slopes

of the two curves at this point of common tangency – P_aP_a' in A and P_bP_b' in B; they will differ between the two countries, of course, because comparative costs of production differ. Production and consumption (in the absence of trade the two must be the same) will be OX_a of X and OY_a of Y in country A, OX_b of X and OY_b of Y in country B.

Now introduce the possibility of trade between the countries. What will happen to the relative prices of X and Y? Clearly the difference between the two countries must disappear; if they did not each product would be bought in the country in which

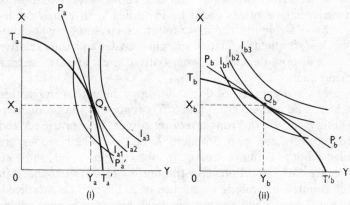

Fig. 29C   Increasing costs

it was relatively cheap and sold in the country in which it was relatively dear, the inevitable result being that price differences would be competed away. So one relative price ratio must apply in both countries. But relative prices must in equilibrium be equal to relative costs in each country – that is, the single price line must be a tangent to the two different transformation curves. How are these two separate conditions satisfied?

The answer is given by superimposing the two transformation curves on the same axes, as is done in the rather complicated Fig. 29D. There will be only one line, PP', which is simultaneously tangential to both curves and this defines the relative price level which will be established by the opening of trade between the two countries; it is the only single price ratio equal to relative marginal costs in each country.

A vital consequence of foreign trade is now discernible. If the indifference map of either country is now added to the diagram – the three from country A are in fact used in Fig. 29D – it will become clear that the points of production equilibrium and of consumer equilibrium are now separated rather than necessarily identical as in the no-trade situation. Production equilibrium occurs at the point Q'_a in country A, since at this point relative prices equal relative marginal costs. Consumer equilibrium

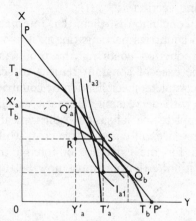

Fig. 29D   Increasing costs and trade

occurs at point S, where relative prices equal relative marginal utilities. Country A, in other words, *produces OX'_a of X* but *consumes* only RY_a of it and *produces OY'_a of Y* but *consumes OT'_a* of it. The triangle $Q'_a R S$, in other words, is the *trade triangle*; country A exports $Q'_a R$ of X and imports in return RS of Y, while country B obviously does the reverse. Trade has freed consumption from the constraints of domestic production and the process of exchange has enabled the country to reach a higher indifference curve, I_{a3}, than it could have attained without trade. This shift from I_{a2} to I_{a3} is a measure of the welfare gain arising from international trade.

One contrast between this situation and that of constant

costs is that with increasing cost total specialisation does not occur. Each country produces *some* of each product although its production pattern will shift in favour of the product in which it has the initial comparative advantage. The effect of trade is to eliminate the least efficient plants in each country but since increasing costs apply the process cannot normally result in one country specialising entirely on the production of either product.

Closely analogous argument would apply in the somewhat improbable case of industries which enjoyed continuously decreasing costs from economies of scale. It is in fact referred to in the succeeding section.

The general conclusion is, then, that international trade will be beneficial to countries participating in it provided that their comparative production costs for the products concerned are different. In the case of constant returns to scale, the process would lead to complete specialisation by countries in their most efficient lines; with decreasing returns it would lead to partial rather than complete specialisation – the typical case in the real world. But differences in comparative cost, while being a *sufficient* condition for the existence of foreign trade, are not a *necessary* condition. Attention must now be turned to the role of demand.

2 THE INFLUENCE OF DEMAND

It was noted earlier that countries differ in their relative preferences between products as well as in their efficiency at making them. Foreign trade, by freeing the pattern of consumption in any country from the pattern of its production, may arise from such demand differences quite apart from differences in comparative costs – although the two influences will obviously operate simultaneously in many cases.

Suppose that the transformation curve in Fig. 29E(i) is the same for both countries A and B but that the relative preferences for the two commodities differ: the preferences in A are embodied in the indifference map I_{a1} and so on and those in B in the indifference map I_{b1} and so on. If no trade is possible, production in A will be determined by the point Q, at which the highest attainable indifference curve is I_{a2} while in B production will settle at the point R. The relative prices of X and Y will obviously differ in the two countries.

Now let trade be opened between the two countries; the two relative price levels must now come together somewhere between the slopes of the previous price lines. Let this after-trade price ratio be PP' in Fig. 29E(ii). Both countries will now produce at point Q; the output of X will fall in country A from X'_a to $\bar{X}'$ while that of Y will increase from Y'_a to $\bar{Y}$ and production will move in the reverse direction in B. Country A is now

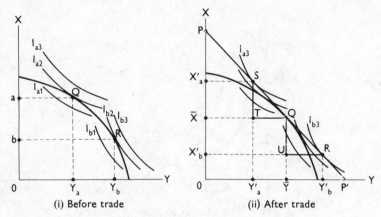

Fig. 29E   Demand and international trade

able to attain a higher indifference curve, I_{a3}, by exporting TQ of Y in exchange for TS of X, B doing the reverse and thus attaining a higher indifference curve I_{b3}. The pattern of exports and imports is reflected in the similar triangles QTS and QUR; the gain in welfare by each country is reflected in the shift of consumption to a higher indifference curve.

Thus a second cause of the gains from international trade is established; even where comparative costs of production do not differ, countries whose demand patterns differ can still gain through the process of exchange. Differences must exist, then, *either* in comparative costs *or* in patterns of demand for international trade to be beneficial.

There is one theoretical – and in practice distinctly unlikely – exception to this general rule. This is the case in which two countries have identical tastes *and* identical production possibilities but where the two products involved are produced under conditions of increasing returns throughout. This is the case illustrated in Fig. 29F, where the transformation curve TT' (convex to the origin throughout to indicate falling costs as the output of either product is increased) and the indifference map, I_1, I_2, etc. are the same for both countries A and B. Without the possibility of trade each country will produce (and consume)

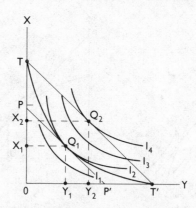

Fig. 29F   The case of increasing returns

the combination of goods defined by Q_1. If trade becomes possible, each country will find it profitable to concentrate production on only one product and obtain its supplies of the other by trade. Thus, in the diagram, country A can produce OT of X, trading TX_2 of X for X_2Q_2 of Y and so reach the higher indifference curve I_4. Trade in this case permits each country to exploit the maximum economies of scale for one product and trade the resulting surplus to the mutual benefit of each trading partner.

All these conclusions concerning the benefits of international trade have been worked out, for the sake of simplicity, in terms of just two countries and two products but the analysis can of course be generalised to cover a world in which there are more than two countries and considerably more than two commodities. National specialisation and foreign trade perform for the international economy the role performed by division of labour and geographical specialisation within an individual economy. So long as differences in tastes or relative costs of production exist between countries, specialisation and trade enable the world as a whole to maximise the output obtained from its scarce resources, given the inability or unwillingness of factors to move across national frontiers so as to be everywhere combined with one another in the optimum proportions.

This is a theoretical conclusion, but it does not follow that in the actual world the productive activities of each country will be solely governed by the operation of these theoretical principles. First, those principles assume the existence of complete freedom of trade; in reality, comparative production costs are distorted, and their effects on trade stultified, by the use of tariffs, quotas and other hindrances to the international exchange of goods and services. Secondly, the effect of transport costs must be allowed for; although a commodity may be more efficiently produced in A than in B, the costs of transporting it from A to B may be so great as to more than offset A's productive superiority, and B will find it preferable to produce the commodity itself despite its lower efficiency. Thirdly, the existence of different levels of efficiency in the production of any given commodity need not result in complete specialisation within a particular country even if constant or decreasing costs apply; the output of any product cannot sensibly be carried beyond the level necessary to meet the entire world's needs for it, so that even the most efficient country in the world will generally require to produce a certain amount of other products at which its comparative efficiency is relatively low.

In general, then, it can be said that countries tend to specialise in the production of those commodities which they produce most efficiently in relation to other commodities, but that in many cases the full working-out of this tendency is prevented by artificial obstacles to trade, by transport costs and by the possibility of variation in average costs of production in different countries as their levels of output change. In so far as they operate, the principles outlined in this section show how free trade between nations, in precisely the same way as division of labour within a nation, can raise the overall real income of society.

3 THE TERMS OF TRADE

The analysis must now return to a question which was left on one side during the discussion of the preceding section. Assuming that countries specialise in producing certain commodities and then carry on trade with one another, how are the relative values of the traded commodities determined?

If the first example quoted in the previous section is considered once again, it will be apparent that the conditions of production in the countries involved will impose definite limits on the rate at which they will exchange goods with one another. The productive abilities of the two hypothetical countries were such that with each unit of resources

Country A could produce 20 loaves or 5 machines
and   Country B could produce 18 loaves or 6 machines.

If A now specialises in producing loaves, it is obvious that it will not exchange more than 4 loaves for a machine, since it could itself produce a machine with the labour it uses in making 4 loaves. If it were to give *more* than 4 loaves for a machine, then, it would be losing rather than gaining from international trade. Similarly B will not be willing to exchange a machine for less than 3 loaves, since it can itself produce 3 loaves with the same amount of resources as it needs to make a machine; rather than accept, say, 12 loaves for 6 machines, it would prefer to employ the resources necessary to make 6 machines in the production of loaves, making 18 loaves as a result. The upshot is, then, that the rate of exchange between loaves and machines cannot be more than 4 to 1 (or A will not trade) and cannot be less than 3 to 1 (or B will not trade).

The rate of exchange must therefore lie somewhere between 3 and 4 loaves to one machine. What decides the exact point at which the relative values of the traded commodities, usually known as the *terms of trade*, will settle? Essentially it is a matter of demand and supply. If, in this example, the supply of loaves from county A is large, relative to the demand for them in B, then A will have to offer something close to 4 loaves in order to obtain a machine. On the other hand, if B's demand for loaves should suddenly rise, or if the supply should be reduced for some reason, B will have to offer more machines for any given quantity of loaves, and the exchange rate will fall closer to 3 to 1.

In this example, the limits imposed by production conditions are so narrow that the terms of trade between A and B (i.e. the value of machines in terms of loaves) cannot vary much. In the world of reality, however, the major imports of the United Kingdom are foodstuffs and raw materials, and the cost of producing British requirements of these products in overseas countries is vastly different from what it would be if Britain had to produce them herself. Similarly, if Britain's major buyers had to produce for themselves the engineering products they now import from Britain, their cost would be much greater than it is at present. The limits to the rates of exchange between British imports and exports set by the production possibilities, therefore, are far apart, with the result that Britain's terms of trade can vary considerably.

Changes in the terms of trade can most easily be measured by a comparison between the average price of exports and the average price of imports. If a country's exports become cheap relatively to its imports, then more goods will have to be exported by that country in order to purchase a given quantity of imports, and the terms of trade are said to have worsened. Conversely a rise in the value of exports in terms of imports – an improvement in the terms of trade – enables a country to purchase a given volume of imports with a smaller volume of exports. The degree to which the terms of trade of the United Kingdom have varied in the present century may be seen from Table 29.1 overleaf.

The 'terms of trade' index in column 3 is obtained by dividing the index number of the average value of exports by

TABLE 29.1   *Terms of trade of the UK 1900–74*
             (1970 = 100)

	1 Average value of exports	2 Average value of imports	3 Terms of trade (1 ÷ 2)
1900	13	17	76
1920	49	55	89
1938	21	20	105
1946	41	42	98
1960	76	76	100
1974	171	215	80

Source: *Key statistics of the British economy, 1900–1966,* London & Cambridge Economic Service; *Monthly Digest of Statistics,* March 1975

that of the average value of imports; a fall in the terms of trade index, therefore, indicates a *worsening* of the terms of trade – i.e. that the prices of the country's imports have risen in relation to those of its exports – while a rise indicates an improvement. As can be seen, between 1900 and 1938 Britain benefited enormously from the change in the relative values of exports and imports; the average value of her exports rose by over 50 per cent while import prices remained almost unchanged. A good many causes underlay this development, the major ones being the large increase in world agricultural production stimulated by the disruption of trade channels during the First World War, the fall in the cost of primary products (i.e. the products of agriculture, mining, forestry and fishing) resulting from rapid technical developments during the 1920s and 1930s, and the collapse of commodity prices during the depression of the 1930s – primary products, being in highly inelastic supply, are liable to marked fluctuations in price in response to shifts in demand.

Between 1938 and 1951 these trends were reversed, largely because of the fact that the production of agricultural commodities had risen substantially less than that of manufactured goods. To some extent this was due to political disturbances in some major sources of agricultural supplies (e.g. Malaya and Burma); more important, however, has been the tendency for countries which were previously almost wholly agricultural to shift their resources into manufacturing to an increasing degree (e.g. Argentina and Australia). The sharp rise in import prices between 1972 and 1974 was a classic example of how the risks involved in international trade are nowadays heightened by political as well as purely economic factors. Over those three years the average price of Britain's imports doubled while the average price of her exports rose by only 60 per cent, the major cause at work being the quadrupling in the price charged by Middle East producers for their exports of crude oil, an increase having no connection with changes in real production costs.

The direct effect of a worsening of a country's terms of trade is bound to be unfavourable, of course. In 1974, Britain's expenditure on imported goods amounted to around £20 000 million, so that a rise of 10 per cent in the price of imports relative to that of exports would add some £2 000 million to the value of exports needed to purchase a constant volume of imports. Obviously this would be a considerable increase in the real burden falling on the economy. However, certain indirect effects of changes in the terms of trade would tend to offset this. First, a rise in import prices represents a rise in the incomes of foreign suppliers, and this will tend to raise their demand for goods exported by other countries. A country whose terms of trade have worsened, therefore, will often find that after a short time-lag the volume, and probably the price, of its exports begin to rise, easing the burden of the increased import bill. Secondly, a country such as Britain has invested a great deal of capital in primary producing countries over the last two centuries, so that some of the increased profits resulting from a rise in the price of primary products will come back to it in the form of increased profit earnings on its foreign assets. These compensating effects are unlikely to offset the direct effect entirely, however, and instability in the terms of trade must always remain a potential source of danger to countries heavily dependent on foreign trade.

4 INTERNATIONAL TRADE AND EMPLOYMENT

In the discussion of the components of aggregate demand in Chapter XXV, the question of foreign trade was left on one side. It is necessary now to fit exports and imports of goods and services into the pattern of income-determination. Exports share many of the features of investment expenditure; like investment, the production of exports results in the receipt of incomes by the factors involved in their manufacture, so that the overall levels of incomes and demand are raised. Again, the production of exports, like that of capital goods, adds nothing directly to the supply of consumer goods available in the home market, so that there is no increase in supply to offset the increased demand generated by the incomes paid out in their manufacture. Like investment expenditure, then, the production of exports is inflationary.

Imports, on the other hand, are the opposite in both respects. The incomes generated by their production do not enter into a country's income flow; they are received by factors of production in some other country. On the other hand, imports *do* add to the supply of goods available in the home market, so that they increase aggregate supply without resulting in any increase in aggregate demand. Imports, then, have a deflationary effect on the economy.

One way to incorporate foreign trade into the analysis of the determination of income and employment is to treat the net excess of exports over imports as an addition to investment expenditure (or as a deduction from investment expenditure if imports exceed exports). The income-determination equation therefore becomes

$$Y = (I + E')\frac{1}{1 - c}.$$

Where E' represents the excess of the value of exports over that of imports ('net exports') and the other symbols represent the same elements as before.

Alternatively, the fraction of income which is spent on imported goods (*the propensity to import*) can be treated as an income 'leakage' exactly comparable with savings, since expenditure on imports prevents the passing-on of income to other members of the economy, just as saving does. The income-determination equation will then be

$$Y = (I + E)\frac{1}{1 - c + m}$$

where E represents the total value of exports and m the fraction of income which people spend on imported goods. Both expressions will give the same answer, of course. For example, assume that in an economy the rate of investment is £100 million, the level of exports is £80 million and imports £60 million and the overall average propensity to consume is $\frac{4}{5}$. The first type of formulation would give (in £ million):

$$Y = (100 + 20)\frac{1}{1 - \frac{4}{5}} = 600.$$

Since imports are £60 million out of a total income of £600 million the propensity to import can be taken as $\frac{1}{10}$ and the second type of formulation gives:

$$Y = (100 + 80)\frac{1}{1 - \frac{4}{5} + \frac{1}{10}}$$

$$= 180 \times \frac{1}{\frac{3}{10}} = 600.$$

The second method has the advantage that by it the tendency to purchase imports is automatically allowed for, whereas with the first method the total expenditure on imports has either to be known or to be estimated separately beforehand.

The importance of foreign trade in the determination of the level of incomes and employment is therefore fairly clear. An export boom will have precisely the same internal effects as a rise in the rate of domestic investment, while a switch in the expenditure of consumers from foreign to home-produced goods will have the same internal effect as a fall in the propensity to save. The inter-relationship of exports and imports must never be forgotten, however. Obviously, for the world as a whole

exports and imports must be equal in value, so that the inflationary effects in one country of a rise in exports (or fall in imports)
must be precisely offset by deflationary effects somewhere else
in the world. As later discussion will show, this fact has considerable importance in assessing the relative advantages of
imposing restrictions on foreign trade.

5 FREE TRADE AND PROTECTION

The analysis of earlier sections led clearly enough to the conclusion that complete freedom of international trade between
countries offers substantial gains from the process of exchange
itself when international comparative costs do not differ, and
from the concentration of output in the most efficient hands
when they do. Theoretically, foreign trade maximises world
welfare. Yet in the real world international trade in goods and
services, so far from being completely free, is conducted within
a network of restrictions and obstacles. Imports are frequently
restricted by various forms of licensing arrangements which
limit the quantities of specified products which may be purchased from overseas; exports are encouraged or discouraged
by subsidies or levies; as will be noted later in the discussion
of the monetary aspects of international trade, the exchange of
currencies against one another is frequently subject to various
forms of official regulation which have the effect of influencing
the flow of imports and exports.

Most important of all, virtually every country operates some
form of *tariff* – that is, a set of taxes on various categories
of imported goods which are not levied on comparable goods
produced within the country concerned. Sometimes these tariff
structures have a preferential aspect, which means that a relatively low rate of tax is imposed on imports from favoured
trading partners in comparison with that imposed on similar
imports from other countries. Historically – and at the present
time also in many developing countries – these duties were
imposed for purely revenue purposes, since the goods concerned
tended to be regarded as luxuries and in any event the collection of tax revenues was relatively easy given the limited

number of points of entry in the countries. Nowadays more
often than not the tariff is used as a *protective* measure; by
making the imported product more expensive to the domestic
consumer, domestic producers are naturally placed at an
advantage even if their costs were relatively high.

Whatever their motivation, there can be no avoiding the
theoretical result that the effect of tariffs is to reduce the welfare
of consumers in the country imposing them. The situation is
shown for an individual commodity in Fig. 29G. Suppose that
the demand schedule for the product is DD' and the supply

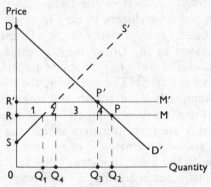

Fig. 29G   The effects of a tariff

curve for domestic producers is SS'. Foreign producers exporting to the country have initially a supply curve RM, so that
they can sell at a price PQ_2. At this price, total consumption
will be OQ_2 but domestic producers will be able to supply only
OQ_1 at this price – at bigger outputs their costs exceed the
market price and this part of the domestic supply schedule is
therefore inoperative. Imports thus amount to Q_1Q_2.

A tariff is now imposed on foreign supplies, raising the
import supply schedule bodily to $R'M'$. Market price rises to P'
and total consumption falls to OQ_3. At this higher price more
domestic production becomes competitive so that domestic
output rises from OQ_1 to OQ_4 and imports fall from Q_1Q_2 to
Q_3Q_4. Total consumers' surplus (the triangle formed by the
demand schedule and the horizontal price line) is reduced by

the area $R'P'PR$. What happens to this reduction in consumer welfare?

The first element, marked 1 in Fig. 29G, is handed over to domestic producers in the form of additional revenues (since market price has risen) in excess of costs – given by the supply schedule: this is the *transfer effect* of a tariff. The second element, 2, is used up in bringing the additional home output, Q_1Q_4, into existence at, so to speak, unnecessary cost. Every unit in this range *could* have been imported at a cost of PQ_2 but is costing something between PQ_2 and $P'Q_3$ to make. This, then, is the *protective effect* of the tariff – its contribution to enabling some home producers to stay in business instead of being pushed out by foreign competition. The third element, 3, is of course passed to the Government in the form of import duties – a tax of PP' on Q_3Q_4 units of imports; this is the *revenue effect* of the tariff. There remains the triangle 4 which is lost to consumers but not transferred to anyone else: it is in fact the net welfare loss imposed by the tariff on society. Elements 1 and 3 are mere transfers *within* the society, from one group to another; element 2 is at least paid over in the form of income to the home industry; element 4, however, just disappears. Thus it emerges that a tariff must necessarily in itself impose some loss of economic welfare. Why then are tariffs so extensive?

To a large extent the reasons are of a political or social, rather than economic, nature. Agriculture is frequently protected by restrictions on imports, for example, mainly on political grounds; it is feared that home agriculture could never survive if it had to face the full competition of imported products, and the extinction of agriculture might prove to be a serious business if a country had a substantial proportion of its population – probably the poorest – with their only livelihood removed. Similarly, industries may be protected because it is felt that they play an important role in the social life of the community, or for no better reason than that the employers or workers of an industry are in a position to bring political pressure to bear on the Government to relieve them of uncomfortable competition from abroad.

Can interference with free trade ever be justified on strictly economic grounds? In general the logic of analysis leads firmly to the conclusion that it cannot. If foreign trade develops, it generally means that one country has at least a relative advantage over another in the production of a given commodity, and interference with the free flow of goods can result only in a sacrifice of some of the benefits which would follow from specialisation. The country restricting its imports is reducing its real income, because it is using resources to produce goods at an unnecessarily high cost.

One exception of an economic nature is frequently quoted, however. This is the case of an *infant industry*. It sometimes happens that a country seeks to develop an industry for which it is potentially well suited, and in which it could effectively compete with foreign producers once the industry was well established. In the early stages of its development, however, the industry is unable to meet competition from abroad; it has of necessity to commence on a small scale, so that it cannot yet reap the full economies of large-scale output, and it has had insufficient time to build up a skilled labour force, specialised marketing and maintenance organisations, or the accumulated experience of well-established entrepreneurs. Hence protection in the early stages of its development would permit it to acquire all these things and to grow into a mature and fully competitive industry requiring no further protection, just as a small child must be protected from the full force of the elements if it is to grow eventually into a healthy and virile adult. In principle, the argument is sound enough; it simply takes account of the fact that in the real world knowledge is not perfect and economic development is not instantaneous. In practice it leaves a good deal to be desired. Industries protected from competition have a habit of never growing up; the sheltering of an industry is not always conducive to the energetic pursuit of maximum efficiency. Furthermore, the removal of protection would tend to injure the employers and workers of the industry concerned, and these, being a relatively small and homogeneous group, would be quick to express organised opposition to the change. Those who stand to benefit by the removal of protection, on the other hand, are the general body of consumers, who are unorganised and frequently unaware of the loss they suffer through protection and the resulting high prices. Changes which arouse fierce opposition from the potential losers but no acclaim from the beneficiaries are seldom regarded as practical politics.

Other arguments of an economic nature advanced in favour of protection have even less real foundation. One of these is that a high-wage country must protect itself against competition (invariably labelled 'unfair') from low-wage countries. The argument usually loses sight of the fact that it is wage-cost per unit which matters in trade, rather than the absolute level of wages; the United States has the highest wage-level in the world, but its labour costs per unit of output are amongst the lowest. Secondly, the argument overlooks the fact that any attempt to shut out goods produced in low-wage countries can only tend to maintain those low wages, or even reduce them further; only in conditions of expanding markets and relatively full employment can real wages be expected to rise. The main weakness of the argument, however, is that a country can only gain by obtaining goods at a low cost, since its real income is raised thereby; if an exporting country chooses to hold down its real income in order to export goods, the loss is the exporter's, not its customers'.

Another argument common in periods of depression is that protection should be imposed in order to stimulate home employment. Although the suggestion has a sound theoretical basis (as has been seen) its attraction is largely illusory. Protection will provoke retaliation, both automatic and deliberate. If a country reduces its imports, the incomes of its suppliers will be reduced, and this is bound to react adversely on their demand for the protecting country's exports if that country plays a major role in world trade. More to the point, protection is a game at which more than one can play; a country placing restrictions on its imports will almost always find that similar restrictions have been placed on its exports in retaliation. Any stimulus to employment in home industry, therefore, is likely to be partly or wholly offset by the damage done to export industries. The experience of the 1930s demonstrated this, if nothing else.

Judged theoretically, then, protection can be adopted only at the cost of a loss of real income. It may be that strategic or social gains are more than sufficient to compensate for this, but restrictions on free trade would be seldom justifiable from a strictly economic point of view, if the assumptions of a perfectly competitive world are satisfied. This, however, is the rub: the world of practice is one in which re-adjustment and transference of resources, especially labour, as between different industries is a slow and painful business, and where the unaided operation of the price mechanism may be weak and wasteful when large and sudden changes are necessary. In a world of perfect competition the case for completely free trade would be unassailable on economic grounds. In the world of reality, where competition is usually far from perfect, the issues are less clear-cut. When unrestricted imports may result in the wastage of capital and unemployment of labour, it is by no means always obvious that the balance of even economic advantage lies unambiguously with completely free trade. Economic welfare may often be augmented, rather than reduced, by temporary protective measures designed to assist and ease a process of transition. It is one of the unfortunate facts of life that such measures have an unhappy knack of establishing themselves as irremovable features of the economic and political landscape, and therefore result in a permanent loss of real income; this loss is no less regrettable because it is not readily apparent to the general public by whom it is suffered.

International Economics

FURTHER READING

R. SHONE *The pure theory of international trade* Macmillan, London 1972

S. J. WELLS *International economics* (rev. edn.), Allen and Unwin, London 1973, Chs. 1–8

I. F. PEARCE *International trade* Book II, Macmillan, London 1970, Ch. 12

P. W. FREVERT *Production and trade* Holt, Rinehart and Winston, New York 1972, Chs. 1–2

J. ADAMS *International economics* Longman, London 1972, Part II

H. KATRAK *International trade and the balance of payments* Fontana, London 1971, Ch. 1

R. FINDLAY *Trade and specialisation* Penguin Books, London 1970

CHAPTER XXX

Foreign Exchange

1 THE MECHANISM OF FOREIGN PAYMENTS

THE conduct of international trade by barter – with producers in different countries exchanging their products directly for one another – would be subject to all the disadvantages of barter in domestic trade. Since the use of money overcomes these disadvantages for transactions between residents of the same country, transactions between those of different countries are naturally also carried out through the medium of money. This permits *multilateral trade* – that is, the sale of goods in one country and the use of the revenues thereby earned for the purchase of goods from another – rather than a system in which exporting countries are forced to purchase their imports from the country in which their goods are sold. As in internal trade, the use of money in international exchanges allows producers to sell in the best market and buy in the best market, whether or not those markets happen to be found in the same country.

In international trade, however, a complication arises which is absent from exchanges within a country. This is that the various independent countries of the world each have their own separate currencies, with separate names, differently valued units and issued on different bases. Even currencies bearing the same name may be found to have different varieties. The Fiji pound, for example, is a different pound from the one circulating in the United Kingdom, while the Tongan pound is distinct from both; there are French francs, Belgian francs and Swiss francs, all with different values.

When an importer has purchased goods from a foreign producer, therefore, he is frequently (although not always) faced with the problem of securing a foreign currency in order to pay for the goods. An importer of American wheat, for example, will find his supplier unwilling to accept payment in pounds sterling; the American cannot use pounds to pay his workers, to build a new factory, or to buy petrol for his car, in a country where dollars, and not pounds, circulate as money. In America the British pound would lack the first attribute of money – i.e. general acceptability. The importer has therefore to secure an adequate supply of the currency used in his supplier's country.

He will do this through the *foreign exchange market*, which is the market in which the different currencies of the world are exchanged for one another. The use of the word 'market' may be a little misleading here, since there is no single institution or locality in which such exchanges are carried out. The foreign exchange market comprises all those persons and institutions who, usually amongst other things, carry on the business of buying and selling foreign currencies; it includes, therefore, Central and commercial banks as well as independent brokers and agents, merchant banking houses and bullion dealers.

An ordinary importer or exporter will usually secure foreign currencies through his bank. For example, if an importer wishes to use his British bank deposit to pay for exports from France and invoiced to him in French francs, his bank will instruct its Paris branch (or a French 'correspondent bank' which has agreed to act as its agent) to credit the exporter with the appropriate amount of French francs. The British bank will reduce the importer's credit in its books, of course, by the equivalent sum in pounds calculated at the current rate of exchange between British pounds (pounds sterling) and French francs.

In the normal course of events, a bank transferring pounds into francs in this way would be receiving a more or less equal amount of business in the opposite direction; its Paris branch, or correspondent, will be exchanging francs for pounds on behalf of *its* customers. If there is a net movement in one direction – say, more pounds are being turned into francs than francs into pounds – then the British bank will find that its balance in Paris is falling, or that its indebtedness to its correspondent French bank is growing. It may therefore need to replenish its holdings of francs by an outright sale of sterling on its own account.

Banks are of course able to handle such sales through their own facilities but it could also be done through a specialist foreign exchange broker (an individual or group of individuals) whose business is the purchase and sale of currencies, rather than the borrowing and lending of currencies. These brokers make their living by performing three functions. First, they carry out routine purchases and sales for clients on a commission basis. Secondly, they conduct complicated *arbitrage* business if differences emerge in cross-exchange rates, and thereby even out such differences. An example may make this clear. Suppose that in both London and New York the current rate of exchange between pounds sterling and dollars is £1 = $2·5, that the rate of exchange between pounds and francs in both London and Paris is £1 = Frs. 10·00, and that in New York the rate of exchange between dollars and francs is $1 = Frs. 4·00. This is an equilibrium situation. But suppose the dollar–franc rate in New York for some reason changes to $1 = Frs. 3·80. The arbitrage operator in London can now buy Frs. 10 with £1 in London, sell the Frs. 10 in New York for about $2·63 and re-convert his $2·63 into pounds, ending up with £1·05. The rush to sell francs against dollars and dollars against pounds will be so great that either the New York dollar–franc rate or the dollar–pound rate (or both) will immediately move, so as to correct the discrepancy. Finally, the foreign exchange broker will buy and sell single currencies on his own behalf, buying currencies whose exchange rate he expects to rise, and selling those whose rate he expects to fall. In this, of course, he hopes to make a profit; in so far as his expectations are based on genuine assessments of the inherent values of various currencies, he carries out the valuable economic function which can be performed by all speculators – the bringing-forward in time and consequent smoothing of future changes. There is in all these respects a close similarity between the activities of the foreign exchange broker and the Stock Exchange jobber.

A final special aspect of the foreign exchange market is that known as *forward exchange*. Many traders and investors find it desirable to have the promise of a certain amount of a specified currency (at a known rate of exchange) well in advance of the date on which they expect to be using it. By placing an order for the future delivery of a currency at an agreed rate they protect themselves against any fluctuations which may occur in the rate of exchange in the meantime. Both banks and brokers therefore buy and sell foreign currencies for future delivery – I can arrange with my bank to transfer pounds into Dutch guilders in three months' time at a rate agreed on now. Naturally the dealers in forward exchange usually quote somewhat less favourable forward rates than the appropriate current rate in order to compensate for the risk they are taking in promising to deliver at a specified rate a currency whose price may have changed considerably when the time comes for them to deliver it.

This is an outline of the bare mechanics of foreign exchange operations. The fundamental question – on what basis is the rate of exchange between one currency and another determined? – has been ignored in giving it and will be examined in Sections 3 and 4 below. But before proceeding to this question another is worth brief examination: why does it matter what the exchange rate is for any currency?

2   THE ROLE OF EXCHANGE RATES

In the long run, every country entering into trade must aim at securing some kind of balance between its imports and its exports. If it persistently imports more than it exports it can do so only by using up its accumulated assets or by running into debt, and neither process can continue indefinitely. There is an exact analogy here with a private individual who persistently spends more than he earns; he can do it by using up his savings or running into debt, but this state of affairs cannot go on for ever. (Less obviously, a country cannot continuously accumulate debtors; if its debtors never repay, the exports are in fact being given away, and no country will accept such a situation indefinitely.) It follows, therefore, that the prices of a country's exports and imports must be such as to at least hold out the promise of ultimate solvency.

Now export and import prices have two components; the price in the country of origin and the rate of exchange between the currency in the country of origin and in the country of sale. For example, British motor-cars are sold in France. Their cost to the French buyer is a combination of (*a*) the British price, and (*b*) the pound–franc exchange rate, and a change in the final cost can result from a movement in *either* factor. If a car is sold at £1 000 to a French importer, and the current exchange rate is £1 = Frs. 10·00, then the cost to the French purchaser will be about Frs. 10 000. That cost could rise to Frs. 11 000 if *either* the cost of production in Britain rose to £1 100 *or* the pound–franc exchange rate moved to £1 = Frs. 11·00. Whichever factor was at work, the price of British cars in France would rise, and the amount of them purchased would therefore fall.

A country which finds that its exports and imports are becoming seriously out of step, therefore, can do one of two things. It can *either* adjust its internal price level in the appropriate direction *or* it can accept some variation of the exchange rate of its currency – or, of course, adopt some combination of the two. If Britain finds that its imports of goods and services exceed its earnings from exports, it can either try to reduce costs of production at home or allow the external value (i.e. the exchange rate) of the pound to fall. If home costs are reduced, exports will be cheaper and normally more of them will be sold abroad; conversely, foreign goods will have become relatively expensive as a result of the cheapening of home products, and imports will therefore tend to fall. The same effects would follow from a reduction in the exchange rate of the pound. If British blankets cost £20 to produce, American refrigerators cost $500 to produce and the current exchange rate is £1 = $3·00 then British blankets will have to be sold in America at about $60 and American refrigerators will sell in Britain at about £167. If the pound is now *devalued* so that the exchange rate falls to say, £1 = $2·00, British producers of blankets will be able to sell in America at about $40, and still cover their costs, while American producers will have to sell refrigerators in Britain at about £250 in order to cover their costs. British exports will be cheaper, and more will be sold; imports into Britain will be dearer and fewer will be bought.

But why should such adjustments of internal prices or exchange rates be necessary? Assuming that the original rates of exchange between different currencies are established at such a level that all countries achieve a proper relationship between their exports and imports, why should not these rates be maintained indefinitely? The answer is that internal price levels in different countries never maintain a fixed relationship with one another for long. One country will increase its level of productivity more rapidly than others, for any one of many reasons, so that its level of costs will become lower in relation to that in other countries; alternatively, countries will vary in the monetary policies they pursue, so that quite apart from productivity differences the original relationship of prices in different countries will inevitably be disturbed. Periodically, then, every country will find that its exports are becoming dear or cheap relatively to those of other countries, so that the initial situation of trade balance will be replaced by one of an import or export surplus. To restore equilibrium, either the internal price level or the external value of its currency will have to be changed.

This should not be taken to mean that a reduction in the exchange rate will necessarily improve the balance of payments: much will depend on the elasticities of the demand for the country's exports and of its demand for imports. Unless the elasticity of demand for exports exceeds unity, the *revenue* from exports will fall as the result of the reduction of their prices in foreign markets brought about by devaluation; equally, expenditure on imports, in terms of foreign currencies, will be reduced significantly only if the elasticity of demand for them within the importing country is sufficiently great to lead to a substantial reduction in consumption as their domestic prices rise as a result of devaluation. In fact it can be shown that a necessary condition for a devaluation to lead to a net improvement in the trade balance, in monetary terms, is that the *sum* of the absolute magnitudes of the demand elasticities for exports and imports should exceed unity. Even this is not a *sufficient* condition; there must be sufficient elasticity in the supply of exports to ensure that the rise in their volume is not associated with such a sharp rise in costs as to eliminate almost immediately the competitive advantage gained from the initial devaluation.

3 EXCHANGE RATES: THE FREE MARKET

Several references were made in the preceding section to the effects, desirable or otherwise, of changes in the rate of exchange between one currency and the currencies of the rest of the world – changes, in other words, in the *price* of a currency expressed in terms of any other currency. How and why do such changes occur? Put another way: is there an equilibrium rate of exchange for any currency at any time such that tendencies towards a change do not exist? If so, what are the factors which determine that equilibrium?

The foreign exchange rate of a currency is its price, and like that of any other commodity the price of a currency would be the outcome of market forces unless government agencies intervened to qualify the effect of market forces in some way. In practice such official intervention is almost universal, but it will be as well to begin by assuming that a free market exists for the buying and selling of currencies: the effects of government intervention can then be superimposed on this framework.

In a free market for any currency there will exist for it a demand schedule and a supply schedule, each indicating the amounts of that currency which people are seeking to buy (offering other currencies in exchange for it) or to sell (in exchange for other currencies) at different prices – i.e. exchange rates. The demand for the currency will be the reflection, so to speak, of the anxiety of foreigners to buy goods and services produced in the country concerned or capital assets (bank deposits, securities, factories and so on) owned by residents of that country. As was seen in the previous section, the higher the exchange rate of a currency the more expensive are these goods and services or assets and hence the smaller the demand for the currency needed to buy them. As the exchange rate falls, so those goods and assets become cheaper and more attractive to the foreign purchaser and the demand for the currency will consequently become greater. Thus in the example shown in Fig. 30A the 'price' of the pound sterling is measured in US

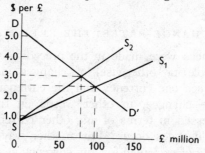

Fig. 30A   A 'free' foreign exchange market

dollars on the vertical axis (although that price could be expressed in terms of any other currency) and the total (say) daily demand for pounds on the part of holders of other currencies is reflected in the downward-sloping demand schedule, DD'.

The supply schedule is, of course, the reverse: it is the outcome of the desire on the part of UK residents to acquire goods or assets denominated in currencies other than the pound sterling – in general, those produced or owned by residents of foreign countries. The higher the exchange rate of the pound, the cheaper those goods and assets become and hence the greater the volume of pounds coming into the market for conversion into foreign currencies in order to purchase them. The supply schedule will be upward-sloping like SS_1 in Fig. 30A. Equilibrium in this market, as in any other market, requires that the amounts offered at any given price should equal the amounts demanded at that price. The equilibrium rate of exchange in the market would thus tend to that defined by the intersection of the demand and supply schedules – about $2·50 in Fig. 30A.

The consequences of any shift in the forces underlying these schedules are analysed easily enough. Suppose, for example, that the price-level of British products fell in relation to that of the outside world. At any given exchange rate, therefore, foreign goods would be less attractive than hitherto, in comparison with domestic products, and the number of pounds coming forward for conversion into foreign currencies would fall accordingly. The supply schedule would thus shift to the left, a movement shown by SS_2 in Fig. 30A, and the exchange rate would tend to rise. For the sake of simplicity the demand schedule is shown as constant in Fig. 30A but in practice the forces which shifted the supply schedule to the left would also – for exactly the same reasons – shift the demand schedule to the right, thus reinforcing the tendency for the exchange rate to rise to a new equilibrium level.

In a free market, then, the equilibrium exchange rate is determined ultimately by the relative prices of goods and assets at home and abroad. Many years ago an attempt to give more precision to this process was embodied in the purchasing power parity theory. This stated that, left to the free play of market forces, the external value of currencies would settle at that level which made the purchasing power of a given unit of currency the same wherever it was spent. For example, if there was only one commodity, bread, and a loaf of bread cost 15p in Britain, 36 cents in the United States and Frs. 1·50 in France, the exchange rates of pounds, dollars and francs would have to be such that $15p = 36$ cents $=$ Frs. 1·50 i.e. £1 $=$ \$2·4 $=$ Frs. 10·00. If this were not so, the theory argued, it would be possible to purchase goods at a low price in one country and resell them at a high price in another, and this one-way trade would continue until the forces of supply and demand brought prices into equality when expressed in the different currencies.

It is undoubtedly true that in the long run the external value of a currency will be determined fundamentally by the relative level of costs and prices in the country concerned. To relate the exchange rates prevailing at any moment of time simply to overall purchasing power, however, is a gross oversimplification. The general price level takes account of a great many goods and services which cannot enter into international trade and whose prices therefore cannot be brought into equality in different countries through the process of one-way trade mentioned above. Secondly, the existence of tariffs, subsidies, transport costs, and import restrictions may result in permanent discrepancies in the prices quoted for the same commodities in different countries, and these also will be incapable of removal through the flow of trade in one direction. Finally, the demand for and supply of a currency may be influenced by a good many causes having nothing whatever to do with price levels or current trade, such as government expenditure overseas, capital movements, relative interest rates and speculative purchases and sales.

This last point is worth a little elaboration. The discussion so far has been conducted in terms of currencies being demanded in order to purchase goods or services or income-earning assets – which of course they are. But in addition to this 'normal' demand there can also be a 'speculative' demand which over short periods of time can reach dimensions far in excess of the normal demand. The speculative buyer or seller of a currency is not in the market to buy goods or undertake long-term investment but to make a short-term capital gain or avoid a capital loss. Suppose that the prevailing exchange rate is £1 = $2·50 and the view spreads amongst the professional dealers in the market (for well-founded reasons or otherwise) that the rate is likely to fall in the near future to £1 = $2·40. The speculator will then unload pounds on to the market – borrowing from the British banking system if necessary – and sell them for dollars which can then be held as bank deposits in the United States until the expected fall occurs; they can then be re-converted into pounds at a comfortable profit. Thus £1 million sold at the rate of £2·50 will bring in $2·5 million when this is converted back to sterling at $2.40, the proceeds will amount to about £1 041 670, bringing in a capital gain of over £40 000 in what might well be a matter of hours. If these speculative movements are large enough, indeed, they are capable of actually bringing about – even if only temporarily – the very movement on which the speculators are gambling. The result may be sudden and substantial instability in the exchange markets having a damaging effect on the international trade and investment of the country whose currency is the object of speculation. To all the 'normal' risks of production for or investment in overseas markets are now added these monetary risks of agreements entered into at one rate of exchange having to be honoured when the rate of exchange may have moved substantially – and adversely.

All that can be said, then, is that when the determination of exchange rates is left to the free play of market forces, the value of a currency will depend on all the factors underlying the purchase or sale of foreign currencies. In the long run, the cost of exports in relation to imports is bound to exercise a dominant influence; if the goods exported by a country are cheap relative to its imports, with the result that an export surplus is achieved, the demand by foreigners for its currency in order to pay for exports will be greater than sales by residents against foreign currencies, and the exchange rate will be driven up until equilibrium is restored. If a country has an import surplus, the external value of its currency will tend to fall. In the short run, however, the flow of capital, trade restrictions, or speculative movements may offset or even reverse these basic tendencies. What is more, the 'free' market in foreign exchange is very much the exception: the exchange rate is too important a factor to any country for the government to be indifferent to what is happening. Hence the prevalence of government intervention in foreign exchange markets, to which the discussion must now turn.

4 EXCHANGE RATES: OFFICIAL INTERVENTION

Broadly speaking, official influence can be exerted on foreign exchange rates either through operations on the supply of or

demand for its currency (in relation to foreign currencies) in the
open market or on the supply of it which the residents of its
country are permitted to sell at any given exchange rate.

In Britain the first type of influence is exerted through the
Exchange Equalisation Account, an official fund held partly
in the form of a balance at the Bank of England and partly in
the form of balances in foreign Central Banks (in the currency
of the country concerned, of course) or in gold which, as
Chapter XXXIII explains, is widely accepted in exchange for
most currencies. Other countries have similar stabilisation
agencies whose primary function is to even out fluctuations in
the external value of a country's currency arising from what
are considered to be purely temporary causes rather than long-
run trends. An exchange rate may oscillate because of seasonal
selling pressures, or speculative sales made in the hope of buying
back at a later date and at a lower value. The Exchange Account
operates with its stock of the home currency and of the major
foreign currencies. For example, if the exchange rate of the
pound is tending to fall because of excess selling pressure, the
British Exchange Account itself enters the market and buys
pounds sterling in exchange for some of its stock of foreign
currencies; conversely, if the pound is tending to appreciate
unduly, the Exchange Account sells pounds and buys foreign
currencies. By adding to the demand for or supply of pounds,
it attempts to offset what are believed to be temporary fluctuations and to maintain a high degree of stability in the external
value of the pound.

The process is illustrated in Fig. 30B. The initial situation
is one in which the daily demand schedule for pounds is given
by D_1D_1' and the supply schedule by SS' : an equilibrium
exchange rate of £1=$2·50 is therefore established. Suppose
now that for some reason – perhaps a rise in U K prices relative
to those of the rest of the world – the demand schedule shifts
back to D_2D_2'. Left to market forces, the exchange rate would
fall to $2·00, but the authorities are determined to maintain a
rate of £1 = $2·50, perhaps in the belief that the loss of Brit-
ish competitiveness is purely temporary. The Exchange Equalisation Account can now enter the market and fill the demand

deficiency of £40 million at the price of $2·50 by selling the equivalent in foreign currencies and, in effect, pushing the demand schedule back to D_1D_1'. In the event of an unwelcome tendency for the price of the pound to rise above the 'official' parity of $2·50, of course, the reverse policy would be adopted with the Exchange Account selling pounds and buying foreign currencies – in effect, shifting the supply schedule to the right.

In the long run, of course, the Exchange Account cannot prevent a movement arising out of the fundamental realities of the country's economic position. If the country persistently runs an import surplus, the Exchange Account could prevent a fall in the exchange rate only by continuously adding to the

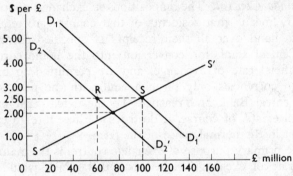

Fig. 30B   Official intervention in the market

demand for pounds by selling foreign currencies in exchange for it. Ultimately, its stock of foreign currencies would be exhausted by this procedure; its powers would then also be exhausted and the inevitable decline would occur in the external value of the pound. The major weakness of the Exchange Account system, indeed, lies in the difficulty of distinguishing in practice between short-term and long-term trends.

If the government of the United Kingdom is pursuing a policy of maintaining a fixed exchange rate for the pound sterling, then, the Exchange Equalisation Account functions as a means of maintaining this rate, rather than as an agency for offsetting purely temporary movements. It operates on 'free' markets (sometimes referred to as 'black' markets) in foreign financial centres such as New York or Zurich where sterling is bought and sold by persons not subject to the British exchange control regulations. The Account' s object is to ensure that the rate for sterling quoted in these free markets does not diverge significantly from the 'official' rate. If sterling fell below that rate in such markets, no one would bring foreign currencies to the Bank of England for conversion into pounds if they could avoid it; they would prefer to buy their sterling at the 'cheap' rate. In this way Britain would suffer a loss of foreign exchange reserves.

The second form of official intervention is known as *Exchange Control.* The imposition of exchange control by a country means that residents of that country are required by law to hand over all their receipts of specified currencies to the Central Bank for conversion into the home currency at the official rate of exchange, and are permitted to buy such foreign currencies only through, and with the permission of, the Central Bank or Treasury. To the extent that exchange control exists, of course, it destroys the free foreign exchange market in the normal sense of the term.

The primary purpose of exchange control is the maintenance of a rate of exchange higher than that which would exist if demand and supply were allowed to work themselves out in freedom. The authorities must believe that, at the rate which they are seeking to maintain, people would wish to sell more of the currency than foreigners would wish to buy. If the United Kingdom was running an import surplus, for example, it might seek to prevent the depreciation of the pound which would normally result by refusing to allow more pounds to be sold against foreign currencies than are currently being demanded by foreigners to pay for British exports. The natural result of this will be, of course, that imports into the United Kingdom will be cut down. If British buyers cannot obtain the foreign currencies necessary to pay for foreign goods, foreign suppliers would continue to send goods to Britain only if they were prepared to accept in exchange pounds which could be used to purchase goods in Britain, but could not be transferred into their own or any other currency. Not many foreign producers would regard such a situation as satisfactory.

Like all impediments to foreign trade, exchange control is bound to cause some loss of real income because of the artificial restraint it imposes on international specialisation. Nevertheless, in certain circumstances exchange control can be justified, and may even be unavoidable. A country at war, for example, obviously cannot allow its residents to transfer scarce foreign exchange reserves to its enemies, or even to use them for relatively frivolous purchases. In view of the dislocation of trade which war involves, foreign currencies are scarce and valuable assets which countries will wish to use only in the interests of the war effort; only by the imposition of exchange control can the authorities ensure that this actually happens.

Another set of circumstances in which exchange control may be considered necessary is that in which the United Kingdom has frequently found itself in recent years. In this instance, the demand for foreign currencies – or, rather, the goods which can be bought only with such currencies – is in excess of what can be paid for from Britain' s current foreign earnings because of the excess pressure of domestic demand. If exchange control was not adopted, the only solution might be a drastic devaluation of the pound *vis-à-vis* the currencies of the rest of the world, and (for reasons discussed in the next chapter) the authorities might prefer not to resort to this. Exchange control enables the expenditure of foreign currencies to be restricted to what are considered to be essential uses.

Finally, exchange control may be used in an attempt to reduce undesirable capital movements. In recent years many currencies have suffered instability because of large-scale movements of capital motivated by the hope of speculative gains in the manner outlined in the previous section. While speculation of this sort can have no long-run influence on the exchange rate, in the short run (and policy-makers are *always* forced to work in a short-run context: in the long run, as Keynes remarked, we are all dead) they can set in motion upward or downward movements in exchange rates which it is beyond the capacity of stabilisation agencies such as the Exchange Equalisation Account to offset. By requiring official approval for the transfer of sterling (or whatever is the appropriate domestic currency) into foreign currencies the authorities can seek to moderate such movements. It has to be admitted, however, that in practice official powers in this respect are severely circumscribed. Exchange control laws can be enforced on the residents of the country applying them but scarcely on non-residents buying or selling the currency concerned in the many financial centres with active foreign exchange markets. Even with residents, the numbers of tricks and techniques by means of which funds can be transferred from one currency to another, given sufficient determination, are virtually infinite. Money capital is the quicksilver of the economic system: controlling its movement is far easier described in theory than effected in practice.

5 FIXED VERSUS FLOATING EXCHANGE RATES

It will have become clear from the two preceding sections that any trading country has a policy choice in relation to its exchange rate. On the one hand it can allow the currency to 'float' in the open market and for its value on any day to be determined by the pressures of unrestricted demand and supply. Some marginal control over such fluctuations might of course be exercised by the various techniques of intervention – a situation known elegantly as 'dirty floating' – but essentially the exchange rate is left to find its own level. On the other hand, a government may determine what is in its view the 'correct' price of its currency and use all its policy weapons to maintain this fixed rate whatever the trend indicated by contemporary market pressures. Of course, such a policy of fixed exchange rates would not exclude occasional and pre-determined adjustments in the official parity; the rate would be 'pegged' at any time but the peg would be adjustable if and when substantial re-alignments in currency values had clearly become necessary.

The relative advantages of fixed and floating exchange-rate

policies have been the subject of a great deal of controversy. Until relatively recently almost every major trading nation in the world followed a form of fixed-rate policy under which the value of a currency was defined in terms of a specified weight of gold or one of the major currencies of the world such as the pound or the dollar, and the Central Bank accepted the responsibility for converting its currency into gold, or vice versa, on demand and at the specified rate of exchange, at least with regard to sales by other Central Banks. The system had the advantage that since the values of all major currencies were defined in terms of a common element, one currency could always be converted into another at a fixed rate, thus stimulating the free flow of multilateral trade with all its benefits.

The stability of exchange rates is of special significance for countries highly dependent on international trade, since the possibility of fluctuations in the foreign exchange market introduces serious risks into the business of exporting and importing. Suppose an exporter of British textiles to Italy agrees to sell for 1 800 000 lire a consignment of goods which has cost him £1 000, at a time when the exchange rate is £1 = 1 500 lire. Under these circumstances he is assured of a reasonable profit; at the current exchange rate, the revenue of 1 800 000 lire can be converted into £1 200, so leaving him a surplus of £200 after paying the cost of the goods. Now suppose that, during the interval between entering into the sale agreement and actually receiving the proceeds, the exchange rate moves to £1 = 2 000 (i.e. the pound sterling appreciates in terms of Italian lire). His 1 800 000 lire will now exchange for only £900, turning his profit of £200 into a loss of £100. International trade is therefore discouraged and hampered by the possibility of exchange-rate fluctuations, and promoted by stability on the foreign exchanges. The same considerations would apply with even more force in the context of the international flow of long-term capital for genuine investment purposes. Variations in exchange rates can have a very serious effect on the real burden of a country's indebtedness to foreign investors and, equally, on the value of its investments abroad. The flow of capital from the relatively rich countries of the world to the less developed countries is a matter of prime importance and anything which renders that process riskier than it need be is to be deplored.

The advocates of fixed exchange rates also attach a good deal of importance to the internal discipline which they believe it imposes on countries pursuing such a policy. If inflation is allowed to proceed more rapidly in one country than in the world generally, that country will inevitably find itself increasing its expenditure on imports and facing a decline in its receipts from exports. The inevitable result of this shifting of the supply curve of its currency to the right and of the demand curve to the left will be a tendency for the exchange rate of its currency to fall. In order to prevent this, and defend the fixed rate, the Exchange Account, or its equivalent, will be forced to intervene on an increasing scale and its reserve of foreign exchange will begin to fall. Since that decline obviously cannot continue indefinitely, the authorities will be forced to adopt some deflationary measures – restriction of the money supply, increased taxes, reduced government spending and so on – until the rate of inflation is reduced and the import–export imbalance removed. A country with a relatively deflationary situation, on the other hand, would face the reverse situation. In order to prevent an appreciation of its currency, it will find itself accumulating unnecessarily large stocks of idle currency reserves, so conveying to the authorities the information that a more expansionary domestic policy is both possible and desirable. The advocates of fixed exchange rates therefore claim for the system a 'built-in' stabilising mechanism which automatically tends to maintain equilibrium.

Unfortunately, the picture is not so attractive in reality. In the first place, although countries accumulating reserves could expand credit, raise incomes and so on, there is no obligation on them to do so, and many countries in fact fail to do so because of the fear of causing or augmenting inflation. The debtor countries are in a different position. The loss of reserves *forces* them to deflate so long as the obligation of maintaining a fixed parity continues, and the failure of other countries to raise their price levels means that debtors have to deflate all the more in order to get their prices back into line with the rest of the world. The system therefore has an inherent deflationary bias.

More important, however, is the assumption of price flexibility implicit in the system. When reserves are lost and deflationary measures adopted, the resulting fall in the level of demand is assumed to cause a similar fall in the rate of inflation. As demand *falls*, workers accept lower increases in money wages, entrepreneurs lower prices and profits and landlords lower rents; if costs are held back in the same proportion as demand, the same level of employment and output can be maintained. As has been seen at an earlier stage, however, the mechanism of inflation is by no means as simple as this. More often than not the deflationary effects of fiscal and monetary policy are felt on the level of output and, in particular, on the rate of growth rather than on the forces pressing upwards on costs and prices. The deceleration in the rate of growth may in fact have the effect of increasing rather than reducing the rise in relative costs, since unit costs rise least when productivity is increasing most rapidly, and productivity tends to rise rapidly in periods of expansion rather than in periods of stagnation. The price of maintaining a fixed exchange rate has thus frequently appeared to be – certainly for Britain – an alternation of modest expansion followed by enforced stagnation and it is by no means clear that in the long run the exchange rate of the pound has been held up in the process.

The argument in favour of freely-floating exchange rates, of course, is largely identical with that against fixed rates. Above all, a country which forgoes the attempt to maintain its currency at a fixed parity with gold or another currency is, theoretically at least, able to design its domestic policy with the primary aim of securing full employment and rapid economic growth at home. If imports exceed exports, it allows its exchange rate to fall, making its exports cheaper and its imports dearer; it makes no attempt to close the trade gap through a reduction in domestic incomes and prices, which would give rise to at least the threat of stagnation and possibly unemployment.

It can also be argued that a floating exchange rate discourages the wild speculative movements which can be so damaging to exchange markets. With a fixed-rate policy, people speculating on the devaluation of a currency have in a sense a guarantee against loss; if they sell the currency in anticipation of a fall in its value they make profit if they are correct in their forecast but suffer no loss if they are wrong – they can always buy back at the fixed rate. A floating rate, on the other hand, implies that a currency may go up as well as down and speculators may find themselves having to buy back at a higher price than that at which they sold.

Yet the absence of a discipline for internal policy cannot be denied. An unduly inflationary policy, leading to an excess of imports over exports, will cause the exchange rate to fall, but (unlike the fixed-rate situation) there is no reason why the authorities should feel themselves impelled to do something about it. The depreciation of the currency will certainly contain in itself the seeds of a corrective mechanism, since imports will become relatively expensive and exports more competitive. But this price mechanism can work – as was pointed out in an earlier section – only if the supply responses are right. Resources must be diverted from domestic consumption to take advantage of the new export competitiveness and with strong inflationary pressure in the economy this may require quite drastic deflationary action which the authorities are under no immediate compulsion to take. What is more, if the demand for imports is inelastic – as is probably the case in Britain – the depreciation of the currency and the resulting increase in the domestic price of imports may well increase rather than reduce internal inflationary pressure as the increased import costs work their way through to the cost of living in the form of higher prices for food and raw materials.

Three conclusions follow. First, the state of the internal economy, meaning the levels of output, employment, prices and growth, is necessarily and inescapably linked with the relationship between imports and exports and no conceivable exchange-rate policy can break that link or even weaken it. There are no simple and easy solutions here, any more than in other areas of economic policy.

Second, the familiar trade-off problem also exists as much

in this policy area as in any other. By a fortunate configuration of circumstances the policy requirements for economic growth, employment and exchange rate may all lie in the same direction. It is much more probable, however, that they will conflict: one policy may be indicated in the context of foreign trade and the rate of exchange while the reverse is desirable in the interests of domestic stability or growth.

Third, of its nature the exchange rate of any currency involves other countries. No single country is free to vary its rate of exchange without thereby affecting the exchange rates of every other. The problem of policy with regard to exchange rates must necessarily be placed in the context of the *international* monetary scene: it can never be a purely domestic matter. Hence the discussion will return to the world monetary system in Chapter XXXIII below.

FURTHER READING

T. SCITOVSKY *Money and the balance of payments* Ch. 13
S. J. WELLS *International economics* Chs. 13–15
J. ADAMS *International economics* Part III, 15–16
H. KATRAK *International trade and the balance of payments* Ch. 2

CHAPTER XXXI

The Balance of Payments

1 THE BALANCE OF PAYMENTS ON CURRENT ACCOUNT

JUST as a company draws up every year a statement of its income and expenditure so a country draws up an annual statement of its current transactions with foreign countries; this is known as the *balance of payments*. The word 'balance' is to be taken here in the sense of a relationship rather than as an exact equality, since it is most unlikely that the goods and services purchased by residents of a country from abroad will be exactly offset by their sales of goods and services to foreigners.

The balance of payments can be drawn up on the basis of *current* transactions (the receipts and expenditure of income which go on year after year), or it can include *capital* transactions (the lending of sums to other countries, borrowing from other countries, or transfers of assets accumulated in the past). The degree to which a country is living within or beyond its current means is best observed from the balance of payments on current account. This includes what are known as *visible* and *invisible* trade. By visible trade is meant the tangible goods which are exported from or imported into a country. Major imports of the United Kingdom, for example, include foodstuffs, such as meat, grains, fruits, coffee and tea, and raw materials – especially petroleum, cotton, wool and metal ores; even so, more than a half of British imports consists of manufactured or semi-manufactured goods. Britain' s major exports are machinery, cars and lorries, chemical products and textiles of all kinds. The difference between a country's expenditure on its visible imports and its earnings from visible exports is called the *balance of trade,* which is said to be 'favourable' if the value of exports exceeds that of imports and 'adverse' if the opposite is true. (The *balance* of trade should never be confused with the *terms* of trade. The former expresses the relationship between the total *amounts* spent on imports and received from exports; the latter refers to the relationship between the *prices* of exports and imports.)

The 'invisible' items included in the current balance of payments are the services paid for by residents of a country or performed on behalf of foreigners, and the property incomes flowing into or out of a country; they are items of income or expenditure which cannot be physically seen or handled at Customs barriers as can the commodities comprising visible trade. The main items involved are earnings from shipping and insurance services, expenditure of tourists outside their home country, government expenditure in foreign countries on embassies, maintenance of troops, etc., and the interest and dividends on investments in foreign countries. Under each heading, of course, a country may *receive* payments from abroad or *make* payments abroad; the United Kingdom, for example, earns a considerable income from the carriage of goods for foreigners by British ships, but it also pays out substantial sums for the transport of British goods in foreign ships. Under each heading, therefore, the net balance of earnings of a country may be positive or negative; it will be the balance of both receipts from other countries and payments to other countries.

If the balance of trade is added to the net receipts from invisible exports and imports, the resulting total constitutes the balance of payments on current account; this is said to be *favourable* if total receipts exceed total payments, and *adverse* if payments exceed receipts. It follows that the balance of trade has no special significance when taken in isolation. A country may continuously export more goods than it imports and yet have a deficit on its overall current balance of payments, if its net expenditure on invisible account is more than sufficient to offset the trade surplus. By contrast, the United Kingdom has run an adverse balance of trade in most years since the middle of the nineteenth century; in some years its invisible earnings have been more than sufficient to compensate for the excess of physical imports over physical exports but in other years they have not been and an overall current deficit has resulted.

2 INTERNATIONAL CAPITAL MOVEMENTS

The transactions included in the current balance of payments are, as the term implies, *current* items of expenditure or revenue; they are part of a recurring flow of national income and expenditure from or in the rest of the world. Like an individual, however, a country may use its resources to acquire capital assets abroad rather than in current consumption and, equally, may experience receipts of wealth from the sale of assets abroad as well as from that of current output. The balance of payments, in other words, must take account of capital transfers as well as current items since the former involve monetary exchanges with the rest of the world just as much as the latter.

An important distinction must be drawn, however, between two very different types of capital movement: those which occur as the result of a deliberate policy decision to make them ('autonomous' movements) and those which are simply a necessary by-product of decisions concerning other types of expenditure ('compensatory' movements). An example may help to clarify the distinction. Suppose that a man decides to purchase £500 of shares and finances it by running down his current account in the bank by that amount. His credit balance in the bank will thus be reduced by £500, but since this results from a conscious decision on his part to change the form of his assets it could be called an autonomous capital movement. If, on the other hand, his current expenditure over the period in question had exceeded his current income by £500, a similar reduction would have occurred in his credit balance; this, however, would be a compensatory capital movement since it was a consequence of his current expenditure behaviour and not deliberately intended as an end in itself.

The distinction is an important one in the context of the balance of payments and, in particular, of the ability of the authorities to defend the exchange rate of the currency. So far as the currency flow is concerned – that is, supplies coming forward seeking exchange into some other currency or the demand by foreigners to obtain it in the foreign exchange market – there is no difference between flows corresponding to current imports and exports and those arising from the purchase and sale of capital assets. Any excess of supply over demand, however, has to be met by 'compensatory' financing by the Exchange Equalisation Account, or its equivalent, if the rate of exchange is to be held at some fixed level, and the extent of these compensatory movements is a measure of the degree of support which the authorities are being called on to provide. It is, in other words, an indication of the strain being imposed on government agencies by the attempt to maintain the rate of exchange at its current level.

Autonomous capital movements are of three main kinds. First, private long-term investment overseas by persons or enterprises in the United Kingdom or, equally, in British enterprises by residents of other countries. The bulk of this takes the form of *direct* investment – that is, the construction or acquisition of real capital assets in manufacturing companies, oil refineries, mines and so on. Another form is known as *portfolio* investment, where the assets concerned are securities of one kind or another which do not involve the actual control of productive assets. A great deal of this private capital flow in fact takes the form of the reinvestment of profits arising in overseas enterprises rather than their repatriation from the country in which they are operating. The recipient country is in effect borrowing capital from the overseas owners of the enterprises. At first sight it may seem dangerous – or at least a sign of weakness – for a country to finance itself out of foreign borrowing just as an individual is ill-advised to finance his current expenditures by borrowing from the bank. This is not necessarily so, however. If the foreign borrowing enables a country to increase its productive powers through capital investment, then the loan can be repaid from the extra income generated by the investment. Almost all creditor countries – the United States and Canada, for example – were at some time debtor countries, running import surpluses financed by foreign borrowing and using the resources thus placed at their disposal to increase their productive capacity. A country which borrows abroad to finance current consumption without carrying out compensating investment, however, is heading for disaster; its balance of payments problem in the future will be made even more intractable because of the interest or dividend payments and capital repayment which it will have to make to the country from which it borrowed.

The second kind of autonomous capital movement takes the form of short-term movements of funds from one financial centre to another in such a form – bank deposits or treasury bills and so on – that movement back again is always possible at short notice. These movements will occur if, for example, money-market rates are significantly higher in one financial centre of the world than in the home market. Alternatively – and more ominously for governments attempting to maintain stability in the exchange rate of their currencies – short-term funds may be moved from one financial centre to another in the hope or, at least, expectation of a fall in the exchange rate of a 'weak' currency and the attainment of capital gains when a currency is bought back at a lower rate of exchange than that at which it was sold. These are the so-called 'hot money' movements which have done so much in recent years to de-stabilise the world's foreign exchange markets.

The third category of autonomous capital movement comprises long-term borrowing and lending by the Government itself. The lending takes the form mainly of relatively low-interest loans to the developing countries of the Commonwealth while the borrowing has tended to reflect the efforts of past governments to defend what proved to be indefensible exchange rates with the aid of loans from foreign governments.

All these autonomous capital movements, then, add to the demand for and supply of pounds sterling in the market at any one time, together with the flows arising from ordinary trade transactions. Unless by some remarkable coincidence demand exactly equals supply at the prevailing exchange rate, the gap between them must be offset by compensatory movements ('official financing') if the exchange rate is not to move from its present level – or if the authorities, while tolerating some variation in the rate, wish to moderate its degree.

Two possibilities are open. First, the authorities may use their own reserves of foreign exchange to bring the demand for their currency up to current supply at the prevailing exchange – or, of course, add to those reserves by selling the domestic currency if demand exceeds supply. There are clearly limits to the extent to which a currency can be supported in this fashion. At the end of 1974, for example, Britain's official foreign exchange reserves totalled around £2 300 million – a considerable sum but none the less vulnerable when experience has shown that 'hot money' movements out of sterling alone have exceeded £1 000 million in a single month. The second possibility is that the Bank of England can itself borrow at short term from other central banks or from the International Monetary Fund (described in Chapter XXXIII below), using the resulting proceeds of foreign currencies to support the demand for its own currency. As will be described in Chapter XXXIII, arrangements for such short-term credit between the central banks of the richer countries of the world are now complex and widespread.

3 THE BALANCE OF PAYMENTS OF THE UNITED KINGDOM

It will be useful to relate the foregoing general discussion of the balance of payments to the actual position in which the United Kingdom has found itself in recent years. The main features of the overall balance may be seen from Table 31.1 for three selected years between 1961 and 1971. The British balance of trade has been typically adverse for many years, a small 'visible' surplus being achieved in only four years since the Second World War. The absolute value of Britain's physical trade rose by some 700 per cent over this period, however, partly because of the marked rise in world prices but also because of an increase in the volume of trade – between 1946 and 1974, the volume of British imports was quadrupled while exports rose even more. Despite the sale of a great many overseas assets, Britain's private invisible earnings have risen steadily over the past 25 years – again, partly because of the worldwide inflation – but a continuing high level of government expenditure overseas has made substantial inroads into the net invisible balance.

The overall outcome of the British balance of payments has oscillated with great violence from one year to another during the past decade: one example was the swing in the 'Total currency flow' from a surplus of about £3 230 million in 1971 to a deficit of about £1 270 million in 1972 – a turn-round of some £4 500 million in twelve months. The three years shown in Table 31.1 cannot therefore be said to be typical – there is no pattern to be typified. They illustrate, however, the mechanism by which different types of situation were accommodated. The years 1961 and 1967, for example, provide examples of situations in which the authorities – then seeking to rigidly maintain a fixed rate of exchange of £1 = $2.80, finally abandoned in favour of £1 = $2.40 in November 1967 – were driven to substantial 'compensatory financing' in support of the pound. In both years the trade balance was in deficit, but the state of the current balance was clearly much less favourable in the latter year. In both years net capital outflows added around £350 million to the supply of sterling in the market. In 1961 the authorities were able to deal with this relatively easily, being able to draw on the International Monetary Fund sufficient not only to offset this excess supply but to add some £31 million to the official reserves. The position in 1967 was very different. The size of the net outflow of sterling was doubled and recourse could not be had to the International Monetary Fund. As a result, substantial short-term borrowing from overseas governments proved necessary and the official reserves were drawn down by £115 million. In the event even this large-scale support was insufficient to keep the pound at its official parity of $2.80.

The figures for 1971 reveal the opposite situation – it was in fact a spectacularly (and short-lived) successful year for the British balance of payments. The trade balance, unusually, was favourable and the current balance was in surplus to the tune of over £1 000 million. In addition, so far from a net capital outflow occurring, nearly £2 000 million of private capital on

TABLE 31.1 *Overall balance of payments of the
United Kingdom, 1961-71*

£ *million*

	1961	1967	1971
1. Current balance			
a. Merchandise imports	4 043	5 681	8 491
b. Merchandise exports	3 891	5 124	8 790
c. 'Visible' balance (b−a)	−152	−557	+299
d. *Invisible items (net):*			
(i) Transport	−11	+10	+2
(ii) Interest & profits	+254	+379	+470
(iii) Tourism	−24	−38	+53
(iv) Government expen-			
diture	−332	−463	−527
(v) Other	+271	+354	+743
e. Total invisible earnings	+158	+242	+741
Current balance (c + e)	+6	−315	+1 040
2. Capital movements (net)			
a. Private borrowing	−322	−490	+1 931
b. Official borrowing	+6	−5	−92
c. Balancing item	−29	+139	+349
d. Total capital inflow	−345	−356	+2 188
Total currency inflow (1 + 2)	−339	−671	+3 228
3. Official financing			
a. Short-term borrowing	+370	+556	−1 692
b. Reduction in reserves	−31	+115	−1 536
Total official financing	+339	+671	−3 228

Source: Based on *United Kingdom Balance of Payments 1972*, HMSO,
London 1972.
The 'balancing item' (2c) is, in effect, the net outcome of all errors
and omissions in the estimates and is a statement of the
discrepancy between independent estimates of 1 + 2a + 2b, on the
one hand, and item 3 on the other.

balance flowed in. The authorities were thus able to repay nearly £1 700 million short-term debt and simultaneously more than double the official reserves of gold and convertible currencies.

The extraordinary contrast between these not-far-separated years illustrates the extreme vulnerability of the British balance of payments to changes in world economic conditions and, in particular, changes in its relative pace of inflation and capital movements substantially influenced by views held in the outside world concerning likely movements in the rate of exchange of the pound sterling. The authorities therefore need policy instruments which can react quickly to the pronounced deterioration in the external payments situation which experience demonstrates is liable to occur at any time. What are these policy instruments and how successful is their application likely to be?

4   DEVALUATION, DEFLATION AND IMPORT CONTROLS

The relative advantages and disadvantages of fixed and variable exchange rates were discussed at some length in the previous chapter. At first sight the case against fixed exchange rates is overwhelming in the modern world; if a deficit in the balance of payments has to be corrected only by a policy of deflation, this is likely to impose burdens which are nowadays considered intolerable. The effects on the internal rate of growth are likely to be especially unfortunate. If deflationary fiscal measures, or a restrictive monetary policy, make their impact on the rate of expansion of investment and output, rather than on the pace of inflation – and British experience suggests that this is far from unlikely – the improvement so gained is a rather hollow victory. That some improvement will follow in the external situation is indeed probable. The first effect of an acceleration in the growth rate is likely to be a sharp rise in imports as stocks of raw materials and semi-manufactures are built up in order to feed the industrial expansion; the increased outputs – and exports – are likely to emerge only after something of a lag. Similarly, the first effect of a slowing-down in the rate of expansion is likely to be an improvement in the trade figures as imports fall (at least relatively) without any immediate effect on exports. The relief is likely to be only a temporary one, however. Once the initial contraction of imports is over, the country is left with a stagnant economy in which productivity is likely to be growing only slowly, if at all; as its efficiency falls further behind that of its more rapidly expanding competitors the payments deficit is likely to build up again and the country is back where it started. The experience of the modern world shows clearly that it is not the stagnant or slow-growing economies which enjoy comfortable balance-of-payments positions and strong currencies but those in which growth rates have been high and productivity gains correspondingly rapid.

Equally, the experience of exchange depreciation would not support the proposition that it offers an easy solution to the problem of a deficit. The pound was devalued in 1949 and again in 1967; in 1972 the attempt to defend a fixed rate was abandoned and the pound duly drifted downwards. In each case, however, payments difficulties reappeared soon afterwards. One reason is that the immediate effect of a devaluation or depreciation is likely to be a worsening of the payments position; the elasticity of demand for exports is likely to be reasonably high, but there is an inevitable time-lag before the competitive advantage given by the depreciation can reveal itself in the form of a volume of sales sufficiently expanded to more than offset the reduced foreign-currency value of each unit of exports. More important, these additional exports will be forthcoming, however competitive their price, only if capacity to produce them exists within the domestic economy – which implies either expanded output or fiscal measures to reduce the usage of resources in domestic consumption, neither of which is by any means automatically forthcoming.

A further difficulty with devaluation has been that by raising the cost of imports to home producers it has tended to result in a rise in the cost of exports – the imports may be raw materials which are subsequently embodied into manufactured exports. The rise in export prices, of course, will automatically lessen the advantage bestowed by devaluation. Finally, and most important, the rise in the price of imported foodstuffs resulting from devaluation may exert such a marked effect on the general cost of living that demands for further wage increases are immediately and not unreasonably inspired. This may accentuate the wage–price spiral and lead to a general rise in the level of costs and prices which offsets, or more than offsets, the initial advantage in foreign markets secured by devaluation.

It must be admitted that in ideal terms – i.e. in terms of a simultaneous achievement of external balance and internal growth – the problem has never yet been solved by the British economy. Yet, difficult and unpleasant though it may be, countries will have to find some way of adjusting their internal output and price level when faced with a deficit on their balance of payments if they are not to run the risks inherent in the continuous rise of prices and corresponding decline of exchange rates. This is not quite the verdict of despair that it might seem at first sight. So long as the general upward trend in money incomes and prices continues throughout the world – and it shows little sign of ending at the moment – a debtor country will be able to bring its costs back into line if it can succeed in moderating the pace of its inflation – perhaps through some form of incomes policy – while that of the creditor countries goes on increasing, without needing to attempt an absolute reduction in the level of money incomes. The same effect of a relative cheapening of exports will be secured. For example, suppose a country succeeds in maintaining a relatively stable level of incomes and prices at a time when world prices in general rise 10 per cent. Its exports would then be 10 per cent cheaper, in comparison with the products of the rest of the world, without any actual fall in the price of its exports. Similarly, if productivity is increasing rapidly – a process which will be assisted by a high rate of internal growth – costs can be reduced by achieving a somewhat slower rise in factor-incomes, resulting in a fall in unit costs of production without the attempt to force a complete standstill in money wages and profits in absolute terms. But even the task of achieving relative stability at a time of rising prices in the outside world, or of increasing productivity rapidly, is an immensely difficult one; it must be admitted that Britain has not yet provided convincing evidence of having mastered it. Nevertheless it is a good deal nearer practical possibility than the task of reducing incomes in absolute terms, and if international trade is to maintain a reasonable degree of freedom and stability it is a task which will have to be accomplished.

One difficulty with policies of this kind – securing adjustment of a deficit through relative price stability at a time of external inflation or rising productivity – is that it must necessarily take some considerable time to achieve success. If world prices are rising at a rate of 2 or 3 per cent a year more than in Britain, or world productivity at 1 or 2 per cent a year less, the costs of British manufacturers will still fall in relation to those of the rest of the world at a pretty slow rate. Several years may elapse before the movement has progressed far enough to close a substantial payments deficit. If the country's exchange reserves are too small to sustain the outflow which will continue in the meanwhile, and if further depreciation in the currency is to be avoided, import controls – either direct quantitative restrictions on specified imports, or the use of exchange control measures – may be resorted to.

The advantage of such controls is that they enable a country to ensure that imports are restricted to the level it can currently afford, and, furthermore, that the imports allowed in are those giving the highest degree of benefit to society as a whole. Just as in a war foreign currencies are mobilised in the interests of the war effort, so in peace direct controls can ensure that foreign currencies in short supply are not being employed to purchase luxury goods rather than essential foodstuffs and raw materials.

As a short-term measure to permit readjustment within the economy import controls may have much to be said for them. There is no other way of ensuring that scarce currencies are not squandered on Cadillacs and vintage champagnes while bread has to be rationed because of a shortage of wheat, or industry is hampered by a lack of raw materials. As a permanent feature of the economy, however, they suffer from all the disadvantages mentioned earlier in connection with protection. In particular, they tend to foster inefficiency by allowing home industries to continue and expand without the foreign competition which would force them to hold down costs to the absolute minimum. In any case, such controls can never be a substitute for a policy aimed at the correction of the fundamental causes of a deficit. In so far as they succeed in reducing imports, the supply of goods available in the home market at a time of full employment is thereby reduced, so that the pressure of demand on prices is accentuated. There are at least some reasonable grounds for arguing that in the last resort there is no satisfactory substitute for a policy which aims directly and honestly at restraining internal demand within the limits which the country can afford. Yet if such a policy is carried to such lengths, or administered in such a way, as to hold the economy below its potential growth path it may well be self-defeating in the long run.

So the policy trade-offs grow and multiply. Full employment, steady growth, stability of internal prices, free collective bargaining, unrestricted international trade, stability of exchange rates – all are intrinsically desirable yet each conflicts with at least one of the others. No policy prescription which claims to guarantee one without specifying the loss of another is either feasible or honest. The problem facing society is not to determine which policy aim it must have but rather to determine what particular mix short of the ideal represents the most desirable practical outcome it is reasonable to expect in an imperfect and uncertain world.

FURTHER READING

T. SCITOVSKY *Money and the balance of payments* Chs. 7–12

S. J. WELLS *International economics* Chs. 11–12 and 16

I. PEARCE *International trade* Book 1, Chs. 4–5

J. ADAMS *International economics* Part III, 12–14

H. KATRAK *International trade and the balance of payments* Ch. 6

B. J. COHEN *Balance of payments policy* Penguin Books, London 1969

CHAPTER XXXII

The European Economic Community

1 THE POST-WAR BACKGROUND

THE history of modern Europe has been distinguished by periodic attempts to create a higher degree of political and economic unity amongst its many independent states. The tremendous human and physical losses which they have succeeded in inflicting on one another through war during the first half of this century inevitably strengthened the political motives behind these attempts; the enormous suffering of the Second World War, and the manifest insecurity of Europe's position after it, naturally resulted in a resurgence of efforts to weld the separate states of Western Europe into some form of political unity.

With one exception, however, these early post-war attempts to establish a political or economic union in Europe came to nothing. The exception was the agreement reached between the governments of Belgium, Luxembourg and the Netherlands, in successive stages between 1943 and 1946, to establish a customs community, and eventually a full economic union, amongst themselves. This union, Benelux, was the only positive result to emerge from the many proposals for European unity; in general, the long tradition of independent political sovereignty and the national rivalries accumulated over many generations proved too formidable for the somewhat idealistic plans for political unification advanced from time to time.

Considerably more progress was made from 1948 onwards, however, with the creation of the Organisation for European Economic Co-operation (OEEC) – renamed the Organisation for Economic Co-operation and Development (OECD) in 1961. This body was set up by seventeen (later eighteen) countries of

Western Europe, with the United States and Canada as associate members, for the purpose of administering the European Recovery Programme (the Marshall Plan) under which the United States provided a series of large annual dollar grants to assist in the reconstruction of the European economy. As part of this process the OEEC countries embarked on a programme of gradual liberalisation of the trade between member countries – i.e. the concerted removal of quantitative restrictions on imports from other OEEC members. By 1956 this programme had succeeded in freeing about 90 per cent of intra-OEEC trade from such restrictions.

This undoubtedly represented a considerable advance towards a reduction of the barriers within the European economy. It did nothing towards a positive integration of the separate economies, however, which many in Europe believed to be the only way in which Europe could attain its maximum potential stability and prosperity. Any movement towards full political union being impracticable, a start towards a gradual 'sector-by-sector' integration was made in 1952 as a result of the initiative of the leaders of the integration movement in Europe. This was the establishment of the European Coal and Steel Community (ECSC), by which six countries – France, Germany, Italy and the Benelux countries – agreed to place their coal and steel industries under the control of an independent High Authority responsible to a European Parliament comprised of members from the six participating countries. A single market for coal and steel was to be established throughout the six countries, and the industries would be run by the High Authority as a single entity, and not as six independent, and sometimes overlapping and duplicating, national units.

The United Kingdom participated in the early stages of the negotiations leading to the establishment of ECSC but ultimately withdrew and declined to join the Community when it was formed. The basic reason is clear. Unlike OEEC, the ECSC was essentially supra-national. Membership of OEEC merely involved negotiation and agreement with other sovereign states, each of which had a veto over decisions of OEEC as a whole. The ECSC, on the other hand, involved the handing over of the management of a sector of the economy to a body, the High Authority, over which member governments had no control and which was answerable only to a European Parliament in which a majority vote would prevail. Sovereignty was clearly sacrificed by membership of ECSC, and the United Kingdom was not prepared to accept this.

In the latter part of the 1950s, then, two quite separate movements were at work in Europe. The OEEC programme of the removal of quantitative restrictions on trade, however, had proceeded virtually to its limit. Further advance towards integration via OEEC could take place only through a reduction in the *other* main type of restriction on trade — i.e. tariffs. Here, however, the 'gradualist' approach of OEEC met a fundamental difficulty. With one exception, all OEEC members were also members of another international body set up after the Second World War to establish an orderly system of rules for the conduct of international trade and to reduce as far as possible hindrances to it — the General Agreement on Tariffs and Trade (GATT). They were therefore bound by a fundamental GATT rule that a preference (i.e. a tariff reduction) cannot be extended by a member unless it is simultaneously extended to *all* GATT members. Since most GATT members are not European, this made the problem of closer *European* integration through tariff reductions apparently insoluble.

There is one important exception to the GATT rule of no-new-preference, however. It is open to GATT members to reduce tariffs on imports from one or more specified countries provided that this takes the form of *the removal of all tariffs* on trade between the countries concerned — i.e. the creation of free trade, or a customs union, between those countries. Foreseeing the situation which would arise as OEEC reached the limit of its liberalisation programme, therefore, the ECSC governments — in which the influence of the proponents of European integration was very strong — began a series of negotiations aimed at the establishment of such a customs union amongst themselves. These culminated in an agreement embodied in the Treaty of Rome, signed in 1957.

The United Kingdom did not feel itself able to join in this

agreement, nor did the other OEEC countries outside the six ECSC members. It is dangerous to over-simplify so highly complex a matter, but in essence it was the ECSC issue over again – the Treaty of Rome involved a sacrifice of sovereignty which the non-participating countries were not willing to make. In 1961 the whole question of the United Kingdom, and other European countries, acceding to the Treaty of Rome was raised again but again the negotiations failed; on this occasion Britain's entry was vetoed by France for political reasons. After a third round of negotiations in 1970–71, however, the hurdles were finally overcome and in January 1973 Britain, together with Denmark and Ireland, became full members of the Community by signing a Treaty of Accession.

2 THE TREATY OF ROME

Two treaties were in fact signed by the same group of countries in Rome in 1957. One of them established a community called Euratom, the aim of which was to achieve in the field of atomic energy the same type of integration amongst the signatory countries that the ECSC was working towards in the coal and steel industries. The term 'Rome Treaty' almost invariably refers to the other treaty which established the European Economic Community (EEC), which itself includes the ECSC and Euratom. Fundamentally the EEC is a political concept; the primary purpose of the Rome Treaty is declared in its preamble to be 'to establish the foundations of an ever closer union among the European peoples'. This discussion will nevertheless be confined to the economic aspects of the EEC only, as befits a work on economic analysis. In any case, the political intentions of the Treaty are stated in the very broadest terms only, and there are considerable differences of opinion within the EEC countries themselves concerning the precise political form which the Community will ultimately take. At one extreme are those who conceive of the EEC as remaining a group of separate political states who pool their sovereignty only in those respects and in that degree necessary to achieve the Treaty's economic ends; at the other extreme are those who see the economic provisions of the Treaty not as ends in themselves but as no more than means to the ultimate political goal – a single, federal United States of Europe in which the members will have ceased to exist as individual sovereign entities just as the states of the United States of America have.

In order to achieve its ends, the Treaty created a system of four main institutions. The first is the *Council of Ministers*, comprised of one Minister appointed by each of the nine national governments; the second is the *European Commission*, composed of fourteen members and having a fairly large secretariat. The fourteen Commissioners are appointed by general agreement amongst the member governments, not more than two being from any one member country, but are entirely independent of their own national governments. Between them, the Council and Commission are at present the essential elements of the EEC structure. In a very broad way they can be likened to the government and civil service of an independent state, except that in most cases the Council can decide only *after* a recommendation has been made to it by the Commission, and the Commission (unlike a national civil service) may act independently of the Council in certain matters. The third institution is the *Assembly* or European Parliament, now consisting of 208 members of the parliaments of the member states nominated in agreed proportions. In theory, the Council and Commission – like the ECSC High Authority and Euratom – are answerable to it; in practice its powers are severely limited, and it seems certain to remain little more than an advisory body for some time to come. Finally, there is the European *Court of Justice* established to decide cases arising out of the provisions of the Treaty or from the operation of any of its institutions.

The essential core of the EEC is contained in the Treaty's provisions for the establishment of a customs union and, ultimately, a common market. A customs union implies two things: first, completely free trade within the customs union area and, secondly, uniformity of tariffs on any product imported into the customs union area. Without the second, the first would be difficult (although not impossible) to administer; if the outer tariff was higher in one part of the customs union than in another, goods would simply flow over the low tariff wall and be re-consigned (under free trade conditions, of course) to the region having a high outer tariff on the commodity concerned.

The procedure laid down in the Rome Treaty for securing free internal trade between EEC members is simple. First, no member was allowed to introduce any *new* duty on its trade with any other member. Second, all existing tariffs were to be cut by 10 per cent by each country so far as imports from other EEC countries were concerned on 1 January 1959. Thereafter this procedure of an all-round reduction of duties on imports from other member countries was to be repeated at intervals not longer than 18 months generally, so that all intra-EEC trade would be duty-free by (at latest) 1 January 1973. This period between the date of the first reduction (1959) and that of the complete removal of all internal duties was known as the 'transitional' period; the Treaty provided that under no circumstances could it exceed fifteen years. In fact the six original members moved ahead of their timetable and all internal tariffs were abolished by July 1968.

The other element of the customs union – the adoption by all members of a common tariff structure for imports from the rest of the world – was to follow a similar programme. The common tariff laid down as the ultimate target was defined to be *in general* the arithmetic average of the tariffs levied on each product by the six member countries on 1 January 1957. For a large number of commodities specified in lists attached to the Treaty, however, it was provided that the final tariff should not exceed stated maximum rates (the commodities were mostly basic raw materials on which the final rates were in general to be comparatively low) or should be the subject of subsequent negotiations. Like the abolition of internal duties, the movement towards the common tariff – involving tariff increases for some countries and reductions for others – was planned in stages over the same transitional period. (The Commission was given power to give reliefs of various sorts for countries experiencing special difficulty in pursuing this programme.) The progress of the EEC on both these fronts was in fact more rapid than that laid down in the Treaty; like the abolition of internal tariffs, the establishment of the common external tariff was in fact completed in July 1968, a year and a half ahead of the original target.

A *common market*, however, implies rather more than an absence of duties and quota restrictions within the area concerned. Hence the Rome Treaty contained a great many provisions designed to remove 'artificial' differences between the economies of the participating countries. All *restrictions* on the movement of people or capital between the member countries are to be removed; an enterprise from one member country must be completely free to operate in any other member country on equal terms with indigenous enterprises and so on. A series of provisions is designed to ensure what is called *fair competition* – the avoidance of 'dumping' (i.e. sales abroad at less than true average cost), of open or concealed subsidies to enterprises of one country rather than another, of differential transport rates which discriminated against enterprises of another member country, or of differences in anti-monopoly legislation. Similarly, provisions seek to establish uniform *social policies* – equal pay for men and women, comparable and transferable social security benefits, consistency in the levying of employees' social security contributions, etc.

One aspect of these special provisions worth noting is the inclusion in the Rome Treaty of an instruction that the Commission should draw up a common *agricultural policy* which would gradually replace the various national agricultural policies then prevailing in the member countries. Agriculture has always been, of its nature, subject to fluctuations of prosperity of a peculiarly violent kind – mainly because of an inelastic demand, a highly inelastic supply and the very large number of small-scale enterprises involved – and for political and social reasons is regulated by government policy to an unusual degree. The Community has now adopted a complex Common Agricultural Policy to which Britain, like all other members, must adhere. The policy consists of a network of highly organised marketing arrangements for each product and a system of guaranteed minimum prices and protection for the farmer by means of variable levies on imports from other countries. As will be seen, the adoption of such a policy for agriculture by the EEC has created special problems for the United Kingdom.

3 GAINS FROM THE COMMON MARKET

The previous section has attempted a very condensed summary of a highly complex organisation — an organisation, furthermore, which is continuing to change and develop as time proceeds. Essentially, of course, the end of all the provisions of the Rome Treaty is the transformation of nine individual countries into what is, for economic purposes at any rate, a single market. The gains to be secured from this transformation are in principle quite clear. Just as the law of comparative costs is the application to international trade of the familiar concept of the division of labour, so the creation of a common market is in effect a widening for each participating country of the area over which the law of comparative costs, or specialisation, is allowed to exert itself. All the gains which are secured by the free working of the price mechanism and specialisation internally can be secured to a higher degree by extending the volume of resources over which hindrances to their free operation are removed.

This is the essence of the thing: the arguments advanced in favour of the particular application of this principle in the form of the European Common Market are no more than practical variations on this theme. For example, it is argued that the countries participating in the EEC will derive benefit from the vastly increased market which will be opened to their industries as a result of membership in that common market. Instead of operating on the basis of nine separate markets each industry has access to a single market bigger in terms of population, as Table 32.1 shows, than the United States; in terms of total income its size is of course smaller in relation to the United States, but it would still be very large. Given such a market, European industry is able to plan for output levels at which economies of scale otherwise denied to it can be exploited to the full.

Secondly, and obviously following from this, it is argued that the Common Market encourages a higher degree of specialisation between the member countries. Given a single, unified market, the production of a commodity can be concentrated in the areas best suited to it and not, as previously, duplicated in national industries of widely varying degrees of efficiency.

TABLE 32.1   *The European Economic Community, 1972*

	Population (mn.)	Gross Domestic Product at market prices	
		Total £ mn	Per head £
1. 'The Six'			
Belgium	9·71	14 201	1 463
Luxembourg	0·35	435	1 243
France	51·70	78 259	1 514
West Germany	61·67	102 806	1 667
Italy	54·34	46 951	864
Netherlands	13·33	18 476	1 386
Total	191·10	261 128	1 366
2. 'The Three'			
Denmark	4·99	6 957	1 394
Ireland	3·01	2 131	708
United Kingdom	55·88	61 539	1 101
Total, EEC	254·98	331 755	1 301
United States	208·84	465 910	2 231
Japan	106·96	117 458	1 098

Source: Based on data in *OECD Observer* No. 68, Paris, February 1974. GDP totals converted into £ at the average rate for 1972.

Finally, it is argued that the removal of national barriers and creation of a single large market exposes industries to a higher degree of competition with salutary effects on their efficiency, while the possibilities opened up to enterprises gives an impulse of dynamic expansion with consequent benefits to the growth of the whole economy. Many would suggest, indeed, that this latter effect was clearly visible during the 1960s for what were then the six members of the Community. During the decade following the signing of the Rome Treaty the rate of economic growth in each of the member countries exceeded that in the United States – being in some cases twice as great – and with the single, and rather special, exception of Germany considerably greater than during the 1950s. One must beware, however, of the fallacy of *post hoc, ergo propter hoc*; that rapid growth followed the creation of the E E C is undeniable, but that the creation of the E E C was the *cause* is a proposition on which views may legitimately differ.

Summing up, then, the protagonists of the E E C would argue that through increased scale of operation, a higher degree of specialisation and more intense competition the Common Market will result in a higher, and more rapidly rising, level of real income for the populations of the participating countries – all the gains, in other words, which the analysis of Chapter XIV suggest would accrue from the free operation of the market economy.

4 DISADVANTAGES OF THE COMMON MARKET

On grounds of pure theory, only one economic consideration can be set against these arguments in favour of the E E C. In so far as it removes internal duties, a customs union such as the E E C will undoubtedly stimulate trade between the member countries. But it may also divert trade, and the net balance of effects may not be wholly favourable. Suppose that countries A and B both have a tariff of 50 per cent on imports of transistor radios; suppose also that B and a third country, C, are producers of transistor radios, C being the more efficient producer with production costs some 20 per cent below those of B. In the initial situation, A and B are independent countries and A will naturally import its transistor radios from C. If A and B now enter a full customs union, A's tariff on imports of tran-

sistor radios from B becomes zero, although it remains at 50
per cent, of course, on imports from C. Consumers in A will
therefore find B's radios cheaper than C's, and the import trade
will shift accordingly from C to B. The effect of the customs
union will thus be to reduce the output of the more efficient
producer, C, and increase that of the less efficient producer, B.
Overall, therefore, resources are allocated less efficiently after
the event than before.

The issues involved may perhaps be seen more clearly from
the diagram in Fig. 32A(i). Suppose that the line DD' represents the demand schedule for some product in country A which
does not itself produce it, that CC' and BB' are the supply
schedules of the product from countries C and B respectively
but that C_tC_t' and B_tB_t' are the effective supply schedules after
the imposition of a standard tariff by A on all imports. The
consumer is therefore able to purchase the product at a price
RM and country B is simply not able to compete at all in that
market.

Let A and B now enter into a customs union so that the tariff
on imports from B disappears. The effective supply curve now
becomes BB' since, without having a tariff levied on its products, country B is able to undersell C which still suffers from
the tariff. Price will therefore fall to NU and imports (ON) will
be drawn entirely from country B. What are the gains and
losses to A? Consumers benefit from the lower price and this

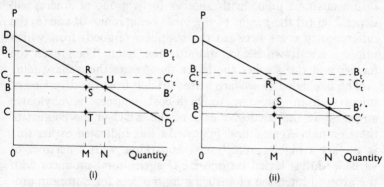

Fig. 32A   The trade diversion effect

gain is represented by the increase in consumer surplus C_tRUB. On the other hand, since no tariff is now levied on imports, the government of A *loses* the tax revenue it previously enjoyed — C_tRTC, the revenue from a tax of RT on the previous OM of imports. Now the area BC_tRS is common to both the gain of consumer surplus and the loss of tax revenue. The overall gain or loss to country A therefore depends on the relative areas of the triangle RSU (net gain of consumer surplus) and the rectangle $BSTC$ (net loss of tax revenue). In the case of Fig. 32A(i) the balance is clearly disadvantageous to country A — the loss incurred in switching to the high-cost source of imports ($BSTC$) obviously exceeds the net consumer gain (RSU). The trade-diversion effect of the customs union has resulted in a loss of welfare to A.

This need not necessarily be the case: it arises in the situation of Fig. 32A(i) essentially because the cost difference between the two import-sources, B and C, is relatively large. In the case illustrated in Fig. 32A(ii) this cost differential is much smaller. In the pre-customs-union situation C still has the cost advantage but the switch to B as a result of the union gives a much larger net consumer gain (RSU) than the net tax revenue loss ($BSTC$). In this instance A's welfare has been raised by the Customs Union despite the diversion of imports to a somewhat less efficient producer. This illustrates the general conclusion that the welfare effects to any country from entering into a customs union with another (or a group of others) will depend on (*a*) the height of the tariff being removed and (*b*) the difference in costs between the suppliers of goods from which imports are drawn before and after the union. The greater the former and the smaller the latter the greater the welfare gain.

The likelihood of welfare losses arising from the diversion of imports from low-cost to high-cost sources is obviously strongest in the particular case of the EEC in the context of the Common Agricultural Policy. As was indicated earlier this is in fact a highly protectionist apparatus, with a network of variable duties levied on non-EEC agricultural products with the avowed intention of ensuring high prices for European producers. The effect is necessarily — and intentionally — to ensure

the survival and, indeed, the expansion of domestic food production in Europe at the expense of (hitherto) low-cost production in the traditional non-European exporting countries. This
point gained especial importance as a result of Britain joining
the EEC. Britain is currently the world's largest importer of
foodstuffs and its previous tariff on food imports had been
either zero or very low in comparison with that of the EEC
countries. Serious repercussions on the pattern of world food
production were therefore inevitable when the United Kingdom
was in effect transformed from a low-tariff to a high-tariff
country *vis-à-vis* agricultural imports from outside Europe.

What the precise magnitude of these effects have been is
exceedingly difficult to say, since in practice the trade-diverting
effects of the EEC have been obscured by the *growth* in EEC
imports from the outside world (despite the obstacle of the
EEC tariff) as a result of its rapid rate of internal growth. One
study of the EEC in the first seven years of its life has indicated that for industrialised countries such as the United States
and Britain this latter effect more than offset the trade-
diversion effect on their exports to the EEC; for the mainly
food-producing countries, however, the trade-diversion effect
was predominant and substantial.

This is without doubt the main immediate economic disadvantage of membership of the EEC, but it is by no means
obvious that the costs of European food will continue to be high
in comparison with those of non-European suppliers. Again,
obtaining the benefits of an extension of a free market across
national boundaries implies the loss of national powers in major
respects. In discussing the policy of maintaining rigidly fixed
foreign exchange rates it was pointed out that the system implicitly assumed sufficient flexibility in price-levels to maintain
international equilibrium. Exactly the same is true within a common market. If costs and prices rise more rapidly in one member
country than another, goods will obviously flow in from the rest
of the area and restrictions on imports cannot be applied to
prevent it; ultimately output and employment in the high-cost
area must decline unless the price discrepancy is corrected. The
power of each country to inflate or deflate independently, in other

words, is lost. Income and output policy has to be a common policy, not a national one. If payments difficulties arise with the outside world, for example, a country might find itself forced to adopt a deflationary policy where, as an independent country, it might have resorted to devaluation or import restrictions. National freedom of action is lost; if differences exist amongst the member countries concerning the relative importance attached to, say, the maintenance of full employment, on the one hand, and price stability, on the other, each country will have to accept the majority view.

This, at least, will be the position when the EEC reaches its goal of full economic union and, in particular, if and when it attains the declared end of full *monetary* union. This would require the currency of each member country to be freely convertible into the currency of every other member at a permanently fixed rate, thus reducing the difference between national currencies to the purely nominal status involved in the difference between a pound note issued by the Bank of Scotland and one issued by the Bank of England. Europe is a good deal short of this state yet and may indeed never reach it; in the meantime member countries retain some degree of freedom in their power to alter the exchange rate – or let the market alter it for them – if and when their domestic price levels get out of line. But it is of the inherent logic of the EEC that ultimately one monetary system should cover the whole of its area just as one does in the United States.

This leads on to the third possible source of danger attached to the common market; unlike the previous consideration, it is a matter of policy rather than principle. To a large degree, the extent to which the EEC secures the benefits of a free market economy will depend on the broad philosophy with which the institutional weapons are used. A large market could develop into an extension of monopoly and cartel powers, for example, if the anti-monopoly provisions are weakly applied; the agricultural policy could be permanently applied to benefit farmers at the expense of consumers without any serious attempt to raise the efficiency of European agriculture; the harmonisation of social security systems could gravitate towards no more than the lowest common denominator; escape clauses could be operated with an eye to internal political exigencies rather than on strict economic grounds, and so on. All this is a matter of opinion rather than analysis; how substantial such anxieties may be only experience can show.

5 BRITAIN AND THE EEC

The considerations set out in the previous sections naturally entered into the decision of the United Kingdom to join the Community in 1973 and it would be a fair statement that that decision was a good deal less than unanimous. The main opposition was naturally political: the inherent logic of the Treaty of Rome is that the sovereignty of the individual member countries, and of their legislatures, will in due course be subsumed into the larger entity of the Community as a whole. To many in Britain this was, and remains, an unacceptable proposition; others, of course, regard it as being, on the contrary, the only realistic prospect for the continuance of British influence on world affairs in any effective form. The disagreement is profound and probably irremovable: it is certainly political rather than economic.

A second peculiarly British problem with the EEC was that of the Commonwealth. From 1932, the Commonwealth countries operated a tariff system under which preferential treatment was given to (i.e. lower tariffs imposed on) goods from other Commonwealth members in comparison with imports from non-Commonwealth countries. This system (the Imperial Preference system) was only one element, of course, in the network of political, economic and cultural ties which bound the Commonwealth together into a flexible but none the less real unity. British membership of the EEC necessarily transformed the position of Commonwealth exporters to the United Kingdom from one of a preferential kind into one in which they were actually discriminated against – i.e. their goods are subject to the EEC's common external tariff, whereas similar goods from other EEC countries enter duty-free. This is particularly far-reaching in the context of the type of imports of foodstuffs produced in the EEC countries (or their overseas territories) which made up a very large element of Commonwealth exports to the United Kingdom. (Indeed, it is not always easy to distinguish between this semi-political Commonwealth problem and the related cost problem – discussed below – imposed on Britain when its sources of duty-free – and hence cheap – raw materials and foodstuffs were suddenly replaced by high-cost European sources or supplies from elsewhere on which substantial import duties are payable.) Many people doubt, in fact, whether the Commonwealth as such will long survive this development.

A great part of this problem was overcome by the negotiation of special agreements covering exports from the developing countries in the Commonwealth, especially in Africa, the Caribbean and the Indian Ocean; in general these countries were given preferential access to the whole EEC area on the same footing as the dependent overseas territories of the Six. For the rest it seems clear that if Britain's entry into the EEC reduces the economic significance of the Commonwealth it will be no more than a reinforcement of a long-established trend. In 1951 imports into Britain from the sterling area (roughly synonymous with the Commonwealth) accounted for about 36 per cent of the total, whereas by 1974 the proportion was down to 17 per cent; similarly, the sterling area took 51 per cent of Britain's exports in 1951 but only 18 per cent in 1974.

Without doubt the issue over which controversy raged most fiercely, however, was the cost imposed on Britain as a result of entry and especially by the financing of the common agricultural policy. To understand this it will be helpful to examine briefly the arrangements for the Community's annual budget initially drawn up by the Commission and ultimately approved by the Council of Ministers. For 1973 the net expenditure items were as shown in the table opposite. Although the future pattern is bound to change, it will be seen that currently by far the greatest part of EEC spending is devoted to the agricultural policy. Basically, guaranteed prices are laid down by the Commission and the sums paid out by way of price supports are the amounts necessary to bridge the gap between these guaranteed

	£ mn.	%
1. *Agriculture:* price supports and other assistance	1 410	84·9
2. *European Social Fund*	100	6·0
3. *EEC Commission:* running cost	88	5·3
4. *Council of Ministers*, Court of Justice and Parliament	27	1·6
5. *Euratom:* research & investment	36	2·2
	1 661	100

prices and actual market prices paid by consumers – the latter in any case being held up to fairly high levels by means of levies imposed on imports from non-EEC sources. Since Britain accounts for only some 10 per cent of the agricultural output of the EEC, it is clear that the share of this total expenditure accruing to Britain will be correspondingly small.

The revenue side of the Community Budget is inevitably complex. Since 1971 all levies on agricultural imports from non-EEC sources (apart from a margin to cover collection costs) are handed over to the Community, as is an increasing proportion of all Customs duties on non-agricultural imports; from 1975 *all* such duties (apart from collection costs) are to be passed to the Community. In addition, from 1975 onwards the Community will be entitled to a proportion of the revenues of the Value Added Tax in all member countries of whatever size is necessary to bring its total receipts up to its total expenditure requirements. From that point on, in other words, the Community will be self-financing in that its revenue will be determined automatically and without the need for special approval by individual member governments.

In the meantime each member country has agreed to make good any deficiency between the Community's expenditure requirements and its import-duty revenues by means of a contribution roughly equivalent to its gross national product; the maximum percentage contribution which Britain may be called on to make to the budget is estimated to rise from just under 9 per cent of the total in 1973 to as much as about 19 per cent in 1977.

What it comes to, then, is that Britain, being a major importer of food, is likely to pay a high proportion of the revenues accruing to the Community from import levies and having a relatively large gross national product is equally likely to make a substantial contribution in other ways; having a relatively small agricultural sector it is likely to receive a small share of the Community's expenditure so long as that is dominated by the costs of the common agricultural policy. The exact magnitude of this net contribution as the years proceed is a matter of considerable disagreement and cannot be accurately forecast: much will depend on the responsiveness of British agricultural output to the spur of high guaranteed prices, the developing efficiency of European agriculture and the extent to which the gap between European farm prices and those of the outside world – from which our imports would alternatively have been drawn – widens or narrows.

Above and beyond this, of course, is the equally unpredictable gain accruing to Britain on the industrial side from the opening-up of the European market to British entrepreneurs and from any acceleration in the overall rate of growth induced by membership of the Community. To a large degree, these are simply unknowns – as, indeed, are the purely political consequences of membership. In the end the debate reduces to a matter of faith rather than statistics – as must any area in which economic consequences may be extensive and important but in which, nevertheless, political aims and attitudes predominate.

FURTHER READING

S. J. WELLS *International economics* Chs. 20–22
H. KATRAK *International trade and the balance of payments* Ch. 5
D. SWANN *The economics of the Common Market* 2nd edn., Penguin Books, London 1972

CHAPTER XXXIII

The International Monetary System

1 THE PROBLEM OF WORLD MONEY

IDEALISTS sometimes argue that the human lot would be a great deal happier and more stable if all the countries of the world used the same currency, just as they are liable to believe that the same results would follow if all the nations of the world spoke the same language. Whether such beliefs are well-founded or not must remain a matter for argument but the facts are that the nations of the world do *not* have a single currency or a common language and are not likely to have them in the foreseeable future. National currencies, like languages, are as important a manifestation of sovereignty as independent legislatures, legal systems or a seat in the United Nations. If and when the nations of the world volunteer to sacrifice their sovereign powers to some supra-national government then a single currency may come into existence — as it did for the United States when a federal government was established and the individual states ceased to be totally self-governing. That day is a very long way ahead.

It might be argued, however, that national currencies could co-exist with an international currency if each national currency was freely convertible into the international currency at some fixed rate — the effect would be the same as using a single world currency. For many years, until 1931, such a system did in fact operate under the name of the international gold standard. Each currency was declared freely convertible into a fixed weight of gold and the rate of exchange between any two currencies was thus automatically defined. In order to maintain this fixed rate of exchange, it was necessary for the central bank of each country to regulate the supply of its own money in accordance with the state of its gold reserves; just as a commercial bank must reduce its deposits if its reserves fall below the requisite level, so on an international plane the central bank could honour its commitment to gold convertibility only by reducing its total liabilities in terms of its domestic money supply whenever its gold reserves fell below some ratio which experience indicated to be adequate.

The analysis of previous chapters has sought to bring out the severe limitations imposed by such a rigidly fixed system of exchange rates, and the experience of the 1930s demonstrated these in terms of harsh reality. Essentially, the commitment to the convertibility of a currency into all others at some fixed rate necessarily creates a conflict between external payments equilibrium and the maintenance of a high level of output, employment and growth in the domestic economy. If the foreign exchange rate is rigidly fixed, any differences which emerge in relative price-levels and productivity must be cured by deflation; if internal wages and price levels are not flexible in a downwards direction, that deflation must work through the level of employment and output. The aggregate demand curve is shifting down against an aggregate supply curve which is immovable: prices may ultimately fall in relation to the outside world, but only at the expense of the level of real national output.

The onset of depression in the United States in 1930, inevitably transmitted to the rest of the world through this fixed-rate system, brought this policy conflict into the open to an unparalleled degree. One after the other, practically all developed countries demonstrated that the state of their internal economies occupied a higher priority than the defence of the gold-standard parity of their currencies. By 1931 Britain and many other countries had abandoned the commitment to convert into gold on demand at a fixed rate and the link between the state of the gold reserves held by the Bank of England and the internal money supply was permanently broken. Ultimately the same was true for the rest of the world.

The years which followed saw the establishment of a system of free exchange rates with major countries intervening to some degree in foreign exchange markets to maintain stability: Britain's instrument in this context was of course the Exchange Equalisation Account. It soon became clear, however, that the abandonment of the gold standard was not in itself the sole answer to the problems of world depression. Reducing the external value of a currency can give a competitive advantage to the export industries of one country, and a degree of protection from foreign competition in the home market, but only for one country in isolation. If *all* countries devalue the trick will not work. Similarly, the creation of a protective tariff – to which Britain resorted also in 1931–32 – will protect domestic industry but will be self-defeating if all other countries follow suit. This was in fact the outcome during the 1930s; competitive and beggar-my-neighbour trade policies merely reduced the overall level of international trade, benefiting none and in fact leaving all worse off. The world had encountered the harsh reality that if all countries are free to devalue their currencies, *no* country is free to do so.

It was against the background of this experience that a conference was held at Bretton Woods towards the end of the Second World War to do for the international monetary system what it was hoped the United Nations would do for the postwar political system: to avoid the errors of the past and to establish a basis whereby necessary adjustments could be secured through reasoned agreement and co-operation rather than self-defeating competition.

As the experts at that conference saw it, three ingredients were necessary to any efficient international monetary system. First, the chaos of unstable foreign exchange markets, at the mercy of large-scale speculative movements of hot money, must be replaced by a system of stable exchange rates but not one which, like the old gold standard system, achieved it at the expense of instability in domestic output and employment. Second, provision must be made for occasional adjustments in the exchange rates of particular currencies when the internal price levels of the countries concerned had drifted seriously and irrevocably out of line – deflation as a technique of restoring a fundamental disequilibrium was to be replaced by occasional, controlled re-alignments of currencies. To avoid the competitive scramble of the 1930s, however, such unavoidable realignments by individual countries having no acceptable alternative must not be followed by a self-defeating repetition by the rest of the world. Third, countries should have some systematic means of short-term borrowing to meet temporary balance-of-payments problems without being forced to resort to currency depreciation or trade restrictions which would have the effect of transmitting the difficulties to other countries through the international multiplier. There needed to be some other source of temporary assistance on which countries could rely while doing running repairs, so to speak, to their balance of payments.

Such were the aims. The instrument devised by the experts to attain them came into operation in 1945 and was called the International Monetary Fund.

2   THE INTERNATIONAL MONETARY FUND

The Charter of the International Monetary Fund (IMF) was inevitably a highly complex document and only the broad nature of its main provisions need be summarised here. It was originally signed by 29 governments but the number of member countries has steadily grown to 126 in 1974 as the number of independent countries has increased. In general it may be said that its membership includes all countries except those in the Soviet bloc.

The first object of the IMF was to achieve stability of foreign exchange rates and this was secured by the agreement of all member countries to maintain a rate of exchange which would lie within + or − one per cent of an official parity notified to the IMF and defined in terms of the weight of fine gold for which one unit of each monetary standard would be sold or purchased by the central bank of the country concerned. The parities so notified in the first instance were the official parities actually prevailing in 1947. The permissible margin around the official parity was subsequently expanded to + or − $2\frac{1}{4}$ per cent.

The second object of the exercise was to make provision for

occasional and individual adjustments in these official parities while preventing retaliatory copying by the rest of the world. It was sought to attain this by an undertaking by each member government that the official parity of its currency would be moved outside the official range allowed only after prior consultation with, and approval by, the Board of Directors of the IMF. The Charter made it clear that approval to alter the official parity of any currency by more than 20 per cent would be granted only for countries who could show that such a change was necessary because of a 'fundamental disequilibrium' in their balance of payments. What exactly constituted a 'fundamental disequilibrium' was carefully left undefined, although the object of the provision was obviously to prevent devaluations brought about purely in retaliation against currency depreciation elsewhere in the system.

The third major set of provisions was designed to ensure the availability of short-term international borrowing facilities which would avoid the necessity for recourse to the drastic and de-stabilising measure of exchange-rate adjustments immediately a country ran into difficulties on its balance of payments. Each member country was given a *quota* – based on a combination of its GNP and its involvement in international trade – which defined both the amount which it could be called on to place at the disposal of the IMF and the amount it could draw out of the IMF if need arose. Technically the quota (25 per cent in gold and 75 per cent in its own currency) defined how much it could be required to *sell* to the IMF in return for other currencies or *buy from* the IMF when in need of foreign exchange; in reality they defined how much member countries could be required to lend to, or entitled to borrow from, the IMF. In June 1947 the total quotas of all members amounted to £1 916 million, of which the United States accounted for about 36 per cent and Britain about 17 per cent; by 1974 the quota total had grown to around £14 700 million.

Taken together, these provisions were designed to prevent the calamities which had followed the First World War and which the designers of the IMF not unnaturally expected to follow the end of the Second World War. These were: a retreat into isolationism by the United States and a continuing trade deficit on the part of the rest of the world *vis-à-vis* the United States, a tendency to international deflation after a short post-war boom, a fairly rapid restoration of free foreign exchange rates and a recurrence, if not checked, of the competitive currency depreciations which had featured the 1930s.

In reality, not a single one of these assumptions proved to be well-founded and the overall result was that the carefully worked out IMF system of regulating the international monetary system never came into operation. So far from retreating into economic and political isolationism, the United States occupied an increasing role in the world economy and poured out vast flows of dollars into the hands of the outside world. In the 1950s this occurred through the European Recovery Programme and US assistance in the defence outlays of its allies through NATO, SEATO and other treaty arrangements; in the 1960s it occurred through an increasing balance of payments deficit on the part of the US itself – in which its own military adventures played a major part – and an enormous outflow of American capital for investment purposes. So far from being a scarce currency obtainable only through borrowing at the IMF, then, the United States dollar became a major direct contributor to the foreign currency reserves of the rest of the world and the IMF was by-passed as its source.

The reality of continuing inflation in contrast with the expectation of deflation had two major consequences. As the monetary value of world trade has risen so has the value of foreign exchange reserves necessary to finance it; these reserves are to a country's foreign trade what ordinary transactions balances are for the individual in his day-to-day spending. The IMF quotas, fixed in relation to 1945 prices, soon became totally unrealistic in relation to the current levels of world trade – another reason for by-passing the IMF. Secondly, maintaining currency prices in terms of gold meant that the real value of gold (the one commodity whose price was fixed in monetary terms) fell continuously as world prices rose, with the result that its supply to official buyers (at official prices) was increasingly discouraged. Two major ingredients in international monetary reserves (IMF quotas and gold) had thus been priced out of the market and the world turned increasingly to the more plentiful dollar as a form of international reserve. Both factors had to some extent been modified by the early 1970s; IMF quotas were successively raised and eventually made subject to annual review, while an increasing resort to floating exchange rates and 'free' gold markets led to a sharp rise in the monetary value of gold. But these changes were too small and too late to affect the basic forces at work.

The results may be seen in Table 33.1. In 1951 holdings of gold by the central banks of the world had constituted well over two-thirds of official exchange reserves whereas in 1973 they accounted for less than 30 per cent. Holdings of dollar balances, by contrast, had moved up from less than 9 per cent of official reserves in 1951 (outside the United States, of course) to not far short of 40 per cent twenty years later. Even

TABLE 33.1   *World monetary reserves, 1951–73*

		\$ *billion*		%	
		1951	1973	1951	1973
1.	Gold	33·9	43·2	68·8	23·4
2.	IMF credit*	1·7	18·1	3·4	9·8
3.	Foreign currencies:				
	a. Dollars	4·2	66·8	8·5	36·3
	b. Sterling	8·2	7·8	16·6	4·2
	c. Other	1·3	48·4	2·7	26·3
	Total	13·7	123·0	27·8	66·8
Total reserves		49·3	184·3	100·0	100·0
As % of imports		67	34		

* Reserve position plus Special Drawing Rights
Sources: International Monetary Fund, *Annual Report*, 1966 and 1974.

so, the growth of world liquidity, despite this massive injection of dollar balances, had not kept pace with the growth of world trade. In 1951, official reserves had amounted to the equivalent of about 8 months' imports but in twenty years the ratio had fallen to only about a half of this. Through the 1960s, in other words, the world was being pushed through a phase of not only major change in the pattern of its foreign exchange reserves but in the size of their overall total relative to the need for international liquidity as measured by the current value of world trade.

The third key assumption behind the IMF — a rapid restoration of free exchange markets and an undesirable tendency for unstable exchange rates as a result — proved especially wide of the mark. The reconstruction of the world economy after the Second World War proved to be, for many reasons, much more difficult and protracted than it had been after the First World War. So far from a rapid re-establishment of free foreign exchange markets, the reality almost throughout the 1950s was a network of tight official controls over foreign exchange and the reliance on the direct regulation of trade and payments rather than on exchange-rate adjustments to maintain or restore balance-of-payments equilibria. Furthermore, and partly as a result of this long period of officially maintained stability in exchange rates, the experience of the 1960s was to reveal a curious and paradoxical resistance of considerable dimensions to either the depreciation or appreciation of exchange rates. Appreciation was resisted by the countries with balance of payments surpluses and strong currencies mainly because appreciation, by making exports dearer and imports cheaper, would bring down on governments the condemnation of industries finding their foreign markets harder to keep and their domestic market threatened by cheaper imports from foreign competitors. Depreciation was equally unpopular since it carried overtones of inflationary dangers and certainly involved loss of political face.

By the early 1970s, then, the world had drifted, by accident rather than design, into a monetary system in which a high degree of rigidity had been built into the network of exchange rates, the IMF machinery had largely rusted away through sheer disuse, and the world was increasingly reliant on holdings of a single currency – the US dollar – to augment (and then inadequately) its stock of international liquidity. Unfortunately the structure contained some inherent and fundamental weaknesses to which the discussion must now turn.

3   THE RESERVE CURRENCY SYSTEM

The principle of one country holding balances in the currency of another as part of its international reserves is by no means a new one. An ordinary British commercial bank, after all, treats the liabilities of the Bank of England – Bankers' Deposits – as part of its cash reserves, confident in the knowledge that those deposits can be turned into legal tender without loss or delay whenever need arises. Similarly it holds another line of reserves in the form of short-term loans in the money market, confident that they too can be turned into cash with a minimum of risk and have the merit of earning income in the meantime.

In much the same way, until 1931 most of the Commonwealth countries preferred to maintain their reserves in the form of short-term deposits in London, confident in the knowledge that the Bank of England stood ready to convert them into gold at any time at a fixed rate; since gold could then be used to purchase any other currency which might be required, balances in London – *sterling balances* – were foreign currencies at one remove which had the additional merit of earning interest, an attribute not possessed by gold bullion stored in underground vaults.

The collapse of the gold standard in 1931 did not seriously disturb this system; in fact it brought it out more clearly into the open and renamed it the *sterling area* system. Even without the formal convertibility into gold, the pound sterling was still the major currency of the world; a quarter of the world's trade was conducted directly through the use of sterling and the pound was still freely convertible on the foreign exchanges into any other currency. Just as a bank is able to safely carry large deposit liabilities on the strength of relatively small cash reserves *so long as it commands public confidence in its power to repay*, so in the late 1930s Britain was able to attract and retain substantial deposits on the strength of relatively small reserves of gold and convertible currencies. As will be seen from Table 33.1, even in 1951 sterling balances of this kind accounted for nearly 17 per cent of the world's international reserves.

The sterling area system worked well enough in the 1930s. Why could an augmented reserve currency system, in which the dollar first joined and then overtook the pound as a major reserve currency, not work equally as well in the post-war world? During the 1950s, indeed, it did work tolerably well, bearing in mind the network of official controls and restrictions which it was noted earlier prevailed in most countries. In the 1960s, however, the essential inconsistencies of the system came increasingly to the fore.

In the first place (and unlike the 1930s), world trade was expanding rapidly in monetary terms and with it was expanding the world need for international liquidity – the transactions balances of foreign trade. Given the inability of the gold supply to meet this need, for the reasons mentioned above, it could be met only through a growth in the holdings by the outside world of dollars and pounds sterling. This implied a continuing deficit (including autonomous capital movements as well as current transactions) on the part of the two countries concerned: there is no other way in which third countries can increase their holdings of the reserve currencies. This meant that the rate of growth of world liquidity was dependent on the size of the payments deficits being run by one or two major countries – clearly an unsatisfactory situation over the long run. More to the point, however, the system implicitly assumed that the creditor countries – i.e. those accumulating dollar or sterling balances – would be prepared to finance these deficits indefinitely by, in effect, lending increasing sums of money to the debtor countries. This was inevitably and increasingly a source of tension and dissatisfaction in the international monetary structure.

A second, and even more fundamental, weakness was associated with this. The essence of the reserve currency system is that the outside world must retain confidence in its ability to convert holdings of the currency concerned into any other currency more or less on demand and without loss. Yet it has just been established that, in order to work, the reserve currency system requires a continuing deficit on the balance of payments of the countries supplying the reserves. The need to maintain confidence and the need to run persistent payments deficits are clearly incompatible: sooner or later the latter must destroy the former. A country cannot simultaneously run a continuing payments deficit and add to, or even maintain, its gold reserves. It is therefore in the position of a bank which adds continuously to its deposit liabilities with a constant, or even declining, stock of reserve assets. In the case of the bank the ratio between reserves and liabilities must sooner or later fall below the minimum required by the authorities; in the case of the country operating a reserve currency it must sooner or later fall below the minimum required to maintain the essential ingredient of international confidence in that country's ability to maintain convertibility at the going rate. And once that confidence is lost, the reserve currency game is irretrievably up.

It is fair to say that for these reasons the credibility of the pound sterling as an international reserve currency had disappeared by the late 1960s. Periodic crises in the British balance of payments since the end of the Second World War inevitably eroded world confidence in the ability of the Bank of England to maintain the current official parity of the pound. On two occasions within twenty years this lack of confidence manifested itself in speculative runs against the pound sterling of such magnitude that the Bank was unable to withstand them and the pound was devalued, in 1949 and again in 1967. From mid-1972, indeed, the attempt to maintain a fixed parity for the pound was abandoned in favour of a 'temporary' floating exchange rate – which led to a further decline in the market valuation of the pound. A substantial proportion of balances still held in London by overseas central banks were in fact retained only because of a guarantee given by the British authorities (with the aid of stand-by credit facilities raised abroad) that their dollar value would be protected in the event of further depreciation in the market value of sterling. The day of the pound as an international reserve currency in its own right was clearly over.

The fate of the dollar has been only a little happier. After maintaining a fixed rate of $35 per fine ounce of gold – with increasing difficulty in the face of large-scale speculative attacks in the later 1960s – continuously between 1934 and 1971 the US authorities have been forced to give ground in the shape of a higher dollar price for gold and, in effect, small but significant devaluations of the dollar. As an international reserve currency the dollar has certainly not yet reached the end of the road but the signs of strain in the reserve currency system are only too obvious.

Apart from these two problems of the world monetary mechanism with which the reserve currency system has grappled unsuccessfully – the problem of ensuring an adequate and acceptable supply of *liquidity* and that of maintaining *confidence* in the underlying standard of exchange value – there is a third problem having widespread implications. Any efficient world system should provide for – or at least be not inconsistent with – some means of *adjustment* for the periodic disequilibria which are bound to recur in the payments positions of all trading nations.

In essence the problem is this. If a serious disequilibrium develops in the balance of payments of any country some means must obviously be adopted to correct it and that process of correction is liable to impose an unwelcome burden on the country undergoing it. The disequilibrium must be removed *either* by the country experiencing the deficit *or* by the country (or countries) which must somewhere be experiencing a corresponding surplus; disequilibrium on the balance of payments exists, after all, when a country enjoys substantial and continuous surpluses just as much as when it suffers continuous deficits. Either the debtor country must reduce its costs and prices relative to the rest of the world, so reducing its imports relative to its exports *or* the creditor country must encourage its price level to rise in relation to the rest of the world and thus ensure that its payments surplus is gradually whittled away. Or, of course, the adjustment process could operate simultaneously on both sides, creditors and debtors coming to meet each other half-way.

The old gold standard system had such an adjustment mechanism in the form of the direct link between external reserves and internal money supply. Theoretically this eliminated disequilibria by automatically setting in motion corrective forces of deflation and inflation. In practice, as was noted in a previous chapter, the burden of adjustment was thrust almost entirely on to the debtors and, ultimately, the strains thus imposed destroyed the system itself. But the necessity for the adjustment of disequilibria remains none the less: no conceivable monetary system can obviate it. If the adjustment is not to be carried out through linkages with the internal money supply then it must be achieved in some other way.

The great defect of the reserve currency system was not that it provided no alternative adjustment mechanism but that it positively hindered it. If and when the United States or Britain incurred deficits there was no automatic pressure on them to do anything about it. The deficits were automatically financed by an addition to the dollar or sterling balances in the hands of overseas creditors which would be a contribution to the latter's external reserves. It was as if, under the gold standard system, a debtor country was able to settle its deficit by effortlessly drawing gold bullion from some inexhaustible internal reserve.

The creditor countries, on the other hand, were under no obligation to indulge in inflationary domestic policies simply because their balances in New York or London had grown and, indeed, showed a marked reluctance to do so. From their point of view they were in effect financing the deficits of the reserve currency countries by a kind of automatic loan. Unfortunately, if the system were to ensure an adequate rate of growth in world reserves, it was essential that they should continue to do precisely this. Not surprisingly, increasing dissatisfaction was expressed by creditor countries at a reserve system which required them to finance indefinitely the profligate spending (as they saw it) of the British on their welfare state or of the Americans on military adventures or capital investment in the outside world.

4 THE PROBLEM OF MONETARY REFORM

This last issue of how payments disequilibria – which are bound to recur repeatedly in a dynamic world – should be corrected, and of how the burden of that correction should be shared between creditor and debtor countries, is at the root of the continuing debate on how the international monetary system should be reformed so as to eliminate the problems experienced throughout the 1960s and early 1970s. These were inevitable with a system which sought to resist any changes in currency exchange rates but simultaneously provided no alternative adjustment mechanism when changes in relative costs and prices between one country and another generated, inevitably, periodic payments disequilibria. The only outcome were periods of frantic efforts to maintain inappropriate exchange rates interrupted, with increasing frequency, by adjustments enforced by speculative movements proving too much for the inevitable panic of borrowing arrangements between central banks desperately trying to keep some semblance of orderliness in foreign exchange markets and the equally inevitable international conferences of Finance Ministers emerging on each occasion with a final solution in which no one really believed.

Creditor countries, in such circumstances, naturally demand changes which will ensure that the debtors are disciplined to mend their erring ways and are prevented from riding on the backs of the better-behaved nations of the world through automatic access to unlimited borrowing. Debtor countries, equally naturally, insist on the vital necessity of borrowing facilities of this kind so that their internal levels of output and employment should not be placed at the mercy of the balance of payments with all the consequent dangers of an international transmission of deflation and depression on the scale of the 1930s. The burden of adjustment, in their view, should be placed on the debtor countries who have created the disequilibrium through an unduly low level of internal demand and prices or an undervalued exchange rate. The conflict is fundamental and in no real sense avoidable. Hence the variety of reforms proposed from time to time for the world monetary system.

At the one extreme of the discipline-the-debtors school are a few voices calling for a return to a full gold standard system, but this is a remedy which finds little support. Quite apart from all the defects noted in the earlier discussion of the gold standard, a full restoration of gold as the only form of international reserve would preserve a system which involves the rather futile process of excavating gold in some parts of the world and burying it again in vaults somewhere else; it would also make the supply and distribution of the world's reserves arbitrary and unpredictable.

A stronger case can be made for a reversion to reliance on the IMF, the quotas being continuously revised to take account of world needs. This has the advantage, to the creditors, that the borrowing rights of deficit countries would be strictly limited and would in fact be under the control of the major creditors. IMF quotas do not represent credit *created* by the IMF but merely rights to purchase existing currencies; the suppliers of those currencies (i.e. the creditor countries) would thus always have the last word in a dispute over whether debtors should or should not be given further credit.

The dangers implicit in this last element, and the fear that a bias towards constraint on the growth of world liquidity would be inevitable amongst creditor countries being asked, in effect, to provide it have led others to a more drastic proposal – that the IMF should be converted into a genuine international central bank with powers to create its *own* world money, as and when need arose, just as a national central bank can create additions to the internal money supply. For the reasons already given, the creditor nations look on proposals of this kind with great suspicion, seeing in them a recipe for unlimited profligacy on the part of debtors. Certainly it is very doubtful if the world is yet ready for the transfer to an international body such as the IMF the degree of economic sovereignty which such a proposal involves.

Compromise is inevitable in a situation of this kind where national interests, in the short run at least, are so diametrically opposed. Hence the creation, by agreement amongst all member countries, of a new kind of international money known as *Special Drawing Rights* (SDRs) by the IMF in 1970. As the name implies, these are additional rights to draw on the IMF to cover payments disequilibria but unlike the normal IMF quota they constitute reserves in themselves and are not merely rights to purchase existing currencies. The central banks of all member countries have agreed to treat these SDRs *as* reserves, so that a borrowing country can transfer some of its SDRs from the IMF to a foreign central bank, the latter accepting the sum transferred as equivalent to gold or any other convertible currency. For the first time, a form of international money exists which is not dependent on the currency of any single country nor the vagaries of the gold mines of the world.

This development did not make the IMF into a genuine international bank, however, since the value of SDRs created is not a matter which the Managing Director of the IMF can decide off his own bat according to his assessment of the needs of individual countries or the world at large. Issues have to be authorised by the Executive Board of the IMF and the voting requirements are such that any increase in SDRs could be vetoed by, say, the United States or the Six of the original EEC voting together. In principle, then, the position of creditor countries has been preserved and they cannot be called on to accept unlimited amounts of some new international money created by resolutions passed against their will at the behest of the chronic debtors of the world. The SDR is so far a relatively small element in total world liquidity; at the end of 1973 they amounted to only £4 420 million, or about 6 per cent of total world reserves.

What the future will hold is, of course, impossible to say. It may well be that the SDR will steadily grow in importance until it becomes the major form of international reserve. Hopefully, the liquidity and confidence aspects of the world monetary system will then be placed on a secure base. The adjustment problem, however, remains and it would be idle to pretend that any international monetary arrangement could change its essential nature. Perfection, in the sense of the elimination of the adjustment problem associated with payments disequilibria, is inherently unattainable. It is merely one aspect of the basic problem which has been the subject of this book – the conflict between scarce means and conflicting ends and the need to balance gains in one direction against losses in another. The problem is inescapable and eternal – or, at least, has a time dimension which coincides with that of humanity itself.

FURTHER READING

G. WALSHE *Monetary reform* Macmillan, London 1971

T. SCITOVSKY *Money and the balance of payments* Ch. 14

S. J. WELLS *International economics* Chs. 17–19

H. G. GRUBEL *The international monetary system* Penguin Books, London 1969

J. MARCUS FLEMING *Essays in international economics* Allen and Unwin, London 1971, Chs. 4–7

Index